J

College o.
Surgeons
of British Columbia

PREVENTING SEXUAL ABUSE
OF PATIENTS

A LEGAL GUIDE FOR
HEALTH CARE PROFESSIONALS

Marilou McPhedran

Wendy Sutton

LexisNexis™
Butterworths

Preventing Sexual Abuse of Patients: A Legal Guide for Health Care Professionals
© LexisNexis Canada Inc. 2004
April 2004

Members of the LexisNexis Group worldwide

Canada	LexisNexis Canada Inc, 75 Clegg Road, MARKHAM, Ontario
Argentina	Abeledo Perrot, Jurisprudencia Argentina and Depalma, BUENOS AIRES
Australia	Butterworths, a Division of Reed International Books Australia Pty Ltd, CHATSWOOD, New South Wales
Austria	ARD Betriebsdienst and Verlag Orac, VIENNA
Chile	Publitecsa and Conosur Ltda, SANTIAGO DE CHILE
Czech Republic	Orac sro, PRAGUE
France	Éditions du Juris-Classeur SA, PARIS
Hong Kong	Butterworths Asia (Hong Kong), HONG KONG
Hungary	Hvg Orac, BUDAPEST
India	Butterworths India, NEW DELHI
Ireland	Butterworths (Ireland) Ltd, DUBLIN
Italy	Giuffré, MILAN
Malaysia	Malayan Law Journal Sdn Bhd, KUALA LUMPUR
New Zealand	Butterworths of New Zealand, WELLINGTON
Poland	Wydawnictwa Prawnicze PWN, WARSAW
Singapore	Butterworths Asia, SINGAPORE
South Africa	Butterworth Publishers (Pty) Ltd, DURBAN
Switzerland	Stämpfli Verlag AG, BERNE
United Kingdom	Butterworths Tolley, a Division of Reed Elsevier (UK), LONDON, WC2A
USA	LexisNexis, DAYTON, Ohio

National Library of Canada Cataloguing in Publication

McPhedran, Marilou
    Preventing sexual abuse of patients : a legal guide for health care professionals / Marilou McPhedran, Wendy Sutton

Includes index.
ISBN 0-433-44194-1

    1. Medical personnel and patient--Ontario. 2. Sex crimes--Ontario--Prevention. 3. Sexually abused patients--Ontario. 4. Medical laws and legislation--Ontario. I. Sutton, Wendy, 1949- II. Title.

KEO616.M36 2004	345.713'0253'02461	C2004-901299-1
KF2905.M36 2004		

Printed and bound in Canada.

ABOUT THE AUTHORS

Marilou McPhedran, C.M., B.A., LL.B., LL.D. (Honoris Causa) has provided strategic counsel in health and human rights to public and private institutions for more than 25 years, including the Pan American Health Organization, the United Nations Division for the Advancement of Women, the Asian Development Bank, Women's College Hospital and Liberty Health (Canada). Ms. McPhedran has chaired several inquiries into the sexual abuse of patients, including Canada's first such panel in 1991. She has been a Member of the Order of Canada since 1985, in recognition of her leadership in the successful campaign to strengthen protection for women and girls in the Constitution of Canada. She has also served as the chief executive officer of the National Network on Environments and Women's Health.

Wendy Sutton, B.A., LL.B., LL.M. is a consulting lawyer with Miller Thomson, LLP, where she acts as Executive Editor of Miller Thomson's eLaw Library of Health Law and writer for the firm's newsletter "Hospital Law". She is an Affiliate Member of the York University Centre for Health Studies, managing editor of the Canadian Journal of Women and the Law and the Assistant Course Director of the part-time LL.M. programme in Health Law at Osgoode Hall Law School. Her work involves consulting, research, writing and education in law for the health sector, with a particular emphasis on the health professions. A frequent lecturer on health law and a regular contributor to the Journal of the Ontario Association of Occupational Health Nurses, Ms. Sutton teaches a continuing education course entitled "Law and the Health Professional" at the Michener Institute of Applied Health Sciences.

Marilou dedicates this book to the memories of Dr. Lois Plumb and Maxwell Goldhar whose love continues to grace my life and to my vibrant, gentle-giant sons who have taught me so much – Jonathan and David McPhedran-Waitzer.

Wendy dedicates this book to her mother, Helen Kendall Nicholson, who has always been there for me, with love.

FOREWORD

I welcome this exhaustive piece of work on sexual abuse of patients. It is easy to understand why one would feel strongly about the issue: as patients, individuals usually are at their most vulnerable. There is no balance or equilibrium in the power relationship between those trained to help and those being helped. And there can be no denial that every health professional is somehow, to an extent that can vary, in a relationship of power and control over his or her patient.

The problem is not new. But now, we can talk of it. We can name, label, categorize, and analyze. And we can draw conclusions. And governments changed legislation, regulatory bodies and professional colleges developed guidelines and codes of conduct, unions organized panels and discussions. Going through the literature in my university office, I realized that otherwise good handbooks for students had not a word on the matter, books that are not 15 years of age. How much of the question of sexual abuse of patients is rooted in our academic and professional curricula, other than an ethics class in passing, I do not know. But a serious approach is warranted, by each of the helping professions. This *Sexual Abuse of Patients: A Legal Guide for Health Care Professionals* is clearly directed towards the practitioners — current and in training — of medicine, nursing, the rehabilitation sciences, to name only a few. But in Ontario at least, the law also includes social workers and teachers, and this book is for them as well. I hope the book also gets in the hands of health administration students and professionals.

Let me applaud the authors for a well-researched manual. The various case studies presented bring real life situations to the analysis and help understand the legal framework around them. I remember when Marilou McPhedran, one of the authors, chaired for the College of Physicians and Surgeons of Ontario, Canada's first task force on the sexual abuse of patients more than a decade ago. With Wendy Sutton, she went on to explore how what used to be the topic of jokes is now framed by the law in a most serious manner. They are right to have written this book: sexual abuses by some are denying normal social emotions by many.

How can society accept such a betrayal of trust?

The Honourable Monique Bégin, PC, FRSC, OC
Former Minister of National Health and Welfare
University of Ottawa

ACKNOWLEDGMENTS

We have undertaken to produce Ontario's first textbook on sexual abuse of patients in order to provide students, professionals, regulators and educators with a tool that we hope will facilitate the understanding and eradication of the problem. We are grateful to the Honourable Monique Bégin for providing us with such a supportive and inspiring Foreword. Over the course of our research and writing, we asked for feedback on drafts of this book from knowledgeable individuals with many perspectives, for example, officials in regulatory colleges, health professionals in practice and in training, educators, legislators, patients, advocates, lawyers and researchers, and so we garnered invaluable comments on the manuscript, to which we have given serious consideration, resulting in numerous changes. To the following individuals who assisted us in this process, we give our heartfelt thanks: Mary Addison, Mary Armstrong, Bimpe Ayeni, Harvey Armstrong, Neil Arya, Jasmine Asseliav, Dody Bienenstock, Carolyn Bennett, Earl Berger, Sheila Berger, Ronda Bessner, Madeline Boscoe, Cindy Campbell, Paula Caplan, Claudette Chase, Gardner Church, Anne Coghlan, Graeme Cunningham, Nancy Curran, Carolyn Dean, Mary Lou Fassel, Irwin Fefergrad, Marc Gabel, Rocco Gerace, Lorraine Greaves, Ruth Grier, Joan Gilmour, Lyndsay Green, Ethel Harris, Milton Harris, Margaret Haworth-Broackman, Tuula Heinonen, Judith Herman, Verna Hunt, Iris Jackson, Karen Katchen, Pam Katz, Melissa Kluger, Catherine Kulisek, John Lamont, Michele Landsberg, Briar Long, Barbara Lent, Suzanne MacDonald, Angela McLeod, Brian MacLeod Rogers, Bill Maurice, Pat Marshall, Tom Marshall, Patrick McNamara, NancyRuth, David Naylor, Darryl Peck, Susan Penfold, Jane Pepino, Bev Richardson, Gail Robinson, Roz Roach, Marcel Saulnier, Carol Scurfield, Gary Schoener, Carol Sinclair, Gail Siskind, Michael Sutton, Regan Tessis, Sari Tudiver, Susan Vella, Patricia Wales, Shayna Watson. We thank them for their contributions. Any errors or omissions are solely those of the authors.

Alison Engel, Jodi Kovitz, and Nicola Simmons provided excellent research assistance and our publishers at LexisNexis Canada, Inc., notably Myrsini Rovos, Teresa Chan and Tina Eng are also due a debt of thanks for suggesting and sustaining this endeavour. We ask readers to note that every case is unique and there are different interpretations to any law, so if particular legal concerns arise, a lawyer should be consulted.

There are many special people without whose support Marilou simply could not have finished this book. As I write this, I am on assignment in South Asia, thus leaving disproportionate responsibility for my intrepid, meticulous co-author, Wendy Sutton, one of the smartest choices in a colleague ever made! Crucial support from friend and mentor Milton Harris made it possible to complete our research, beautiful safe places to write were provided by Lyndsay Green and NancyRuth, generous encouragement came from Sally Armstrong, Caroline Bamford, Carolyn Bennett, Margo Birch Blackwell, Margot Franssen, Val Monroe, Ede McPhedran and Patrick Watson, which, combined with the 5 a.m. coffees, late-night dinners at my computer and unstinting affection from Darryl Peck, made it all possible.

Wendy would like to thank her family Michael Sutton, Kendall Sutton, Mollie Sutton and Helen Nicholson for their encouragement, faith, assistance and patience, in this, my first full-fledged endeavour to write a book. But for them, and the initial invitation and inspiration of, and confidence placed in me by my co-author Marilou I would not have this wonderful opportunity to learn, grow and contribute, much less complete the task.

March 2004

TABLE OF CONTENTS

INTRODUCTION
HOW THIS GUIDE CAN HELP YOU

This book is about the intersection of law and practice affecting health professionals and students in the health professions in Ontario regarding sexual abuse of patients — behaviour that has re-emerged in law in the last ten years as a matter for concern. This law, the *Regulated Health Professions Act, 1991 (RHPA)*[1] pervades daily practice for thousands of health professionals and their patients, often in ways that are invisible or subtle. But the most comprehensive survey of Ontario's health professionals published to date (in 1999) clearly indicated a low level of awareness of the law generally and particularly of the amendments of the law regarding the sexual abuse of patients.[2]

Although Canadian researchers have published a variety of studies and some educators affiliated with professional programs in colleges and universities have developed some good educational materials about sexual abuse of patients, no general textbook geared to the needs of health profession students or graduates registered to practice in Ontario had been produced. This Guide has been written on the premise that students, professionals and patients — who all make up the "public" — will benefit from a book of this nature being readily available.

---

[1] S.O. 1991, c. 18.

[2] PricewaterhouseCoopers, *Evaluation of the Effectiveness of the Health Professional Colleges' Complaints and Discipline Procedures with Respect to Professional Miscon-duct of a Sexual Nature and Status of the Colleges' Patient Relation Program*, Vol. 3: College Member Survey (July, 1999). PricewaterhouseCoopers, National Survey Centre estimated 229,889 professionals were registered in 21 Ontario regulatory colleges in 1998, based on membership lists provided by the colleges under strict confidentiality agreements for a mail-in survey, commissioned by the Health Professional Regulatory Advisory Council (HPRAC) of Ontario.

A. ONE LAW AFFECTS MORE THAN 225,000 HEALTH PROFESSIONALS AND THEIR PATIENTS

In Ontario, there are more than 225,000 men and women in 24 professions[3] who are regulated by 21 colleges under one law — the *RHPA* – and there are thousands of students enrolled in degree programs for these 24 professions.[4] The majority of health professionals rely on payment for their services from institutions or agencies that receive government funding. The sexual abuse of patients by health care professionals has, in the last dozen years, come into prominence as an issue that concerns the public, patients, health care practitioners and their colleges, the government and the legal professions. Initially profiled in large part by the findings of the Task Force on Sexual Abuse of Patients Final Report commissioned by the College of Physicians and Surgeons of Ontario in 1991 (1991 Task Force),[5] sexual abuse in this context is a complex concept. As the chair of the Ontario government's advisory council on the health professions, which conducted an extensive impact analysis of the *RHPA* in 2001 noted, "When the *RHPA* was passed in 1991, it represented a shift from profession-centred regulation to public interest regulation."[6]

In 1993, the Government of Ontario introduced Bill 100,[7] with extensive amendments to the *Regulated Health Professions Act* – to deal specifically with the sexual abuse of patients and sexual misconduct of health professionals. On the occasion of those amendments being introduced to the Legislature of Ontario, then-Minister of Health, the Honourable Frances Lankin, said,

> I am confident we all have the same goal. We here in the Legislature, health professionals and members of the public — women, children and men — all want to stop sexual abuse. Patients and health professionals need to know that sexual abuse of patients is never acceptable and must not be tolerated. If the trust between

---

[3] *Ibid.*

[4] Note that naturopaths are a regulated health profession, not under the *RHPA*, but under the *Drugless Practitioners Act*, R.S.O. 1990, c. D.18. Teachers and social workers have also recently been granted self-regulation status. See the *Ontario College of Teachers Act, 1996*, S.O. 1996, c. 12, and the *Social Work and Social Services Work Act, 1998*, S.O. 1998, c. 31.

[5] M. McPhedran, H. Armstrong, R. Edney, B. Long, P. Marshall & R. Roach, *The Final Report of the Independent Task Force on Sexual Abuse of Patients* (Toronto: College of Physicians & Surgeons of Ontario, 1991).

[6] Health Professions Regulatory Advisory Council, *Adjusting the Balance: A Review of the Regulated Health Professions Act* (Queen's Park: Government of Ontario, March, 2001) in Foreword (R. Alder, Chair).

[7] *Regulated Health Professions Amendment Act, 1993*, S.O. 1993, c. 37.

a patient and a health care professional is abused, the consequences are devastating. People need to know that their right not to be victimized in this way is backed by law.[8]

In the wake of the sexual abuse amendments, the colleges, the bodies that regulate the regulated professions,[9] were required to respond with programs to prevent sexual abuse, customized for each profession, to educate both professionals and the public about the problem. The approved amendments used the term "patient" to remain consistent with the rest of the Act, even though some professions and the public tend to use different terms, such as "client." In both the professional and public realms, there remains a great deal of confusion, misunderstanding and, on occasion, ignorance about exactly what sexual abuse is, how often it occurs and when it should be tolerated or accepted, if at all. For instance, the Health Professions Regulatory Advisory Council (HPRAC)[10] surveyed Ontarians and found that two out of three respondents were not certain of where or how to file a complaint regarding sexual misconduct by a health care professional.[11]

B. ASSISTING HEALTH PROFESSIONALS IN THE PREVENTION OF SEXUAL ABUSE

This Guide aims to provide clear information as a primary means of assisting health professionals in preventing and avoiding sexual abuse. Written by lawyers with experience in the teaching and analysis of sexual abuse prevention, this Guide is designed to be a practical, intelligible and instructional resource for those who practise as health care professionals, for those who educate and regulate them, and for their

---

[8] Ontario, Legislative Assembly, *Official Report of Debates (Hansard)*, L064 (8 October 1992) at 2542 (Hon. Frances Lankin).

[9] As we describe further in Chapter 2, each regulated profession is managed by an organization known as a "college" (not to be confused with the educational kind of college), which is given responsibility under the *RHPA* for regulating the activities of its members. The health professions that are regulated under the *RHPA* in Ontario include: audiology; speech-language pathology; chiropody; chiropractic; dental hygiene; dental technology; dentistry; denturism; dietetics; massage therapy; medical laboratory technology; medical radiation technology; medicine; midwifery; nursing; nursing assistants; occupational therapy; opticianry; osteopathy; pharmacy; physiotherapy; podiatry; psychology; and respiratory therapy.

[10] HPRAC is a body set up by the *RHPA* for the purposes of providing various kinds of advice to the Minister of Health and Long-Term Care regarding the regulated health professions.

[11] HRPAC, *Adjusting the Balance, supra* note 6, at 81.

patients and the public at large. In order to accomplish this goal, the authors have consulted widely: we have worked with expert advisors from the regulated health professions and subjected our work to their scrutiny; we have engaged in consultation with a variety of groups, including students, patients, lawyers, educators and professional colleges; we have endeavoured to ensure that our research is as thorough, up to date and relevant as it can be. In doing so, we wish to underscore that the problem of sexual abuse is by no means confined to one profession and is of concern to all professions. For this reason, we have surveyed all of the health care professions in our search for examples of and solutions to the problem.

Perhaps most importantly, given that so much of what underpins the problem of sexual abuse is defined by legal concepts, we have tried to write this Guide in a style and language that anyone who needs to know about what sexual abuse is and its impact can understand. It is our hope that we have created a work that will assist readers to better inform themselves and those with whom they interact, so that the problem can be constructively, knowledgeably and confidently addressed, prevented and ultimately eliminated.

C. STRUCTURE OF THIS GUIDE

This Guide is structured in the following manner. We begin by exploring the problem of sexual abuse in the context affecting most health professionals. In trying to encourage an understanding of and prevention of sexual abuse, we use case studies and examples as a way to look at causes, prohibitions and prevalence, and to explore the impact that sexual abuse can have on its victims — some of whom are also health professionals — as well as on the professionals who are perpetrators. We also look at various reactions to the problem — from governments, professionals and their colleges, and the public — including some of the still-existing misconceptions about the issue. We conclude our overview chapter with a summary of the law relating to sexual abuse of patients by health care providers. Each chapter ends with discussion points, and the overview chapter contains questions about one recent sexual abuse case, encouraging readers to explore three different perspectives:

1. a voluntary membership professional association,
2. a regulatory college, and
3. an appeal court responding to opposing arguments from the first two.

We then guide the reader through a more detailed survey of the current legislative framework for self-regulation of health professionals in Ontario, the mechanisms within it to respond to sexual abuse and the context of administrative law when health professions are given the privilege and responsibility to self-regulate in the public interest.

The next section of the book concentrates on how sexual abuse complaints are addressed in the *RHPA*, in particular its *Schedule 2*: the *Health Professions Procedural Code* (the *"Code"*)[12] as well as the legislation that specifically governs each profession. This is followed by an explanation of the complaints and disciplines process for which the colleges of each profession are legally responsible. Because the legal procedure that occurs when a sexual abuse complaint is processed by a regulatory college under the *RHPA* is just one possible scenario facing a professional, we then describe what occurs when the professional is sued for harm caused as a result of alleged sexual abuse in the civil courts. And because each sexual abuse scenario can produce three possible, sometimes overlapping legal actions against a professional named as an alleged abuser, we move the discussion from legal actions in civil law to what happens when a professional is charged by the police with sexual assault of a patient under the *Criminal Code of Canada*.[13] Here again, we provide case studies involving sexual abuse, some that have been heard by the Supreme Court of Canada and others by lower levels of the courts.

The next part of the Guide deals with strategies for the prevention of sexual abuse, with a strong emphasis on more effective education and training. It will be evident that much of this book has been written out of concern that students and practitioners in the regulated health professions need and deserve more and better education on the dynamics, sequelae and countermeasures to sexual abuse. We outline various approaches to assist in developing

- policies and procedures for the recognition and prevention of sexual abuse in the workplace,
- essentials for effective continuing education of regulated health professionals,
- components for curricula, and

---

[12] *Health Professions Procedural Code*, being Sch. 2 to the *Regulated Health Professions Act, 1991*, S.O. 1991, c. 18.
[13] R.S.C. 1985, c. C-46.

- guidelines by various colleges of the regulated professions as they apply to both the patient/practitioner relationship and relationships in the workplace.

We conclude by summarizing the implications of the law — and processes triggered by the law — for regulated health professionals, for patients and for the public at large. And finally, in the appendices, we provide some practical tools for your use in the future, including excerpts of current legislation; good examples of codes and policies on zero tolerance of sexual abuse of patients; sample checklists of sensitive care options for students and practitioners; guidance on where to seek help; draft workplace policies; a tutorial guide based on the case studies in each chapter of the book and a list of highly recommended readings. Some of our advisors for this book were patients who have experienced the reality of sexual abuse and the legal processes that can flow from taking action after sexual abuse has occurred. These patients and a number of health professionals who provide care to survivors of childhood sexual abuse and sexual abuse by health professionals urged us to add the "Handout for Patients" at the end of the book. We know that some patients will want to use this book too. One of our reviewers is, a patient who went through a college complaint, an appeal to the Health Professions Appeals Review Board, and a civil lawsuit — all related to one sexual abuse case. She told us,

> [a]s a victim of therapeutic abuse, I would have welcomed such a book. I had to search for answers from many individual sources such as the college and the legal system, try to understand what happened to me, try to get well. And equally important — I didn't have real cases to refer to. Because I am the type of person that needs proof of things, I truly believe it would have been helpful if my doctors or lawyers could have provided me with one source of information to read and digest.

D. WHY "REAL LIFE" CASE STUDIES ARE USED IN THIS GUIDE

Educators have noted that many students and practitioners seem to give little thought to the possibility that they might cross a sexual boundary as a form of exploitation of one or more patients.[14] While this attitude is

---

[14] See, for example, the results of the Institute for Clinical Evaluative Sciences (ICES) study conducted of medical students: "Sexual Abuse of Patients" in College of Physicians and Surgeons of Ontario, *Members' Dialogue* (November/December 2002) online, College of Physicians and Surgeons of Ontario <http//www.cpso.on.ca/Publications/Dialogue/1102/study.htm>.

"only human" and understandable, it is also dangerous for professionals and patients. Bluntly put, ignorance is not a defence in matters of professional competence, and a finding of sexual abuse of a patient is not only indication of professional misconduct, it can also signal that the professional has been incompetent and is liable for substandard care. In this Guide, every case study quotes from an actual case on the public record so that we can challenge the "but, not me" attitude that insulates many health professionals from learning skills they need to have. Some of these cases leave no doubt that dedicated professionals who may have contributed much to their communities and helped many of their patients have nevertheless made the mistake in judgment that brought life-changing legal interventions they did not expect, or welcome. It is our sincere hope that this Guide will have long-standing value for those who come across it: in practice, in the classroom, in the workplace and out of a genuine interest to learn and — as a result — that more professionals and patients will gain the knowledge and skill needed to prevent sexual abuse of patients.

Chapter 1

THE PROBLEM OF SEXUAL ABUSE

The "problem" may be seen as sexual abuse of patients, but without an understanding of the "cause," our society will be unable to find solutions by addressing and changing the factors contributing to this phenomenon. Extending beyond regulated health care providers who cross long-established professional boundaries and cause harm, others in trusted professions like law, teaching and the clergy, and the systemic mechanisms that often shield perpetrators, are increasingly being exposed and held accountable.[1] Every chapter in this book presents case studies that track events leading up to formal legal findings of guilt, and each case study adds information to the quest for a solution by implicitly asking, "why was this harm caused and how can we stop it from happening again?" No reader of this book is exempt from being involved in responding to this phenomenon, either as participant in the problem or participant in the solution.

A. NOTE ABOUT TEACHING WITH THE CASE STUDIES IN THIS BOOK

For ease of reference, the case studies are referred to at the beginning of each chapter, although they might not be discussed until later on. At the end of each chapter, we provide questions and issues raised by the cases as a way to facilitate individual learning and group discussions. Appendix IV contains a compilation of the case studies and related discussion points. Many of the issues raised require thoughtful, sophisticated analysis and lend themselves well to interactive learning through professionally courteous, vibrant debate. To augment accuracy and longer term understanding of

---

[1] See *Doe v. O'Dell*, [2003] O.J. No. 3546 (S.C.J.) at para. 174, a case in which the court ordered a priest and his diocese to pay $1.4 million to a victim of sexual abuse. Madam Justice Katherine Swinton is quoted in the article: "In this case, there can be no doubt that Father O'Dell committed numerous acts of battery against the plaintiff... Given the facts of the case, I find there was a significant connection between the employment of Father O'Dell and the abuse."

the regulatory framework within which each member of the regulated professions in Ontario must practise, the full text of Schedule 2 of the *Regulated Health Professions Act, 1991* (*RHPA*), the *Health Professions Procedural Code* (the *Code*)[2] is reprinted in Appendix I, and a chart summarizing the offences and penalties defined under the *Code* can be found in Chapter 3.

B.   CASE STUDY: DR. W, A MEDICAL DOCTOR IN VANCOUVER

This case, which will be referred to in its short form as *Norberg*, is featured as the book's first case study because it is the leading statement of the Supreme Court of Canada regarding sexual abuse by a health professional.[3] In 1988, a medical doctor, Dr. W, was sued by his former patient, Laura, but she lost her case in both the British Columbia trial and appeal courts because those courts held she had consented to the sexual contact.[4] Her final appeal to the Supreme Court of Canada, however, reversed the lower courts and held that Laura had not consented to the secual contact given the power imbalance between the patient and the doctor. The Court found Dr. W liable for paying damages to his patient for harm done to her as a result of his abrogation of his duty as a health professional. The Supreme Court decision in *Norberg* stands as the definitive analysis by our highest court (as of January 2004 when this book was published) on the fiduciary duty owed by health professionals to their patients and on how the Court found the doctor's defence argument that the patient gave her "consent" to sexual contact to be "inherently suspect."[5]

Dr. W had been in practice for many years and maintained his office in conjunction with his home. The patient, Laura, came to see Dr. W, complaining of severe headaches, for which previous physicians had prescribed strong medications, such as Fiorinal. It became clear that she wanted greater access to such drugs and when Dr. W confronted his patient, she admitted to him that she was addicted. Dr. W made suggestions of a sexual nature by pointing upstairs where his apartment

---

[2]   *Regulated Health Professions Act, 1991*, S.O. 1991, c. 18 [hereinafter *RHPA*], the *Health Professions Procedural Code*, being Sch. 2 to the *Regulated Health Professions Act*, S.O. 1991, c. 18 [hereinafter "the *Code*"].

[3]   *Norberg v. Wynrib*, [1992] 2 S.C.R. 226.

[4]   *Norberg v. Wynrib* (1988), 27 B.C.L.R. (2d) 240 (S.C.), aff'd (1990), 44 B.C.L.R. (2d) 47 (C.A.).

[5]   *Norberg v. Wynrib*, *supra* note 3, at 255.

was located, but he did not at any time use physical force. Initially Laura resisted, but after trying and then failing to obtain enough medication from other doctors, Laura returned to Dr. W. An exchange of sex for drugs evolved, continuing for more than a year, and included sexual behaviour that consisted of fondling and simulated intercourse, prior to the patient receiving a prescription renewal or a supply of medication from the doctor.

Dr. W refused to prescribe to Laura when he learned that she was under criminal investigation for "double doctoring," but when she visited upstairs with him, he continued to give her pills. Laura told Dr. W that she needed help with her addiction. Dr. W advised her to "just quit." Laura stopped coming to him and took the initiative to enter a rehabilitation centre after being charged with obtaining narcotic prescription drugs without disclosing particulars of prescriptions from other doctors.

Some time after entering treatment, Laura sued Dr. W in a civil suit[6] on the grounds of negligence, breach of fiduciary duty,[7] breach of contract and sexual assault as the tort[8] of battery, which is the intentional infliction of force on another person. Laura lost her case at trial and again on appeal to the British Columbia Court of Appeal. However, the judges of the Supreme Court of Canada unanimously agreed that the lower

---

[6] A civil suit is a legal action that does not rely on criminal law, initiated by one party against another, in pursuit of rectification of a particular dispute, usually by way of monetary compensation known as "damages."

[7] Fiduciary duty is defined in law as follows:

    (1)   The fiduciary has scope for the exercise of some discretion or power.

    (2)   The fiduciary can unilaterally exercise that power or discretion so as to affect the beneficiary's legal or practical interests

    (3)   The beneficiary is peculiarly vulnerable to or at the mercy of the fiduciary holding the discretion or power [*Frame v. Smith*, [1987] 2 S.C.R. 99 at 136 per Wilson J.].

[8] Tort is a historical English word, still used to include an offence in civil law (not criminal) that has been defined in *Black's Law Dictionary*, 6th ed. (St. Paul: West Publishing, 1990) 1489 as a " ... legal wrong committed upon the person or property independent of contract. It may be either (1) a direct invasion of some legal right of the individual; (2) the infraction of some public duty by which special damage accrues to the individual; (3) the violation of some private obligation by which like damage accrues to the individual." Generally, a plaintiff must prove "a violation of some duty owing to the plaintiff," and generally such duty must arise by operation of law and not by mere agreement of the parties. Specifically, the tort of "battery" is the "consummation of a wrongful assault" and battery always includes an assault on the person. There is also a criminal offence of "assault" in s. 265 of the *Criminal Code of Canada*, R.S.C. 1985, c. C-46.

courts were wrong and ordered the doctor to pay damages as well as legal costs to the patient.

We chose *Norberg* as the first case study because of its unique position in Canadian civil law as the only Supreme Court of Canada decision so far to focus on sexual abuse of patients. Laura, the patient, was clearly vulnerable and in dire need of medical care at the time the abuse occurred. The Court made note of the fact that Laura had testified that she thought Dr. W was "lonely" — a description that might be considered an indication that Dr. W was vulnerable in his own way as well. Other case studies in this Guide provide more examples of serious mistakes in judgment that health professionals have made, sometimes during times of disruption and stress in their own personal lives. Certainly, the evidence in a number of the case studies indicated the presence of illness contributing to unprofessional, predatory behaviour. This is not to excuse the professional or blame the patient. But the "real life" facts in these cases serve to underscore the importance of 1) effective education with ongoing training and support in professional conduct and boundaries, and 2) enforcement of clear, consistent and widely disseminated standards of professional conduct — combined to serve as the primary means of preventing damage to patients (and professionals) due to sexual boundary crossing by health professionals.

C. UNDERSTANDING THE PROBLEM: QUESTIONS AND ANSWERS

The dynamics of sexual contact between health professionals and their patients or the effect of sexual exploitation of patients by health professionals are not popular topics in society at large or, for that matter, in much of the curricula of schools for health professionals. In attempts to understand the nature of sexual abuse of patients and what can be done to prevent its occurrence, a number of questions recur, such as:

- What constitutes sexual abuse?
- How extensive is the problem?
- How many patients are affected by sexual abuse at the hands of health care providers and, when they are, just what damage is done?
- Are there any situations in which sexual relations between health care provider and patient can be sanctioned?
- What actually happens to a health professional when there are allegations of sexual abuse?

The answers to these questions are not simple and the various perspectives brought to answering them differ. However, policies and legislation in Ontario provide some clear guidelines and requirements that merit close attention from individual students and practitioners in the health professions and their related organizations.

1. Sexual Abuse Defined

The term "sexual abuse" in relation to patients is now defined by Ontario legislation in the *RHPA*, which specifies three types of the offence, in the following detail:[9]

1. sexual intercourse or other forms of physical sexual relations between the member and the patient;
2. touching of a sexual nature of the patient by the member; or
3. behaviour or remarks of a sexual nature by the member towards the patient.

In addition to defining these three types (some might call them "levels") of sexual abuse, subsection 51(5) 2 the *Code* of the *RHPA* defines specific acts of sexual abuse which, upon a finding of guilt, trigger mandatory revocation of the professional's certificate of registration (which is required to practise in Ontario).[10]

The goal of this Guide is to provide current, relevant, understandable information to answer the kinds of questions just described in a format that supports learning and educating by health professionals.

2. Causes of Sexual Abuse of Patients

Is sexual contact between patients and health professionals treating them a recent or rare phenomenon? Certainly not, but relatively little focused research has been done on this phenomenon. Public understanding of the causes, prevalence and the consequences of this boundary violation in professional health care has shifted and expanded in recent years.

---

[9]   *Regulated Health Professions Act, Health Professions Procedural Code, supra* note 2, s. 1(3).

[10] Clauses 51(5) 92 (i) through (v).

(a) Transference and Counter-transference

As shown in some of the case studies in this Guide, transference and counter-transference are described as strong elements in boundary crossing by professionals, many of whom have not been adequately educated or trained in the dynamics at work when such abuse occurs. As Susan Penfold, Professor Emeritus in Psychiatry at the University of British Columbia, describes it,

> [t]ransference arises from a tendency to exclude new information, cling to what is familiar, and see the past in the present. Childhood experiences, which may be forgotten, are powerful influences on current attitudes and behaviours. … The interaction between a health professional and a patient seeking [care?] has some parallels with that between a parent and a child. The patient is in a trusting, vulnerable, childlike position, and the health professional is the parent-surrogate. In this situation, the patient displaces onto the health professional feelings that she had, as a child, about parents or other significant figures.[11]

As a result of their lack of understanding about transference, some professionals can make very serious errors in judgment and believe that they are not placing their patient at risk of harm by crossing a sexual boundary because they feel that they are merely responding to their own (and the patient's) autonomous sexual desires. This is termed "counter-transference" and Dr. Penfold described it as

> [f]eelings stirred up in the health professional by the patient. The emotions relate to the patient's attitude, appearance, personality, and behaviour, and are also influenced by the health professional's own past life experiences. The professional's countertransference is increased by life stresses and unresolved emotional conflicts. Countertransference can lead to inappropriate over-involvement with patients, or unhelpful negative reactions. For instance, patients may remind health professionals of their own traumatic life experiences as children, or of hated parents or ex-spouses…. all health professionals can benefit from recognizing how their personal issues impact on patient care….[12]

Professionals need education, training and support to recognize and respond to transference dynamics — *before* they can apply the knowledge and skill needed, especially when they find themselves in life situations that are stressful or unhealthy, which in turn can increase the risk of crossing sexual boundaries and causing harm.

---

[11] S. Penfold, *Sexual Abuse by Health Professionals: A Personal Search for Meaning and Healing* (Toronto: University of Toronto Press, 1998) at 20, 21.
[12] *Ibid.*, at 22.

3. Prevalence of Sexual Abuse of Patients: Just a Few "Bad Apples"?

The identification of sexual abuse of patients as a serious problem affecting a significant number of patients and health professionals is quite recent. Some health professionals struggle with the persistent belief that reports of sexual abuse have been caused by "just a few bad apples." Seeking more and more precise quantification of the extent of sexual abuse by health professionals is useful, but we know enough already about "the numbers" to acknowledge that this is a problem amongst health professionals that is real, that is deep and that causes serious harm, and that these numbers do not need to be huge to signal a significant and serious problem.

(a) Canadian Research

(i) INCIDENCE

The first task force in Canada (the 1991 Task Force)[13] to hold public and private hearings on the question of sexual abuse of patients was commissioned in 1991 by the regulatory body that governs all licensed medical doctors in the province of Ontario, the College of Physicians and Surgeons of Ontario (CPSO), in response to media and public criticism of how patients' complaints were being handled.[14] When the independent task force issued its preliminary report in 1991, it found that no Canadian data was available, but research from the United States indicated that from 6 to 13 percent of patients had likely experienced some form of sexual contact with doctors.[15] The methodology in these American studies varied, with some being based on anonymous "self-reporting" by doctors and others on surveys of patients.

Like any other group of offending health professionals, those who sexually abuse their patients represent a small but significant minority of the members of their respective professions. Patients who are sexually

---

[13] M. McPhedran, H. Armstrong, R. Edney, B. Long, P. Marshall & R. Roach, *The Final Report of the Independent Task Force on Sexual Abuse of Patients* (Toronto: College of Physicians & Surgeons of Ontario, 1991).

[14] P. Taylor, "Probe into Boy's Death Reaching Conclusion", *The Globe and Mail* (13 November 1990) A11.

[15] N.K. Gartrell, J. Herman, S. Olarte *et al.* "Psychiatrist-patient sexual contact: results of a national survey I: prevalence" (1986) 143 Am. J. Psychiatry 1126-31; S.H. Kardner, M. Fuller & I.M. Mensh, "A survey of professionals' attitudes and practices regarding erotic and non-erotic contact with patients" (1973) 130 Am. J. Psychiatry 1077-81.

abused are much greater in number than the professionals involved in the abuse, yet they represent a limited percentage of all patients in Ontario.

In consultation with the CPSO, statistician Dr. Earl Berger conducted the first Canadian sexual abuse of patients survey in 1991. In this survey of 549 Ontario women, 7 percent of respondents reported inappropriate watching or sexualized comments by a professional and 2 percent reported sexual abuse involving physical contact. In total, 8 percent reported either or both experiences.[16] The figures were much higher among women with a university education. Twelve percent of these women reported inappropriate watching or comments, 4 percent reported sexual contact and 15 percent reported either or both experiences. In Dr. Berger's opinion, the 15 percent figure was a more reliable estimate of the extent of sexual abuse by professionals.[17] In a study conducted by the British Columbia College of Professionals and Surgeons in 1992, 8 percent of male doctors acknowledged sexual contact with patients.[18]

In a survey conducted by PricewaterhouseCoopers Inc. (PwC) in 2000 for the Ontario Health Professions Regulatory Advisory Council (HPRAC), male and female adult patients in Ontario were asked about direct experiences with sexual boundary crossing by a health professional during the first five years after the *RHPA* was enacted. The survey reported on the incidence of "inappropriate behaviour/remarks and/or sexual contact/touching" by health professionals during 1994 through 1999.[19] One percent of the respondents to this study reported having experienced sexual contact or touching by a health professional and 2 percent had experienced inappropriate behaviour or remarks.[20] One approach to understanding this survey is to hypothesize that about 8 million of the 10 million people living in Ontario were represented in this survey (because children were not included). This leads to an estimate that well over 200,000 Ontarians, taking into account the likelihood of underreporting, have experienced sexual abuse at the hands of health professionals. Do these results — which indicate lower rates of sexual abuse than reported in Dr. Berger's 1991 survey of adult women —

---

[16] E. Berger, *Canada Health Monitor*, PriceWaterhouse Canada (Toronto, 1991) 3.
[17] *Ibid.*
[18] Committee on Professional Sexual Misconduct, *Crossing the Boundaries* (Vancouver: College of Physicians & Surgeons of British Columbia, November, 1992) Introduction.
[19] PricewaterhouseCoopers, *Evaluation of the Effectiveness of the Health Professional Colleges' Complaints and Discipline Procedures with Respect to Professional Misconduct of a Sexual Nature and Status of Colleges' Patient Relations Program*, Vol. 3, College Member Survey (Toronto: HPRAC, 1999).
[20] *Ibid.*

mean that fewer health professionals were guilty of sexual abuse in that five-year period?

Perhaps, but there are reasons to believe that other factors contributed to the lower rate of sexual abuse reported by PwC. For example, the PwC survey sampled both men and women and, according to Dr. Berger, older men and women are much less likely than "baby boomers" to report any kind of abuse. Further, older men and women in general are consistently less likely to report unpleasant experiences.[21] Dr. Berger has suggested that underreporting could be as high as 25 percent, when taking into account the evidence of underreporting in surveys of other forms of abuse.[22] If we look at the issue using 2 percent as a moderate estimate of the percentage of Ontario men and women patients who have experienced some form of sexual abuse, the extent of the problem becomes clearer. Other evidence of prevalence indicate that women are more likely than men to be sexually abused by health professionals.[23] It should also be noted that the PwC survey asked respondents about their experiences for the limited time between 1994 and 1999, while the 1991 survey asked whether sexual activity or contact of any kind had ever happened to them in the past. According to Dr. Berger, the 1991 and 1999 figures are not inconsistent with one another,[24] and in any event, the data clearly indicate that sexual abuse by health professionals remains a problem of considerable proportion — for professionals, patients and our society at large.

To understand the impact of this failure to maintain high standards of practice, it is worth considering the ripple effect. The reach of the problems caused by the sexual abuse of patients is far greater than most observers could ever contemplate. To help illustrate this, the Special Task Force on Sexual Abuse of Patients, appointed by Ontario's Minister of Health in 2000 and reporting in 2001 (the 2001 Task Force),[25] published findings on the range of professions and locations that patients who communicated with the Task Force identified with experiences of sexual abuse by health professionals. Of some 60 reports heard by the 2001 Task Force, abuse was reported to have occurred in the following Ontario locations: Barrie, Brantford, Burlington, Cambridge, Chatham,

[21] Berger, *supra* note 16.
[22] *Ibid.*
[23] 2001 Report 3.
[24] Berger, *supra* note 16.
[25] M. McPhedran, H. Armstrong, B. Long, P. Marshall & R. Roach, *What About Accountability to the Patient? The Independent Final Report of the Special Task Force on Sexual Abuse of Patients* (Toronto: Ministry of Health & Long-Term Care, 2001).

Fort Erie, Gloucester, Kincardine, London, Manila, Metro Toronto, Mississauga, Niagara, Ottawa, Penetanguishene, Shelbourne, St. Catharines, Thornhill and Windsor. The following health professions were identified as having subjected their patients to sexual abuse: chiropractors, dentists, medical laboratory technologists, nurses, massage therapists, physicians, psychiatrists, psychologists, psychotherapists, physiotherapists and registered practical nurses.

The 2001 Task Force noted that self-reported rates of sexual contact by professionals ranged from 0 percent (Canadian psychiatric residents, 1991) to 13 percent (U.S. professionals, 1973).[26] However, there are problems with these particular data because the surveys were based on self-reports and other literature confirms,[27] that sexual offenders tend to deny or to underreport the number of times they offend. Furthermore, response rates to the surveys, which ranged from 19 to 78 percent, may not be truly representative of professionals in general. In particular, there is reason to believe that low response rates may tend to underestimate prevalence, because professionals who are abusing may be less likely to respond to such questionnaires.[28]

There is also reason to believe that what professionals have self-reported as sexual abuse may be different and more limited than the current definitions in the *RHPA*. For example, in a 1994 study of Canadian obstetrician-gynaecologists, Lamont *et al.* found that 10 percent of their sample reported knowledge of a colleague who was sexually involved with a patient, but 23 percent reported awareness of sexual involvement that would be viewed as sexual abuse or impropriety as defined by the CPSO.[29] It should be noted that all of these studies asked respondents whether they had ever had "sexual contact" (which was defined in a variety of ways). As a result, there is inadequate information on how frequently new instances of sexual contact occur or how rates may be changing over time.

---

[26]   *Ibid.*, at 3.
[27]   *Ibid.*, at 4.
[28]   The authors wish to acknowledge Dr. Briar Long and Dr. Nick Kates for their analysis of these studies as provided to the 2001 Task Force.
[29]   J. Lamont & C. Woodward, "Patient-physician Sexual Involvement: A Canadian Survey of Obstetrician-gynaecologists" (1994) 150 C.M.A.J. 1433 at 1434.

(*ii*) DIVERSITY

With some exceptions, such as the study of female physicians who reported abuse/harassment by patients[30] and the reports of female medical students surveyed for their experiences of abuse/harassment by instructors and supervisors,[31] prevalence of abuse within professions is an under-researched area.

As well, little of the research has been analyzed by gender, race, age, class or other such social determinants. A quick review of the gender breakdown within the two largest regulated health professions in Ontario, and then within the sub-group of professionals charged with sexual abuse by each college, shows that the field for more gender-based analysis is rich with possibility. For example, the College of Nurses of Ontario (CNO) reported that in 1997, although its membership was 97.2 percent female nurses, male nurses accounted for 58 percent of the respondents in the 48 sexual abuse cases investigated by the CNO between 1994 and 1998. As an anecdotal observation, the percentage of women medical students in Ontario universities has increased substantially over the past two decades and women doctors have begun to be represented relatively more frequently in the summaries of Discipline Committee findings of guilt for sexual abuse, regularly reported at the back of the CPSO magazine, *Members' Dialogue.*

Indications are that patients who are disadvantaged socially and economically, including those with childhood sexual abuse histories, may be at higher risk of sexual abuse and re-abuse by persons who are in positions of power over them, including health professionals. As an example of the sort of inquiry lacking in sexual abuse of patients research, consider a Winnipeg study of 1003 women patients over about a two-year period (between November 1992 and March 1995), in which over a third (36.5 percent) of the respondents reported having been sexually abused, 74 percent of those incidents having occurred during childhood. The prevalence was higher among Aboriginal women than among non-Aboriginal women (44.8 percent versus 30.1 percent, p <0.001). Although the researchers did not ask a specific question on re-abuse, they did conclude that a history of sexual abuse was associated with other clinical, lifestyle

---

[30] M.S. Schneider & S.P. Phillips, "A Qualitative Study of Sexual Harassment of Female Doctors by Patients" (1977) 45:5 Social Science and Medicine 669-76; S.P. Phillips & M.S. Schneider, "Sexual Harassment of Female Doctors by Patients" (1993) 329:26 N. Engl. J. Med. 1936-9.

[31] R. Moscarello, K.J. Margittai & M. Rossi, "Differences in Abuse Reported by Female and Male Canadian Medical Students" (1994) 150:3 C.M.A.J. 357-63.

and reproductive factors, suggesting that sexual abuse may be associated with subsequent health behaviours, beyond specific physical and psycho-social disorders. They found that Aboriginal and non-Aboriginal women who have suffered sexual abuse showed substantial differences in their subsequent health and health-related behaviours.[32]

D. PROHIBITION OF PROFESSIONAL/PATIENT SEXUAL CONTACT

There is quite a range of popular opinion as to whether sexual contact between a health professional and a patient should be prohibited,[33] even though prohibition is the standard of practice for all health professions in every jurisdiction in Canada and the United States. See, for example, the Canadian Medical Association (CMA) policy discussed later in this chapter. However, the socio-medical research on assessing the damage done to patients as a result of professional-patient sex is now consistent in concluding that when sexual words, gestures or acts occur between a caregiver and patient, they are usually influenced by a psychological state known technically as transference or counter-transference — unconsciously influencing professionals who allow intimate boundaries to be breached — at great risk of harm to their patients and often, to themselves and others in the lives of both professional and patient, who will be affected by the transgression.[34]

Numerous organizations, in a number of jurisdictions, have reached the conclusion that violations of professional standards and of the trust implicit in the caregiving relationship are not good for patients and are outside the boundaries of acceptable standards of professional care. A 1992 editorial in the *British Medical Journal* asserted that sexual contact between doctors and patients was almost always harmful to the patient,[35] and an article in the *Journal of Medical Ethics* of New Zealand argued in support of a regulatory framework that focused on *risk of harm*, referencing the policy of "zero tolerance of sexual abuse of patients"

---

[32]   T. Kue Young & Alan Katz, "Survivors of sexual abuse: clinical, lifestyle and repro-ductive consequences" (1998) 159 C.M.A.J. 329-34.

[33]   Margaret Wente, "Are Women Moral Idiots?", *The Globe and Mail* (6 September 2001) A21.

[34]   See for example Judith Herman, M.D., "A Healing Relationship" in *Trauma and Re-covery: The aftermath of violence — from domestic abuse to political terror* (New York: Basic Books, 1997) at 134-49.

[35]   T. Fahy & N. Fisher, "Sexual contact between doctors and patients" (1992) 304:6841 Brit. Med. Assoc. J. 1519-20.

initially proposed by the first Canadian task force in 1991. At the time, the New Zealand author, described as a medical doctor in general practice, uses the following logical construct to test the higher standard, "risk of harm" in the medical context:

> When this premise is accepted as fact and used to draw the conclusion that sexual contact should never take place between doctors and patients, the argument takes the following form ...
>
> Proposition 1. Thalidomide is **almost always harmful.**
>
> Hypothesis Proposed. It is impossible to predict who will not be harmed by thalidomide.
>
> Proposition 2. Almost always harmful drugs **where it is impossible to predict who might be harmed** ought never to be used.
>
> Conclusion. Thalidomide ought **never to be used**. [Emphasis added.][36]

The author goes on to note how justifying sexual contact(s) with a patient, as a "special case," needs to be scrutinized:

> The doctor who wishes to make an exception for himself has claimed to be able to identify Miss Jones as someone who will not be harmed by sexual contact with him. Medicine has a history of charlatans who claim to be able to distinguish the "special cases" who will benefit from interventions that are, in general, dangerous. They claim skills not shared by their peers, and from which they make a personal gain. It is difficult to see how the doctor who wishes to make an exception for himself escapes the charge that he is behaving like a quack.[37]

A study conducted by the Institute for Clinical Evaluative Sciences (ICES)[38] of final-year medical students in Ontario in 2002, commissioned by the CPSO found that

> ...the vast majority of students knew that having a relationship with a current patient is always unacceptable, however, a substantial minority of medical students fail to recognize that sexual relationships with current patients, regardless of who initiates them, always constitute sexual abuse, and that physicians are responsible for preventing such relationships, even if patients appear to consent.... Moreover,

---

[36] R.M. Cullen, "Arguments for zero tolerance of sexual contact between doctors and patients" (1999) 25 J. of Med. Ethics 482 at 483.

[37] *Ibid.*

[38] College of Physicians and Surgeons of Ontario, "Sexual Abuse of Patients" *Member's Dialogue* (November/December 2002), online, College of Physicians and Surgeons <http://www.cpso.on.ca/Publications/Dialogue/1102/toc.htm>.

> 28% of the students either disagreed or were uncertain if they would report sexual abuse when they worked closely with the physican.[39]

even though they are required to do so by law.

1. Why Patient "Consent" is Not a Defence

The medical profession has been under a stronger spotlight than the other health professions on issues of sexual abuse. In the recent ICES study of medical students for the CPSO, mentioned above, a number of disturbing observations were made. Only 66 percent of the students reported that they had formally discussed sexual abuse of patients in their courses.[40] Whereas about half agreed that the Ontario laws and guidelines on sexual abuse of patients are fair, almost 10 percent believed that a physical relationship between doctor and patient was not sexual abuse if the patient initiated the relationship.[41] Five percent agreed that as long as both were "consenting adults" then sexual relationships between patients and professionals could be kept private.[42]

With a few exceptions, including the College of Nurses of Ontario, the other regulatory bodies have not attempted the range of programs developed or encouraged by the CPSO, so when medical students display the level of ignorance evident in the 2002 study, it is understandable that the results of this study have generated concern among educators, not only in medical schools but in the other training centres for regulated health professions in Ontario.[43]

Douglas Anderson, a CPSO spokesperson, gave the rationale for this emphasis on education of students on sexual abuse issues, by noting that:

> [e]nsuring that the issue of sexual misconduct is incorporated into the medical curricula will decrease the need of having to devote attention and resources toward the more difficult task of dealing with offenders later in their career and helping victimized patients.[44]

---

[39]   *Ibid.*, at 2.
[40]   *Ibid.*, at 1.
[41]   *Ibid.*, at 2.
[42]   *Ibid.*
[43]   There are 23 health professions regulated under the *RHPA*. Naturopathic doctors are also a regulated profession in Ontario, under a different regime the *Drugless Practitioners Act*, R.S.O. 1990, c. D.18, which among other things makes no specific mention of sexual abuse.
[44]   "Sexual Abuse of Patients", *supra* note 38.

2. "Consent" as Defined in Criminal Cases

Although the level of the power imbalance may vary from health profession to health profession, the Parliament of Canada recognized the inherently suspect nature of "consent" in power relationships by amending the sexual assault provisions of the *Criminal Code of Canada*,[45] which state that "consent is never a defence" when a trust relationship is found to exist. A 1999 decision by the Ontario Court of Appeal reviewed arguments by the defendant that his patients had consented to sexual contact but upheld a two-year prison sentence for a psychologist charged under the *Criminal Code* for engaging in sexual relations with two of his patients.[46] The Court noted that the patients' consent was induced by the exercise of authority arising from the psychologist-patient relationship, observing, "[a]n unequal distribution of power is frequently a part of the doctor-patient relationship."[47]

3. What is the Impact of Sexual Abuse on Patients?

(a) Risk of Harm

While there is still a debate among researchers on such boundary crossing when the patient-professional relationship has been terminated, researchers on professional standards clearly conclude that the *risk of harm* to patients is sufficiently great to warrant the setting of clear and strict boundaries regarding sexual contact with both current and past patients. Patients have to give up a certain amount of personal autonomy and often a great deal of privacy in order to get the kind of treatment that they need for their health care. Protective status in society often disappears when patients have to take off their clothes, answer very personal questions or submit to invasive bodily treatments. But giving up autonomy and transferring trust are part of the professional-patient healing dynamic, enhanced because of the safe context created by reliance on professional standards in the regulatory framework established through democratic governance in the larger public interest.

---

[45]   R.S.C. 1985, c. C-46, s. 273.2 [am. 1992, c. 38, s. 1].
[46]   *R. v. Matheson* (1999), 44 O.R. (3d) 557 (C.A.).
[47]   *Ibid.*, at 18 as cited by LaForest J., in *Norberg v. Wynrib, supra* note 3, at 258.

(b) Secondary or Vicarious Victimization

Experts note that sexual abuse also produces trauma in people who are not directly involved. Dr. Gary Schoener uses the descriptive term "associate victims."[48] Dr. Harvey Armstrong has explained that:

> Secondary or vicarious victimization occurs when a second person, on learning of the extent and severity of a person they care about and are involved with, become traumatized themselves and develop post traumatic symptoms.[49]

4. What is the Impact of Sexual Abuse Allegations on Health Professionals?

At the time of learning that allegations of sexual abuse have been made, the respondent health professional has no way to be sure whether the case will stay within the civil regulatory process. If the complaint of sexual abuse is taken to the police and criminal charges are laid, and also taken to a regulatory college and an investigation is commenced (an administrative/civil law process), then it is possible that the respondent/professional and the complainant/patient will find themselves enmeshed in complex, stressful and lengthy procedures in parallel or sequential processes governed by rules of procedure in both the civil and criminal spheres of the law.

As explored in more detail in Chapter 3, the risk of significant damage to a professional's livelihood, family and community status is considerable — under either or both civil or criminal systems. Being a member of a self-regulating health profession in Ontario is predicated on assumptions of trustworthiness and skill, which in turn can convey to the professional certain benefits and respect, but the "flip side" for a professional is experienced when the due process of self-regulating procedures starts to impact on the professional's practice and personal life.

---

[48]   Personal communication with M. McPhedran, March 19, 2000.
[49]   M. McPhedran, *et al.*, 2001 Task Force, *supra* note 25 at 12.

E. FORMAL BOUNDARIES: PROFESSIONAL AND ETHICAL STANDARDS

1. The Hippocratic Oath — Then and Now

Ethical prohibitions against sexual relationships date back at least to the Hippocratic Oath, which was probably written in the fourth century BC and has been translated as follows:

> I swear by Apollo Professional and Asclepius and Hygieia and Panaceia and all the gods and goddesses, making them my witnesses, that I will fulfil according to my ability and judgment this oath and this covenant:
>
> . . .
>
> *Whatever houses I may visit, I will come for the benefit of the sick, remaining free of all intentional injustice, of all mischief and in particular of sexual relations with both female and male persons, be they free or slaves.*[50]

While it is common knowledge among members of the lay public that many doctors take an oath that states a fundamental principle like "First, do no harm," the fact is that not all medical schools require their graduating doctors to take the Hippocratic Oath and use of the Oath has changed over time. Out of 157 deans of allopathic and osteopathic schools of medicine in the United States and Canada that were surveyed in 1992, 98 percent reported using some kind of oath or promise, but a relatively small number reported that the Hippocratic Oath was used.[51] The British Medical Association, in 1997, published a draft revised Hippocratic Oath that is still under discussion while being considered by the World Medical Association.[52]

2. Contemporary Professional Standards Regarding Sex with Patients

For many professionals and students in the health professions in Ontario, the sexual abuse of patients is thought of as a relatively recent issue on

---

[50]   Translation from the Greek by Ludwig Edelstein, *O Temkin & Cltemkin eds.* (Baltimore, Md.: Johns Hopkins Press, 1967) at 6 [emphasis added]. See further, M.L. Campbell, "The Oath: an investigation of the injunction-prohibiting professional-patient sexual relations" (1989) 32 Perspect. Bio. Med. 300-8.

[51]   Robert D. Orr, M.D. & Norman Pang, M.D., *et al.* "Use of the Hippocratic Oath: A review of twentieth century practice and a content analysis of oaths administered in medical schools in the U.S. and Canada in 1993" (1997) 8:4 J. of Clinical Ethics 374 (Courtesy of the Gersten Institute).

[52]   *Ibid.*

which little research has been done. This is sometimes cited as an explanation for an absence of or slight reference to the topic in course materials and training sessions. It is true that the *RHPA* was the first statute in a regulatory framework in Ontario to "name" and define sexual abuse of patients, and to legislate mandatory measures as a means of acknowledging the serious nature of the problem and developing more effective measures directed at deterrence and reduction of such abuse. One of North America's pioneers in researching trauma and recovery in this generation, Dr. Judith Herman of Harvard Medical School, observed:

> The study of psychological trauma has a curious history — one of episodic amnesia. Periods of active investigation have alternated with periods of oblivion. Repeatedly in the past century, similar lines of inquiry have been taken up and abruptly abandoned only to be rediscovered... Though the field has in fact an abundant and rich tradition, it has been periodically forgotten and must be periodically reclaimed.[53]

(a) Examples of Policies on Zero Tolerance of Sex with Patients

Since this book is written primarily for an Ontario audience, we will look briefly at some background to the amendments of the *RHPA* that were specifically introduced to counter the sexual abuse of patients in what might be seen as the beginning of a period of "reclamation" and, ideally "active investigation."

(*i*) MEDICAL DOCTORS

Although Hippocrates recognized the problem of sexual exploitation long ago, and addressed it in his prohibition against sexual contact with patients, in our time, the issue gained the formal acknowledgement of the American Psychiatric Association (APA) in 1973 with an explicit prohibition of sexual contact with patients in the APA code of ethics.[54] The Canadian Psychiatric Association followed the APA 12 years later with this policy statement, which is still operative:

> That the Canadian Psychiatric Association emphatically reaffirms its resolute policy that sexual relations in all its forms between a psychiatrist (as with all professionals), and his/her patient is a grave violation and abuse, on the part of the psychiatrist (as with all professionals) of the patient/doctor relationship. Further, the

---

[53] Herman, *supra* note 34, at 7.
[54] American Psychiatric Association, *Code of Ethics* (1973).

Canadian Psychiatric Association unequivocally condemns such misconduct and deems it totally unacceptable under any and all circumstances.[55]

The Ontario Medical Association (OMA) does not have a code of ethics but the Canadian Medical Association (CMA) reviewed policies and initiatives of its provincial and territorial divisions and other professional associations, then released an updated policy on "The Patient-Physician Relationship and the Sexual Abuse of Patients (Update 2000)" including some guidelines, educational and preventive strategies.[56] In the CMA policy, the sexual abuse of patients is defined as "any behaviour that transgresses the patient-physician relationship in a sexually exploitive manner by a physician's words or actions." The CMA policy also states:

…it is vital to recognize that it is the responsibility of physicians to establish and maintain the boundaries or limits of behaviour for themselves and for their patients.

…Physicians should never be sexually or romantically involved with their current patients.

…The CMA believes that sexual abuse never has a place in the patient-physician relationship. Furthermore, when physicians have reasonable grounds to believe that sexual abuse has occurred in any patient-physician or other patient-provider relationship they have an ethical responsibility to protect the patient from harm by taking every reasonable step to ensure that such behaviour is reported to the appropriate authority.

Unlike the OMA and CMA, where membership is optional, membership in the regulatory colleges of the health professions under the *RHPA*, such as the College of Physicians and Surgeons of Ontario, is a requirement. The creation of guidelines as part of the educational responsibilities of the colleges, as mandated by the *RHPA*, will be discussed in more detail in Chapter 6, Education. The colleges are required under the *RHPA* to develop guidelines for preventing sexual abuse of patients, whereas the creation of a code of ethics, or a policy on sex with patients, by a professional association such as the OMA or the Ontario Psychological Association (OPA) is voluntary. The voluntary

---

[55] Statement approved by the Board of Directors of the Canadian Psychiatric Association (1 June 1985).

[56] Canadian Medical Association, "The Patient-Physician Relationship and the Sexual Abuse of Patients (Update 2000)." Copies of the full policy can be obtained from the Member Service Centre of the CMA, 1867 Alta Vista Drive, Ottawa, Ontario K1G 3Y6; call toll-free: 1-888-855-2555; fax: 1-613-236-8864; or online at <http://www.cma.ca>.

nature of this commitment is demonstrated when a professional association articulates a different position, as was done in 1998 by the OMA (discussed in more detail at the end of this chapter). In 1993, OMA representatives responded to the Ontario government's Bill 100,[57] which proposed a legislated prohibition on sex with patients. The OMA presented its submission to members of the Standing Committee on Social Development of the Ontario legislature, stating:

> The OMA strongly agrees that sexual intercourse and touching of a sexual nature are serious abuse and an exploitation of the professional and trust relationship between the doctor and the patient, and are clearly unjustifiable in the clinical encounter. [58]

(*ii*) PSYCHOLOGISTS

All codes of ethics for psychologists prohibit sexual exploitation of patients. The *Canadian Code of Ethics for Psychologists* of the Canadian Psychology Association (CPA) — which has been adopted by the OPA — specifies the prohibition and provides specific guidance to members of the profession.[59] The CPA's *Canadian Code of Ethics for Psychologists* is currently in its third edition,[60] and was the first such code developed for health care providers. It provides a means of deciding ethical ambiguities based on a "decision tree" process.

(*iii*) CHIROPRACTORS

By early 1996, the Council of the College of Chiropractors of Ontario adopted comprehensive policies related to informing its members about sexual abuse. The policies are complemented by supportive literature,

---

[57] *An Act to amend the Regulated Health Professions Act, 1991*, S.O. 1993, c. 37.

[58] Ontario Medical Association Submission to the Standing Committee on Social Development Regarding Bill 100, an *Act to Amend the Regulated Health Professions Act* (November 1993) at 8.

[59] I. Jackson, "The Psychological Support Program of the Ontario Psychological Association" (Paper presented to the 104th Annual Convention of the American Psychological Association. Toronto, August 9, 1996) [unpublished]. (With permission of the author.)

[60] Used as a model by the Association of States and Provincial Psychology Boards, the North American Federation of regulatory bodies in psychology, the first edition of the CPA *Canadian Code of Ethics for Psychologists* was developed by Dr. Carole Sinclair and Dr. Jean Pettifor in the mid 1980s.

videos and risk self-assessment tools.[61] Of those professions that have adopted a policy such as that of the College of Chiropractors, some have not necessarily followed through with implementation measures. In its 2000 study of the effectiveness of the patient relations programs of the colleges, HPRAC looked at the extent to which each college had provided guidelines for its members. It categorized 16 of the colleges as having "integrate[d] robust and fully developed components into College activities," four colleges as having met "requirements in a way that reflect[ed] the intent of the legislation," and one college (Opticians) as having met only "minimal or narrow definition of legislated requirements."[62]

(*iv*) ONTARIO HOSPITAL ASSOCIATION

At the time of writing, some of the bodies representing health professionals and health care institutions in Ontario had adopted clear policy statements against sexual contact with patients, even though there is no statutory requirement to do so. For example, the philosophy of zero tolerance that was adopted by the CPSO Governing Council in May of 1991 has been taken up by other organizations and institutions, including the Ontario Hospital Association (OHA), thus affecting the many hospitals that make up the OHA membership. The OHA confirmed its commitment to the philosophy of zero tolerance of sexual abuse with "a mandate to develop comprehensive guidelines for hospitals to use in the development or revision of their own policies on abuse."[63]

---

[61] College of Chiropractors of Ontario, "Prevention of Sexual Abuse of Patients" *Guideline G-001*, Patient Relations Committee, Approved by Council (18 February 1996).

[62] Health Professions Regulatory Advisory Council, *Effectiveness of Colleges' Patient Relations Programs: Advice to the Minister of Health and Long-Term Care* (May 2001) Appendix A at 6, online, Health Professions Regulatory Advisory Council <http://www.hprac.org/downloads//patientrelations/PatientRelationsPrograms.pdf>.

[63] Ontario Hospital Association, "Guidelines for the Development of Hospital Policies on Managing Abuse: Roles and Responsibilities of Hospital Boards;" Publication H302, <http://www.oha/ohapubl.nsf>.

F.   RESPONSES TO THE PROBLEM OF SEXUAL ABUSE IN CANADA

We need to look back more than three decades to find the earlier research on sexual abuse of patients — in the United States.[64] But in Canada, when the College of Physicians and Surgeons of Manitoba established an internal committee to look into the issue in the 1980s, it became the first Canadian regulatory health organization to take such an initiative.[65] However, no contemporary Canadian research was available until 1991 when the first national survey in Canada on sexual abuse of patients by physicians was directed by statistician Dr. Earl Berger.[66] The survey was partially the result of the decision of the College of Physicians and Surgeons of Ontario that year to commission an independent task force (meaning that the majority of the task force members were not doctors) with the "mandate to seek information from the public, the College, and individual doctors through public and private hearings in various cities in Ontario."[67]

Generally speaking, the regulatory framework for health professional self-regulation is much the same in Canadian provinces and territories, with decision-making authority delegated by statute to the regulatory bodies of specific health professions by the provincial or territorial governments. Each regulatory body has staffed offices with a process for receiving complaints from the public and uses a system of peer judgment to reach conclusions on guilt and penalty in a range of professional misconduct situations, with one major variance. Only Ontario has placed 24 of the regulated health professions under the same umbrella of legislation, the *RHPA*, which requires that their colleges all follow the same procedural code and reporting standards, as a condition of self-regulation.

Following the CPSO initiative in 1991, doctors' regulatory colleges in a number of other provinces (for example, British Columbia, Alberta, New Brunswick, and Prince Edward Island) established inquiries into the sexual abuse of patients and thereafter some provincial legislatures (for

---

[64]   See for example, J. Marmor, "The Seductive Psychotheropist" (1970) 31 Psychiatry Digest 10-16; S. Kardener, M. Fuller and I. Mensch, "A Survey of Physicians' Attitudes and Practices Regarding Erotic and Nonerotic Contact with Patients" (1973) 130 American Journal of Psychiatry 1077-81.

[65]   College of Physicians and Surgeons of Manitoba <http://www.umanitoba.ca/colleges/cps/>.

[66]   Berger, *supra* note 16.

[67]   Resolution of the Council of the CPSO, January 28, 1991.

example, Prince Edward Island and British Columbia) created new, stricter laws in response to sexual abuse of patients by doctors. However, only Ontario extended the legislation with its adjudication requirements to include so many health professions in addition to physicians.[68]

1. Reports and Policies in the Context of Zero Tolerance

(a) *Leadership by the College of Physicians and Surgeons of Ontario*

In May 1991, the CPSO, followed the recommendation of the first Ontario task force and became the first regulatory body to adopt a clear "zero tolerance" policy, as follows:

> The Council of the College of Physicians and Surgeons of Ontario confirms its commitment to the safety of the public by affirming the philosophy of zero tolerance of sexual abuse and, in accordance with that philosophy, to develop policies, procedures, practices and education programs that support it.[69]

(b) *Government Responses — The Regulated Health Professions Act, 1991*

Section 3 of the *RHPA* states that individuals are to be treated with sensitivity and respect in their dealings with health professionals, colleges and the Health Professions Appeal and Review Board. When the then-Minister of Health, the Honourable Ruth Grier, presented the amendments including definitions and specific penalties regarding sexual abuse to the *RHPA* to the Ontario Legislature in 1993, she stated that the underlying principle was "zero tolerance of sexual abuse" noting that the purpose of the amendments was

> ...to make health professionals — and this bill applies to all of the regulated health professions — aware that if the trust between a patient and a health practitioner is abused, the consequences will be serious. People seeking health care have the right to expect that the treatment they receive from a health care provider will be proper, not improper, and caring, not damaging.[70]

---

[68] *Medical Practitioners Act*, R.S.B.C. 1996, c. 285; *An Act to Amend the Medical Act*, S.P.E.I., 1997 c. 30.

[69] CPSO Governing Council Motion, May 21, 1991.

[70] Ontario, Legislative Assembly, *Official Report of Debates (Hansard)* L057B (29 July 1993) at 2979 (Hon. Ruth Grier).

(c) The Health Professions Procedural Code of the RHPA

Ontario's *Health Professions Procedural Code* (the *Code*)[71] is Schedule 2 of the *RHPA*: "[T]he all important ... Procedural Code consists of the rules to be followed by the governing bodies in registering members, handling complaints, conducting investigations and conducting discipline and fitness to practise proceedings."[72] It is explicitly stated in the *RHPA*[73] that the *Code* "shall be deemed to be part of each health profession Act." Thus, most health care professionals and most administrators of health care institutions (because of their management responsibilities) in Ontario are governed or affected by the *RHPA* and its *Code*, as well as any specific professional Act that regulates their respective health profession. It should be noted, that while regulated, the profession of naturopathic doctors in Ontario is not explicitly mentioned in the *RHPA*, but is governed instead by the *Drugless Practitioners Act*.[74]

It is clear from section 3 of the *RHPA* that the overriding objective of the legislation is to ensure that health professionals are regulated in the public interest. Similarly, subsection 3(2) of the *Code* states that "[i]n carrying out its objects, the College has a duty to serve and protect the public interest." The *Code* also delineates the objectives of the sexual abuse provisions:[75]

> The purpose of the provisions of this Code with respect to sexual abuse of patients by members is to encourage the reporting of such abuse, to provide funding for therapy and counselling for patients who have been sexually abused by members and, ultimately, to eradicate the sexual abuse of patients by members.

The term "sexual abuse" is defined in the *RHPA* and consists of the following three components:

(a)   sexual intercourse or other forms of physical sexual relations between the member and the patient,

(b)   touching, of a sexual nature, of the patient by the member, or

(c)   behaviour or remarks of a sexual nature by the member towards the patient.[76]

---

[71]   *Supra* note 2 [am. 1993, c. 37].

[72]   L. Bohen, *Regulated Health Professions Act: A Practical Guide* (Aurora: Canada Law Book, 1994) 9.

[73]   *Ibid.*, s. 4.

[74]   *Supra* note 43.

[75]   *Health Professions Procedural Code*, *supra* note 2, s. 1.1.

[76]   *Ibid.*, sub. 1(3).

It is clear that the concept of zero tolerance and the notion of breach of trust are embodied in the legislation.[77] As lawyer Richard Steinecke states in *A Complete Guide To The Regulated Health Professions Act*, "this definition of sexual abuse presumes that consent to sexual conduct is irrelevant; …where there is a practitioner/patient relationship, the conduct is wrong."[78]

(d) Professional and Institutional Responses

The *Code* requires each college to establish a Patient Relations Program to address "measures for preventing or dealing with sexual abuse."[79] Each Patient Relations Program is to include the following elements:

(a)   educational requirements for members;
(b)   guidelines for the conduct of members with their patients;
(c)   training for the College staff;
(d)   provision of information to the public.

2. Principles for Prevention of Sexual Abuse

(a) Coverage

To be consistent with legislation that set standards for public safety and public interest, Laskin and Klein, in *Sexual Abuse Prevention Plans of the Regulated Health Professions: Recommended Approaches and Evaluation Methods*,[80] observe that a prevention program will be successful only if it is directed at all the target groups. These target groups include the health professionals who abuse or are at risk of abusing patients, colleagues of the offenders, the institutions that govern the professions (colleges) and that employ the professionals (for example, hospitals, universities, clinics), supervisors and administrators who oversee the work of the health care professionals, college staff who

---

[77]   See further, L. Melanson, "The Long Road to Reform: Discipline of Sexually Abusive Professionals in Ontario" (1997) 10 Can. J. Admin. L. & Prac. 307 at 347; and S. Rodgers, "Health Care Providers and Sexual Assault: Feminist Law Reform?" (1995) 8 Can. J. Women & Law 159 at 182.

[78]   R. Steinecke, *A Complete Guide To The Regulated Health Professions Act*, looseleaf (Aurora, Ont.: Canada Law Book, updated January 2000) at 10-4.

[79]   *Health Professions Procedural Code*, *supra* note 2, s. 84.

[80]   B. Laskin & P. Klein, *Sexual Abuse Prevention Plans of the Regulated Health Professions: Recommended Approaches and Evaluation Methods: Report to the Health Professions Advisory Council* (Health Professions Regulatory Advisory Council, Toronto: December 1996) at 11.

receive and deal with complaints, clients/patients, and the public. Laskin and Klein noted that each prevention program must include an explanation of the nature of the fiduciary relationship and a thorough presentation of boundaries, as well as the impact on the patient of boundary violations.[81]

(b) Regulatory College Programs

In 2001, HPRAC conducted an assessment of prevention programs in each of the regulatory colleges under the *RHPA*, and found that all but one of the colleges had met requirements reflecting the intent of the legislation with the majority of them (14) integrating their programs well into their activities.[82] Despite this, however, HPRAC concluded that more work was needed and stated the following:

> In assessing the likelihood of effectiveness of patient relations activities in achiev-
> ing the objective of enhancing relations between members and patients, HPRAC
> regards compliance with the statutory provisions as necessary but not sufficient for
> effectiveness. Despite compliance by most Colleges, Ontario does not have a pub-
> lic that is well-informed on matters such as the rights and responsibilities of pa-
> tients, the public interest mandate of Colleges, and where to make inquiries or pre-
> sent concerns about an individual health professional.[83]

(c) Key Questions to Ask

The following impact analysis of transference, consent and relationship boundaries, as described by Ontario medical researchers, provides a useful basis for analysis:

> [T]wo other issues are paramount:
>
> 1.   Whether a doctor-patient relationship that places the patient in a vulnerable
>   position ever evolved and,
> 2.   whether there is capacity for mutual consent.
>
> These issues are removed from time elements and are much more related to con-
> cepts of transference and its effects on idealization, identification and dependence.
> All therapeutic encounters are evocative of transference feelings.... It is thus illogi-
> cal to presume that there is *ever* a time frame within which mutual consent would

---

[81]   *Ibid.*, at 21-2.
[82]   *Effectiveness of Colleges' Patient Relations Programs, supra* note 62, Appendix A,
        Table 1: HCA Ratings for Overall Patient Relations Programs at 4.
[83]   *Ibid.*, Executive Summary at i.

be possible once a doctor-patient relationship is established. Romantic involvement would always imply a breach of trust.[84]

In the Dr. AB case study profiled in Chapter 4, Dr. Iris Jackson, a former president of the Ontario Psychological Association, was relied upon as an expert witness in a civil lawsuit brought by a victimized patient against her former therapist, in which the judge assessed whether the patient could have truly consented, as follows:

> [The patient] could not have made a free choice to consent in sexual relationship with (her therapist). She was in a sexual relationship with a man who had power over her psychological state of mind and her treatment process. He had initiated erotic contact after a process of grooming her for exploitation and slowly eroding her personal, physical and psychological boundaries and implying that she was special to him and that he "loved her although he was not in love with her."

> [The patient] was in the throes of transference of a love more analogous to that for a father than that for a husband or lover. She was confused, anxious and vulnerable to him and afraid that, if she displeased him, she would lose him and thereby lose not only his attention but also her treatment for the emotional pain that originally brought her to him. There was a power, physical size and social status differential that placed [the patient] at a distinct disadvantage to [her therapist]. In no way could she have freely consented to a sexual relationship with him.[85]

(d) Who's to Blame?

A male physician in general practice in a small Ontario city was one of the many reviewers of the manuscript for this book. He wrote:

> In fact in many cases a physician is actually vulnerable. I certainly think that many in that situation may lose perspective — often physicians in College cases have suffered recent set-backs especially in their personal life or with substance abuse. Many have had insufficient boundaries themselves as children, when they are vulnerable to approaches by others — who then is to blame?

Dr. Susan Penfold is a professor in the Department of Psychiatry at the University of British Columbia and the author of a book on sexual abuse by health professionals. She notes:

> On the whole, our society is not particularly sympathetic to victims, and people often assume that victims cause and deserve their problems. Sympathy for child victims of sexual abuse is more readily evoked, but adolescents and adults may have little credibility. When society lacks an understanding of the fiduciary duty of health professionals, or fails to recognize the enormous power imbalance between

---

[84] P. Garfinkel, B. Dorian, J. Sadavoy & M. Bagby, "Boundary Violations and Departments of Psychiatry" (1997) 42:7 Can J. Psychiatry 764 at 766 [emphasis in original].

[85] *C.(N.) v. Blank*, [1998] O.J. No. 2544 (Gen. Div.) (QL).

health professional and patient, misinterpretations, biases and harsh judgments abound. For instance, the abuse is reinterpreted as "consensual" — an "affair". The victim may be thought to have seduced the health professional. The character of the victim is often maligned and he or she is seen as a dangerous, vindictive, seductive, manipulative person who has outwitted and trapped the health professional in a sexual relationship or grossly exaggerated or lied about an appropriate encounter.[86]

G. THE LAW

This chapter is entitled "The Problem of Sexual Abuse." To understand the problem requires understanding the purpose and function of the regulatory framework that has been legislated in Ontario to respond to sexual abuse of patients. Dr. Gail Robinson has described the need for clear regulatory standards as "another form of transference," in that such legislation or policy is geared to serve the public interest so that people can place (transfer) their trust in health professionals as part of the healing relationship and rely on professionalism not to cross boundaries that *may* cause harm.[87] Defining this boundary in legal and ethical terms and as an appropriate standard of care in the *RHPA* means that even when patients are attempting to encourage the crossing of such personal boundaries, the individual patient's interest and the larger public interest are served when the health professional understands the potential sexual dynamics in a healing relationship and is professionally competent so he or she can be relied on not to cross that boundary.

1. Judicial Decisions and Shifting Perceptions

The philosophy of zero tolerance of sexual abuse was transformed from words to paper when it was woven into legislation that states the view that sexual abuse of patients is never acceptable and must not be tolerated in our society.[88] The *RHPA* recognizes that the risk of harm caused by sexual abuse, which can result in serious long-term damage that is both psychological and physical in nature, cannot be tolerated.[89]

---

[86]   Susan Penfold, "Introduction" in M. McPhedran, *et al.*, 2001 Task Force, *supra* note 25 at xxvii.

[87]   Personal Communication with M. McPhedran, May 16, 2002.

[88]   The authors wish to express appreciation to Ronda Bessner, with assistance from Valerie Markidis and Angela McLeod for background legal research and writing for *What About Accountability to the Patient?*, the 2001 Task Force report (*supra* note 25) that provided the foundation for this section.

[89]   The statement of purpose in s. 1.1 of the *Health Professions Procedures Code* of the *RHPA* reads as follows:

The actual implementation of the zero tolerance principles requires education of both health care professionals and members of the public regarding appropriate behaviour and attitudes in order to ensure that abuse is not committed as a result of ignorance of the ethical and legal boundaries.[90]

In this initial chapter, the case study of "Dr. W" is based on the facts of the civil lawsuit cited as *Norberg*, which is the definitive decision on sexual abuse of patients and the nature of "consent" by the Supreme Court of Canada to date. In their concurring judgment[91] in this 1992 case, Justices Beverly McLachlin (who is now the Chief Justice of the Supreme Court) and Claire L'Heureux-Dubé (who is now retired) accepted the reasoning in the final report of the 1991 Task Force that physicians owed their patients the highest possible legal standard of care.[92] Justice McLachlin described this fiduciary relationship as " ...trust of a person with inferior power that another person who has assumed superior power and responsibility will exercise that power for his or her good and only for his or her good and in his or her best interests."[93]

Although referred to by only two of the nine judges hearing the case, this Supreme Court decision has helped to clarify that a health care professional in Canada is obligated to provide service consistent with the standards associated with a fiduciary relationship — loyalty, good faith, and avoidance of conflict of duty and self-interest — and addressed "the unequal power between the parties and the exploitative nature of the [sexual] relationship."[94] In this case, the Supreme Court found "consent" by a patient to be "inherently suspect" and rejected the argument that the patient can be found responsible for a sexual assault by a professional.[95]

> The purpose of the provisions of this Code with respect to sexual abuse of patients by members is to encourage the reporting of such abuse, to provide funding for therapy and counselling for patients who have been sexually abused by members and ultimately, to eradicate the sexual abuse of patients by members.

[90] M. McPhedran, "Investigating Sexual Abuse of Patient: The Ontario Experience" (1992) 1 Health Law Review 3 at 8-9; Health Professions Regulatory Advisory Council (HPRAC), *Adjusting the Balance, A Review of the Regulated Health Professions Act* (Toronto: HPRAC, 2001) Recommendations 1 and 2 in Appendix B at 1.

[91] A concurring judgement is one written by some members(s) of the court who agree with the final disposition of the case, but do so based on different reasons.

[92] *Norberg v. Wynrib, supra* note 3, at 272. See generally M. Litman, "Fiduciary Law and For-Profit and Not-for-Profit Health Care" in T. Caulfield and B. Von Tigerstrom, eds., *Health Care Reform and the Law in Canada* (Edmonton: University of Alberta Press, 2002) 85.

[93] *Ibid.*

[94] *Ibid.*, at 261.

[95] *Norberg v. Wynrib*, [1992] S.C.J. No. 60, para. 60 *ff*. See also P. Hughes, "Women, Sexual Abuse by Professionals, and the Law: Changing Parameters" (1996) 21

In Chapter 4, we use a case study of Dr. AB, a psychologist who went through both the College disciplinary process and a civil suit brought against him by the patient he abused. The judge in the civil suit discussed the onus on professionals for maintaining boundaries, as follows:

> Exploitation did occur in this case, and the sole responsibility for that rests with Dr. B. There can be no doubt that [the therapist] owed fiduciary obligations to [the patient] when he took her on as a client within his clinical psychology practice. It is also equally clear that he breached those obligations by totally ignoring what were appropriate therapist-client boundaries and particularly by initiating and maintaining a sexual relationship with her. The obligation was on him and him alone to ensure the appropriate boundaries were maintained. By breaching them, he put his own needs ahead of those of [his patient].[96]

2. Sexual Abuse Cases in Civil Law Compared to Criminal Law

(a) Civil Lawsuits Between Private Parties

Within the civil law sphere, a professional can face two different and distinct kinds of legal proceedings that run on different tracks, even though they arise from the same set of facts. The first is an administrative (civil) law process and involves an investigation and possibly a disciplinary hearing conducted by the professional's College, responding to a complaint that the professional has sexually abused a patient or patients. In the College process, the primary issue is whether sexual abuse, as defined by the *RHPA*, occurred. In the second situation a professional may be made a defendant to a civil lawsuit brought by a patient who alleges that the professional has been abusive and harmed her.

(b) Involving the State: Criminal Charges of Sexual Assault

The following excerpts from section 265 of the *Criminal Code* can be applied to include a scenario where a health professional could be found guilty of the crime of sexual assault because "consent" or submission to sexual activities with a health professional was procured or induced by the professional's exercise of authority:

265. (1)   A person commits an assault when

         (a)   without the consent of another person, he applies force intentionally to that other person, directly or indirectly;

Queen's L.J. 297 at 335; and S. Rodgers, "Health Care Providers and Sexual Assault: Feminist Law Reform?" (1995), 8 Can. J. Women & Law 159 at 176.

[96] *C.(N.) v. Blank, supra* note 85, at paras. 174-5, per Aitken J.

. . .

(3)   For the purposes of this section, no consent is obtained where the complainant submits or does not resist by reason of

. . .

(d)   the exercise of authority.

(*i*)   EXAMPLE: CASE STUDY IN CHAPTER 4 — DR. M, THE TORONTO PSYCHOLOGIST

The criminal case of Dr. M, the psychologist in Chapter 4, is an example where the courts (at trial and on appeal) found "the intentional exercise of such a position of authority to obtain any sexual activity [was] criminal...."[97] The appeal court in that case went on to say that "[U]nder those circumstances, when proven to be genuine, consent is no defence," so the professional is found guilty of the crime of sexual assault.[98]

H.   LEARNING ISSUES AND DISCUSSION POINTS: SEX WITH PATIENTS — THREE PERSPECTIVES ON THE LAW

This chapter has provided an overview of the issues raised for health professionals by sexual contact with patients. The case studies and commentary in the following chapters will help readers to explore these issues in more depth and to have ready access to the laws, policies and procedures affecting the standards of practice in their respective health professions.

To stimulate thought and discussion, this chapter concludes with three quotations from a case involving two regulated health professionals — a medical doctor in general practice who billed the Ontario Health Insurance Plan for psychotherapy with a patient with whom he was also having sex — a woman who was a registered physiotherapist, an employee of the doctor's for a time and also, with her husband, a social acquaintance.[99] This case study is featured in more detail in Chapter 3,

---

[97]   *R. v. Matheson, supra* note 46, at 9.
[98]   *Ibid.*
[99]   *Mussani, Re,* [1998] O.C.P.S.D. No. 15 (QL). Dr. Mussani and the OMA lost their appeals of the CPSO findings [*Mussani v. College of Physicians & Surgeons (Ontario)* (2003), 64 O.R. (3d) at 641 (Div. Ct.)] and in October 2003, both Dr. Mussani and the OMA appealed further to the Ontario Court of Appeal. At the time of publication of this Guide, the Ontario Court of Appeal had not yet rendered its decision in this appeal.

but for this chapter, the focus is on learning from discussion that explores some tough issues raised by differing perspectives on the appropriate professional sexual boundary between a doctor and his patient (referred to previously in this chapter under the heading "Examples of Policies on Zero Tolerance of Sex with Patients").

This first chapter is an overview of the "problem of sexual abuse," including some examples of codes and policies on professional conduct (and definitions of misconduct) that have been developed voluntarily by professional associations, but also some of the guidelines regarding sexual abuse mandated by the *Code* of the *RHPA*.

Consider this information as part of the discussion for this chapter: In 1998 the voluntary membership professional association — the OMA — intervened in the above-mentioned doctor's discipline case, challenging the constitutionality of certain provisions in the *RHPA* related to sexual abuse of patients. In taking up the constitutional challenge, the stance on prohibition of doctor-patient sex articulated by the OMA in its court documents differed markedly from its policy statement in 1993 to a provincial legislative committee that was holding hearings on proposed amendments to the *RHPA*.[100]

The following three quotations on the question of when, if ever, sex with a current patient should be considered acceptable under the law reflect three perspectives:

1) the voluntary professional association,
2) the regulatory college, and
3) the unanimous judgment of the court to which the doctor appealed the college finding of guilt, in which the association was given permission to intervene and make its own separate arguments.[101]

Read the three quotations below and then respond to the questions that follow, on the relative merits of each perspective. For the most part, the arguments of the doctor and of the OMA were the same, except that the OMA also challenged the sections of the *RHPA* that stated its purpose and definition in relation to "sexual abuse" asking that these provisions

---

[100] *Supra* note 58.
[101] An "interested party" can apply to a court hearing a case, requesting permission to present arguments relevant to the issues before the court, on the grounds that, as intervenor (in this case, the OMA), it can bring additional arguments and evidence through its "intervention" that will assist the court in deciding on the issues raised by the case. A court (or an administrative tribunal, for example, a discipline committee of a regulatory college) can decide whether it wishes to allow the intervention, or not.

all be considered to be "mandatory revocation provisions" in the law and that all these sections of the law be ruled unconstitutional.[102]

QUOTATION ONE: an excerpt from arguments filed by the OMA. The CPSO has allowed the OMA to intervene (for the first time in a CPSO discipline case) to make constitutional arguments for a health professional's right to engage in "consensual" sex with patients, under certain circumstances despite the provisions in the *RHPA* to the contrary. The following quotation is taken from the OMA factum filed with the CPSO Discipline Committee (that is, the document used in proceedings containing a statement of facts and law):

> No other jurisdiction in the world has comparable provisions *requiring* a disciplinary body to revoke a physician's certificate in cases of sexual abuse, or indeed in any case of professional misconduct....[Paragraph 9]

> The OMA submits that the mandatory revocation provisions violate two aspects of the right to liberty: first, the right to enter into consensual sexual relations; and second, the right to carry on a profession. [Paragraph 23]

> The OMA submits that the mandatory revocation provisions have the effect of preventing physicians from entering into personal relationships, no matter how consensual and no matter what their true nature, and thereby violate their freedom of association. [Paragraph 40]

> The OMA submits that... there is no rational basis on which to conclude that a requirement that the Panel revoke a physician's licence would either encourage reporting of sexual abuse, provide funding for therapy and counselling, or eradicate sexual abuse of patients. [Paragraph 45][103]

QUOTATION TWO: from the decision of a panel of the Discipline Committee of the regulatory college, the CPSO, in responding to the constitutional arguments made by the OMA and the respondent doctor:

---

[102] The OMA is not alone in its opposition to the mandatory revocation requirement upon a finding of sexual abuse as defined in clauses 51(5) 2 (i) to (v). For example, the College of Nurses of Ontario (i.e., the legislated regulatory body, not the Registered Nurses Association of Ontario (RNAO), which is the nurses' association that is equivalent to the OMA) wrote to the Health Professions Regulatory Advisory Council (HPRAC) in 1999, recommending removal of the five-year mandatory revocation requirement for the specified acts of misconduct of a sexual nature, explaining, "...(a)ny incident of sexual abuse needs to be dealt with as a grave violation of trust and professional ethics. However, the mandated penalty precludes the discipline panel from considering the facts of the case and any mitigating circumstances in setting an appropriate and fair penalty." [As quoted in a written communication dated April 28, 2000 from the College of Nurses to Marilou McPhedran, in her capacity as chair of the Special Task Force on the Sexual Abuse of Patients.]

[103] Factum of the Ontario Medical Association as Intervenor in *Mussani, Re*, before the CPSO in 1998.

Section 51(5) of the Code does not regulate sexual relations per se: it regulates the way in which a doctor may practise medicine. The right to practise a profession is characterized as an economic interest rather than a legal right, and so is not the type of liberty which section 7 [of the *Canadian Charter of Rights and Freedoms*[104] in Canada's constitution] is intended to protect. It is the view of the Committee that the proper characterization of subsection 51(5) is not to deprive professionals of their liberty, but rather to regulate the practice and behaviour of doctors within the practice of medicine. The practice of medicine in Ontario is a privilege, which brings with it certain obligations both to their patients, (to refrain from sexual relations), the public and to fellow members of the profession.[105]

QUOTATION THREE: taken from the unanimous decision by three judges of the Ontario Superior Court of Justice on the appeal by the doctor and the OMA of the CPSO Discipline Committee finding of sexual abuse and mandatory revocation of the doctor's certificate of registrations required to practise in Ontario:[106]

Further hypotheticals put forward by the OMA posit a position where the patient makes a "fully consensual" decision to engage in the sexual activity, or the closely related hypothetical of where the physician "has not acted in an exploitative or abusive manner." Both the evidence presented to this court as well as the previous jurisprudence demonstrate that these two scenarios are inherently suspect.... Both the Supreme Court and the Court of Appeal have held that a power imbalance inherently exists between physicians and patients, that patients under the care of a medical doctor are frequently vulnerable, that physicians have a duty to treat patients for the good of the patient and in the patient's best interest, that sexual contact with a patient can cause great harm, and that acquiescence by a patient to sexual relations with his or her physician may not amount to "consent" because of the dynamics of the physician-patient relationship....[at para. 156].

The OMA argues that the Discipline Committee erred in law in concluding that the Mandatory Revocation Provisions do not violate freedom of association. It submits that the freedom of an individual to enter into consensual sexual relationships as he or she desires is protected by section 2(*d*) of the *Charter*, and that the Mandatory Revocation Provisions violate this guarantee [para. 165]....

There is no Canadian jurisprudence which has held that the guarantee of freedom of association extends to the right to have intimate personal relationships.... The purpose of s. 2(*d*) is to promote social interaction and collective actions not private sexual relationships. The courts have repeatedly refused to find that intimate personal relationships are protected under s. 2(*d*) [para. 168]....

---

[104] Part I of the *Constitution Act, 1982*, being Schedule B to the *Canada Act 1982* (U.K.), 1982, c. 11.

[105] *CPSO v. Mussani*, 29 October 1999, page 14, unreported, copy of decision obtained from CPSO.

[106] *Mussani v. College of Physicians & Surgeons (Ontario)* (2003), 64 O.R. (3d) 641.

Lastly, there was nothing in the impugned provisions that absolutely prohibited Dr. Mussani from associating or establishing a relationship with A.K. He simply was required to decide which relationship he wished to have with her, sexual or professional. This was not a difficult choice. Instead, he knowingly undertook the risk of having both relationships [para 170].

I. QUESTIONS FOR DISCUSSION

In your discussion, consider the different perspectives that are brought forth in answering the following questions:

1. Under what circumstances does the law allow a professional to have sexual contact with a patient? With a former patient?
2. What right does a professional have to earn his or her livelihood as a registered and regulated health professional under the *Charter of Rights and Freedoms* and/or the provincial regulatory framework, such as the *RHPA* or the *Drugless Practitioners Act?*
3. What should a professional reasonably expect from his or her professional association when charged with sexual abuse by their regulatory college?
4. Where does the public interest fit into cases like this? Who should be responsible for ensuring that the public interest is protected in such cases?

Chapter 2

THE ONTARIO REGULATORY FRAMEWORK AND SEXUAL ABUSE

In Ontario, most regulated health professionals are governed by the *Regulated Health Professions Act, 1991*,[1] which includes the *Health Professions Procedural Code* (the *Code*),[2] a Code of statutory rules, 21 profession-specific companion statutes, and regulations for each of the 23 regulated professions. In order to assist readers to comprehend fully the implications of the *RHPA*, as applied to the prevention of, or responses to sexual abuse, this chapter is an overview of why and how the Ontario regulatory framework has been constructed. The chapter after this — Chapter 3 — looks specifically at actual sexual abuse cases and how the regulatory process is activated and applied.

A.   CASE STUDY: DR. G, AN ONTARIO PHYSICIAN WORKING IN ARIZONA[3]

Every year, the College of Physicians and Surgeons of Ontario (CPSO) asks each of its members to complete a questionnaire as a requirement of having his or her membership renewed. When Dr. G, a physician registered in Ontario but working in Arizona, completed his 2000 questionnaire, he provided a number of negative answers to questions about any disciplinary actions in which he was involved, when in fact he was immersed in a disciplinary process conducted by the Arizona State College. When the CPSO became aware of the Arizona process and its outcome, which found Dr. G guilty, and noted that Dr. G had misinformed the College when he responded to its questionnaire, the

---

[1]   S.O. 1991, c. 18. The *RHPA* came into force on December 31, 1993.
[2]   S.O 1991, c. 18, Sch. 2.
[3]   *Goldenthal, Re*, [2002] O.C.P.S.D. No. 10 (QL).

CPSO commenced an investigation and subsequently set a date for a disciplinary hearing. Dr. G pled not guilty to the charges.

The disciplinary panel ruled on two allegations against Dr. G. The first involved the determination on whether, by falsifying his questionnaire responses, he was guilty of professional misconduct under the *RHPA*.[4] Second, the panel considered whether the finding of professional misconduct in Arizona and the fact that Dr. G had disobeyed the Arizona Board's orders constituted a similar finding under the Ontario legislation.

Dr. G did not attend the hearing and the panel relied on evidence that it had gathered in its investigation. The panel concluded that Dr. G was guilty, and ordered that a reprimand be placed on the register against him and that he pay costs in the amount of $5,000.

B. CASE STUDY: DR. NMRC, AN ONTARIO PSYCHIATRIST PRACTISING IN QUEBEC

Dr. NMRC was a member of the CPSO at the same time that she was practising in the province of Quebec. She had been treating Mr. A for anxiety and alcohol-related problems for several years, when he called her for help. Dr. NMRC advised Mr. A to come to her home so that she could assess his condition. After seeing Mr. A, Dr. NMRC urged him to go to hospital, but he refused. Instead, Dr. NMRC administered Ativan, which is used to treat anxiety, and allowed Mr. A to stay in her home, which he did. Dr. NMRC continued to lodge Mr. A and treated him as an employee by providing him with a variety of jobs. Mr. A had stayed with Dr. NMRC for a month when the relationship between them became sexual and it continued for the next six months.

Dr. NMRC was eventually convicted under Quebec law of professional misconduct as a result of her relationship with Mr. A. The matter came to the attention of the CPSO, which convened a disciplinary hearing and rendered a decision in July of 2001. The grounds for the hearing were based on the requirements under the *Code*, subsection 51(1), which states:

> A panel shall find that a member has committed an act of professional misconduct if,

. . .

---

[4]   *Supra* note 1.

   (b)   the governing body of a health profession in a jurisdiction other than Ontario has found that the member committed an act of professional misconduct that would, in the opinion of the panel, be an act of professional misconduct as defined in the regulations;

   (b.1) the member has sexually abused a patient....

Dr. NMRC admitted her guilt and the disciplinary panel found that she had committed an act of professional misconduct as alleged. It ordered that her certificate of registration be revoked immediately and that she be reprimanded and that the reprimand be recorded in the College register.

Although the case about Dr. G did not appear to involve issues of sexual abuse, we include it along with the study of Dr. NMRC to open this chapter for two reasons. First, both cases provide a concrete example to show how the elements of legislation work together and second, they demonstrate the reach of health professional legislation in Ontario. Each of the allegations against these health professionals were founded on different parts of the *RHPA*. As it pertains to the legislative framework, when it considered Dr. G's disobedience of the orders of the Arizona regulator, the Ontario discipline panel relied on paragraph 51(1)(b) of the *Code*, which addresses professional misconduct in the following way:

   51. (1) A panel shall find that a member has committed an act of professional misconduct if,

   (a)   the member has been found guilty of an offence that is relevant to the member's suitability to practise;

   (b)   the governing body of a health profession in a jurisdiction other than Ontario has found that the member committed an act of professional misconduct that would, in the opinion of the panel, be an act of professional misconduct as defined in the regulations;

   (b.1) the member has sexually abused a patient; or

   (c)   the member has committed an act of professional misconduct as defined in the regulations.

This section tells us a great deal. Paragraph (b) provides the specific foundation for the panel's findings and demonstrates the power a college has in disciplining its members even for conduct found to be improper in other jurisdictions. Of particular relevance to this Guide is the addition of paragraph (b.1), an amendment made when the sexual abuse provisions were added to the *RHPA,* and which specifically cites sexual abuse as a form of professional misconduct and captures the circumstances of Dr. NMRC. The section also includes in paragraphs (a) and (c) broad bases for the finding of professional misconduct that are subject to further definition, such as paragraph (c) referring to further regulations that can be made under the legislation.

As an example of how regulations affect the process, the panels relied on the specific definition of professional misconduct as defined in the regulations under the *Medicine Act, 1991*.[5] Unlike a section of a statute, which is written by the legislature, regulations are written when authorized in a piece of legislation as the more specific details that a legislature does not engage in but rather delegates, within the legislation, to a specific authority such as a college with the final approval of Cabinet. For example, the regulation-making powers assigned to each college as stated in the above section of the *Code* enables the college to define what it means by professional misconduct as the offence applies to its particular members. Under the *Medicine Act*, Ontario Regulation 856/93 lists 34 different forms of professional misconduct, among them being:

> (1)   The following are acts of professional misconduct for the purposes of clause 51 (1) (c) of the Health Professions Procedural Code:
>
> . . .
>
> 33.   An act or omission relevant to the practice of medicine that, having regard to all the circumstances, would reasonably be regarded by members as disgraceful, dishonourable or unprofessional.

It was this portion of the regulation upon which the Ontario panels relied in concluding that both Dr. G and Dr. NMRC had committed acts of professional misconduct when the former falsified his responses on completion of his annual questionnaire for the College and the latter engaged in sexual impropriety with her patient, Mr. A.

C. REGULATION OF HEALTH PROFESSIONALS IN ONTARIO

This chapter proceeds by establishing the early foundations of professional self-regulation in Canada and then explores the predecessor legislation to the *RHPA*, the *Health Disciplines Act* (*HDA*).[6] Following this is a more comprehensive look at the *RHPA* itself, involving the main statute, and its two Schedules including the *Health Professions Procedural Code* (the *Code*),[7] with particular emphasis placed on how the *RHPA* addresses the issue of sexual abuse. Finally, an overview is provided of the *Drugless Practitioners Act* (*DPA*),[8] which governs

---

[5]   S.O. 1991, c. 30.
[6]   R.S.O. 1980, c. 196.
[7]   *Supra* note 2.
[8]   R.S.O. 1990, c. D.18.

naturopathic doctors, who are not included in the *RHPA*, and comments are provided about a number of statutes affecting the reporting requirements of health care institutions.

1. The Constitutional Roots of Professional Self-Regulation

The regulation of health professionals is based on the constitutional division of powers between the federal and provincial governments, which can be traced back to the *Constitution Act, 1867.*[9] Section 92(13) of the *Constitution Act* attributes authority over "property and civil rights" to the provinces rather than to the federal government. This is a jurisdictional right that has been upheld by the Supreme Court of Canada since 1907.[10] In 1990, in the case of *Knutson v. Registered Nurses' Assn. (Saskatchewan)*, the Court clearly stated that "[i]t can hardly be contended that the province by proper legislation could not regulate the ethical, moral and financial aspect of a trade or profession within its boundaries."[11] Hence, because the provinces each possess this control, their bodies of legislation have evolved in substantively different ways, and at different times, as each of the provincial jurisdictions have defined the manner in which health professionals were to be regulated within provincial boundaries. Thus, when regulated health professionals move to a different province, they also move to the regulatory regime of that province.

Health professional organization in Canada first emerged in 1867 when physicians grouped together to form the Canadian Medical Association (CMA), designed to operate as the national advocacy or political arm of the profession as opposed to its regulatory body.[12] As more professions have come on stream, this model has been reflected at a

---

[9] (U.K.), 30 & 31 Vict., c. 3, reprinted in R.S.C. 1985, App. II, No. 5.

[10] *Lafferty v. Lincoln*, [1907] 38 S.C.R. 620. For an example of how the courts have upheld the disciplinary process of colleges as not incurring on federal criminal law, see *Landers v. Dental Society (New Brunswick)* (1957), 7 D.L.R. (2d) 583 (N.B. C.A.). Note in contrast, however, that in the case of *Morgentaler v. New Brunswick (Attorney General)* (1994), 117 D.L.R. (4th) 753; (N.B.Q.B.), aff'd (1995), 121 D.L.R. (4th) 431 (N.B. C.A.), the New Brunswick Court of Appeal ordered the government of New Brunswick to recognize the penalization of the performance of out-of-hospital abortion as contrary to federal criminal law. See further, P.W. Hogg, *Constitutional Law of Canada* (3rd ed.) (Scarborough: Carswell, 1992) and M. Jackman, "The Constitutional Basis for Federal Regulation of Health" (196) 5 Health Law Review 3.

[11] (1990), 46 Admin. L.R. 234 at 238 (Sask. C.A.).

[12] C.D. Naylor, *Private Practice, Public Payment* (Kingston: McGill-Queens University Press, 1986) 20.

provincial level for each of the regulated professions; that is, in each province, each of the regulated health professions has both a regulatory body (usually known as a college) and an advocacy association, sometimes combined as one body. Some health professions, specifically medicine, nursing, dentistry and pharmacy have been regulated since the late 19th century.[13] During this period, most of the thrust for regulation came from the professions themselves, principally medicine, on the basis of the desire of professionals to secure the autonomy of self-regulation a professional monopoly (that is, exclusive scope of practice) and control over, and independence from, other competing professions.[14] It was not until 1906 that the first health professional licencing statute was enacted. The *Canada Medical Act*,[15] though federal in origin, was hinged on provincial approval of a national system of licencing physicians.

2. The Regulatory Framework in Ontario

In 1974, the government of Ontario passed the *Health Disciplines Act*,[16] which created five professional colleges: medicine, nursing, pharmacy, dentistry and optometry. A guiding principle of this legislation was that each profession was "self-regulating"; that is, the college of each profession was granted total authority to define its respective scope of practice and regulate its respective members. Under the *HDA*, each profession was governed by a council, which was empowered to pass:

a)   regulations concerning various matters including standards of practice, discipline, and defining professional misconduct, subject to the approval of the Lieutenant Governor in Council (the legal term for the Cabinet of the government of Ontario) and with prior review by the Minister of Health;[17] and

---

[13]   By these dates, at least five provinces had regulated these professions: Physicians and surgeons, 1870; dentists, 1889; pharmacists, 1891; nurses, 1917. R.G. Evans & W.T. Stanbury, *Occupational Regulation in Canada* (Toronto: University of Toronto, 1980) 3.

[14]   See further, G.M. Torrance, "Social-Historical Overview: The Development of the Canadian Health System," in D'Arcy Coburn & G.M. Torrance, *Health and Canadian Society: Sociological Perspectives* (Toronto: University of Toronto Press, 1998) 3-22 at 7; and see more generally, C.D. Naylor, "The Canadian Medical Profession" *Private Practice, Public Payment* (Montreal: McGill-Queen's University Press, 1986) Chapter Two.

[15]   R.S.C. 1906, c. 137.

[16]   S.O. 1974, c. 47.

[17]   *Health Disciplines Act*, R.S.O. 1980, c. 196; Dentistry, s. 25; Medicine, s. 50; Nursing, s. 73; Optometry, s. 94; and Pharmacy, s. 119.

b) by-laws relating to the administrative and domestic affairs of the college, on its own initiative and without ministerial approval.[18]

The supervision of each college was conducted by the Minister of Health, who may "review" the activities of the council, "request" it to act in a certain manner, "require" it to provide information, and "advise" it on various matters including the implementation of policies, regulations and procedures.[19] This ministerial authority fell within the broader scope of the minister's duty to "ensure that the activities of health disciplines are effectively regulated…in the public interest."[20]

The legislation entitled each college to provide for the office of Registrar to administer its activities.[21] In addition to duties delegated to the Registrar by the college council, under the *HDA*, the Registrar was charged with a number of specific duties, such as, with the approval of the Executive Committee, order one or more persons to investigate a member when the Registrar has reasonable and probable grounds to believe that an act of professional misconduct including allegations of sexual abuse had taken place.[22] It should be noted that the *HDA* made no mention at all of sexual abuse by health professionals. Instead, the Discipline Committee of each college had the power to make a finding of guilt and determine the penalty, on the basis of "professional misconduct" or "impropriety."[23]

In addition to the council of each college, the *HDA* also provided for the activities of five committees within each college structure: the Executive Committee, the Registration Committee, the Complaints Committee, the Discipline Committee and the Fitness to Practise Committee.[24]

The *HDA* was superseded in 1993 by the *RHPA*. As the omnibus legislation that currently governs most of the health professions in

---

[18] *Ibid.*; Dentistry, s. 26; Medicine, s. 51; Nursing, s. 74; Optometry, s. 95; and Pharmacy, s. 120.

[19] *Ibid.*; Dentistry, s. 24; Medicine, s. 49; Nursing, s. 72; Optometry, s. 93; and Pharmacy, s. 118.

[20] *Ibid.* sub. 3(1).

[21] *Ibid.*; Dentistry, s. 24; Medicine, s. 49; Nursing, s. 72; Optometry, s. 93; and Pharmacy, s. 118. Note that with respect to nurses, this individual was called a Director.

[22] *Ibid.*; Dentistry, s. 40; Medicine, s. 64; Nursing, s. 72; Optometry, s. 93; and Pharmacy, s. 118.

[23] *Ibid.*; Dentistry, sub. 37(3); Medicine, sub. 60(3); Nursing, s. 84a; Optometry, s. 108; and Pharmacy, s. 133.

[24] *Ibid.*, sub. 53(1).

Ontario,[25] the *RHPA* is the source of a much more complicated and comprehensive regime, compared to the *HDA* with its inclusion of additional professions, additional committees and sexual abuse provisions. But before beginning a further discussion of the *RHPA*, a further exploration of the often-competing principles that underpin the notion of self-regulation is warranted. As will be evident, this will better explain the distinctions between the rationales behind both the *HDA* and the *RHPA*, which are relevant to appreciating how sexual abuse of patients is treated in the *RHPA*.

3. Principles of Self-Regulation

As more and more professions entered the health care field, as the public became more knowledgeable about health care, and as the public funding of health services continued to increase, year by year, the focus on professional regulation shifted away from one of professional self-interest. Rather, it moved more toward regulation in the public interest, particularly by ensuring that individuals had the freedom to choose their type of caregivers, with confidence in the fact that the professionals they chose were competent. Creating balance between these two underlying principles of health professional function has been seen as the job of government, through its power to regulate.[26] Government interventions into market activities generally occur when there is the belief on the part of legislators that unregulated activities will result in some form of inequity or imbalance or harm that significantly undermines the public interest. In theory, when a market operates perfectly, individuals have complete knowledge and freedom to make their choices as consumers, without coercion, and without their choices adversely affecting others. When one of these elements is not present, then government may step in with the purpose of correcting or re-balancing the operation of the market.

---

[25]   The health professions that are regulated under the *RHPA* in Ontario include: audiology; speech-language pathology; chiropody; chiropractic; dental hygiene; dental technology; dentistry; denturism; dietetics; massage therapy; medical laboratory technology; medical radiation technology; medicine; midwifery; nursing; occupational therapy; opticianry; osteopathy pharmacy; physiotherapy; podiatry; psychology; and respiratory therapy.
[26]   See further L. Bohnen, *Regulated Health Professions Act: A Practical Guide* (Aurora: Canada Law Book, 1994) 1 *ff*.

The provision of health care is of particular interest in this context.[27] The individual does not freely "purchase" health care in all situations: he or she often cannot anticipate when a health crisis may arise. When the individual comes into contact with the health professional, there is a clear imbalance between the two when it comes to their respective knowledge and skill in health care about health status and the condition of the individual. Depending on the circumstances, the individual may not have a choice in the form or provision of the care that he or she receives or from whom.

It is out of recognition of these market-model inequities that governments have been motivated to choose a legislative framework for professional self-regulation over non-regulation of the health professions. As a principal drafter of the *RHPA* notes, finding the appropriate balance is a challenge:

> The contradiction between these two policies lies in the fact that mechanisms aimed at protecting consumers from practitioners who do not know what they are doing necessarily limit those consumers' freedom of choice. A system that tries to ensure that practitioners can be utilized is inherently inegalitarian and tends to make the whole system less fluid and less receptive to change. In simplest terms, the contradiction is between regulation in order to protect patients from quacks and incompetents, and deregulation in order to restore a competitive market in health services. Historically, most governments have opted for public protection at the expense of competition. With the RHPA, the Ontario government aimed to have both. ... [In the result]... the government chose to preserve self-regulation in the RHPA. However, governing bodies would be required to function more openly and with greater accountability to the public.[28]

But this discussion is incomplete without further exploring what is meant by the term "self-regulation" itself. The idea of self-regulation is founded on trust in the ability of the profession to establish and operate its own governing body, removed from the direction of government. Current theories of self-regulation suggest that it can be approached one of two ways. Either control is directed at *who* can be regulated, or, control can be exercised over the *service* rather than the service provider. The first method, resembles what used to operate under the *HDA*. The

---

[27] For a more detailed discussion, see further L. Bohnen, *Regulated Health Professions Act: A Practical Guide* (Aurora: Canada Law Book, 1994) 1 *ff.*; L. McNamara & E. Nelson, "Regulation of Health Care Professionals," in J. Downie & T. Caulfield, eds., *Canadian Health Law and Policy* (Toronto: Butterworths, 1999) 54-56; R.G. Evans & W.T. Stanbury, *Occupational Regulation in Canada* (Law and Economics Workshop Series, University of British Columbia, 1980) 8 *ff.*

[28] L. Bohnen, *Regulated Health Professions Act: A Practical Guide* (Aurora, Ont.: Canada Law Book, 1994) at 2.

RHPA, on the other hand, consistent with the growing public desire for increased protection of the public interest, placed more emphasis on regulating the provision and quality of services rather than the service providers.[29]

Under the *HDA* the five professions of medicine, nursing (including "nursing assistants") pharmacy, dentistry and optometry were designated to be self-regulating. The *HDA* prescribed that each of the professions had the exclusive authority to define and govern its own scope of practice and the members it regulated. The *HDA* was criticized on a number of levels for giving too much power to the five regulated professions. It was said to verge on "...a monopoly that was broader than could be justified by the need for public protection, a monopoly paid for by the public purse in higher fees to physicians and in less efficiently run health care institutions."[30] Moreover, the regime was criticized for being "sexist and elitist. The professions that had monopolies were predominantly male, and they wielded great power within the health care system..."[31]

A major objective of the drafters of the *RHPA* was to overhaul how professional regulation operated. In place of the *HDA*, the Ontario government created a new form of regime in which the most widely recognized professions are governed by one overarching statute, supported by an Act specific to each of the professions regulated under the *RHPA*. In these profession-specific Acts, each profession is granted a defined scope of practice and those "controlled acts" that fall within that profession's scope of practice. This is in contrast to the tenets of the *HDA*, under which each profession possessed the authority to determine the scope of its practice. As a further distinction from the *HDA*, under the *RHPA*, each profession is required to consult with the other professions in instances where there is overlap in professional scopes of practice, and an overseeing body, the Health Professions Regulatory Advisory Council (HPRAC) has been put into place to ensure an effective inter-professional process, consistent with the new framework.

---

[29]   L. McNamara & E. Nelson, "Regulation of Health Care Professionals," *supra* note 27, at 56-64.

[30]   L. Bohnen, *supra* note 28, at 21.

[31]   *Ibid.*

(a) The Regulated Health Professions Act, 1991

The *RHPA* is a more comprehensive regime than the *HDA* was.[32] Unlike the *HDA*, the *RHPA* is more than just a simple statute; it is comprised of five distinct parts:

1. The omnibus or umbrella statute: the *Regulated Health Professions Act*, as well as:
2. Schedule 1: the list of regulated health professions,
3. Schedule 2: the *Health Professions Procedural Code* (the *Code*) along with:
4. 21 Profession-Specific Acts[33] and
5. Regulations under each Act.

Structurally, the first part of the *RHPA* legislation, which applies to all of the health professions equally, is the portion to which the two Schedules are appended and to which each of the 21 profession-specific Acts relate. The *RHPA* outlines the requirements of all of the professions with respect to defining the procedures or "controlled acts"[34] each is entitled to conduct and the titles each is permitted to use.[35] The "harm clause" is designed to prohibit individuals who are not registered with a regulated college from performing one of the controlled acts.[36] The *RHPA* sets out the powers accorded to the Minister of Health[37] and provides for a body that oversees various issues affecting all the professions, the Health Professions Regulatory Advisory Council.[38] The

---

[32] On the operation and origin of the *RHPA* and the system of regulation elsewhere in Canada, see further J. Gilmour, M. Kelner and B. Wellman "Opening the Door to Complementary and Alternative Medicine: Self Regulation in Ontario" (2002) 24 Law & Policy 149 at 153-57.

[33] *Audiology and Speech-Language Pathology Act, 1991*, S.O. 1991, c. 19; *Chiropody Act, 1991*, S.O. 1991, c. 20; *Chiropractic Act, 1991*, S.O. 1991, c. 21; *Dental Hygiene Act, 1991*, S.O. 1991, c. 22; *Dental Technology Act, 1991*, S.O. 1991, c. 23; *Dentistry Act, 1991*, S.O. 1991, c. 24; *Denturism Act, 1991*, S.O. 1991, c. 25; *Dietetics Act, 1991*, S.O. 1991, c. 26; *Massage Therapy Act, 1991*, S.O. 1991, c. 27; *Medical Laboratory Technology Act, 1991*, S.O. 1991, c. 28; *Medical Radiation Technology Act, 1991*, S.O. 1991, c. 29; *Medicine Act, 1991*, S.O. 1991, c. 30; *Midwifery Act, 1991*, S.O. 1991, c. 31; *Nursing Act, 1991*, S.O. 1991, c. 32; *Occupational Therapy Act, 1991*, S.O. 1991, c. 33; *Opticianry Act, 1991*, S.O. 1991, c. 34; *Optometry Act, 1991*, S.O. 1991, c. 35; *Pharmacy Act, 1991*, S.O. 1991, c. 36; *Physiotherapy Act, 1991*, S.O. 1991, c. 37; *Psychology Act, 1991*, S.O. 1991, c. 38; *Respiratory Therapy Act, 1991*, S.O. 1991, c. 39.

[34] *Regulated Health Professions Act*, *supra* note 1, s. 27.
[35] *Ibid.* s. 33.
[36] *Ibid.*, s. 30.
[37] *Ibid.*, ss. 2, 3 and 5.
[38] *Ibid.*, s. 7.

RHPA also continues the Health Professions Board (now called the Health Professions Appeal and Review Board),[39] the role of which is to review certain decisions by the regulating colleges. Requests for review (appeals) are made by members of those colleges, for example, when a college refuses to issue a registration, or by patients, such as when a complaints committee of a college declines to forward the patient's complaint on to a discipline hearing in a sexual abuse or other type of complaint. Finally, provision was made in the *RHPA* to exempt provision of services by Aboriginal healers and Aboriginal midwives to Aboriginal peoples in the province.[40] These key features of the *RHPA* are described in more detail below.

(i) THE "CONTROLLED ACTS"

Section 27 of the *RHPA* delineates 13 specific "controlled acts," qualified in two ways. First, unless a profession is regulated under the legislation, it is illegal for any of its members, or an individual for that matter, to perform any of these acts. Second, within each of the profession-specific statutes, each profession is assigned some combination of acts correlating to the profession's specific scope of practice.[41] The *RHPA* also takes into account the ability of a professional to delegate controlled acts or circumstances in which a controlled act cannot be completed without the authorization of another professional.[42] An example of the latter would be the order of an optometrist to an optician to dispense corrective eyewear.

According to the *RHPA*, a "controlled act" is any one of the 13 following activities done with respect to an individual:

1. Communicating to the individual or his or her personal representative a diagnosis identifying a disease or disorder as the cause of symptoms of the individual in circumstances in which it is

---

[39]   Section 18 of the *RHPA* provided for the original name. The new name was created by the *Red Tape Reduction Act, 1998*, S.O. 1998, c. 18, Sch. H, s. 1.

[40]   *Regulated Health Professions Act, supra* note 1, s. 35.

[41]   It is of note that no profession, including medicine, is entitled to perform all 13 of the acts. The controlled acts under medicine do not include the "Fitting or dispensing a dental prosthesis, or an orthodontic or periodontal appliance or a device used inside the mouth to protect teeth from abnormal functioning." [*Dentristry Act, 1991*, S.O. 1991, c. 24, s. 4.] On the other hand, the profession-specific statutes governing dental technology, dietetics, massage therapy and occupational therapy are assigned no controlled acts.

[42]   *Regulated Health Professions Act, supra* note 1, s. 28.

    reasonably foreseeable that the individual or his or her personal representative will rely on the diagnosis.

2. Performing a procedure on tissue below the dermis, below the surface of a mucous membrane, in or below the surface of the cornea, or in or below the surfaces of the teeth, including the scaling of teeth.

3. Setting or casting a fracture of a bone or a dislocation of a joint.

4. Moving the joints of the spine beyond the individual's usual physiological range of motion using a fast, low amplitude thrust.

5. Administering a substance by injection or inhalation.

6. Putting an instrument, hand or finger,
   - beyond the external ear canal,
   - beyond the point in the nasal passages where they normally narrow,
   - beyond the larynx,
   - beyond the opening of the urethra,
   - beyond the labia majora,
   - beyond the anal verge, or
   - into an artificial opening into the body.

7. Applying or ordering the application of a form of energy prescribed by the regulations under this Act.

8. Prescribing, dispensing, selling or compounding a drug as defined in subsection 117(1) of the *Drug and Pharmacies Regulation Act*,[43] or supervising the part of a pharmacy where such drugs are kept.

9. Prescribing or dispensing, for vision or eye problems, subnormal vision devices, contact lenses or eyeglasses other than simple magnifiers.

10. Prescribing a hearing aid for a hearing-impaired person.

11. Fitting or dispensing a dental prosthesis, orthodontic or periodontal appliance or a device used inside the mouth to protect teeth from abnormal functioning.

12. Managing labour or conducting the delivery of a baby.

13. Allergy challenge testing of a kind in which a positive result of the test is a significant allergic response.

---

[43] R.S.O. 1990, c. H.4.

(*ii*)   THE "HARM" CLAUSE

As added protection for the public, section 30 of the *RHPA* states that :

> No person, other than a member treating or advising within the scope of practice of his or her profession, shall treat or advise a person with respect to his or her health in circumstances in which it is reasonably foreseeable that serious physical harm may result from the treatment or advice or from an omission from them.

The penalty for violations of this prohibition can be a fine of up to $25,000 and/or up to a six-month prison sentence.[44] A number of exceptions do apply to the harm clause. They include such things as the administration of emergency first aid and appropriately delegated acts from one professional to another.[45]

(*iii*)   TITLE PROTECTION

Under the *RHPA*, five professions have been granted the use of the title "Doctor." They include medicine, psychology, dentistry, optometry and chiropractic. This aspect of the legislation means that anyone who does not belong to one of these professions, or is involved in an unregulated profession or service, is prohibited from using the title of "Doctor." Each of the other profession-specific acts also designate a title for use by that profession; for example, the *Pharmacy Act* protects the titles of apothecary, druggist, pharmacist and pharmaceutical chemist for use only by those duly registered members of the College of Pharmacy.

(*iv*)   THE ABORIGINAL EXEMPTION

The *RHPA* exempts Aboriginal healers and Aboriginal midwives from its application.[46] The rationale behind this exemption is based on the recognition that Aboriginal health care is based on specific, culturally-based practices that differ significantly from the predominant health care system in the province. Aboriginal healers and Aboriginal midwives are entitled under the legislation to offer traditional services to any Aboriginal person or to individuals who live in an Aboriginal community.

---

[44]   *Regulated Health Professions Act, supra* note 1, sub. 40(1).
[45]   *Ibid.*, s. 29.
[46]   *Ibid.*, s. 35.

(*v*)   MINISTERIAL RESPONSIBILITIES UNDER THE *REGULATED HEALTH PROFESSIONS ACT*

Under the *RHPA*, the Minister of Health is assigned the ultimate responsibility for the administration of the legislation,[47] and in doing so must

> … ensure that the health professions are regulated and co-ordinated in the public interest, that appropriate standards of practice are developed and maintained and that individuals have access to services provided by the health professionals of their choice and that they are treated with sensitivity and respect in their dealings with health professionals, the Colleges and the Board.[48]

However, the thrust of the Minister's authority is directed at how the professions perform, within their colleges, as opposed to the exertion of control over individual health professionals. Under the *RHPA*, the Minister may inquire into the state of practice of a profession, review council activities, require reports or information from a college, or order that a college carry out any activity consistent with the administration of the legislation.[49] The Minister also retains ultimate authority over the regulation-making power each college proposes. The Minister may require a college to make, amend or revoke regulations to the *RHPA*.[50]

(*vi*)   THE HEALTH PROFESSIONS REGULATORY ADVISORY COUNCIL

The Health Professions Regulatory Advisory Council did not exist prior to the *RHPA*. It is composed of between five and seven members who are appointed by the provincial Cabinet for two-year terms[51] and who must not be regulated health professionals or provincial civil servants.[52] Under the legislation, the duty of HPRAC is to advise the Minister of Health as to:

- whether an unregulated profession should be regulated (at the time of writing several were under consideration, including Naturopathy, Acupuncture and Ultrasound);
- whether a currently regulated profession should be deregulated;
- whether amendments should be made to the legislation or its regulations; and

---

[47]   *Ibid.*, s. 2.
[48]   *Ibid.*, s. 3.
[49]   *Ibid.*, s. 5.
[50]   *Ibid.*, s. 3.
[51]   *Ibid.*, ss. 7 and 9.
[52]   *Ibid.*, s. 8.

- matters concerning the Quality Assurance and Patient Relations programs of the professions.[53]

The Minister may also direct HPRAC to investigate and report on any matter related to the regulation of the professions.[54]

(vii) THE HEALTH PROFESSIONS APPEAL AND REVIEW BOARD

The role of the Health Professions Appeal and Review Board is to conduct hearings or appeals regarding matters of registration or complaints.[55] The Board is entitled to hear expert evidence and call upon its own independent experts.[56] Originally comprised of five to seven members, the Board is now composed of between 12 and 20 Cabinet-appointed individuals.[57] Ineligible for appointment are those employed by the provincial government, and any individual who has been, or is currently a member of a college or its council.[58]

(viii) THE COLLEGE COUNCILS

Within the context of self-regulation, the *RHPA* provides that a college be established for the governance of each of the professions. The work of each college is the ultimate responsibility of the college council, which reports to its members.[59] Further details of this function are set out in the *Health Professions Procedural Code*, as discussed below. However, as mentioned, under the *RHPA*, the Minister has the authority to make various demands of the councils relating to such things as regulations and reporting.[60] The Minister also has the discretion to provide the councils with funding[61] and this was done following enactment of the *RHPA* to assist some of the smaller new colleges, such as midwifery.

---

[53] *Ibid.*, s. 11.
[54] *Ibid.*, s. 12.
[55] *Ibid.*, s. 23.
[56] *Ibid.*, s. 24.
[57] *Ibid.*, s.18, as amended by the *Red Tape Reduction Act, 1998*, S.O. 1998, c. 18, Sch. H., s. 3.
[58] *Ibid.*, s. 19.
[59] *Ibid.*, s. 4.
[60] *Ibid.*, s. 5.
[61] *Ibid.*, s. 5(5).

(b)   Schedule 1: Self-Governing Health Professions[62]

Schedule 1 of the *RHPA* lists each of the 23 professions recognized under the legislation with their corresponding profession-specific statutes.

Health Profession Acts	Health Professions
Audiology and Speech-Language Pathology Act, 1991	Audiology and Speech-Language Pathology
Chiropody Act, 1991	Chiropody (including Podiatry)
Chiropractic Act, 1991	Chiropractic
Dental Hygiene Act, 1991	Dental Hygiene
Dental Technology Act, 1991	Dental Technology
Dentistry Act, 1991	Dentistry
Denturism Act, 1991	Denturism
Dietetics Act, 1991	Dietetics
Massage Therapy Act, 1991	Massage Therapy
Medical Laboratory Technology Act, 1991	Medical Laboratory Technology
Medical Radiation Technology Act, 1991	Medical Radiation Technology
Medicine Act, 1991	Medicine (including Osteopathy)
Midwifery Act, 1991	Midwifery
Nursing Act, 1991	Nursing (including nusing assistants)
Occupational Therapy Act, 1991	Occupational Therapy
Opticianry Act, 1991	Opticianry
Optometry Act, 1991	Optometry
Pharmacy Act, 1991	Pharmacy
Physiotherapy Act, 1991	Physiotherapy
Psychology Act, 1991	Psychology
Respiratory Therapy Act, 1991	Respiratory Therapy

(c)   Schedule 2: Health Professions Procedural Code (the Code)

The *Health Professions Procedural Code*[63] provides a set of procedures to which all of the regulated health professions must conform and it is the primary source for specific statements and procedures in Ontario related to complaints of sexual abuse. The *Code* requires the establishment of a

---

[62]   *Ibid.*, Sch. 1.
[63]   *Supra* note 2.

governing college for each profession and defines its role and composition. Each college must also have a set of standing committees, which in addition to an Executive Committee, are designed to govern specific areas of professional conduct including registration, complaints, discipline, fitness to practise, patient relations and quality assurance. The *Code* also sets out the procedures and powers in disciplinary hearing including hearings into allegations of sexual abuse by professionals. A "Miscellaneous" section of the *Code* addresses such things as regulation and by-law making powers of the college, legal procedures to which the college is entitled, and the right to use the French language.

(*i*)   REGULATORY COLLEGES

The *Code* sets out the requirements for each regulated profession to be governed by a non-profit, corporate body called a college.[64] The *Code* cites the overriding duty of the college as the duty to protect and serve the public interest.[65] Beyond this, the *Code* outlines eight key areas of authority and responsibility for each college:

1.   To regulate the practice of the profession and to govern the members in accordance with the profession-specific Act, this Code, the *Regulated Health Professions Act*, and the regulations and by-laws;

2.   To develop, establish and maintain standards of qualification for persons to be issued certificates of registration;

3.   To develop, establish and maintain programs and standards of practice to assure the quality of the practice of the profession;

4.   To develop, establish and maintain standards of knowledge and skill, and programs to promote continuing competence among the members;

5.   To develop, establish and maintain standards of professional ethics for the members;

6.   To develop, establish and maintain programs to assist individuals to exercise their rights under this Code and the *Regulated Health Professions Act*;

7.   To administer the profession-specific Act, this Code and the *Regulated Health Professions Act* as it relates to the profession and

---

[64]   *Ibid.*, s. 2.

[65]   *Ibid.*, sub. 3(2).

to perform the other duties and exercise the other powers that are imposed or conferred on the College.

8.   Any other objects relating to human health care that the Council considers desirable.[66]

(*ii*)   COMPOSITION OF THE COLLEGE

Among the 21 health professional colleges governed by the *RHPA*, there are big differences in the size of memberships. The College of Nurses, for example, has 140,000 members while the College of Midwives has about 140 members.[67] To accommodate this reality, the *Code* defines the composition of college councils in very general terms, leaving the details to be determined by the profession-specific Acts and the by-laws of each profession. The council of a college, or its "Board of Directors" is charged with overall governance of its affairs. The size of each council is relative to the size of the college, but in all cases, the council is comprised of a combination of professionals elected by the members, and lay persons appointed by the Lieutenant Governor General in Council. Members of the specific profession make up the majority of council members, but usually by only a 50 percent majority plus one member.[68] This structure ensures that each council is comprised of a substantial number of public members, a provision that was incorporated into the *RHPA* in order to reflect its objective of protecting the public interest and ensuring professional accountability. Some colleges are also

---

[66]   *Ibid.*, sub. 3(1).

[67]   Health Professions Regulatory Advisory Council, *Final Report to the Minister of Health and Long-Term Care, Effectiveness of Colleges' Complaints and Discipline Procedures for Professional Misconduct of a Sexual Nature* (Toronto: HPRAC, 2000) at 15.

[68]   This is addressed by each of the profession-specific statutes. For example, the *Respiratory Therapy Act, 1991*, S.O. 1991, c. 39, states the following:

7.(1) The Council shall be composed of,
  (a)   at least seven and no more than 10 persons who are members elected in accordance with the bylaws;
  (b)   at least five and no more than eight persons appointed by the Lieutenant Governor in Council who are not,
    i.   members,
    ii.   members of a College as defined in the Regulated Health Professions Act, 1991, or
    iii. members of a Council as defined in the Regulated Health Professions Act, 1991.

See generally L. Bohnen, *Regulated Health Professions Act: A Practical Guide* (Aurora: Canada Law Book, 1994).

required to have members from affiliated educational institutions.[69] Each member of a council serves for three years and may be re-elected or appointed but for no longer than nine consecutive years.[70] The professional members of a council may be remunerated by the college, but the *Code* provides for the payment of public appointees at public expense.[71]

The *Code* states that any person who is registered with a college is a member of that college.[72] When a member is suspended by a college, he or she also loses the certificate of registration,[73] although the college retains authority over members in this situation for reasons of professional misconduct or incompetence during the time the person was a member or was under suspension.[74]

Each college is entitled to hire employees and must appoint one as Registrar.[75] The *Code* also stipulates that all meetings of the college council must be open to the public and that reasonable notice of all meetings must be given to both its members and the public at large.[76] There are, however, some specific exceptions to open council meetings. The public may be excluded in instances which involve public security, sensitive personal information or financial matters; prejudice to another criminal or civil proceeding; personnel matters, property acquisitions, or instructions to the college by its solicitor.[77] In any event, the council must first deliberate the closure of a meeting before the public can be excluded,[78] and its reasons must be noted in the council's minutes.[79]

(*iii*) COMMITTEES OF THE COLLEGE COUNCIL

The *Code* requires that each college establish seven permanent committees, the memberships of which are defined by the by-laws of

---

[69] For example, the *Medicine Act, 1991*, S.O. 1991, c. 30, para. 6(1)(c), requires that three members of the council of the College of Physicians and Surgeons be selected from and by members of the college who are members of a medical faculty in an Ontario university.

[70] *Health Professions Procedural Code, supra* note 2, sub. 5(2).

[71] *Ibid.*, s. 8.

[72] *Ibid.*, sub. 13(1).

[73] *Ibid.*, sub. 13(2).

[74] *Ibid.*, s. 14.

[75] *Ibid.*, s. 9.

[76] *Ibid.*, sub. 7(1).

[77] *Ibid.*, para. 7(2)(a) to (e).

[78] *Ibid.*, para. 7(2)(f).

[79] *Ibid.*, sub. 7(4).

each college[80] and members appointed by the council.[81] Committees are required to submit annual reports to the college outlining their activities, although detailed or sensitive information, such as the details of the disciplinary process, is not to be included. The committees of the college are: Executive, Registration, Complaints, Discipline, Fitness to Practise, Quality Assurance and Patient Relations.[82] Each is described below.

(*iv*) Executive Committee

The Executive Committee of the college's council is empowered to act on behalf of the council in order to conduct the affairs of the council between council meetings that, in the Executive Committee, require immediate attention (exclusive of changes to the college regulations and by-laws, although it can make recommendations in these areas). If the Executive Committee exercises a power of council, it must report its activities to the council at the next meeting of the council and any prudent Executive Committee would ask that the council ratify such actions.

The Executive Committee also plays a role in the college's disciplinary and its fitness to practise processes. In either case, it is the sole authority of the Executive Committee to make decisions about the interim suspension of members before or while their cases are being heard.[83] If the Executive Committee orders an interim suspension, the *Code* requires that the member's hearing be expedited.[84]

(*v*) Registration Committee

Any individual wishing to be registered as a member of a college must first make application to the college's Registrar.[85] It is when the Registrar refers an application to it that the Registration Committee plays a role. The Registrar can refer an application on one of three bases related to registration required before a member can practise in Ontario: (1) the Registrar has "reasonable doubts" about whether an applicant fulfills the college's requirements for registration; (2) the Registrar believes that there should be some terms, conditions or limitations imposed on the

---

[80] *Ibid.*, sub. 10(3).
[81] *Ibid.*, sub. 10(2).
[82] *Ibid.*, sub. 10(1).
[83] *Ibid.*, 36, 37 and ss. 58, 61 and 62.
[84] *Ibid.*, sub. 37(2).
[85] *Ibid.*, sub. 15(1).

66   PREVENTING SEXUAL ABUSE OF PATIENTS

registration; or (3) the Registrar proposes to refuse the registration.[86] On receipt of a referral, the Registration Committee will strike a panel, which will conduct a formal hearing into the matter. Appeals of the Committee's decisions may be made to the Health Professions Appeal and Review Board,[87] and if needed further, to the court.[88]

(*vi*) COMPLAINTS COMMITTEE

In any instance in which a complaint is made to a college registrar, the first consideration takes place before the Complaints Committee, which will then strike a panel to investigate.[89] The panel must be composed of at least three members (one of which must be a lay member) to investigate the complaint.[90] The Committee is expected to render a decision as to the disposition of the complaint within 120 days.[91]

When this part of the process is concluded, the Complaints Committee has a number of options. If it does not decide to dismiss the complaint, the Committee must either deal with the matter directly or refer it to another college committee, depending on the nature of the complaint.

Complaints involving professional misconduct or incompetence may be referred to the Discipline Committee.[92] Complaints involving incapacity may be referred to the Executive Committee.[93] Complaints involving comments or behaviours of a sexual nature may be referred to the Quality Assurance Committee, but the Complaints Committee may also receive a sexual abuse complaint, before deciding whether or not to send it on for a discipline hearing.[94] The Compaints Committee cannot assess credibility or make findings of professional misconduct or reprimand the member. As a screening committee, it provides advice and guidance to the member. When the Complaints Committee does not refer a complaint and instead chooses to deal with the complaint itself, the Committee has the power to take any action it feels appropriate, so long as the action is consistent with the statutes, regulations and by-laws in the *RHPA* regime. In specific complaints of sexual abuse, only the

[86] *Ibid.*, para. 15(2)(a) to (c).
[87] *Ibid.*, sub. 21(1).
[88] *Ibid.*, sub. 70(1).
[89] *Ibid.*, sub. 25(1).
[90] *Ibid.*, sub. 25(2).
[91] *Ibid.*, sub. 28(1).
[92] *Ibid.*, sub. 26(2) 1.
[93] *Ibid.*, sub. 26(2) 2.
[94] *Ibid.*, sub. 26(3).

Discipline Committee has the authority to order mandatory revocation of a member's certificate upon a finding of guilt after a finding of professional misconduct.[95]

(*vii*) DISCIPLINE COMMITTEE

In addition to receiving and considering referrals of specified allegations of professional misconduct from the Complaints Committee, the Discipline Committee may also receive a specific allegation regarding a member's professional incompetence or misconduct, including sexual misconduct, from the Executive Committee.[96] A panel is appointed by the chair of the Discipline Committee[97] to hear a specific case and it can be comprised of between three and five members.[98] One member on a discipline panel must be a member of the college's Council,[99] and no person can be appointed a member if he or she has had any previous involvement with the complaint.[100] While a discipline panel has a quorum of three, a panel is comprised of five, two of whom are public members and is not operable unless at least one public member is present.[101]

The process of the Disciplinary Committee hearing is based on principles of due process in administrative law and as a result, the hearings are quite formal, involving:

- the identification of who can participate in the hearing, and their roles
- rules regarding evidence including what must be disclosed and when, and
- jurisprudence establishing who bears the burden of proof and what standard of proof must be met. [102]

---

[95] *Ibid.*, sub. 51(1)(b.1).

[96] *Ibid.*, s. 36.

[97] *Ibid.*, sub. 38(1).

[98] *Ibid.*, sub. 38(2).

[99] *Ibid.*, sub. 38(3).

[100] *Ibid.*, sub. 38(4).

[101] *Ibid.*, sub. 38(5).

[102] Administrative law involves law affecting the relationship between the individual and the state, such as the rules applying to a health professional appearing before a government-sanctioned tribunal, like a college discipline committee. A wide variety of procedural rules have been developed over the years, for example, procedural fairness, the right to be heard and freedom from bias, so that those appearing before tribunals are fairly treated. For more insight into the realm of administrative law, see for example, L. Braverman, *Administrative Tribunals: A Legal Handbook* (Aurora, Ont.: Canada Law Book, 2001); D.J. Mullan, *Administrative Law* (Toronto: Irwin Law, 2001).

The *Code* also states that hearings must be open to the public unless the panel decides that, in the public interest, an exception should be made for reasons such as public security or personal safety.[103] Each college is required to give reasons for disciplinary decisions[104] and make at least a summary of each decision available to the public in its annual report.[105]

The Discipline Committee has the authority under the legislation to make findings of professional misconduct against a member. When it does, the Committee can impose a number of penalties. For example, the Discipline Committee may:

- reprimand a member,[106]
- order the suspension or revocation of a registration;[107]
- attach conditions to a continued registration, and/or[108]
- impose a fine of up to $35,000.[109]

Special provisions regarding penalty exist in circumstances in which a member's misconduct is based on a finding of sexual abuse and these provisions are described in more detail below. Applications for reinstatement of a registration are made to the Registrar, who then refers the matter to a reviewing panel of the Discipline Committee.[110] Normally, a member seeking reinstatement must wait one year before reapplying, unless the misconduct was found to be sexual abuse, in which case the member must wait five years before reapplying.[111] Appeals of the decisions of the Discipline Committee — by either the member or the college, but not the complainant (patient) — are taken to the Divisional Court of Ontario.[112]

(*viii*) FITNESS TO PRACTISE COMMITTEE

The *Code* recognizes that there may be questions about the professional capacity of a member that do not appropriately fall within the disciplinary process. The idea is that public safety must be protected in

---

[103] *Health Professions Procedural Code, supra* note 2, subs. 45(1), (2).
[104] *Ibid.*, s. 54.
[105] *Ibid.*, s. 56.
[106] *Ibid.*, sub. 51(2) 1.
[107] *Ibid.*, sub. 51(2) 2.
[108] *Ibid.*, sub. 51(2) 3.
[109] *Ibid.*, sub. 51(2) 5.
[110] *Ibid.*, ss. 72(1), 73(1)(a).
[111] *Ibid.*, s. 72.
[112] *Ibid.*, s. 70.

instances where a member is incapacitated, either physically or mentally. The role of the Fitness to Practise Committee is to deal with questions of incapacity among existing College members, but concerns as to capacity that arise in the initial registration application are dealt with as part of the registration process.

When a complaint about the capacity of a member arrives at the College, it is reviewed by the Registrar, who may refer it to the Executive Committee.[113] If the results then go forward to the Executive Committee, or if the Committee receives a complaint from the Complaints Committee querying a member's capacity, it will strike a board of inquiry.[114] This board reports its findings back to the Executive Committee, which may then turn the matter over to the Fitness to Practise Committee for a full hearing.[115] Unlike the requirement of the disciplinary process, the hearings of the Fitness to Practise Committee are not open to the public unless the member before it specifically makes the request.[116] An application for reinstatement can be made one year after the member's registration was revoked or suspended (unless a longer revocation or suspension period was specified by the Discipline Committee).[117] If the application is accepted, the Registrar refers the matter to the Fitness to Practise Committee for a hearing.[118] Any appeal from the Fitness to Practise Committee's decision is taken to the Health Professions Appeal and Review Board and then only to the Divisional Court.[119]

(ix) QUALITY ASSURANCE COMMITTEE

An addition to the *RHPA* over the earlier professional regulatory regime was the requirement that each college create regulations to develop and implement a quality assurance program to be overseen by the Quality Assurance Committee.[120] The initiative grew out of a number of concerns including the desire of the government to ensure that the services

---

[113] *Ibid.*, s. 57.
[114] *Ibid.*, sub. 58(1).
[115] *Ibid.*, ss. 60, 61.
[116] *Ibid.*, s. 68.
[117] *Ibid.*, sub. 72(1), (2).
[118] *Ibid.*, para. 73(1)(b).
[119] *Ibid.*, sub. 70(1).
[120] *Ibid.*, s. 80.

provided to patients were both effective and appropriate to the patient's individual needs.[121]

The *Code* authorizes each college to utilize quality assessors — individuals empowered to inspect the practices and records of members of the college.[122] Every member who is approached by an assessor is required under the legislation to be cooperative.[123] If the Quality Assurance Committee concludes that there are problems with a member's practice as a result of an assessment, then it can meet with the member and endeavour to address and resolve the problem, for example, by having the member agree to a remediation program appropriate to the problem.[124] If a plan of remediation is refused by the member, the Quality Assurance Committee may impose terms, conditions or limitations on the member's certificate of registration for up to six months.[125]

The *RHPA* also provides that the Quality Assurance Committee may deal with issues of sexual abuse by a professional that fall within its definition in section 1(3), including intercourse or other forms of physical contact or touching, of a sexual nature of the patient.[126] In these cases, the Committee has the same power to require the member to take remedial steps or face penalties.

(x) THE SEXUAL ABUSE PROVISIONS

The sexual abuse provisions of the *RHPA* were a late but important and comprehensive addition to the legislation. Their inclusion was predicated on the findings of the 1991 Task Force on Sexual Abuse of Patients[127] commissioned by the Ontario College of Physicians and Surgeons, which raised awareness about the prevalence of sexual abuse of patients by physicians, and prompted a private member's bill in the provincial

---

[121] Bohnen notes that "[t]he Ministry of Health's interest in QA in the broader sense was fuelled by studies showing that certain procedures like Caesarean section and gall bladder surgery were being performed much more frequently in Ontario than in other jurisdictions." L. Bohnen, *supra* note 26, at 102 [footnotes omitted].

[122] *Health Professions Procedural Code*, *supra* note 2, s. 81.

[123] *Ibid.*, sub. 82(1).

[124] *Ibid.*, sub. 95(2).

[125] *Ibid.*, para. 95(2.1)(b).

[126] *Ibid.*, ss. 26, 79.1.

[127] M. McPhedran, H. Armstrong, R. Edney, B. Long, P. Marshall & R. Roach, *The Final Report of the Independent Task Force on Sexual Abuse of Patients* (Toronto: College of Physicians & Surgeons of Ontario, 1991) [hereinafter "1991 Task Force"].

legislature.[128] These activities led to months of extensive governmental consultations with the public and professions, as part of the development of the amendments. As a result of the high level of public concern, the provincial government amended the *RHPA* to deal specifically with complaints about sexual abuse of patients and applied it to all of the health professions regulated under the Act.[129] As Bohnen described it,

> Many of these changes reflect[ed] the policy objectives of increasing public in-
> volvement in the regulation of the health professions and of making college proc-
> esses more open. Some of the changes also reflect[ed] the government's view that
> both colleges and courts [had] been too lax in punishing professionals who sexu-
> ally abuse their patients.[130]

The changes to the *RHPA* include both a statement of the purpose of the sexual abuse sections of the Act and a concise definition of the term "sexual abuse."[131] The amendments also include new responsibilities for both the colleges and their members to reflect the added statement of purpose on eradication of sexual abuse by health professionals. Colleges are required to develop and maintain a Patient Relations Program directed at eliminating sexual abuse[132] and are also expected to finance and administer a program to compensate sexual abuse victims for their therapy or counselling.[133] The legislation also contains strong mandatory reporting or "whistle-blowing" requirements for professionals,[134] and for those who employ them, who have reasonable grounds to suspect that sexual abuse is occurring.[135] In addition, the amendments made to the *RHPA* detail a number of changes to the disciplinary process, some of which are directed at making it more responsive to those bringing sexual abuse allegations. Finally, the legislation also provides for stiff penalties for those found guilty of forms of sexual abuse including the imposition of a mandatory five-year revocation of the professional's certificate of

---

[128] Resolution 35: "Sexual Abuse of Patients" Hansard 12 December 1991, 1st Session, 35th Parl. 98A at 4153, Ernie Eves.

[129] *Regulated Health Professions Amendment Act, 1993*, S.O. 1993, c. 37.

[130] L. Bohnen, *supra* note 28, at 63.

[131] *Health Professions Procedural Code*, *supra* note 2, s. 1(3).

[132] *Ibid.*, sub. 84(1).

[133] *Ibid.*, sub. 85.7(1).

[134] *Ibid.*, s. 85.1. As you will see in Chapter 3, we prefer to use the term "truth telling" rather than "whistle-blowing" because the purpose of the mandatory reporting provisions is to share responsibility for maintaining the highest possible professional standards, as distinct from acting in an underhanded manner typically referred to as a "fink" or a "snitch."

[135] *Ibid.*, s. 85.2.

registration[136] in instances in which overt contact takes place. The *RHPA* describes this contact as follows:

(i)   sexual intercourse,

(ii)   genital to genital, genital to anal, oral to genital, or oral to anal contact,

(iii) masturbation of the member by, or in the presence of, the patient,

(iv)   masturbation of the patient by the member,

(v)   encouragement of the patient by the member to masturbate in the presence of the member.[137]

(*xi*) THE PURPOSE OF THE SEXUAL ABUSE PROVISIONS

The amendments to the legislation set out the purpose of the sexual abuse provisions in section 1.1:

> The purpose of the provisions of this Code with respect to sexual abuse of patients by members is to encourage the reporting of such abuse, to provide funding for therapy and counselling for patients who have been sexually abused by members and, ultimately, to eradicate the sexual abuse of patients by members.

As Richard Steinecke notes, it is unusual for legislation to have this kind of internal provision, which is usually reserved for more general opening statements of purpose in a statute, and, because of this, it is likely that courts will give it more weight than they would if it were in the preamble of the *RHPA*.[138] This is important as the legislation clearly expects professionals to have a rationale, soundly based in clinical standards, when touching a patient's body.

(*xii*) "SEXUAL ABUSE" DEFINED

The term "sexual abuse" is carefully defined in the *RHPA* to include activities that range from verbal comments to sexual intercourse:

•   sexual intercourse or other forms of physical sexual relations between the member and the patient;

•   touching of a sexual nature of the patient by the member; or

---

[136]   *Ibid.*, sub. 72(3).

[137]   *Ibid.*, sub. 51(5).

[138]   R. Steinecke, *A Complete Guide to the Regulated Health Professions Act*, looseleaf (Aurora, Ont.: Canada Law Book, updated November 2001) at 10-1.

- behaviour or remarks of a sexual nature by the member towards the patient.[139]

While adopting a very broad definition of what might constitute sexual abuse, the legislation provides reasonable and practical protection to health professionals by explicitly stating that the term "sexual nature" included in the definition "does not include touching, behaviour or remarks of a clinical nature appropriate to the service provided."[140]

(*xiii*) CHANGES TO THE COLLEGE STRUCTURE — PATIENT RELATIONS

The sexual abuse amendments required each college to establish a Patient Relations Committee to develop and administer a Patient Relations Program for the purposes of preventing or dealing with the sexual abuse of patients by college members.[141] Specifically, the Committee is charged with identifying measures that include educational requirements for members; guidelines for conduct of members with their patients; training of college staff; and the provision of information to the public about sexual abuse issues.[142] In addition, it is the role of the Committee to oversee the funding program set out in the legislation directed at paying for the counselling or therapy required by patients who have been sexually abused.[143]

The purpose of this fund is to provide compensation for counselling or therapy costs incurred by a patient[144] that the college's Discipline Committee determines has been sexually abused by a member of that college.[145] Compensation is specifically directed at any non-insured costs the patient accumulates for therapy or counselling as a result of the abuse. Each college is expected to finance the costs of this program and it is to be administered by the Patient Relations Committee of each college.

---

[139] *Regulated Health Professions Act, supra* note 1, sub. 1(3).
[140] *Ibid.*, sub. 1(4).
[141] *Health Professions Procedural Code, supra* note 2, subs. 10(1); 84(1), (2).
[142] *Ibid.*, sub. 84(3).
[143] *Ibid.,* sub. 85.7(3).
[144] *Ibid.*, sub. 85.7(1).
[145] *Ibid.*, sub. 85.7(4).

(xiv) MANDATORY REPORTING

There are a variety of circumstances in which the sexual abuse of a patient must be reported. Subsection 85.1(1) states: "A member shall file a report.... if the member has reasonable grounds,[146] obtained in the course of practising the profession, to believe that another member of the same or a different College has sexually abused a patient." Scenarios falling within the parameters of this provision could include the discovery by a professional that a colleague in his or her institution or profession has committed sexual abuse or the discovery by a psychiatrist that a patient receiving therapy from that psychiatrist has been abused at the hands of another health professional.

A comparable provision applies to persons operating a facility which employs regulated health professionals.[147] When sexual abuse is identified, the operator is bound to report the offending professional to his or her college. Similarly, it is incumbent on any employer of health professionals to report the termination of a professional for reasons of misconduct, including sexual abuse.[148]

All reports of sexual abuse must be in writing and include the name of the person submitting the report, the name of the suspected offender, an explanation of the abuse, and the name of the patient who was abused, if that is known, and written evidence that the patient has agreed to have his or her name stated when the name is known.[149] The person reporting is required to submit the report within 30 days of discovering the problem, or immediately if he or she believes that there is the possibility of further abuse occurring within that time.[150]

Section 92.1 was added to the *RHPA* as a protection for "whistle-blowers." The section states:

> No person shall do anything, or refrain from doing anything, relating to another person's employment or to a contract providing for the provision of services by that other person, in retaliation for that other person filing a report or making a complaint as long as the report was filed, or the complaint was made, in good faith.

---

[146] It is important to note that "reasonable" constitutes a lower threshold of belief than does "reasonable and probable," the standard that the Registrar must apply to ordering an investigation into a complaint (see the section "Basics of a College Response to a Complaint" in Chapter 3).
[147] *Ibid.*, s. 85.2.
[148] *Ibid.*, s. 85.5.
[149] *Ibid.*, sub. 85.3(3).
[150] *Ibid.*, sub. 85.3(2).

In the same vein, the legislation has also been amended to protect whistle-blowers from the institution of any action or other legal proceedings being brought against him or her.[151] On receipt of a report, the college registrar can commence an investigation if he or she believes there are reasonable and probable grounds to do so. In a situation when the name of the patient is not known, the registrar may choose to hold the report pending receipt of more information or further reports about the alleged offender.[152]

(*xv*) DEALING WITH COMPLAINTS AND THE IMPOSITION OF PENALTIES

The *RHPA* provides that sexual abuse complaints of a non-touching nature (see definition of sexual abuse in section C.1 of Chapter 1) be referred to the Quality Assurance Committee. The rationale for this is that non-physical abuse is better dealt with by means of rehabilitative actions rather that through punishment.[153] Accordingly, the Quality Assurance Committee is authorized to impose orders for continuing education or to place terms, conditions or limitations on a member's certificate of registration for up to six months.[154] Physical actions of sexual abuse are dealt with by the Discipline Committee, which on a finding of guilt is required, at the least, to both reprimand the member and revoke his or her certificate of registration for no less than five years.[155] In addition, the Committee has the power to impose monetary fines of up to $35,000,[156] have the abuser pay the college's costs of the disciplinary process including the hearing[157] and order the abuser to pay the costs of the victim's counselling and therapy into the compensation fund.[158]

(*xvi*) PROTECTIONS FOR VICTIMS

The changes to the *RHPA* took into account concerns for the patient. Among them are the right of an abused patient who is testifying to have

---

[151] *Ibid.*, s. 85.6.
[152] *Supra* note 138, at 10-12.
[153] *Ibid.*, at 10-14.
[154] *Health Professions Procedural Code*, *supra* note 2, sub. 95(2.1).
[155] *Ibid.*, sub. 51(5).
[156] *Ibid.*, sub. 51(2).
[157] *Ibid.*, sub. 51(2).
[158] *Ibid.*, s. 53.1.

his or her name kept in confidence[159] and to submit a victim impact statement.[160] The issue of penalty is under consideration. The victim is also entitled to ask the Discipline Committee to be made a party to the hearing (that is, formally participate in the proceedings),[161] and to have a guaranteed level of access to expert evidence prior to the start of the hearing.[162]

4. Profession-Specific Legislation

As part of the regulatory framework of the *RHPA*, each profession is also governed by a statute specific to that profession.[163] Each of these statutes recognizes the application of the *RHPA* and its Schedules.

The profession-specific statutes define the scope of practice for each profession. The scope of practice defines what the profession can do and it is the foundation for what controlled acts are assigned to it.[164] For example, the scope of practice for the *Medicine Act, 1991* is as follows: "The practice of medicine is the assessment of the physical or mental condition of an individual and the diagnosis, treatment and prevention of any disease, disorder or dysfunction."[165] The scope of practice of the *Dental Technology Act, 1991* states: "The practice of dental technology

---

[159] *Ibid.*, s. 47. This section empowers the panel, at the patient's request to impose a publication ban prohibiting publication of the patient's name or information that might identify the patient.

[160] *Ibid.*, sub. 51(6).

[161] *Ibid.*, s. 47.

[162] *Ibid.*, s. 42.1. The provision states:

> 42.1. *Disclosure of evidence* — Evidence of an expert led by a person other than the College is not admissible unless the person gives the College, at least ten days before the hearing, the identity of the expert and a copy of the expert's written report or, if there is not written report, a written summary of the evidence.

[163] *Audiology and Speech Language Pathology Act, 1991*, S.O. 1991, c. 19; *Chiropody Act, 1991*, S.O. 1991, c. 20; *Chiropractic Act, 1991*, S.O. 1991, c. 21; *Dental Hygiene Act, 1991*, S.O. 1991, c. 22; *Dental Technology Act, 1991*, S.O. 1991, c. 23; *Dentistry Act, 1991*, S.O. 1991, c. 24; *Denturism Act, 1991*, S.O. 1991, c. 25; *Dietetics Act, 1991*, S.O. 1991, c. 26; *Massage Therapy Act, 1991*, S.O. 1991, c. 27; *Medical Laboratory Technology Act, 1991*, S.O. 1991, c. 28; *Medical Radiation Technology Act, 1991*, S.O. 1991, c. 29; *Medicine Act, 1991*, S.O. 1991, c. 30; *Midwifery Act, 1991*, S.O. 1991, c. 31; *Nursing Act, 1991*, S.O. 1991, c. 32; *Occupational Therapy Act, 1991*, S.O. 1991, c. 33; *Opticianry Act, 1991*, S.O. 1991, c. 34; *Optometry Act, 1991*, S.O. 1991, c. 35; *Pharmacy Act, 1991*, S.O. 1991, c. 36; *Physiotherapy Act, 1991*, S.O. 1991, c. 37; *Psychology Act, 1991*, S.O. 1991, c. 38; *Respiratory Therapy Act, 1991*, S.O. 1991, c. 39.

[164] *Dental Technology Act, 1991*, S.O. 1991, c. 23, s. 3.

[165] *Medicine Act, 1991*, *supra* note 69, s. 3.

is the design, construction, repair or alteration of dental prosthetic, restorative and orthodontic devices."

The legislation also sets out the controlled acts that each profession is authorized to perform. In the *Medicine Act*, for example, 12 of the 13 acts appear.[166] Absent is the controlled act specific to some dental specialties that refers to the fitting or dispensing of dental appliances for the purposes of protecting the function of the teeth. In contrast, the *Dental Technology Act* contains no reference to any controlled acts because this profession does not have direct contact with patients.

5. Other Legislation

(a) Drugless Practitioners Act

The *Drugless Practitioners Act (DPA)*[167] came into effect in 1925 and governed chiropractic, massage therapy, naturopathy, osteopathy and physiotherapy. In 1991, when the *RHPA* was enacted, all of those professions regulated by the *DPA* except naturopathy were absorbed by the new legislation.[168] Naturopathy remains as the sole profession under the *DPA* and has since continued to propose that it be recognized and regulated under it. In 2001, HPRAC recommended to the Minister of Health that the profession be regulated by the *RHPA*, but at the time of writing, the Minister has not acted on the recommendation.[169]

Like the *RHPA*, the *DPA* makes no specific provision for the profession to discipline its members for the sexual abuse of patients, only referring more generally to "misconduct," "ignorance" or "incompetence."[170] The profession has nonetheless undertaken to bring its practices in line with the *RHPA* by developing a comprehensive policy against sexual abuse and boundary violations.[171]

---

[166] *Medicine Act, 1991, supra* note 69, s. 4.

[167] *Supra* note 8.

[168] On the regulation of Naturopathy, see further J. Gilmour, M. Kelner & B. Wellman, "Opening the Door to Complementary and Alternative Medicine: Self Regulation in Ontario" (2002) 24:2 Law & Policy 149 at 157 *ff*.

[169] See further, Health Professions Regulatory Advisory Council, *Naturopathy: Advice to the Minister of Health and Long-Term Care* (Toronto: HPRAC, 2001), online, Health Professions Regulatory Advisory Council <http://www.hprac.org/downloads//naturopathy/Naturopathy-ReporttoMinister.pdf>.

[170] *Drugless Practitioners Act, supra* note 8, s. 6; R.R.O. 1990, Reg. 278, s. 30.

[171] Board of Directors of Drugless Therapy — Naturopathy, "Policy on Prevention of Sexual Abuse," No. A.15-1, June 1999 (reproduced in Appendix II of this Guide).

(b) Institutional Legislation

When the 2001 Task Force made its report, it included specific recommendations with respect to health care institutions such as public hospitals and mental health facilities. Specifically, the 2001 Task Force recommended that the legislation governing such facilities be amended to include a *positive obligation* on hospital administration to

- annually report to the Minister about specific information on safeguards being taken to prevent sexual abuse and deal with complaints;
- maintain the highest possible level of education for its staff; and
- report complaints against professionals to their respective colleges.

The 2001 Task Force also recommended that sanctions against hospital administrators that did not comply include a fine of $5000 to be paid into funds supporting the counselling and therapy of patients who were sexually abused.[172] To date, no such amendments have been introduced by the Ontario government.

D. LEARNING ISSUES FROM THIS CHAPTER

This chapter has taken a detailed look at the framework of health professional regulation for 23 professions in Ontario. In light of this, consider the following:

Dr. G's case dealt with professional misconduct that was also confirmed by a regulatory body in another jurisdiction. What would be the implications if the issue was the discovery by an Ontario college that one of its members was guilty of sexual abuse outside the province but that the abuse was not recognized by the regulator in the foreign jurisdiction?

1.   Would the Ontario college have any jurisdiction over Dr. G if he had not renewed his membership in it? If he returned to the province?

2.   Several other professions who wish to be, are not governed by the *RHPA*; for example naturopathic doctors, homeopaths, acupuncturists, ultrasound technologists and those practising

---

[172]   M. McPhedran, H. Armstrong, B. Long, P. Marshall & R. Roach, *What About Accountability to the Patient? The Independent Final Report of the Special Task Force on Sexual Abuse of Patients* (Toronto: Ministry of Health & Long-Term Care, 2001) Recommendation 53 at 52-53 [emphasis in original].

traditional Chinese medicine. These are also professions that are not captured by the *RHPA* provisions relating to sexual abuse of patients. The Ontario Association of Naturopathic Doctors, for example, makes the case that it fulfills the criteria for inclusion in the *RHPA*, stating that "[a]lthough the current regulation of [naturopathic doctors] under the [*Drugless Practitioners Act*] does offer substantial consumer protection, this can be improved by making sure that naturopathic doctors in Ontario have the same demanding regulation as all other health professionals."[173] Specifically, the Association calls for the application of the *RHPA* sexual abuse provisions to its members. "The [*Drugless Practitioners Act*] contains no specific sexual abuse provisions (although there are standards) and, in particular, no ability to provide a counselling fund for victims, which is explicitly demanded under the... *RHPA*."[174] What are the issues associated with the regulation of a new profession? Do the existing protections offered by the *RHPA* make the regulation of existing professions more compelling?

3.   Compare the cases of Dr. G and Dr. NMRC. While they are similar in the jurisdictional sense, how do they differ? Do you think the penalties are appropriate given the differences you have identified?

---

[173]   Ontario Association of Naturopathic Doctors, *Natural Path* (Summer, 2003) at 1.
[174]   *Ibid.*, at 2.

Chapter 3

WHAT HAPPENS WHEN A COLLEGE COMPLAINT IS FILED?

In this chapter, we take a more comprehensive look at how the legislation as well as the complaints and disciplines process conducted by colleges relate to sexual abuse cases. Two different approaches by two different discipline committees are compared — each with very different results — and are presented at the end of this chapter to facilitate discussion.

A. UNSETTLING NEWS: FINDING OUT THAT A COMPLAINT HAS BEEN MADE

The day that a health professional is notified that someone (a patient or the College) has completed the process of filing a complaint with the professional's regulatory college is a time of significant stress and uncertainty. It may be that the professional has no recollection of the circumstances described by the complainant, or feels that there is a huge gap between what the complainant has alleged and what was experienced or intended by the professional. Nevertheless, the professional's world changes on that day and the all-too-human reaction can be one of denial. This can occur on several levels: denial of the allegations, or of the need to respond to the notice of a complaint to the college, or of the need to plan for time and resources to respond. It is very much in the professional's best interest to seek immediate advice and support at the earliest opportunity. Some professions, for example, medical doctors, maintain group insurance through the Canadian Medical Protective Association, but the majority of the professions do not have this kind of mutual defence fund and a professional often has to take full responsibility for finding appropriate assistance and representation in responding to a filed complaint.[1] Regardless, one of the first steps a professional should take on becoming aware of a complaint against him or her, is to contact the insurer. Once the professional begins to appreciate how much time will be used up in resolving most complaints, it becomes clear that time, money and other resources have to be dedicated to the response process. While the best possible representations need to be made on behalf of both patient and professional, professionals understand that both their reputation and their capacity to earn their chosen livelihood can be considerably undermined in a college proceeding.

B. INITIATING COMPLAINTS

There are several sources for complaints of sexual abuse. Delays in making a complaint for a considerable time after the abuse is alleged to have occurred are not unusual.

1. Limitation Periods

For a patient (or representative) pondering how to proceed with allegations of sexual abuse, in any of the three possible processes: regulatory college, civil lawsuit for damages, or sexual assault charges under the *Criminal Code of Canada*.[2] There are no limitation periods. Section 89 of the *Regulated Health Professions Act, 1991* (*RHPA*)[3] used to provide a limitation period[4] on complaints but that has been repealed.

2. Who Are the Complainants and Respondents in a Complaint?

Once a complaint has been made, the patient in question (or a representative) is usually referred to as the "complainant" and the professional as the "respondent." At the complaint stage, the college is the "regulator" in charge of conducting the investigation and the Complaints Committee is responsible for the disposition of a complaint,

---

[1]   For the list of professional associations that offer some support to members complained against, see Appendix II for contact information.
[2]   R.S.C. 1985, c. C-46.
[3]   Section 89 of the *Regulated Health Professions Act, 1991*, S.O. 1991, c. 18, was repealed by the *Justice Statute Amendment Act, 2002* (known as the *Limitations Act, 2002*) S.O. 2002, c. 24, Sch. B, s. 25, which came into effect on January 1, 2004.
[4]   A limitation period is the period of time, as set out in a statute, in which a claim must be made.

as part of the college's role in using administrative law for self-regulation of health professionals under the *RHPA* in Ontario. At the disciplinary hearing stage, although a college is a full party, it also plays a dual role because lawyers paid by the college act as the prosecutor on behalf of the college. But the professional is always a full party with specified rights that the patient does not necessarily have. For example, a discipline panel only needs to send its decisions to a patient/complainant "if the matter had been referred to the Discipline Committee by the Complaints Committee" but not if the Executive Committee or the Quality Assurance Committee made the referral.[5] At the investigation stage, the complainant and the respondent are afforded opportunities to review and comment on a college investigator's record of their statements made in interviews, before being faced with the record in the midst of the college hearing.

Although the Ministry of Health and Long-Term Care (Ministry of Health) received recommendations from the 2001 Task Force[6] and from the Health Professions Regulatory Advisory Council (HPRAC) that complainants merited full "party status", that is, full right to participate in the proceeding,[7] in sexual abuse cases before a college discipline committee, no changes to the legislation have yet been made. Thus the decision as to the extent that a complainant will be allowed to participate in a hearing, for example, to make oral or written submissions, introduce evidence directly (without having to rely on the college prosecutor to do this) or cross examine witnesses at the discipline hearing is at the discretion of the discipline panel hearing the case.[8] However, while either

---

[5] *Health Professions Procedural Code*, being Sch. 2 to the *Regulated Health Professions Act*, *supra* note 3, s. 54.

[6] M. McPhedran, H. Armstrong, B. Long, P. Marshall & R. Roach, *What About Accountability to the Patient? The Independent Final Report of the Special Task Force on Sexual Abuse of Patients* (Toronto: Ministry of Health & Long-Term Care, 2001).

[7] A party in a legal proceeding, such as a regulatory college investigation and hearing into a complaint of sexual abuse, has the right to present evidence, examine the evidence presented to the discipline panel by another party, and cross examine the other party. At present, the complainant is a witness in the proceeding with no right to take the kind of direct action in the proceedings just described, although discipline panels do have the discretion to allow complainants to present evidence of impact (victim impact statements) and to present evidence or arguments about the character of the respondent that may be relevant to the panel having to decide the extent to which its members can rely on what the respondent has told them. This is in comparison to other evidence that panel members must also consider before reaching their decision as to whether the professional did commit sexual abuse as defined in the *RHPA*.

[8] Authors' communication with the Ministry of Health and Long-Term Care, August 2003.

the Complaints Committee or the Executive Committee is in charge of the process — prior to the discipline hearing stage — both patients and professionals are treated as parties and both can appeal the decision of a complaints committee to the Health Professions Appeal and Review Board (HPARB), unless the Complaints Committee recommends the complaint be referred to the Discipline Committee (incompetence or professional misconduct or the Quality Assurance Committee (incapacity).[9]

3. Complaints by Patients

Contrary to what is often assumed,[10] many patients do not easily take the step of initiating a complaint to a college. The 2001 Task Force reported to the Ontario Minister of Health that many of the patients who presented testimony at public and private hearings stated that the primary reason for making a complaint was that they feared that the abusing health care provider was a continuing danger to other patients. The 2001 Task Force also found that patients initiated a complaint often only after learning that the health professional had also abused others.

4. Third-Party Complaints

There are some circumstances in which the patient in question cannot or will not, or do not know they have grounds to make a complaint to a college. As a result, third parties have the right to file a sexual abuse or other complaint directly with the alleged offending professional's college. The right of third parties (individuals or groups who are not the patient who has experienced the alleged abuse) to make a complaint to a college has been one area of debate, with some colleges recommending that third-party complaints should be limited to certain conditions. In its review of the *RHPA*, HPRAC recommended that third-party complaints continue to be allowed because

> [p]rofessions are regulated in the public interest and if a member of the public wishes to bring a complaint forward, he or she should be able to do so in further-ance of the public interest as well as in the interests of the patient/client. There are clearly instances of patients/clients who, for whatever reason, do not wish to bring a complaint forward, or cannot do so. At the same time however, there is a broader

---

[9]   Section 29(2).
[10] Some believe, for example, that false accusations are a fundamental basis for sexual abuse allegations. See for example, "Wrongly Accused MDs Suffer Grief Symptoms" *Medical Post* (12 February 2002) <http://www.medicalpost.com/mpcontent/art...nt/ content/extract/rawart/3806/14A.html>.

public interest at stake that seeks to protect from harm all members of the community. Third party complaints are one method by which this tension between the public and private can be reconciled, at least in some cases.[11]

5. Multiple Complaints Against Professionals

In our case studies in Chapter 4 of the chiropractor and the psychologist who were convicted on criminal charges for sexual assault of certain patient/complainants, a number of patients had also made sexual abuse complaints against these professionals to their respective regulatory colleges, as well as to the police. In order to safeguard due process for the complainant and the respondent professional, the *Health Professions Procedural Code* of the *RHPA*[12] contains or adopts certain rules of civil legal procedure that apply in college proceedings.[13] In college and in criminal processes, defence counsel for professionals can raise concerns about collusion when more than one patient has complained about the same professional.[14] Because professionals can appeal to Divisional Court when not satisfied with a college disciplinary decision, the judges hearing some of these appeals have had an opportunity to respond to defence challenges to the college process based on allegations about collusion among multiple complainants. For example, in a case where physicians appealed College of Physicians and Surgeons of Ontario (CPSO) findings of guilt for sexually abusing more than one patient, the court found that there were sufficient safeguards in the college process for testing the veracity of the multiple complaints and that collusion meant more than complainants having a conversation with each other.[15] Typically, each complaint triggers its own initial investigation, but as the college investigation proceeds, the complaints committee can decide to merge them. In cases where the complaints committee sends the complaint(s) on for a disciplinary hearing, they are usually merged and heard by the one discipline panel.

---

[11] Health Professions Regulatory Advisory Council, *Adjusting the Balance*: *A Review of the Regulated Health Professions Act* (Toronto: HPRAC, 2001) at 62.

[12] *Health Professions Procedural Code*, *supra* note 5.

[13] Sections 41 to 50 provide procedural rules relating to the discipline hearing.

[14] For information on criminal charges of sexual assault and procedures under the *Criminal Code* refer to Chapter 4 of this Guide.

[15] *Deitel v. College of Physicians & Surgeons of (Ontario)* (1997), 99 O.A.C 241 (Gen. Div.). However, note that in another recent case the court stated that once a hearing commences, the Notice of Hearing could not be amended to include charges by new complainants. New complainants must go through a separate process: *Henderson v. College of Physicians and Surgeons* (2003), 65 O.R. (3d) 146.

C. MAIN SOURCES OF COMPLAINTS

Any complaint to a college must be "in writing" or "recorded on a tape, film, disk or other medium" but the content of the complaint is not specified in the *Code*,[16] nor is there any statutory definition that puts a limitation on who can or cannot make a complaint. A complaint may result from an investigation issued by the College Registrar.[17] There are three other external sources of complaints that lead to investigations by regulatory colleges:

1. patients (one individual or several individual patients, with each complaint initially treated as separate), or those representing a patient, or third parties connected to the patient in some way;
2. the professional's employer may be obliged to make a report to the appropriate college, which in turn may trigger a complaint or investigation; or
3. other health professionals who are required by the *RHPA* to file a report when they have a reasonable belief that another professional may be abusing or when a patient has reported sexual abuse by another professional and has named the alleged offender.

Since 1994, every regulated health professional in Ontario (including those providing care to other health professionals or employing other health professionals) is under a statutory obligation to report knowledge of alleged sexual boundary crossing (and other prescribed acts of misconduct, incompetence and incapacity) by another professional, as discussed in more detail later in this chapter.[18]

1. Reports and Mandatory Reports

(a) Who May and Who Must Report?

The "whistle blowing" (or as we prefer "truth telling") provisions of the *RHPA* are quite clear and extensive.[19] Because the *RHPA* was drafted

---

[16] *Health Professions Procedural Code*, *supra* note 5, sub. 25(4).
[17] *Code*, s. 75.
[18] Section 85.1(1).
[19] The authors use the term "truth telling" rather than "whistle-blowing" because the purpose of these provisions is to share responsibility for maintaining the highest possible professional standards, as distinct from someone acting in an underhanded manner who is typically referred to as a "fink" or "snitch." See sections 85.1 through 85.4 of the *Code*.

with the explicit commitment by the Ontario government that it was legislation designed to operate "in the public interest,"[20] and because reducing risk of harm to patients was seen as very much in the public interest, the onus in the *RHPA* is on health professionals to contribute to the protective role required of the regulatory colleges — not only in regard to alleged sexual abuse of patients. The *RHPA* introduced mandatory reporting when health professionals form a reasonable belief that another health professional(s) has sexually abused a patient. In their Final Report in 1991, members of the independent task force commissioned by the CPSO explained that their recommendation for mandatory reporting (on which the subsequent amendments to the *RHPA* were based) was strongly influenced by testimony from doctors to the task force:

> A number of physicians came to the Task Force on a confidential basis and told us of the anguish they have experienced as a result of not reporting sexual abuse by colleagues. Indeed, it was the physicians who came to the Task Force who most consistently urged us to recommend mandatory reporting of sexual abuse. One study found that knowledge of sexual misconduct with a patient by a colleague was extremely stressful on practising professionals.[21]

(b) Reports from Facilities Where Health Professionals Practise

Similar reporting requirements are imposed on persons operating facilities where health professionals practise.[22] Thus, any professional who has reasonable grounds to believe that another professional is or has been making sexual contact with a patient is required by the *RHPA* to report the name of the allegedly offending professional to the appropriate

---

[20]   See note 71 in Chapter 1 referring to the public interest purpose, s. 3 of the *RHPA*.

[21]   M. McPhedran *et al. supra* note 6, at 84, with reference to the study by R. Brigham, *Psychotherapy Stressors and Sexual Misconduct: A Factor Analytic Study of the Non-offending and Offending Psychologists in Wisconsin* (Doctoral dissertation, Wisconsin School of Professional Psychology, Milwaukee, Wisconsin, 1989) [unpublished].

[22]   Section 85.2 of the *Code, supra* note 5, stipulates:

> (1) A person who operates a facility where one or more members practise shall file a report in accordance with section 85.3 if the person has reasonable grounds to believe that a member who practises at the facility has sexually abused a patient.
>
> *When non-individuals have reasonable grounds*
>
> (2) For the purposes of subsection (1), a person who operates a facility but who is not an individual shall be deemed to have reasonable grounds if the individual who is responsible for the operation of the facility has reasonable grounds.
>
> *If name not known*
>
> (3) A person who operates a facility is not required to file a report if the person does not know the name of the member who would be the subject of the report.

college, regardless of their respective membership in any one college, so long as the reporting professional "has reasonable grounds, obtained in the course of practising the profession, to believe that another member of the same or a different College has sexually abused a patient."[23] Many professionals feel considerable angst about the level of certainty that they need to have before making a report. But section 85.5 of the *Code* is clear that the reporting professional does not need to obtain proof before filing the required report.

(c) Reporting by Psychotherapists

The legislation makes specific reference to those professionals involved in forms of psychotherapy who discover that a patient has allegedly been abused by a professional in another college, including when the source of information is the professional who is being treated. However, both the needs of the professional being treated and the public safety interest have been specifically recognized in the *RHPA* through reporting requirements in the following sections of the *Code*:

> 85.3 (5) If a member who is required to file a report under section 85.1 is providing psychotherapy to the member who would be the subject of the report, the report must also contain the opinion of the member filing the report, if he or she is able to form one, as to whether or not the member who is the subject of the report is likely to sexually abuse patients in the future.

> 85.4 (1) A member who files a report in respect of which subsection 85.3 (5) applies, shall file an additional report to the same College if the member ceases to provide psychotherapy to the member who was the subject of the first report.

> (2)   The additional report must be filed forthwith.[24]

(d) Obligation on Employers and Business Partners to Report

Sexual abuse is treated as professional misconduct (and in certain circumstances, as incompetence). Even where an employer or business partner is not a health professional regulated under the *RHPA*, the legislation imposes a reporting obligation on employers when a professional's relationship as an employee or partner is limited or terminated for reasons of professional misconduct, incompetence or incapacity.[25]

---

[23]   *Health Professions Procedural Code*, *supra* note 5, s. 85.1.
[24]   The psychotherapy reporting requirements are found in sections 85.3 and 85.4 of the *Code*.
[25]   Subsections 85.5(1) through (3) of the *Code* stipulate that:

(i) MANDATORY REPORTS: WHEN AND WHAT?

The mandatory report must be filed with the college governing the alleged offender within thirty days after the "obligation to report" arises, which is when the professional first learns of the alleged abuse.[26] The report must contain the following:

    a.   the *name of the professional* filing the report;

    b.   the *name of the member* who is subject to the report;

    c.   a *description* of the circumstances of the alleged sexual abuse;

    d.   the *name of the patient, only* if the reporting professional knows who the patient is *and* has secured the *patient's written consent* to include the name.[27]

Professionals who choose to ignore this obligation are themselves subject to disciplinary review and if convicted they can be fined by their respective colleges.[28]

D. WHAT WILL A COLLEGE DO WITH A REPORT ALLEGING SEXUAL ABUSE?

The answer to this question is rather like a prism, with at least 21 points because there are that many colleges. Among them are some dramatic

---

(1) A person who terminates the employment or revokes, suspends or imposes restrictions on the privileges of a member or who dissolves a partnership, a health profession corporation or association with a member for reasons of professional misconduct, incompetence or incapacity shall file with the Registrar within thirty days after the termination, revocation, suspension, imposition or dissolution a written report setting out the reasons.

(2) If a person intended to terminate the employment of a member or to revoke the member's privileges for reasons of professional misconduct, incompetence or incapacity but the person did not do so because the member resigned or voluntarily relinquished his or her privileges, the person shall file with the Registrar within thirty days after the resignation or relinquishment a written report setting out the reasons upon which the person had intended to act.

(3) This section applies to every person, other than a patient, who employs or offers privileges to a member or associates in partnership or otherwise with a member for the purpose of offering health services.

Note that this applied to sexual abuse by a professional of a patient but not of an employee. In the latter case, the professional misconduct would be captured by the *Code* s. 51(1)(c) in that the member had committed an act of professional misconduct, generally prescribed by regulation as "disgraceful, dishonourable or unprofessional".

[26] *Health Professions Procedural Code, supra* note 5, sub. 85.3(2).

[27] *Ibid.*, sub. 85.3(3).

[28] See the Chart of Offences and Penalties in the section "Offences, Penalties and Protections" in this chapter.

AN OVERVIEW OF THE COMPLAINTS PROCESS

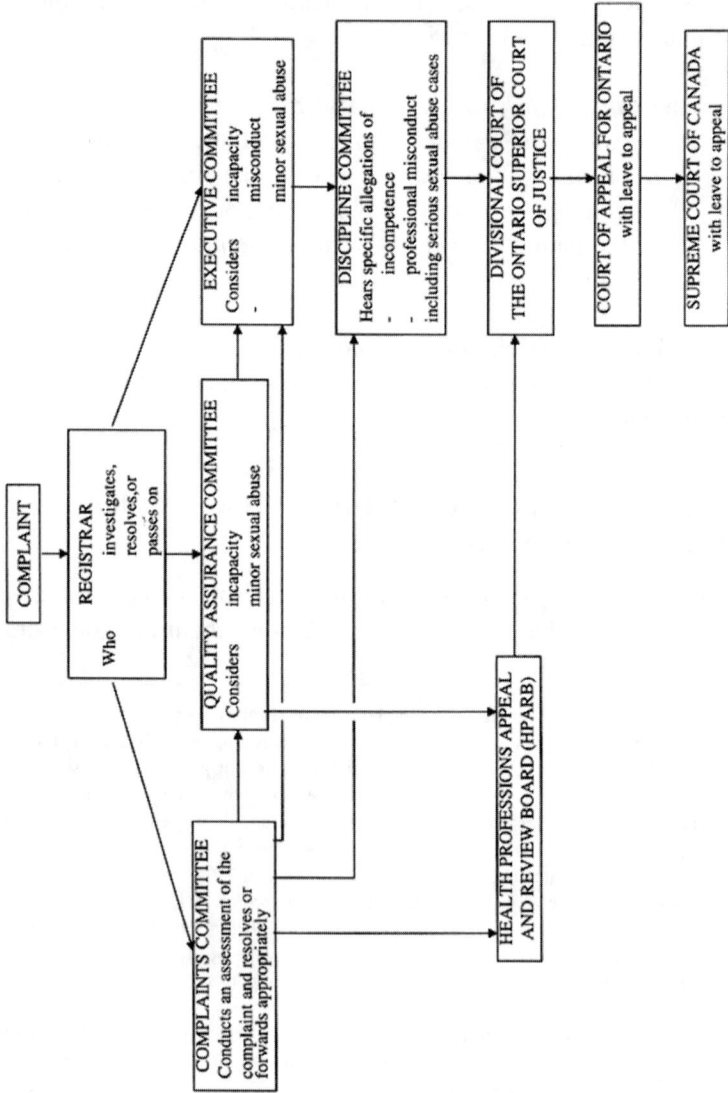

COMPLAINT

REGISTRAR
Who investigates, resolves, or passes on

COMPLAINTS COMMITTEE
Conducts an assessment of the complaint and resolves or forwards appropriately

QUALITY ASSURANCE COMMITTEE
Considers
- incapacity
- minor sexual abuse

EXECUTIVE COMMITTEE
Considers
- incapacity
- misconduct
- minor sexual abuse

DISCIPLINE COMMITTEE
Hears specific allegations of
- incompetence
- professional misconduct including serious sexual abuse cases

HEALTH PROFESSIONS APPEAL AND REVIEW BOARD (HPARB)

DIVISIONAL COURT OF THE ONTARIO SUPERIOR COURT OF JUSTICE

COURT OF APPEAL FOR ONTARIO
with leave to appeal

SUPREME COURT OF CANADA
with leave to appeal

differences in resources and infrastructure that have produced quite a variance among their responses to complaints of sexual abuse. As HPRAC, the advisory council to Ontario's minister of health, concluded: "patients/clients and members of the general public cannot be sufficiently protected unless the *Regulated Health Professions Act* (*RHPA*) contains adequate provisions for achieving this outcome and regulatory Colleges put them into practical effect."[29]

Indeed, there might be a different answer, in some cases, to the question posed at the beginning of this section if we asked, "What *should* a college do?" The *RHPA* is young, in legislative terms, and the disparity of staffing and income levels among the colleges was highlighted in the PricewaterhouseCoopers [PwC] surveys conducted for HPRAC in the initial stage of the effectiveness review. The five-year review was required under the *RHPA* to determine whether patient relations programs effectively fulfilled *RHPA* requirements. The PwC surveys monitored whether colleges' implementation of the 1993 amendments did contribute to a Zero Tolerance of Sexual Abuse policy; and further, where a college did accept a Zero Tolerance policy, whether there was an actual decrease in the numbers of sexually abused patients in Ontario.[30]

1. Basics of a College Response to a Complaint

The one employee that every college must have is the Registrar.[31] As outlined in Chapter 2, the *Code* sets out a close working relationship between a registrar and the committees that each college is also required to establish, as well as its governing body or "council." If a college registrar, on receipt of a report of alleged sexual abuse under section 85.1(1) of the RHPA against a named patient, considers the allegation to have a reasonable and probable foundation, an investigation will be ordered.[32]

---

[29] Health Professions Regulatory Advisory Council, *Weighing the Balance: A Review of The Regulated Health Professions Act* (Toronto: Government of Ontario, 1999) at 12.

[30] PricewaterhouseCoopers LLP, *Evaluation of the Effectiveness of the Health Professional Colleges' Complaints and Discipline Procedures with Respect to Professional Misconduct of a Sexual Nature and Status of the Colleges' Patient Relations Programs*, Vol. 5 (July 1999).

[31] *Health Professions Procedural Code*, *supra* note 5, sub. 9(2).

[32] *RHPA*, s. 75.

(a) Putting a Hold on a Reported Complaint

For patients refusing to be named, the registrar may hold the report pending receipt of further information or allegations against the professional in question. It is possible for a registrar and executive of a college to review the information available and decide, on a case-by-case basis, to initiate an investigation, even without identification of the patient(s).[33]

(b) When a College Initiates a Complaint

Even before the *RHPA* was enacted, regulatory colleges had considerable discretion as to initiating an investigation of a member of the college (the health professional) without waiting for formal patient complaint(s).[34] With the government's shift through the *RHPA* emphasis on colleges governing in the public interest,[35] the following six elements of the regulatory framework defined the public interest:

1. Protection of the public from the risk of harm,
2. Accountability,
3. Accessibility,
4. Equality,
5. Equity,
6. Quality of care.

E. DISPOSING OF A COMPLAINT

1. Role of the College Registrar and Staff

In most cases, it is the job of college staff, particularly its registrar to whom staff report, to support and facilitate the work of a panel set up by the college Complaints Committee to dispose of a complaint within 120 days of it being filed with the college.[36] This process includes college staff in many different roles — reception, intake, interviewing, investigation, facilitating access to information and support to the professional and the patient/complainant — but ultimately it is up to

---

[33]   A college-initiated investigation is dealt with in s. 75 of the *Code, ibid.*

[34]   *Health Disciplines Act*, R.S.O. 1980, c. 196, s. 40 (dentistry); 64 (medicine); 84(a) (nursing); 108 (optometry); and 133 (pharmacy).

[35]   See s. 3 of the *RHPA*, *supra* note 3, and s. 1.1 of the *Code, supra* note 5, for statements of purpose that emphasize the public interest in self-regulation by health professionals. See also the discussion in Chapter 1 of this book.

[36]   *Health Professions Procedural Code, supra* note 5, sub. 26(2).

members of the Complaints Committee to assess the complaint and decide whether it will be referred further on into the college process, to one of two other college committees: the Quality Assurance Committee or the Discipline Committee.

2. How the Complaints Committee Operates

When the Complaints Committee receives a complaint, it is up to the members to decide whether the complaint stops with them. In casual parlance, discipline committees are often seen as the "heavy hitters", the disciplinarians in the regulatory college process, but the majority of complaints are actually dealt with by the complaints committees, often with very little public awareness of how the complaint has been handled although the complainant and respondent are informed.[37] The statutory powers of a Complaints Committee are detailed in Chapter 2, with the general proviso that it can take any action that its members consider appropriate, as long as the action is "not inconsistent" with the *RHPA*, its *Code* and other related regulations and by-laws. For complaints of sexual abuse, a Complaints Committee has responsibility to:

- oversee the investigation of a complaint,
- decide to take no action on complaints that the Committee members find to be "frivolous, vexatious, made in bad faith" or otherwise "an abuse of process",[38]
- decide whether or not to refer a complaint to be heard by a panel of the college's Discipline Committee, or refer it to the Quality Assurance Committee, or
- deal with it within the Complaints Committee itself.

The *RHPA* is clear that the Complaints Committee must deal with "any complaint." The panel of the Complaints Committee has the discretion not to refer a complaint on to a discipline hearing,[39] and the criteria to be applied by a Complaints Committee when making such a decision are not specified in the *RHPA*. When a Complaints Committee panel decides not to refer a complaint on for a discipline hearing, this is one of the points in

---

[37] For example, in its 2002 Annual Report, the College of Nurses of Ontario reported receiving 759 complaints. Of those, the Complaints Committee disposed of 403, and, of those 28 were referred to the Discipline Committee. College of Nurses of Ontario, "Annual Report, 2002" <http://www.cno.org/docs/general/45006_2002annrpt.pdf> at 11.

[38] *Ibid.*, ss. 25, 26.

[39] *Ibid.*, ss. 26, 36.

the process when a complainant/patient can appeal to the HPARB.[40] In that case, the request must be made within 30 days, accompanied by the Panel's written decision.[41]

(a) A Patient's Perspective on Appealing a Complaints Committee Decision

In one case study, a patient was a victim of childhood incest and then, in her adolescence, she was sexually abused by her General Practitioner (GP). As an adult, she went to another GP and disclosed her traumatic history. This GP had not been in practice very long, but as he was [and still is] fully entitled to do under the Ontario Health Insurance Plan, nonetheless engaged in regular psychotherapy with the patient. There were sexually charged sessions, which the doctor felt he could handle. Eventually, the doctor discontinued treatment. The patient believed she was in love and felt extreme betrayal, alleging that her GP had played on the prior sexual abuse in her history, exacerbating her condition due to his ignorance, which in turn required even more therapy with a different professional, just to deal with the mishandling of the transference. As a result, her original problems of incest and childhood abuse could not be the focus of treatment until the most recent experience of betrayal had been competently addressed.

The patient filed a complaint with the college, alleging sexualized conduct, exploitation of the healing relationship and negligent treatment. The college conducted an investigation; the Complaints Committee dismissed the complaint, exercising its discretion not to send the complaint to the Discipline Committee.

At this point, the patient had three options: 1) abandon the complaint, 2) hire counsel or personally appeal the college's dismissal of her complaint (to the predecessor of what is now the HPARB), and/or 3) hire counsel to commence civil litigation, as did Laura against Dr. W in the first case study in Chapter 1. The patient pursued her second option and her counsel argued on appeal that the college investigation was inadequate, pointing out that the college could have, but did not, consult with the General Practice Psychotherapy Association or access an expert GP to assess the methodology of the respondent, or to assess the propriety of his conduct in the psychotherapy sessions. In the words of counsel for the patient in this case:

> So, the patient now has to engage legal counsel and pay for it, and also has to en-
> gage an expert GP Psychotherapist and appeal the college's decision not to send

---

[40]   *Ibid.*, sub. 29(2).
[41]   *Ibid.*, s. 29.

the matter forward to a hearing to what was then the Health Disciplines Board. The patient had to pay for all of this.[42]

On appeal the board found flaws in the investigation of the college, sent the matter back to the college, and gave directions as to key aspects of an appropriate investigation, including hiring an expert to review the respondent's records and provide an opinion as to propriety of the conduct reflected in them.

F. OFFENCES, PENALTIES AND PROTECTIONS

Any professional failing to file a report where it is reasonable to believe that sexual abuse has occurred between another professional and a patient is subject to a fine of up to $25,000. As a protection to "truth tellers," the *Code* expressly states that anyone making a report in good faith and on the belief that there were reasonable grounds is protected from retaliation.[43] The *RHPA* also recognizes any intentionally false report against a professional as an offence. Navigating the *Code* to sort out what offences connect to which penalties can be somewhat challenging because the related sections are not all in one place. Although section 93 refers to most of the penalties with their respective potential fines, it does not describe the nature of the offence, but only refers to the number of the section. For these reasons, we have included the summary chart below, organized by related sections of the *Code*, with emphasis added by underlining key phrases.

1. Chart of Offences and Penalties Related to Allegations of Professional Misconduct including Sexual Abuse

OFFENCE	PENALTY per s. 93 of the Code
Orders preventing public disclosure **45**. (1) A hearing shall, subject to subsection (2), be open to the public. (2) The panel may make an order that the public be excluded from a hearing or any part of it if the panel is satisfied that, (a) matters involving public security may be disclosed;	"Every person who contravenes an order made under section 45" is liable to a fine of $10,000 for a first offence and $20,000 for a subsequent offence.

---

[42] S. Vella, Transcript of Public Hearing of the Special Task Force on the Sexual Abuse of Patients (May 12, 2000) Toronto.
[43] *Health Professions Procedural Code*, *supra* note 5, s. 92.1.

(b) financial or personal or other matters may be disclosed at the hearing of such a nature that the desirability of avoiding public disclosure of those matters in the interest of any person affected or in the public interest outweighs the desirability of adhering to the principle that hearings be open to the public;
(c) a person involved in a criminal proceeding or in a civil suit or proceeding may be prejudiced; or
(d) the safety of a person may be jeopardized.

(3) In situations in which the panel may make an order that the public be excluded from a hearing, <u>it may make orders it considers necessary</u> to prevent the public disclosure of matters disclosed at the hearing, <u>including orders banning the publication or broadcasting of those matters.</u>

Protection of Identity of Witness
47. (1) A panel shall, on the request of a witness whose testimony is in relation to allegations of a member's misconduct of a sexual nature involving the witness, make an order that no person shall publish the identity of the witness or any information that could disclose the identity of the witness.[44]

"<u>Every person</u> who contravenes an order" under section 47 is liable to a fine of **$10,000 for a first offence** and **$20,000 for a subsequent offence**.

College Powers of Investigation of Professional
76. (1) An investigator may inquire into and examine the practice of the member to be investigated and has, for the purposes of the investigation, all the powers of a commission under Part II of the *Public Inquiries Act*.
(2) An investigator may, on the production of his or her appointment, enter at any reasonable time the business premises of the member and may examine anything found there that is relevant to the investigation.
(3) <u>No person shall obstruct an investigator or withhold or conceal from him or her or destroy anything that is relevant to the investigation.</u>

"<u>Every person</u> who contravenes subsection 76(3)" is liable to a **maximum fine of $10,000**.

NOTE RE: RECORDS CONFIDENTIALITY
(4) This section applies despite any provision in any Act relating to the confidentiality of health records.

---

[44] An example of an actual publication ban being ordered can be found in the Dr. AEK case, where the patient was male and the professional was female. College of Physicians and Surgeons of Ontario (Disc Com) (23 June 2003) <http://www.cpso.on.ca> at 2 (this case is discussed in more detail in Chapter 6 "Education"): "The Committee ordered a publication ban pursuant to s. 47(1) of the *Health Professions Procedural Code* (the "Code") which is schedule 2 to the *Regulated Health Professions Act, 1991*, S.O. 1991, c. 18, that no person shall publish the identity of the complainant or any information that could disclose the identity of the complainant and pursuant to s. 45 of the Code prohibiting the publication of the name of the female co-worker of the complainant identified in the testimony of the complainant."

Section 36 of the RHPA requires that all individuals involved in the administration of the Act "shall preserve secrecy with respect to all information that comes to his or her knowledge"

...

with a number of exceptions including...

(b) ... "in connection with anything relating to... complaints against members..." such as an investigator's inspection.

Under section 40(4), anyone who is found to have breached section 36(1) is liable to a fine of not more than $25,000.

Cooperation with Quality Assurance Committee
82. (1) Every member shall co-operate with the Quality Assurance Committee and with any assessor it appoints and in particular every member shall,

(a) permit the assessor to enter and inspect the premises where the member practises;

(b) permit the assessor to inspect the member's records of the care of patients;

(c) give the Committee or the assessor the information in respect of the care of patients or in respect of the member's records of the care of patients the Committee or assessor requests in the form the Committee or assessor specifies;

(d) confer with the Committee or the assessor if requested to do so by either of them; and

(e) participate in a program designed to evaluate the knowledge, skill and judgment of the member, if requested to do so by the Committee.

Inspection of Professional's premises (2) Every person who controls premises where a member practises, other than a private dwelling, shall allow an assessor to enter and inspect the premises.

Inspection of records (3) Every person who controls records relating to a member's care of patients shall allow an assessor to inspect the records.

Exception for Patients (4) Subsection (3) does not require a patient or his or her representative to allow an assessor to inspect records relating to the patient's care.

Confidentiality Override (5) This section applies despite any provision in any Act relating to the confidentiality of health records.

85.1(1) Reporting by members A member shall file a report **in accordance with section 85.3** [Mandatory Reporting — see below] if the member has reasonable grounds, obtained in the course of practising the profession, to believe that another member of the same or a different College has sexually abused a patient.

"Every person who contravenes subsection 82 (2) or (3)" is liable to a maximum fine of **$5,000 for a first** offence and not more than **$10,000 for a subsequent** offence.

Every person who contravenes subsection 85.1 (1), 85.2 (1), 85.4 (1) or 85.5 (1) or section 92.1 is guilty of an offence and on conviction is liable to a fine of **not more than $25,000.**

85.3 Mandatory Reporting (1) A report required under section 85.1 or 85.2 must be filed in writing with the Registrar of the College of the member who is the subject of the report.

Timing of report, sexual abuse (2) The report must be filed within thirty days after the obligation to report arises unless the person who is required to file the report has reasonable grounds to believe that the member will continue to sexually abuse the patient or will sexually abuse other patients, in which case the report must be filed forthwith.

Contents of report (3) The report must contain, (a) the name of the person filing the report;
(b) the name of the member who is the subject of the report;
(c) an explanation of the alleged sexual abuse;
(d) if the grounds of the person filing the report are related to a particular patient of the member who is the subject of the report, the name of that patient, subject to subsection (4).

Patients not named without consent (4) The name of a patient who may have been sexually abused must not be included in a report unless the patient, or if the patient is incapable, the patient's representative, consents in writing to the inclusion of the patient's name.

If reporter providing psychotherapy (5) If a member who is required to file a report under section 85.1 is providing psychotherapy to the member who would be the subject of the report, the report must also contain the opinion of the member filing the report, if he or she is able to form one, as to whether or not the member who is the subject of the report is likely to sexually abuse patients in the future.

85.2(1) A person who operates a facility where one or more members practise shall file a report in accordance with section 85.3 if the person has reasonable grounds to believe that a member who practises at the facility has sexually abused a patient. **[NOTE: 85.3 is quoted in the cell above.]**

Amendments in 2001 to the *RHPA* have extended its reach to **health profession corporations**, declaring them to be **"jointly and severally liable"** with a professional for "all fines, costs and expenses that the member [of a college] is ordered to pay."

85.4(1) A member who files a report in respect of which subsection 85.3 (5) applies, <u>shall file an additional report to the same College if the member ceases to provide **psychotherapy**</u> to the member who was the subject of the first report. **[NOTE: see 85.3 (5) above.]**

85.5(1) A person who terminates the employment or revokes, suspends or imposes restrictions on the privileges of a member or who **dissolves a partnership, a health profession corporation or association** with a member for reasons of professional misconduct, incompetence or incapacity shall file with the Registrar <u>within thirty days</u> after the termination, revocation, suspension, imposition or dissolution <u>a written report</u> setting out the reasons.

PROTECTION FROM RETALIATION

92.1 No person shall do anything, or refrain from doing anything, relating to another person's employment or to a contract providing for the provision of services by that other person, in **retaliation** for that other person filing a report or making a complaint as long as the report was filed, or the complaint was made, in good faith.

2. Timelines and Appeals

(a) Health Professions Appeal and Review Board (HPARB)

If the complainant (patient) or the respondent (professional) has applied to the HPARB, section 28 of the *Code* gives the HPARB the explicit power to extend the time limit imposed on colleges to dispose of complaints within 120 days.[45] But no such power is given to the colleges. However, in practice this timeline, imposed on a panel of the college Complaints Committee to dispose of a complaint within 120 days after it has been filed, is often not met.[46]

Regardless of the cause(s) of such delays, they are stressful to all parties involved, and health professionals should not rely on the 120-day (about four months) limit when estimating the impact that a complaint can have on their daily activities for many months after the investigation begins.

During the five-year review of the *RHPA* that HPRAC was required by the Act to conduct, a number of colleges reported that it is often difficult to comply with the 120-day timeline for disposing of complaints

---

[45]   *Health Professions Procedural Code, supra* note 5, sub. 28(1).
[46]   *Adjusting the Balance, supra* note 11, at 64.

specified in the *RHPA*.[47] As well, patients reporting to the 2001 Task Force expressed frustration at the failure of some colleges to resolve complaints within the specified 120 days, and most were unaware of their right to ask the HPARB for intervention when colleges fail to meet the 120-day timeline.[48] However, some patients and some colleges, such as the CPSO, also reported that HPARB itself often did not meet its own specified timelines for disposition of appeals, causing additional difficulty for patients and professionals who are in the midst of the complaint process.[49] In 2002, however, HPARB reported to HPRAC that its backlog had been significantly reduced.[50]

3. The Role of the Quality Assurance Committee

As discussed in more detail in the previous chapter, the Quality Assurance Committee of the College is one referral option when the Complaints Committee is disposing of a complaint about sexual misconduct. Where the Complaints Committee has found that the sexual abuse involved inappropriate behaviour or remarks, but not physical sexual contact between professional and patient, the Quality Assurance Committee can direct remediation; for example, the Quality Assurance Committee can order a professional to attend a continuing education program, and if not satisfied with the arrangement, the Committee can refer the case on to the Discipline Committee.[51] However, the Quality Assurance Committee does not have a clear obligation to report on the outcome to both the patient and the professional. In fact, its decisions on remedial training are not required to be placed on the public record of a college's register.[52] Thus the patient/complainant often has no way of determining what happened to his or her complaint when handled by the Quality Assurance Committee.

---

[47] In *Adjusting the Balance*, the HPRAC report to the Minister of Health, the following colleges indicated that the 120-day limit was unrealistic: Psychologists Massage Therapists, Occupational Therapists, Dieticians, Medical Radiation Technologists, Physiotherapists and Dental Technologists. Health Professions Regulatory Advisory Council, *Adjusting the Balance: A Review of the Regulated Health Professions Act*, *supra* note 11, at 65.

[48] Section 26 of the *RHPA*, *supra* note 3, gives the HPARB the explicit power to extend time limits and particularly the obligations, under sub. 28(1) of the *Code*, *supra* note 5, to dispose of complaints within 120 days. No such power is given to a college.

[49] *Adjusting the Balance*, *supra* note 11, at 70.

[50] *Ibid.*, at 71.

[51] *Health Professions Procedural Code*, *supra* note 5, s. 79.1.

[52] *Code*, s. 23.

This imbalance prompted the Federation of Health Regulatory Colleges to note that this disparity "…can leave the complainant feeling unsatisfied with the process. It is reasonable for a complainant to be informed about the decision of the Quality Assurance Committee."[53] The CPSO further clarified the problem by noting:

> If the matter is sent to the Quality Assurance Committee, the College cannot provide any further information to the complainant. Agreements and undertakings by members are not generally public. Supervised practice arrangements are often not public. Remediation or educational arrangements are not public. In the era of increased public expectations about access to information, the Colleges need legislative direction to provide more information to the public about their activities.[54]

G. THE DISCIPLINE COMMITTEE PROCESS

Recommendations of the 1991 Task Force and consultations conducted by the Ministry of Health led to amendment of the *RHPA* (in Bill 100) to include adaptations to the disciplinary process where a sexual abuse complaint was under review. These changes were made because heightened difficulties and sensitivities associated with bringing sexual abuse allegations forward were identified, prompting amendments to the *Code*, including:

1. closing hearings to the public for the purposes of protecting witnesses who report having experienced sexual abuse;
2. limiting participation by interveners to testifying as to the good character of the accused;
3. expanding the requirements for disclosure of evidence, particularly with respect to expert witnesses, by both a college, as prosecutor, and by the professional, as the respondent in a disciplinary hearing;
4. allowing victim impact statements in the penalty phase of a hearing;
5. setting out mandatory penalties including reprimand and a revocation of licence for five years for overt sexual offences;
6. setting out additional monetary penalties, including fines up to $35,000, orders to reimburse the compensation fund, orders for security deposits and in some cases, costs, all payable by the respondent professional when found to be the abuser.

---

[53] Health Professions Regulatory Advisory Council, *Adjusting the Balance: A Review of the Regulated Health Professions Act, supra* note 11, at 14.

[54] *Ibid.*

1. Pre-Hearing Conferences

It is only fair to bear in mind that the procedures outlined in the *RHPA* and its *Code* are relatively new to the colleges. Some of the larger colleges are reporting steady improvement on the length of time being taken by the discipline process. For example, the CPSO reported considerable success with pre-hearing conferences, with most of them scheduled within four months of the professional receiving notice of a complaint. By the year 2000, the Discipline Committee was hearing the same number of cases as in 1999, but in half the number of days required for hearing time.[55]

2. What's On and What's Off the Public Record of Colleges?

Although public expectations about access to information are increasing, at the time of writing this book, the *RHPA* prohibits health regulatory colleges from publicly reporting many of their activities with the general exception of Disciplinary Committee hearings.[56]

For example, in cases where the member elects to resign in the context of sexual abuse allegations, the *RHPA* has been interpreted as requiring colleges to keep the related information confidential. Many of the colleges as well as HPRAC have recommended that all undertakings and agreements with resignations should be a matter of public record on the colleges' registers.

The fact is, even today, some sexual abuse complaints are still being processed under the old *Health Disciplines Act* (*HDA*) because those offences occurred while the *HDA* was still in force, and as a result, some of the procedural requirements of the *RHPA* cannot be applied to disciplinary proceedings under the *HDA*. But, the new legislation, college disciplinary panels and executive committees of the colleges are required to revoke the registration of a member's certificate to practise, upon a finding of sexual abuse by the member involving sexual intercourse between the professional and the patient or sexual touching of the patient by the professional.

---

[55] College of Physicians and Surgeons of Ontario, *Annual Report*, 2002 at 13. Available online <http:www.cpso.on.ca> (Jan./Feb. 03).

[56] While disciplinary hearings must be open to the public (s. 45(1)), a panel may close hearings for reasons such as personal or public security. See *Code*, s. 45(2).

3. The Role of the Patient Relations Committees

The addition of a Patient Relations Committee to the structure of the colleges of each of the regulated health professions was a new component included in *RHPA*, after the second reading of Bill 43.[57] Although this committee is given broad scope to address the relationship between patients and members of the college, the main role of the Patient Relations Committee as set out in the Act is to develop a Patient Relations Program directed at "preventing *or* dealing with" (emphasis added) the sexual abuse of patients — a choice of words that has had an unfortunate consequence, in that some colleges have taken the position that they can choose one or the other, and still be within the letter of the law.[58] Specifically, the legislation requires that each college must include in the Patient Relations Program the following measures:

(a) education requirements for members;
(b) guidelines for the conduct of members and their patients;
(c) training for the College's staff; and
(d) the provision of information to the public.[59]

In the first stage of the effectiveness review conducted for HPRAC in 2000, the reviewers noted that:

> As the legislation is written in terms of "preventing **or** dealing" with sexual abuse, those Colleges who choose to focus on either preventing or dealing are meeting the requirement of the legislation, but not the full intent. Dealing with sexual abuse may be interpreted as having a process to manage the complaints and discipline process. If this interpretation is used, the eventual goal for eradication of sexual abuse will not be achieved.[60]

(a) Recommendations for Therapeutic Support to Patients

It is also the responsibility of the Patient Relations Committee to administer a funding program for the funding of therapy and counselling of patients who were sexually abused by members.[61] Eligibility for funding occurs when the Discipline Committee of a College finds a

---

[57] *Health Professions Procedural Code*, *supra* note 5, sub. 84(1). Bill 43 introduced the *RHPA*.
[58] *Ibid.*, sub. 84(2).
[59] *Ibid.*, sub. 84(3).
[60] PricewaterhouseCoopers LLP, *supra* note 30, at 1.
[61] *Health Professions Procedural Code*, *supra* note 5, sub. 85.7(1).

member guilty of sexual abuse of a patient[62] or funding may be applied to therapy that was undergone during the course of a hearing in which the practitioner was found guilty.[63] The patient is then entitled, without having testified in the hearing,[64] or without any further investigation into the request, to make application for counselling or therapy from a person of their choice,[65] either regulated or unregulated for the equivalent of up to 200 half-hour sessions of psychotherapy with a psychiatrist for up to five years following the date of eligibility.[66] While all colleges have established a fund for therapy and counselling, the process for accessing the funds differs by college. By 1999, all 21 colleges combined had provided some level of funding to a total of 32 patients in the five years following enactment of the sexual abuse prevention provisions in 1994.[67]

When this funding mechanism was first proposed by the Task Force on Sexual Abuse of Patients in 1991 as a "Survivors' Compensation Fund," it was conceived as functioning independently of the colleges. Noting that some practitioners who sexually abuse patients were collecting fees from OHIP as they committed their abuses, the Task Force stated:

> So that the perpetrators of sexual abuse do not continue to profit from their offences, and so that victims have access to a more meaningful remedy than just a finding of "guilty," we recommend that the... [government] ... determine the most appropriate way for all monies paid as a result of fines... [for sexual abuse] ... go into the Fund. In addition, the doctor must pay into the... [Fund] ... the equivalent amount of fees paid by OHIP as "services" when in fact the doctor was sexually abusing the patient. Patients whose doctors have been found guilty... may then apply for financial assistance in their attempts to recover from the harm done to them.[68]

(b) Therapeutic Funding Stipulated in the RHPA

The funding mechanism proposed by the 1991 Task Force was not the process that the government adopted. Instead, each college was charged

---

[62]   *Ibid.*, para. 85.7(4)(a).

[63]   *Ibid.*, sub. 85.7(10).

[64]   *Ibid.*, sub. 85.7(13).

[65]   *Ibid.*, sub. 85.7(7). The provision excludes family members [para. 85.7(7)(a)] and anyone who is known to have committed sexual abuse [para. 85.7(7)(b)]. If the patient chooses an unregulated professional, the college has the authority to ask the patient to sign a document indicating understanding that the counsellor or therapist he or she has chosen is not subject to professional discipline [para. 85.7(7)(c)].

[66]   O. Reg. 59/94, pursuant to sub. 85.7(2) of the *Code*.

[67]   PricewaterhouseCoopers LLP, *supra* note 30, at 1.

[68]   M. McPhedran, *et al.*, *supra* note 6, at 194.

with the administration and financing of its own funding program.[69] The effect of this decision results in the potential for inconsistency of the program from college to college. The effectiveness review conducted as part of the five-year report on the *RHPA,* for which HPRAC was responsible, flagged the value of consistent and appropriate training about the program across disciplines, to both professional and public members of college councils and committees.[70] In practical terms, splintering the funding source means that the money to compensate the victims of sexual abuse by members of a particular college must be found by that college, despite the disparity in their sizes, without government assistance. However, there are significant limitations on what recourse a patient has in these situations. Because many professionals provide support, advice and care to patients affected by the complaints and discipline process, it is sometimes necessary to inform a patient who is a complainant that the matter is settled when a college refuses to appeal a panel decision that has rejected the patient's allegation of sexual abuse, or when the patient is convinced that a panel has erred in law.[71] And although a patient's claim under the *Code* to be reimbursed for therapeutic expenses incurred to deal with the psychological damage sustained from abuse will be truncated if the panel finds against the patient, the patient has no right to appeal that disciplinary panel decision, because the patient is not a party to the proceeding.

(c) The Chain of Reporting Requirements on Patient Relations

The Patient Relations Committee is accountable to both the College Council and HPRAC. The legislation requires that the Committee "advise the Council with respect to the patient relations program."[72] It is also stipulated that the Committee must give HPRAC " ...a written report describing the patient relation program and, when changes are made to the program, a written report describing the changes."[73] For its part, HPRAC is

---

[69] *Health Professions Procedural Code, supra* note 5, s. 85.7.

[70] Harry Cummings & Associates, *Evaluation of the Effectiveness of the Patient Relations Program of the Ontario Colleges of Health* (Toronto: HPRAC, 2001) at 37.

[71] A. Coté, *Recommended Approach to Evaluating the Effectiveness of Complaints and Discipline Procedures with Respect to Professional Misconduct of a Sexual Nature: Report to the Health Professions Regulatory Advisory Council* (Toronto: December 1994) at 53.

[72] *Health Professions Procedural Code, supra* note 5, s. 85.

[73] *Ibid.,* sub. 84(4).

required by the *RHPA* to "monitor each College's Patient Relations Program and ... advise the Minister about its effectiveness."[74]

As a further requirement, HPRAC was given a five-year report of the effectiveness of each college's Patient Relations Program, along with similar reports on the complaints and discipline procedures of each college as they relate to professional misconduct of a sexual nature.[75] In anticipation of its first five-year report to the Ministry of Health, HPRAC commissioned a study entitled "Evaluation of the Effectiveness of the Patient Relations Program of the Ontario Colleges of Health," which was produced by Harry Cummings & Associates and released in March of 2001.[76] This study was the second stage of the effectiveness review that began with the report from PricewaterhouseCoopers discussed earlier in this chapter.[77] It was designed to describe and evaluate the effectiveness of the Patient Relations Programs of each of the colleges for the purpose of determining "...whether each College's patient relations programs are [sic] likely to be effective in fulfilling the requirements and intent of the *RHPA* in protecting the public from harm and treating individuals with sensitivity and respect,"[78] recognizing that the process for implementation of the program is still in the development stages with the goal of using the reports' findings to increase college effectiveness.

(d) Good News, Bad News

Some of the findings in the Harry Cummings & Associates 2001 report ("the HCA Report") are in many ways very encouraging.[79] The HCA Report notes that all of the colleges have taken the issue of patient relations seriously and that there has been "a high level of collaboration among them"[80] in doing so. Every college has developed standards, guidelines and a code of ethics related to patient relations both in general and as they relate to the sexual abuse of patients. The prevention of abuse is strongly emphasized and considerable attention has been paid to boundaries and boundary violations, informed consent and professional-patient relationships and power imbalances. In addition, there is evidence that the colleges have taken an integrated and decidedly efficient

---

[74] *Ibid.*, sub. 11(2).
[75] *Regulated Health Professions Act, supra* note 3, sub. 6(2).
[76] Harry Cummings & Associates, *supra* note 70.
[77] PricewaterhouseCoopers LLP, *supra* note 30.
[78] Harry Cummings & Associates, *supra* note 70, at 1.
[79] *Ibid.*, 5.0 Summary and Conclusions — paragraph paraphrases finding in 5.1 "Strengths of the Patient Relations Programs" at 37.
[80] *Ibid.*, Part I at 37.

approach to implementing patient relations programs within their overall operations.

There are also findings in the HCA Report that are troublesome. Most importantly, it suggests that the colleges have not been terribly successful in "providing information to the public in general, and more specifically to patients."[81] Rather, the efforts of most of the colleges[82] have been focused more inwardly to the colleges themselves and their members. The HCA Report states that "[a]lthough most Colleges recognize the broad nature of PR and the importance of communications, many Colleges seem to have interpreted communications to focus on publicity campaigns designed to generate better *Public Relations* for their Colleges."[83]

(e) Is There a Disconnect Between Colleges and the Public?

For the purposes of this Guide, the following finding should cause considerable concern. The HCA Report concludes that "[f]ewer Colleges have provided information about sexual abuse itself — what it is, how to recognize it in the context of a health care relationship, and what to do in situations where one feels uncomfortable or vulnerable."[84]

If one accepts that in the first few years of development of the patient relations program, health care providers have gained more knowledge about sexual abuse, but patients have not, then the goal of rebalancing the power relationship between the two remains unmet. The HCA Report further states that with a few exceptions, little has been accomplished in the education of marginalized groups who are more vulnerable and less likely to report abuse or of the professionals who deal with them.[85] In order to improve some of these shortcomings, the Report notes the need for improved standardized and collaborative planning and evaluations processes within and among the Colleges. With this Guide, we have included a "handout" written with patients in mind. As a public service, our publisher has waived any payment requirements related to copying this handout (but not copyright itself) and we encourage health

---

[81] *Ibid.*

[82] The Royal College of Dental Surgeons of Ontario cites numerous attempts to achieve broader coordination. Personal communication with W. Sutton from Irwin W. Fefergrad Registrar, October 30, 2003.

[83] *Ibid.* [emphasis in original].

[84] *Ibid.*, Part I at 37.

[85] HCA report at 38.

professionals to copy the handout and make it directly available to their patients.

(f) Changing College Patient Relations Committees

In making its recommendations to the Minister of Health and Long-Term Care in May of 2001,[86] HPRAC, the minister's advisory committee, recommended that the *RHPA* be amended to remove the requirement for a Patient Relations Committee in each College but maintain and enhance the patient relations program.[87] Despite this elimination recommendation, HPRAC underscored the importance of public education by citing the need to make available broadly provided, publicly funded and legislated toll-free telephone numbers and written information to enable the public to make inquiries and register complaints about health professionals.[88] Implementation of the legislated requirement that colleges provide public education is certainly a longstanding challenge for self-regulated health professions. The HCA Report, which recommended enhanced public education, was completed more than ten years after the first task force on sexual abuse of patients. The 1991 Task Force made the following recommendation on public education in order to

> actively promote public awareness of its role, policies and procedures, the Zero Tolerance standard, and the entire complaints and discipline process in as many ways as possible, beginning with production of a poster and a brochure... that these be available in languages appropriate to consumers of health services in Ontario and in Braille and on tape... in cooperation with the Ontario Hospital Association, ensure the brochure is available in every location where [professionals] practise and encourage and reward the display of the poster there... that [colleges] encourage display of the poster and brochure in other locations [health and treatment centres, health clubs, community centres and public centres] and make them available to these locations.[89]

Notwithstanding the HCA Report's conclusion that the Colleges had been better at educating themselves and their members as opposed to the public, HPRAC recognized the continuing need by making the following recommendations regarding member education:

. . .

---

[86] Health Professions Regulatory Advisory Council, *Effectiveness of Colleges' Patient Relations Programs: Advice to the Minister of Health and Long-Term Care* (May 2001).

[87] *Ibid.*, Appendix C at 1.

[88] *Ibid.*, at 16.

[89] McPhedran, 1991 Task Force, at 112.

5. That Colleges work closely with professional training schools to ensure that appropriate training on communication with patients, including that related to non-clinical aspects of care, is covered in pre-service curriculum.

6. That Colleges work closely with professional training schools to ensure that the appropriate training on risk management for sexual abuse of patients is covered in pre-service curriculum.

7. That Colleges be required to evaluate knowledge and competencies related to the prevention and reporting of sexual abuse and effective patient relationships as a requirement of entry-to-practice.

8. That Colleges be required to develop and implement a systemic way to regularly obtain public/patient feedback about the quality of patient-professional relationships within the profession and be required to use this feedback to development [sic] member education activities as part of their patient relations program.[90]

4. Learning Issues and Discussion Points

(a) *Mandatory Revocation: the Penalty for Subsection 51(5) Sexual Abuse Offences*

Most patients who reported to the 1991 Task Force and the 2001 Task Force said that the damage they experienced was life diminishing. Patients' experience of the severity of harm created and their concern about risk to other patients produced strong, clear support for mandatory revocation of a member's licence to practice upon being found guilty.

Discipline Committees in a number of colleges have grappled with the harsh nature of mandatory revocation. Most of them have decided that revocation is the only appropriate penalty where they found sexual contact with patient(s). For example, in a discussion affirmed by appeal to the Divisional Court, the mandatory revocation penalty in paragraph 72(3)(a) of the *Code* was examined by the CPSO Discipline Committee in the context of the *Canadian Charter of Rights and Freedoms*[91] in a recent case involving a physician and a physiotherapist.[92] The Committee reviewed the arguments from both sides, but in the end, held that revocation was the only appropriate penalty regardless of the mandate in the *RHPA*. The CPSO Discipline Committee relied on decided case law

---

[90] Health Professions Regulatory Advisory Council, Effectiveness of Colleges' Patient Relations Programs/Advice to the Minister of Health and Long-Term Care (May, 2001) at 16.

[91] Part I of the *Constitution Act, 1982*, being Schedule B to the *Canada Act 1982* (U.K.), 1982, c. 11.

[92] *Mussani, Re*, [1998] O.C.P.S.D. No. 15 (QL).

and held that the constitutional protection addressed social freedom of association, not sexual intercourse, and in any event, subsection 51(5) did *not* violate any of the following constitutional rights and freedoms:

- the right to life and liberty (section 7);
- the right not to be subjected to cruel and unusual punishment (section 12); and
- the freedom of association (section 2(d)).

(b) Question on "Freedom of Association"

In discussing the right of "freedom of association" conveyed by section 2(d) of the *Charter*, do you think that this section should go beyond its current protection of an individual's right to participate in collective labour or social activity?

5. Comparing Two Different Approaches by Colleges and Courts

(a) College of Physiotherapists

The Melunsky case, involving a physiotherapist and her patient, stated that the mandatory revocation provision in the *RHPA* did not have to be respected because, in the opinion of a majority of the members of the discipline panel, mandatory revocation contravened the section 12 constitutional rights of the respondent who became sexually involved with her patient and subsequently married him.[93] With respect to section 12 (cruel and unusual punishment), the majority of the panel was of the opinion that the imposition of the mandatory penalty of five years revocation is cruel and unusual punishment in these circumstances. The panel did not comment on section 7 or section 2(d) of the Charter.

The panel then went on to consider whether section 1 of the Charter, the proviso that the rights and freedoms are guaranteed subject only to such reasonable limits prescribed by law, saved the mandatory penalty provision. It was the opinion of the majority of the panel that in this unique case, the proportionality of the penalty, a mandatory revocation of the member's certificate of registration for a minimum of five years, did not fit the magnitude of the offence and accordingly constituted cruel and unusual punishment. Accordingly, while the member was found guilty of

---

[93] The Melunsky case was appealed and upheld on grounds other than the constitutionality of mandatory revocation: *Melunsky v. College of Physiotherapists of Ontario*, [1999] O.J. No. 148 (Div. Ct.).

professional misconduct for having breached section 51(1)(b.1) of the Health Professions Procedural Code, the majority of the panel were of the opinion that the mandatory penalty under Section 51(5)(2.i.) (revocation of licence) for a minimum of five years could not be invoked by reason of the Charter of Rights.

The panel stated in their reasons that they believe that the message conveyed to the profession and the public is of utmost importance. The member has been found guilty of sexual abuse of a patient while under her care. The fact that this patient is now her husband was, in the opinion of the panel, irrelevant. This action cannot be condoned, therefore, the panel made the following order:

- that the member's certificate of registration should be suspended for a period of six months commencing immediately,
- that the member appear before the Committee for a reprimand.[94]

(b) The College of Physicians and Surgeons

The CPSO committee in the *Mussani* case,[95] which is discussed in Chapter 1, differed with the disciplinary panel in the *Melunsky* case,[96] concluding, "the [College of Physiotherapists] decision is of very little assistance" and noting that:

> The Discipline Committee has found Dr. Mussani guilty of sexually abusing a patient. If subsection 51 (5) of the Code is given force and effect, the Discipline Committee must revoke Dr. Mussani's certificate of registration based on its findings. That is to say, the Discipline Committee may not exercise discretion in the penalty, even if for some reason, it did not consider revocation appropriate.... Having considered the authorities, the Committee is not persuaded that the right to enter into a sexual relationship is a right protected by section 7 of the Charter.[97]

Then the panel of the Discipline Committee of the CPSO thoroughly reviewed the arguments for and against mandatory revocation and concluded that:

> While the Committee is prepared to accept that Section 12 (of the *Canadian Charter of Rights and Freedoms*) may apply to professional discipline hearings, it was not persuaded that the penalty of revocation was grossly disproportionate to the of-

---

[94] *Melunsky v. College of Physiotherapists of Ontario* <http:www.collegept.org>.

[95] *Mussani, Re*, [1998] O.C.P.S.D. No. 15 (QL).

[96] *Melunsky v. College of Physicians & Surgeons (Ontario)*, [1999] O.J. No. 148 (Div. Ct.).

[97] Health Professions Regulatory Advisory Council, *Effectiveness of Colleges' Patient Relations Programs*, *supra* note 86, at 12, 14.

fence. Sexual abuse of patients is a very serious matter which is deserving of a very serious penalty. A doctor does not have an unconditional right to practise medicine and it is appropriate that the right be circumscribed (by way of mandatory revocation) if the doctor sexually abuses a patient. Such a penalty, while severe, protects the public and the integrity of the profession.[98]

6. Question on Discretion of College Discipline Panels

1. What range of discretion is appropriate in a self-regulating system?
2. How important is deterrence in prevention of sexual abuse of patients?

---

[98] *Mussani, Re, supra* note 95.

Chapter 4

WHAT HAPPENS IN CIVIL OR CRIMINAL CASES?

A. DIAGRAM: THREE POSSIBLE LEGAL ACTIONS ON SEXUAL ABUSE COMPLAINT[1]

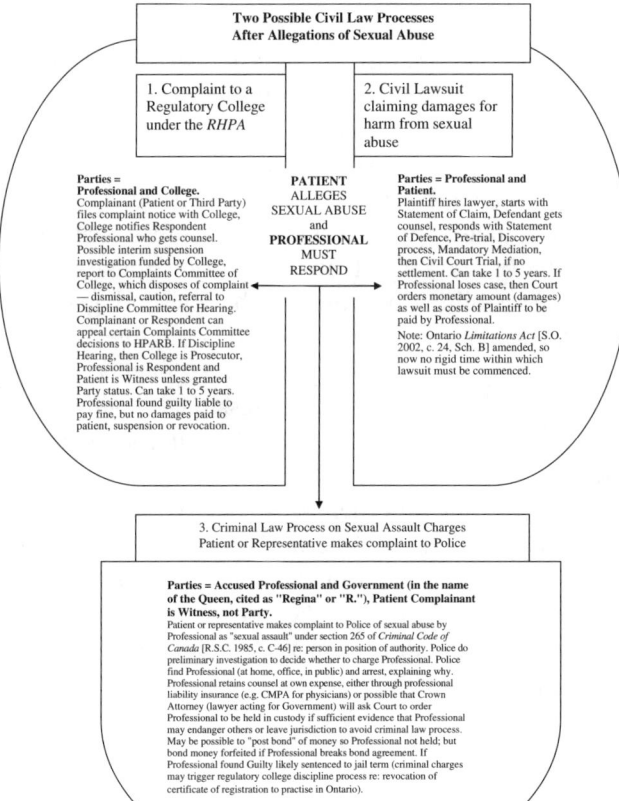

Two Possible Civil Law Processes After Allegations of Sexual Abuse

1. Complaint to a Regulatory College under the *RHPA*

2. Civil Lawsuit claiming damages for harm from sexual abuse

PATIENT ALLEGES SEXUAL ABUSE and PROFESSIONAL MUST RESPOND

Parties = Professional and College. Complainant (Patient or Third Party) files complaint notice with College, College notifies Respondent Professional who gets counsel. Possible interim suspension investigation funded by College, report to Complaints Committee of College, which disposes of complaint — dismissal, caution, referral to Discipline Committee for Hearing. Complainant or Respondent can appeal certain Complaints Committee decisions to HPARB. If Discipline Hearing, then College is Prosecutor, Professional is Respondent and Patient is Witness unless granted Party status. Can take 1 to 5 years. Professional found guilty liable to pay fine, but no damages paid to patient, suspension or revocation.

Parties = Professional and Patient. Plaintiff hires lawyer, starts with Statement of Claim, Defendant gets counsel, responds with Statement of Defence, Pre-trial, Discovery process, Mandatory Mediation, then Civil Court Trial, if no settlement. Can take 1 to 5 years. If Professional loses case, then Court orders monetary amount (damages) as well as costs of Plaintiff to be paid by Professional.

Note: Ontario *Limitations Act* [S.O. 2002, c. 24, Sch. B] amended, so now no rigid time within which lawsuit must be commenced.

3. Criminal Law Process on Sexual Assault Charges Patient or Representative makes complaint to Police

Parties = Accused Professional and Government (in the name of the Queen, cited as "Regina" or "R."), Patient Complainant is Witness, not Party. Patient or representative makes complaint to Police of sexual abuse by Professional as "sexual assault" under section 265 of *Criminal Code of Canada* [R.S.C. 1985, c. C-46] re: person in position of authority. Police do preliminary investigation to decide whether to charge Professional. Police find Professional (at home, office, in public) and arrest, explaining why. Professional retains counsel at own expense, either through professional liability insurance (e.g. CMPA for physicians) or possible that Crown Attorney (lawyer acting for Government) will ask Court to order Professional to be held in custody if sufficient evidence that Professional may endanger others or leave jurisdiction to avoid criminal law process. May be possible to "post bond" of money so Professional not held; but bond money forfeited if Professional breaks bond agreement. If Professional found Guilty likely sentenced to jail term (criminal charges may trigger regulatory college discipline process re: revocation of certificate of registration to practise in Ontario).

---

[1]   All three actions can be proceeding at the same time.

This diagram has been prepared to try to give a one-page overview of the "whole" range of actions that can involve a professional against whom a complaint of sexual abuse is made. It is important to keep in mind that it is possible to be involved in all three of these actions at the same time: a college complaint under the civil law rules, mostly found in the *Regulated Health Professions Act, 1991 (RHPA)*,[2] a civil lawsuit against the professional for monetary damages, and criminal law proceedings based on the charges of sexual assault under the *Criminal Code of Canada*.

B. PART I: CIVIL LAW

No health professional looks forward to a day that he or she might be notified of a pending civil suit for damages.[3] But should that day arrive, it is important to appreciate the contrast between the two most common civil actions (see diagram above) that a professional may face when sexual abuse of a patient is alleged, which are:

1. *the regulatory college process* dealing with a complaint made against the professional by the "complainant" (usually a patient) where the two main parties are the professional as the "respondent" to the complaint and the professional's college, which has responsibility to prosecute by presenting evidence against the professional to members of the Discipline Committee of the college sitting as a panel (usually three members) to hear the case and to decide whether the professional is guilty and, if so, what the professional's penalty should be, in accordance with the *RHPA*; and/or

2. *the civil lawsuit for damages* (damages being money that a court orders to be paid as a result of harm done) that is to be argued before a judge in a civil, not criminal, court because the suit has been initiated by a "plaintiff" as the person (likely the patient) alleging damage as a result of sexual abuse by the professional, and claiming compensation from the professional, who is the "defendant."

---

2   S.O. 1991, c. 18.
3   See the description of damages in a civil suit based on allegations of sexual abuse at note 6 in Chapter 1.

1. Case Study: Dr. AB, a Psychologist in Ottawa

Dr. AB (his actual initials) was a prominent, respected member of Ottawa's professional community for many years. In addition to his private practice as a registered psychologist, he lectured at a university and was often invited to speak at conferences and meetings. The identity of the patient who brought the civil lawsuit against him for harm caused due to his sexual abuse in the course of her treatment was protected by court order. She will be named "Nora" and her husband will be named "James" in this case study.

Nora first consulted Dr. AB in 1990 because she wanted help in dealing with a number of stresses in her life including disease and death in her family and a major change in her job situation.

Following more than two years of care — and after slowly eroding "Nora's" personal, physical and psychological boundaries and grooming her for sexual exploitation — her therapist initiated a sexual relationship. Nora was in a state of deep transference. She was convinced that she was in love and was important and special to him. At that time, Nora told herself that she "willingly" consented to the "relationship" and was reassured when he said that he "loved" her too.

Nora sued Dr. AB and the court found him to be in breach of his duty as a health professional in a position of authority and to have been grossly negligent in the standard of care he provided to Nora.[4]

The following quote from Nora is from her statement to the Ontario Special Task Force on Sexual Abuse of Patients. She describes in her own words her experience of transference exploitation and one aspect of the harm caused by her psychologist's exploitation of her trust:

> When I heard the expert witness describe how he turned me into a little girl, I flashed on how he kept trying to get me to perform oral sex on him in his office and I could only nod my head "no" back and forth, back and forth, like a little girl. Listening to the expert, I realised then that he planned all along to be able to abuse the little girl in me. Even now, years later, I wake up in a sweat remembering. I feel raped. When he had sex with me, he was raping me. He knew what he was doing, but he didn't care.
>
> It never leaves me. Never a day goes by that I think about it, but now I see it for what it was. I have never felt such deep, deep pain to the core of my being.[5]

---

[4]   *C. (N.) v Blank*, [1998] O.J. No. 2544 (Div. Ct.) (QL).
[5]   M. McPhedran, H. Armstrong, R. Bessner, B. Long, P. Marshall & R. Roach, *What About Accountability to the Patient? The Independent Final Report of the Special Task Force on Sexual Abuse of Patients* (Toronto: Ministry of Health and Long-Term Care, 2001).

Dr. Iris Jackson, a psychologist herself and former president of the Ontario Psychological Association, assessed Nora's situation and gave expert testimony in the lawsuit explaining how "consent" could not have been given:

> (Nora) could not have made a free choice to consent in the sexual relationship with (her therapist). She was in a sexual relationship with a man who had power over her psychological state of mind and her treatment process. He had initiated erotic contact after a process of grooming her for exploitation and slowly eroding her personal, physical and psychological boundaries and implying that she was special to him and that he "loved her although he was not in love with her."[6]

2. Secondary Victims: Trauma to People Who Have Not Been Sexually Abused

Dr. Gary Schoener, a psychologist based in Minnesota who is widely consulted on sexual abuse of patients, uses the term "associate victims" to describe the people close to the victim who can be emotionally affected. Dr. Harvey Armstrong, one of Canada's foremost authorities on treating sexual abuse survivors, notes that:

> Secondary or vicarious victimisation occurs when a second person, on learning of the extent and severity of the trauma of a person they care about and are involved with, becomes traumatised and develops post traumatic symptoms.[7]

(a) Nora's Husband, James

Nora also made a complaint to the College of Psychologists of Ontario — a process that went on longer than the civil lawsuit. In his testimony to the Special Task Force, Nora's husband, "James," spoke of his experience:

> It is only recently that I understand that I am a victim of this abuse....
>
> The college process affects the whole family, not just the victim. There are many victims within a family unit. I felt impotent because I could not protect my wife through the process. I had no power to act — to fulfil my role as her husband. It was all done through another party, like a puppeteer.[8]

---

[6]   C. (N.) v. Blank, supra note 4, at 18.
[7]   Task Force Report, supra note 5, at 12.
[8]   Ibid., at 12.

3. A Judge's Perspective on Dr. AB

Few patients reach the point of being able to marshal their resources to sue for damages, separate from or in addition to the college process and possibly also the criminal law process. Few judicial decisions have examined the dynamics of sexual abuse by a health professional thoroughly. The following excerpt is from the judgment in Nora's civil lawsuit against Dr. AB, rendered by Justice Aitken of the Ontario Court of Justice (General Division) in 1998.

> She went to him for help at a time when she was particularly vulnerable and insecure. He had the professional knowledge to help her, but instead used that knowledge to manipulate the situation to his own advantage, playing on [her] lack of confidence, her search for a positive father-figure and her sexual inhibitions. In these circumstances, as has been attested by Dr. Jackson and Dr. Freebury, [the patient] could not exercise free will. Her participation in sexual activities with Dr. B. [a psychologist] was not based on any understanding on her part as to what was really happening. He kept her in a constant state of confusion as to whether his advances were part of her treatment, evidence of his love for her, or something else. This was coupled with her overwhelming dependency on him, which he let develop unchecked, so that she was rendered incapable of coming to her own assessments or conclusions. There could be no genuine consent in these circumstances. Therefore everything from the initial touching to the hugging, kissing, fondling, masturbating and finally intercourse were all forms of battery. I agree with McLachlin J. that "...where such a power imbalance exists it matters not what the patient may have done, how seductively she may have dressed, how compliant she may have appeared, or how self interested her conduct may have been — the doctor will be at fault if sexual exploitation occurs." [*Norberg v. Wynrib* [1992] 2 S.C.R. 226, 92 D.L.R. (4th) 449 at p. 497]. Exploitation did occur in this case, and the sole responsibility for that rests with Dr. B. There can be no doubt that [the therapist] owed fiduciary obligations to [the patient] when he took her on as a client within his clinical psychology practice. It is also equally clear that he breached those obligations by totally ignoring what were appropriate therapist-client boundaries and particularly by initiating and maintaining a sexual relationship with her. The obligation was on him and him alone to ensure the appropriate boundaries were maintained. By breaching them, he put his own needs ahead of those of [his patient]. He did not do this on just one occasion. He did it repeatedly from August 1990 to August 1995, and arguably beyond.[9]

(a) An Example of Damages Awarded to a Patient /Plaintiff

Madame Justice Aitken concluded her written decision by quantifying the damages Dr. AB was ordered to pay as a result of the harm done to his patient. The judge's disapproval of what Dr. AB was found to have

---

[9]   *C. (N.) v. Blank, supra* note 4, at 39, 40.

done is reflected in the fact that Dr. AB was ordered to pay several types of damages, to demonstrate how repugnant his abuse was to the Court. The Court awarded the plaintiff damages of $326,275.98, including aggravated damages of $100,000, punitive damages of $25,000, and special damages of approximately $200,000. The Court awarded the plaintiff's husband $30,000 in damages as compensation for the losses he had suffered and would suffer in the future as a result of the defendant's treatment of his wife. The judge noted that the plaintiff's injuries were the foreseeable result of the defendant's negligence. In assessing damages, the Court started from the premise that absent the defendant's involvement, the plaintiff would have been living a normal, healthy life by December 1993. She would have been working full time. She may have needed supportive counselling from time to time, but nothing in the nature of the intensive psychotherapy she had required since December 1993, and continued to require. The judge was of the opinion that Dr. AB had breached virtually all standards of professional conduct; that his negligence was so reckless and audacious as to shock the Court, meriting aggravated damages, in addition to the other kinds of damages also awarded.

4. "Parties" in the Two Civil Law Processes: 1) Lawsuit and 2) College Complaint

(a) Parties in a Civil Suit

As the diagram at the beginning of this chapter illustrates, the professional is a "party" in both civil law proceedings. When a professional is sued, as Dr. W (in Chapter 1) and Dr. AB were, the main parties are the "defendant" professional and the "plaintiff" patient (or the party claiming damages as a result of the alleged sexual abuse). In some cases, the person who initiates a civil suit may not be the patient if the patient is unable to take direct action or if someone close to the patient feels he or she has cause to claim monetary compensation from the professional as a result of the harmful impact of the alleged sexual abuse. For example, in the case of the civil suit against Dr. AB (the Ottawa case study described above) the husband of the plaintiff patient also claimed damages as a "secondary victim" of Dr. AB's abuse of his wife and the court awarded $30,000 in damages as compensation for the losses he had suffered and would suffer in the future.

(b) Parties in Regulatory College Proceeding

By contrast, the main "parties" in a complaints and discipline proceeding of a regulatory college are the "respondent" professional and the college itself, which funds the investigation and the hearing, if any, including retaining and paying the prosecutor for the college. The participation of the complainant and his or her lawyer as a party in a college proceeding is at the discretion of the disciplinary panel.[10]

5. Key Issues in the Two Civil Processes: Harm and Guilt

(a) Harm is the Key Issue in a Civil Suit

In a civil suit, the key issue is harm caused by the professional to the patient, and where proven, what financial compensation the court will order the professional to pay to the patient.

(b) Guilt is the Key Issue in a Regulatory College Complaint

In a regulatory college process, the impact or harm done to the patient may be considered by the discipline panel, but the focus of the proceedings is on whether the sexual abuse as defined in the *RHPA* actually occurred. If there is a finding of guilt, then the college discipline panel must decide on a penalty in accordance with the *RHPA*. In certain cases, the professional can be ordered by the discipline panel to pay a fine.[11]

6. Do Some Professions Have a Propensity to be Sued?

Actuarial evidence suggests that the more trust that is built between the patient and the professional, the less likely it is that the patient will come back later with a complaint.

Depending on the risk level of the practice, some professionals may be more prone to legal suits than others because of the risks of the nature of the practice itself. Of physicians, for example, an obstetrician/gynaecologist has a greater chance of being sued than does a dermatologist. Similarly, physicians overall are more likely to experience

---

[10] *Health Professions Procedural Code*, being Sch. 2 to the *Regulated Health Professions Act, supra* note 2, s. 41.1 [hereinafter "the *Code*"].

[11] *Ibid.*, sub. 93(4), which sets the maximum fine at $25,000 for offences of sexual abuse defined in subs. 85.1(1), 85.4(1), 85.5(1) or 92.1.

legal complaints because of the comprehensive nature of their practices, when compared to other professionals such as dieticians or opticians.[12] In 2001, the Canadian Medical Protective Association (CMPA), the insurer for physicians across Canada, reported a total of 14,868 new files opened against physicians across Canada, of which a small number were based on allegations of sexual abuse. This is in contrast with 13,531 in 1999 and 11,462 in 1997.[13] As the CMPA notes, "[w]ith slightly less than two members named in each legal action this represents a risk of one in 27 members being named in a new legal action in 2001."[14] The propensity of legal actions against medical doctors is softened when the figures are reviewed in more detail. In 2001, of the nearly 15,000 files opened by the CMPA, 1308 new legal actions were commenced. In the final analysis, approximately 60 percent of these cases did not proceed because the cases were abandoned or withdrawn by the plaintiff and approximately 30 percent were settled before the trial by means of a payment to the plaintiff. Of those remaining cases that did go to trial, the courts found in favour of the plaintiff in about one in three decisions. Recognizing that court cases usually take three to four years to complete explains the approximations; however, these final numbers can be estimated at 74 decisions in favour of physicians in contrast with 25 in favour of patients.

7. Impact of Civil Law Reform Initiatives

It is difficult to predict whether these two civil law processes just discussed (that is, a complaint to a health regulatory college under the *RHPA or* a civil lawsuit for monetary damages initiated by and at the expense of a patient against a health professional as a private action, with no involvement of a regulatory body) will remain essentially as described in this Guide. There are several trends emerging in other jurisdictions that may trigger law reform there and could, in turn, impact on regulated health professionals in Ontario. For example, see the case study of Dr. W

---

[12] See further, Gerald B. Hickson, James W. Pichert, Charles F. Federspiel & Ellen Wright Clayton, "Development of an Early Identification and Response Model of Malpractice Prevention" (1997) 60 Law and Contemporary Problems 7.

[13] Canadian Medical Protective Association, *2001 Annual Report* "The Year in Numbers" online, CMPA homepage <http://www.cmpa-acpm.ca/portal/pub_index.cfm?FILE=HOME_MAIN&LANG=E>, click on "resource centre" to access annual reports (Date accessed 10 August 2003), unpaginated [hereinafter "CMPA 2001 Report"].

[14] *Ibid.*

in Chapter 1, who was sued by his former patient and ordered to pay damages to her for the harm done by his sexual abuse. In Canadian civil law, the patient's statement of claim framed the sexual abuse as an assault that amounted to the tort of battery, which originated in English law hundreds of years ago.[15] But in the United States, the state of California has clarified the high threshold for health professionals by creating a civil cause of action for harm caused to a patient by sexual contact during treatment *and* for two years after termination, regardless of whether the parties thought the sex was "consensual."[16] As well, the California Business and Professions Code makes sexual exploitation criminal.[17] And although self-regulation by health professionals through their colleges is the norm in Ontario under the *RHPA*, many states, such as Minnesota, New York, and Texas, press criminal charges for sexual abuse of patients in addition to using the civil regulatory process.[18] As well, the government of British Columbia, elected in 2002, announced a review of the scope of independence in self-regulation by the professions.[19]

8. Insurance Coverage for Professionals Charged by their Colleges

Each profession has different programs. The longest running legal defence fund is the CMPA, which is available only for medical doctors. When a complaint is made to the College of Physicians and Surgeons of

---

[15] See Chapter 1 at note 8 for a more complete explanation of the tort of battery.
[16] California Civil Code §43.93 creates the cause of action; the California Code of Civil Procedure §51.9 makes sexual harassment of patients illegal; and the California Business and Professions Code, §726 allows for the civil penalty of Licensing Board sanctions (J. Winer, *12 Answers re: Therapist Abuse and Therapist Malpractice Cases* online <http://www.AdvocateWeb.org/hope/ap12commonquestions.asp> (Accessed 27 August 2003).
[17] California Business and Professions Code, §729.
[18] For more information, go to <http://www.advocateweb.org>, "Its Never Okay: Consider the Options — Criminal Complaint." This is a U.S. website providing resources to victims of abuse by health and other helping professionals.
[19] On the introduction of legislation in 2003, the British Columbia Minister of Health stated:
> These amendments aim to increase public confidence in health care professionals and to ensure that professional colleges have direct responsibility for ensuring patient safety. For example, the public will have greater access to complaints about individual health care practitioners, health care professionals will be required to report to their professional college a health professional who poses a public safety risk, and the colleges will be required to implement quality assurance programs to improve health services for patients.
Legislature of British Columbia Hansard, 4th Sess., 37 Parl., 15 No. 11, page 6728, May 13, 2003 *per* Hon. S. Hawkins.

Ontario (CPSO) about sexual abuse or impropriety within the context of what the CMPA considers to be the practice of medicine, then the doctor receives assistance in defending against the allegations. But the CMPA normally does not fund any legal defence for a doctor when sexual abuse or harassment allegations are made by direct employees of the physician or employees in a private clinic. However, even in cases where legal defence has been provided, the CMPA does not pay any awards, settlements or fines that may be levied against a doctor if the Discipline Committee of the CPSO makes a finding of guilt.[20]

9. Alternative Dispute Resolution and Settlement

(a) What is ADR?

Although there are strongly differing views on the use of mediation or other forms of alternative dispute resolution (ADR) in complaints about sexual abuse to regulatory colleges, this complaint resolving process is becoming more widely considered and used by many of the colleges. "ADR" is just what the term suggests: an alternative to the relatively more expensive quasi-judicial process that can end with peer judgment by the discipline committee of a college (which can be appealed to a court by the respondent professional, but not by the complainant patient).

Instead of proceeding through the three possible main stages governed by the *Code* for resolving a complaint — 1) investigation, 2) Complaints Committee's review and 3) possible referral to Discipline Committee for hearing to determine guilt and penalty, if any — the complainant patient and the respondent professional agree to engage in a confidential process of discussion and negotiation guided by trained mediators with the shared goal of reaching a resolution of the complaint that is acceptable to both.

As the *RHPA* does not define a specific standard for a referral to the Discipline Committee,[21] there is also no standard for when a complaint can be redirected to ADR. The fact is, neither the Executive nor the Complaints Committee of a college is charged with adjudicating the

---

[20] Canadian Medical Protective Association, *2002 Annual Report*, online, CMPA home-page <http://www.cmpa-acpm.ca/portal/pub_index.cfm?FILE=HOME_MAIN&LANG=E>, click on "resource centre" to access annual reports.

[21] Subsection 26(2) of the *Code*, *supra* note 10, does say that the Complaints Committee is to decide whether or not to send a complaint on to the Discipline Committee after "investigating a complaint... considering or making reasonable efforts to consider all records and documents it considers relevant to the complaint...".

evidence on any complaint, except to decide 1) if enough of the information would be admissible in a typical discipline hearing, and 2) if the nature of the complaint is serious enough to have the complaint sent on into the process leading to a hearing by a panel of that college's Discipline Committee. However, ADR is not even mentioned in the *RHPA*, and there seems to be considerable variance among colleges as to:

- when it is used,
- what it is called (ADR, mediation or remediation being some of the terms), and
- the degree of transparency of process and outcome related to ADR.[22]

(b) Differing Points of View on the Use of ADR by Colleges

In its 2001 report to Ontario's Minister of Health, the Health Professions Regulatory Advisory Council (HPRAC) noted that some colleges had advised HPRAC that "early resolution of complaints through mediation offered the possibility of increasing both efficiency and complainant satisfaction in knowing the complaint had been dealt with in a timely manner…" and that "frivolous and vexatious complaints ought to be 'dismissed' earlier rather than later in the complaints process to achieve administrative efficiency and fairness to the respondent."[23]

HPRAC members decided that they could see a place for ADR in the general college complaint process, recommending that an addition be made to the *Code*.

> to specifically provide that ADR may be used only to deal with complaints of the following nature: poor communications; inaccurate or poor documentation and/or record-keeping; rude behaviour not indicative of serious practice deficiencies; isolated standards of practice failures not resulting in serious harm; breach of confidentiality; conflicts of interest; and behaviours not indicative of a pattern of practice deficiencies.[24]

HPRAC specifically reported to the minister on use of ADR in cases of professional misconduct of a sexual nature, and made the following recommendations:

> To clarify when it is appropriate to permit resolution of a report or complaint of sexual abuse outside of a discipline hearing, it is recommended that:

---

[22] Health Professions Regulatory Advisory Council, *Adjusting the Balance: A Review of the Regulated Health Professions Act* (Toronto: HPRAC, March 2001) at 68, 69.

[23] *Ibid.*, at 67.

[24] *Ibid.*, at 69.

25. The Minister direct that colleges never use ADR involving a person who was allegedly the subject of sexual abuse by a member (of a regulated health profession under the *RHPA*) for cases of sexual abuse as defined in s. 51 (5) 2 of the [*Code*].

26. The [*Code*] be amended to require that all settlements or undertakings reached with members as a result of a complaint or mandatory report alleging sexual abuse be subject to approval by a committee or panel. [25]

Members of the 2001 Special Task Force on Sexual Abuse of Patients were also asked by the Minister of Health to give their advice and recommendations on the use by colleges of mediation in cases of sexual abuse.[26] In cooperation with the Federation of Health Professional Regulatory Colleges, the Task Force convened a roundtable of college representatives in May 2000, and the issue of ADR was raised. The CPSO and the Royal Society of Dental Surgeons reported to the Task Force that ADR was never used in sexual abuse cases. One of the college representatives at the roundtable, Dr. Dody Bienenstock, explained that the CPSO had conducted a pilot project with four cases, and had "decided that this was not the route for sexual abuse cases. We do not use formal ADR for sexual abuse cases any more, period."[27]

The case of one of the patients who reported to the Task Force in 2000 was also one of the four cases that had been determined by ADR in the CPSO pilot project. She told the Task Force that, while her overall experience was negative and she concluded that ADR was not a good option in her case, there were both positive and negative elements to the experience. She explained to the Task Force that

> [w]hen this option was presented, I felt it was a good one because I wanted to confront the [health care provider] face to face and I had high hopes for us to reach an agreement. I also felt strongly about trying mediation because of our religious convictions. The actual confrontation part of the mediation was a positive experience for me, but there were major disappointments with the process of the mediation, the mediator himself, and, of course, the unsatisfactory outcome.[28]

This patient communicated her concerns to the CPSO and pointed out some serious problems in her mediation experience, including, especially, one incident where she was left alone with her abuser:

---

[25] *Ibid.*, Appendix B at 7.

[26] M. McPhedran, H. Armstrong, R. Bessner, B. Long, P. Marshall & R. Roach, *What About Accountability to the Patient? The Independent Final Report of the Special Task Force on Sexual Abuse of Patients* (Toronto: Ministry of Health & Long-Term Care, 2001). Question 8 at page ix, discussed in Chapter 6 at 58-62.

[27] *Ibid.*, at 59.

[28] *Ibid.*

Please, if you are ever in another mediation, do ensure that the patient is never left alone with the member. [The patient] is still vulnerable. This vulnerability makes being firm and clear, in my case, very difficult.... For a brief time during one point in the mediation, I was left alone with [the respondent health professional] as everyone left the room. During this time, we exchanged some words and he affirmed me in a way that made me feel linked to him again and definitely more desiring to please him.... I didn't realise this at the time but, after the mediation, I had a considerable emotional setback...[29]

Before making its final recommendation to the Minister of Health on the use of ADR, the Task Force consulted Dr. Barbara Landau, a lawyer, psychologist and professional mediator, who made a number of general points, on the basis of what she called "the one key premise — *safety is the most important criterion.*"

- mediation must not be used in a way that would undermine patient or public safety;
- a responsible mediator would discourage mediation in cases of obvious transference;
- each case requires a thorough screening process with specially trained mediators if sexual dynamics are present in the complaint; and
- skilled mediators would never meet at the same time with the two parties in such cases.[30]

In contrast to the HPRAC recommendation on the use of ADR, the Task Force recommended an addition to the *Code* "to state that any procedures considered to be Alternative Dispute Resolution or Mediation are not to be used to attempt to resolve complaints of sexual abuse."[31]

In his book, *A Complete Guide to the Regulated Health Professions Act*, lawyer Richard Steinecke raised some questions and concerns about the use of ADR, including:

(1) The primary motivation of the college in mediation is to reduce the costs associated with discipline hearings. Colleges may be subordinating their public protection mandate to save money.

(2) Mediation is inappropriate for some complaints. Serious allegations ought to be dealt with through discipline in order to deter practitioners and to express disapproval of the alleged conduct.

(3) Complainants may be vulnerable in the mediation process. They may not have a full appreciation of their right to insist that the matter be dealt with through the discipline route. Complainants are often unrepresented by lawyers and may

---

[29] *Ibid.*, at 60.
[30] *Ibid.*, at 60 and note 23.
[31] *Ibid.*, Recommendation 25.0 at 62.

not have the same confidence and ability to express themselves that practitioners have.

(4) The mediation process is confidential. Often the result of the mediation is either not published or does not identify the practitioner. The resulting secrecy makes it difficult for others to scrutinize the process.

(5) Mediation can result in additional delay and expense if it is unsuccessful.

There is developing pressure upon the colleges using mediation to have clear, public guidelines for its use.[32]

10. Privacy Concerns

The *RHPA* requires each college to maintain a register, with public and non-public information. After a finding of guilt on sexual abuse charges, a college must place on the public register the name of the professional, the grounds for the finding of guilt and the penalty imposed by the Discipline Committee.

The cases in this chapter all involved criminal charges as well as a college disciplinary process. Where criminal charges have been laid and a criminal court has used its authority under the *Criminal Code* to order a publication ban to protect the identity of the complainant and/or witnesses, then the ban is extended to non-criminal related proceedings. As well, the *Code* in the *RHPA* provides the discretion to a college council to protect identity and privacy by ordering exclusion of the public and media from *a meeting* of a college if considered necessary to prevent the public disclosure of matters discussed in the meeting. This can include banning publication or broadcasting of those matters.[33] More specific to sexual abuse cases, the *Code* provides that a discipline panel has the authority to order a publication ban and "order that the public be excluded from a hearing or any part of it if the panel is satisfied that, (a) matters involving public security may be disclosed; (b) financial or personal or other matters may be disclosed at the hearing of such a nature that the desirability of avoiding public disclosure of those matters in the interest of any person affected or in the public interest outweighs the desirability of adhering to the principle that hearings be open to the public; (c) a person involved in a criminal proceeding or in a civil suit or proceeding may be prejudiced; or (d) the safety of a person may be jeopardized."[34]

[32] R. Steinecke, *A Complete Guide To The Regulated Health Professions Act*, looseleaf (Aurora, Ont.: Canada Law Book, updated January 2000) at 6-98.1.
[33] Subsections 7(2), (3) of the *Code*, *supra* note 10.
[34] *Ibid.*, subs. 45(1), (2), (3).

(a) Evidence Admissible in a Civil Lawsuit

For both the patient and the professional, loss of privacy is usually a major concern, regardless of which legal process is triggered by a sexual abuse complaint. Although the purpose is not clearly stated, subsection 36(3) of the *RHPA* creates a barrier around information related to a college proceeding, stipulating that "no record of a proceeding" under the *RHPA* and "no report, document or thing prepared for or statement given" and "no order or decision made" in a college proceeding is admissible in a civil lawsuit between private parties (that is, patient and professional). The practical effect of this amendment to the *RHPA* is that the evidence needed in a civil suit by a plaintiff to "build the case" when suing a professional for the harm caused by the alleged sexual abuse must be freshly gathered, even if the identical evidence has already been produced in a college proceeding related to the same fact situation between the same patient and professional. Similarly, the professional cannot introduce evidence from a college proceeding on occasions when such information might be helpful to the professional's defence in the civil suit. This prohibition does *not* apply to criminal cases and was inserted into the *RHPA* as a subsequent amendment following suggestions from some of the regulatory colleges.

(b) Privileged or Protected Personal Information

For both the professional and the patient and other potential witnesses, there are concerns about disclosure of information normally considered to be confidential (discussions with one's therapist, for example) or at least private (OHIP billings and other such accounting). In both civil law processes — a lawsuit or a college complaint process — there is little that is protected by any privilege recognized in law for those engaged in such legal procedures. Members of a Discipline Panel and judges in a civil lawsuit have the discretionary power to determine whether personal information is relevant to the issues in the case that has to be decided, and to order that the information be disclosed.

In college cases, appeals against such decisions can be made to the Health Professions Appeals Board (HPARB).[35] In civil lawsuits, a judge has the authority to hold someone who refuses to provide relevant information under that person's care or control in contempt of court.[36]

---

[35] *Ibid.*, ss. 29 and 32.
[36] *Rules of Civil Procedure*, R.R.O. 1990, Reg. 194, r. 60.11.

(c) Dealing with the Media

A quick search of the main media Internet sites is an ample demonstration of the fact that sexual abuse cases often generate media attention and that professionals who must respond to charges against them are usually fully identified. By contrast, the *RHPA* specifies that the professional making a mandatory report and the college processing a complaint about "a patient who may have been sexually abused" must ensure that the patient's name is not included in such a report *unless* the "patient or if the patient is incapable, the patient's representative, consents in writing to the inclusion of the patient's name."[37]

11. Learning Issues and Discussion Points

(a) Questions About Civil Lawsuits Against Health Professionals

1. What is the first step for a professional to take when notified that a patient or patient's representative has commenced a lawsuit?
2. What difference does it make if the professional being sued is a doctor or a denturist?
3. What protections of a professional's privacy are possible after a civil lawsuit has been commenced? What about for the patient who has initiated the suit? What about for other patients that may be called as witnesses — by either side?

(b) Questions About Complaints to Colleges Against Health Professionals

1. What are the advantages to a professional of engaging in the ADR process rather than proceeding through the complaints and discipline process specified in the *Code*?
2. Why is ADR not recommended for sexual abuse cases?
3. Why do you think that there is a difference of opinion among colleges, researchers and mediators about the use of ADR in sexual abuse cases?

In the next section, we move to a completely different area of the law — criminal charges for sexual assault by a person in a position of authority.

---

[37] Subsection 85.3(4) of the *Code, supra* note 10.

C. PART II: CRIMINAL LAW

The two key sections of the *Criminal Code of Canada* that usually form the basis of criminal charges against a health professional alleged to have had sex with his or her patient(s) are section 271, which is specific to sexual assault, and section 265.

1. Section 271

    (1)   Every one who commits a sexual assault is guilty of

        (a) an indictable offence and is liable to imprisonment for a term not exceeding ten years; or

        (b) an offence punishable on summary conviction and liable to imprisonment for a term not exceeding eighteen months.

2. Section 265

    (1)   A person commits an assault when

        (a) without the consent of another person, he applies force intentionally to that other person, directly or indirectly;

        . . .

    (2)   This section applies to all forms of assault, including sexual assault, sexual assault with a weapon, threats to a third party or causing bodily harm and aggravated sexual assault.

    (3)   For the purposes of this section, no consent is obtained where the complainant submits or does not resist by reason of …

        (a) fraud; or

        (b) the exercise of authority.

3. Three Case Studies: Criminal Charges Against a Chiropractor, a Psychologist and a Nurse

(a) Case Study: Dr. B,[38] a Chiropractor in St. Catharines

Dr. B negotiated guilty pleas on nine charges of sexual assault committed while he was purporting to treat nine women in his capacity as a licensed chiropractor. His abusive conduct took several forms, including breast fondling, genital manipulation, digital penetration of the vagina and digital penetration of the rectum. Dr. B persisted in the sexual misconduct despite being questioned about it by some of his patients, and despite being warned to stop, once by a senior medical practitioner from the community and once from the College of Chiropractors. Victim impact statements were filed at the criminal trial, detailing the harm suffered as a result of Dr. B's mistreatment of those patients, including: sexual dysfunction, termination of marriages and long-term relationships, disharmony within the family, loss of trust in the health professions, loss of self-worth and dignity and overwhelming feelings of shame, humiliation and embarrassment.

The trial judge gave Dr. B an 18-month conditional sentence plus three years' probation. The Crown appealed the conditional sentence and asked the Court of Appeal to use its authority to replace the conditional sentence with a prison sentence of nine months because the conditional sentence failed to "adequately reflect the principles of general deterrence and denunciation and that it is manifestly unfit having regard to the gravity and seriousness of the offences and the respondent's degree of moral blameworthiness."[39]

The trial judge had decided on the conditional sentence after taking into consideration evidence about Dr. B's particular circumstances as a popular practitioner in a small Ontario city. The trial judge heard testimony from a noted psychologist who reported that Dr. B had marital problems and that he suffered from a sexual disorder known as "toucherism." The psychologist told the judge that, in his expert opinion, Dr. B needed therapy to prevent relapsing but that he did not present a danger to the community at large. The trial judge also took into account the remorse that Dr. B expressed at trial and the fact that he acknowledged assaulting 13 patients over a ten-year period, and that he entered nine

---

[38]   *R. v. Bedard* (23 May 2001) Doc. No. C35494 (Ont. C.A.), online <http://www.canlii.org/on/cas/onca255.html> (Accessed 13 Sept. 2003).

[39]   *Ibid.*, per Moldaver J.A. at para. 2.

guilty pleas at trial, which in turn spared the victims from having to re-live their experiences in a public forum.

The three Court of Appeal judges unanimously decided to set aside the conditional sentence and substitute a sentence of nine months' imprisonment, while keeping the terms of three years' probation and a weapons prohibition put in place by the trial judge. In giving reasons for the Appeal Court making this decision, Moldaver J. said:

> The crimes committed by the respondent were extremely serious. As indicated, over the course of ten years, he sexually assaulted thirteen female patients and in doing so, he repeatedly broke the sacred bond that forms the essence of a doctor/patient relationship. By any measure, this was a gross breach of trust and, as is all too often the case, it has resulted in tragic consequences for the victims.[40]

(*i*) DR. B, THE CRIMINAL COURT AND THE COLLEGE

A "360 degree" view of these cases, such as with Dr. B's, is difficult to achieve. Each of his patients had a unique experience that traumatized them and affected their personal circles extending out into the community at large. Dr. B expressed remorse over his violations of professional standards and the trust of his patients. He was married with children; his family had to make the best of their lives in the same community as his victims, without his financial support. And like many professionals found guilty of sexually abusing one or some of their patients, Dr. B was popular with many of his patients and generally well regarded, which set up another kind of dissonance within the community at large. This was recognized by the trial judge, and on appeal Moldaver J. noted:

> Because these offences occurred in a small Ontario community, many of the victims harbour concerns about meeting the respondent in public. For some, this has led to a form of self-imposed house arrest. For example, Ms. H states: '...[I] have felt petrified to go out in public, even with my family because I'm afraid I'll run into him and I don't know how I would react. So ever since the charges were laid against [Dr. B] last year I haven't really been out other than doctors [sic] appointments and medical tests and on occasion since we have a new 24 hours grocery store my husband will take me at 1:00 or 2:00 a.m. All this worry and stress has made my physical condition much worse....'
>
> Another example is found in Ms. S's victim impact statement: '...Or when you go out into a mall and the whole time you're looking around to see if you are going to run into someone who works at the chiro [sic] office or [Dr. B] himself which has

---

[40] *Ibid.*, per Moldaver J.A. at para. 18.

happened to me at Christmas and you completely lose it in a public place. I find that I tend to avoid a lot of situations…'[41]

Moldaver J. also acknowledged the impact of community dissonance on the victims:

In addition to feeling like prisoners in their own community, several of the victims report that because of the respondent's [Dr. B] otherwise unblemished professional reputation and his strong support in the community, they have had to contend with comments from others, including relatives and friends, to the effect that the respondent is innocent and that the charges against him have been concocted for purposes of personal gain.[42]

After the criminal process was well underway, the College of Chiropractors followed up in accordance with the mandate given under the *RHPA*. Some colleges take the position that it is better to wait until a criminal process is complete before undertaking the college complaint process under civil law. Other colleges decide — on a case-by-case basis — whether or not to use executive authority to temporarily suspend a professional's practice, out of concern for immediate harm to patients. There is no set rule as to what colleges must do when one or more complaint is received about a member of that college. The decision to intervene is left to the judgment of the Registrar and the Executive Committee of the particular college.

The following excerpts, from testimony given to the 2001 Task Force by one of the women victimized by Dr. B and her husband, a police officer, are taken from the transcript of a public hearing held by the Task Force in Toronto on May 9, 2000, to illustrate some of what was experienced by them as a result of the College's decision to have the criminal investigation proceed in advance of the college process. Brenda and Rod asked that their real names be used.

Brenda commented on her experience of the college process, after she had participated in the criminal trial,

His other victims and I were put through the criminal process; he finally came before the college where he admitted guilt in all cases. Along with other victims, I was at the college hearing when they revoked his licence for five years. This whole process continues to be like a nightmare — weird and hard to predict. It's been a real eye opener for me to see how these people being paid good money to process our cases treat victims — they act like they're doing us a big favour, they

---

[41] *Ibid.*, per Moldaver J.A. at para. 8.
[42] *Ibid.*, at para. 9.

take months to respond, months to proceed on very serious charges and months to reimburse our expenses.[43]

At the public hearing, Rod expressed concerns from his perspective as a husband, a member of the community and a police officer:

> I have been a policeman for 25 years and continue to be one. For eight of the years, I specialised in investigating sexual assaults. Because of the difficulty in dealing with such cases, each of us that investigate sexual assaults is forced to undergo extensive training. Police receive training in cognitive interviewing skills. Yet, the person who interviewed Brenda in the hotel room had no training, no video, no recording.
>
> ...
>
> The only sanction placed on this man was by the courts — controlling his behaviour with other patients. The college has yet to do a single thing. He's allowed to resign. If that isn't a PR move...
>
> When a complaint comes from a member of the same college, it must have been the hardest thing that member has to do, to complain about a fellow college member in a small community. He knows this man personally.
>
> Mandatory revocation of an abuser's license is a must in order to instill any confidence in the public. These are the procedures already in place, but it seems there is no standardisation that happens between the colleges. From our experience, we've gone into great detail and we've been pushed on this right to the hills.
>
> At the date that the information is officially sworn in court, he is officially charged with the criminal offences, yet there are no sanctions from the college to protect the public from this man. Since the college has interviewed the victims, not a single thing has been done. It seems illogical that the college wouldn't act upon the charges being officially laid and have an interim sanction in place pending the outcome. This is not one isolated incident. At the time, there were at least nine other victims. It's now a matter of law whether this person is going to be found guilty or not. But there's [sic] reasonable grounds to believe, as far as the college goes, that something has to be done, first to protect the public and the second, to protect the remaining members of the profession who are truly doing a decent job.[44]

(b) Case Study: Dr. M,[45] a Psychologist in Toronto

Dr. M was the chief psychologist at a large general hospital in Metropolitan Toronto and he maintained a private practice. He was 47 years old when he was charged with two counts of sexual assault of two patients — U and V — whose names were protected by publication bans made by the trial judge. Both patients were married with families and

---

[43] McPhedran *et al.*, 2001 Task Force, *supra* note 26, at 18.

[44] *Ibid.*, at 17, 18.

[45] *R. v. Matheson* (1999), 44 O.R. (3d) 557 (C.A.).

both had histories of sexual abuse, which they disclosed to Dr. M early in their psychotherapeutic relationship with him.

Dr. M chose not to testify at his criminal trial.

(*i*) What Happened with Patient U

In 1987, Ms. U was dismissed from her job of 22 years. She was devastated. She could not sleep or eat and felt suicidal when she was referred to Dr. M. She commenced seeing him twice a week at his office at the hospital and disclosed her personal background, including the fact that as a young person she had been physically and sexually abused while under the care of the Children's Aid Society.

The trial judge accepted her testimony when she described the gradual process that led to sex with Dr. M. During therapy, U and the appellant would sit in chairs facing each other. As time passed, he would move closer while she would push her chair away from him. During particularly difficult sessions, when Ms. U discussed painful incidents, the appellant would touch Ms. U on the foot or leg with his own foot or leg. He told her that it would be easier for her to talk if he touched her. In July 1988, Dr. M asked for a kiss because it was his birthday. Ms. U presented her cheek but he turned her face and kissed her on the lips. In therapy, when Ms. U described her husband as a person with problems of his own who was not supportive of her, Dr. M told her that she would never get better unless she left her husband. In late July 1988, Dr. M first came to his patient's house, at night, uninvited. Thereafter the appellant returned to Ms. U's house several times, sometimes with food and wine. On one such occasion, he told his patient that his marriage was a mistake and that he was in love with her. Ms. U told Dr. M that it would not be difficult for her to get a lover, but that what she wanted and needed was a therapist. Nonetheless, Dr. M started coming to U's house every night and eventually they started having sexual intercourse there. She continued to see him at the hospital for therapy. After about a month of the visits, Dr. M went to Europe to attend an International Society of Hypnosis meeting. Before he left, U told him again that she only wanted him to be her therapist. He agreed. However, while he was gone, she received a barrage of letters and postcards, some with sexual messages on them. She also received telephone calls and gifts from him. When Dr. M returned from Europe, both the sexual and therapeutic relationships resumed. Ms. U said she had had no intention of continuing with the sexual relationship.

Ms. U repeatedly asked to be sent to another therapist. Furthermore, when she was suicidal, she asked him to admit her to the hospital's psychiatric unit. The trial judge described Dr. M's response: "He would explain about the length of time it took to develop trust with him and to talk about what had happened in her background," noting that "whatever the accused said to her made sense to her."[46] More than a year after sexual contact with Dr. M had begun, Ms. U and her husband separated. The sexual contact with Dr. M continued for almost four years after that, during which time the therapeutic relationship ended. Finally, in September 1992, the sexual relationship ended when Ms. U found Dr. M in bed with another one of his patients.

(ii) WHAT HAPPENED WITH PATIENT V

Ms. V was a 29-year-old registered nurse, who was married to a medical doctor and was the mother of two children, when she became a private patient of the appellant in March 1992. She remained his patient for only seven months. Ms. V had been sexually victimized as a young girl, which caused depression and suicidal tendencies. As a teenager, Ms. V had been unable to refuse sexual overtures. As an adult, these earlier traumatic events contributed to a depression that affected her sexual relationship with her husband. Her husband suggested hypnotherapy and they sought a female hypnotist who had experience dealing with survivors of child sexual abuse. The Ontario Society for Clinical Hypnosis recommended they contact Dr. M because he had a female associate who might be available. Ms. V approached her first appointment with Dr. M carefully. Before seeing him, she sent him a fax in which she outlined in detail her background and present difficulties. At their initial meeting Ms. V told Dr. M that she wanted a female therapist. She agreed to let Dr. M hypnotize her, under which she was returned to a child-like state in which she felt the experience of desperately needing someone to rescue her. Ms. V agreed to continue seeing Dr. M because she believed hypnosis would be helpful. During those initial therapy sessions, there was non-sexual touching by Dr. M, which comforted Ms. V when she talked of something troubling or painful. However, over time, the touching grew more intimate. Dr. M started to rest his hand on her knee or shoulder and he pulled his chair closer, placed his arm around her and pulled her onto his lap, in a manner

---
[46] *Ibid.*, at 562.

that the patient found comforted her and allowed her to speak freely about difficult issues. Dr. M suggested that they embrace at the outset of each meeting in order that she would feel comfortable right away, and Ms. V complied.

During one session, while the patient recounted childhood abuses, Dr. M stroked her arm. When she told him that she was sexually aroused by this, he responded that it was normal for patients to develop strong feelings for their therapists. Ms. V told the appellant that she felt guilty and distressed because she did not want to have sexual feelings for him. Dr. M knew of her sexual difficulties as a teenager and he also knew that she valued her 12 years of fidelity to her husband. In spite of knowing how she felt, he continued to touch her in this manner, explaining to her that she needed therapy and he was helping her. After one of these sessions, Ms. V decided to send Dr. M a fax saying that she wanted to end therapy with him because it was having a harmful effect on her. She also told her husband how she felt about the touching, but he did not agree that she should end the therapy, telling her the touching was a therapeutic tool used to trigger positive feelings of comfort. Her husband encouraged her to discuss her feelings with Dr. M. After that, her sessions were increased to two a week, even though she realized that the touching had nothing to do with her comfort, but was really about his desire for sex. However, she was unable to talk to anyone about her realization and felt powerless to alter the course of action. Thus began the three-month period of psychologist-patient sexual contact in the course of psychotherapy.

During one session, the appellant embraced V and stroked her while she spoke of the childhood abuse. She asked him to touch her because she was upset. He told her he did not want to do anything to hurt her. She asked if his touching would hurt her. He said he did not know. He touched her breasts and she rubbed his chest for ten or 15 minutes. The subsequent session began in the same manner. They eventually started touching each other, then stood up, took off their clothes and had sex on the floor of his office. After that previous session, the patient anticipated that Dr. M would want to have intercourse so she brought a condom. After the sex, Ms. V told Dr. M that she felt very distressed and he assured her he was going to provide her with therapy.

By the next session, the patient decided that sex was not a price she wanted to pay for therapy. She wanted to phone the appellant to tell him but feared that her husband would again intervene. Instead, she went to the appellant's office. She placed her chair as far away from him as she could and would not look at him. She was crying while she told him how terrible she felt about what they had done and said that they could not do it again. She said she needed therapy and that she did not want him to touch her. She also told him she did not want to have sex with him. Dr. M told Ms. V that she did need therapy, that she was very close to being better and that he could help her. He told her she did not have to disclose anything to her husband. He sat on the floor next to her and touched her knee. She kept telling him she did not want him to touch her. He spoke to her throughout in a very reassuring tone, repeatedly telling her that he cared a great deal for her and was going to help her.

By the end of the session, Ms. V had agreed to continue seeing Dr. M twice a week, one day for sex and the other for therapy. She later told him that if sex was going to continue she did not want to have sex on the floor of his office because she found it humiliating. She "agreed to" and did have the "sex sessions" in his apartment about five times. Her next attempt to stop the sex came when she sent Dr. M a fax telling him that she desperately needed therapy, but that he had betrayed her, that she felt he had manipulated her and was not helping her. Ms. V told Dr. M that she felt trapped because there was nobody else in the world she could talk to except him. Once again he assured her that she was getting better.

In August, Dr. M went away for three weeks. While he was gone, Ms. V resolved once again that she was not going to resume therapy with him. Upon his return, Dr. M called Ms. V at her home and she agreed to meet him because she did not want to be rude. They met and had sex, after which she had a panic attack, rolled off the bed and pulled a blanket around herself. She told Dr. M that she was very frightened and to leave her alone. Again, he was very reassuring. As always, he told her that it was all right, and that he was going to help her, and that she did not have anything to fear. The following month, seven months after she first saw Dr. M, Ms. V read the book, *Sex in the Forbidden Zone*, which explained transference and made it clear why a therapist cannot have sex with a patient and provide competent therapy to that patient at the same time. Ms. V gave this book to Dr. M and told him that what he had done was harmful. He became apologetic and acknowledged that he had done something wrong, and he offered to find her another therapist. After this meeting, Ms. V did not see the appellant again.

As is standard in sexual assault trials, Ms. V was closely questioned about her willingness to have sex with Dr. M. She acknowledged that Dr. M had not expressly asked for sex; she testified that she "always went more by his actions and behaviour than his words."[47] Ms. V also testified that during the time that the sexual activity was happening she never in any way evidenced that she did not wish to have it, explaining that she did not believe that she could stop Dr. M from touching her or having sex with her.

(*iii*) WHY THE COURTS DECIDED AGAINST DR. M

A primary defence argument on behalf of Dr. M was that both women patients "consented" to sex with him, over a considerable period of time, when they could have declined or walked away. The reasons for judgment at trial and on the appeal by Dr. M against his conviction focused on whether there was consent on the part of the two patients. The judges had to look at whether there was consent and whether it could be recognized as genuine and mutual consent or whether it was the kind of "consent" that was vitiated by the authority held by professionals. According to paragraph 265(3)(d) of the *Criminal Code*, "no consent is obtained where the complainant submits or does not resist by reason of... the exercise of authority." Dr. M's defence counsel argued that the relationship of therapist and patient does not involve authority and that the patients in question consented freely to their sexual relationship with their therapist.

The central issue raised by this appeal was about the meaning of the word "authority" as used by Parliament in enacting paragraph 265(3)(d). Dr. M's argument was that as a psychologist he had neither the power nor the right to enforce obedience, and thus he did not have "authority," therefore his conduct could not fall within the ambit of paragraph 265(3)(d). His defence counsel pointed out to the trial judge that "authority relationships" are numerous, for example, parent and child, teacher and pupil, employer and employee, and superior and junior ranks in military and other organizations, and in each of these organizations there is a power or right to enforce obedience in some respect — but that is not true of the doctor-patient relationship nor of the therapist/patient relationship. The doctor may prescribe, but he or she has no power or right to enforce obedience.

Dr. Gail Robinson was one of the expert witnesses at trial and her explanation of the transference and the power dynamics in psychotherapeutic relationships was accepted by the trial judge, and respected by the appeal judges in their conclusions that the boundaries crossed by

---

[47] *Ibid.*, at 565.

Dr. M brought his exercise of his professional authority within the meaning of the *Criminal Code*. The courts noted the following explanation of transference with approval, citing Phyllis Coleman's article on sexual abuse:

> Transference refers to the phenomenon whereby the patient begins to relate to the psychotherapist as if he were a parent or some other significant person in her life. The degree of transference involved places this relationship close to that of the parent-child on the continuum of exploitation.

> To benefit from psychotherapy, the patient must reveal intimate information about herself. Because these revelations are so personal, and often involve information which could be damaging to the patient, she must develop a strong sense of trust in her psychotherapist before she makes such disclosures. Consequently, she is likely to "fall in love" with her psychotherapist, fantasizing that he will be able to make her well. The patient's fantasy is similar to the belief of a child that the parent can solve any problem. As a result of the transference, adult patients may attempt to change the relationship from therapeutic to sexual. Such behaviour is analogous to the "flirtatious" behaviour of a daughter with her father. Nevertheless, just as the father must encourage his daughter to develop her sexuality without responding to her in an overtly sexual manner, the psychotherapist must deny the patient sexual gratification while providing a safe place for exploration of her sexual nature.

> ...

> The therapist must reject any overt response to sexual feelings because, as a result of transference, the patient's consent to a sexual relationship is inherently suspect. As with the child incest victim, coercion ordinarily is not required. The dependent person's "consent", or even her initiation of sexual contact, is not voluntary because she cannot make a mature decision based on existing information. Rather, she "agrees" as a result of unconscious factors, and therefore lacks the state of mind necessary to consent. Sex under these circumstances is tantamount to sex without consent and should result in liability for damages [Phyllis Coleman, "Sex in Power Dependency Relationships: Taking Unfair Advantage of the 'Fair' Sex" (1988), 53 Alta. L. Rev. 95 at 103-04].[48]

In its judgment on whether the trial judge had erred, the Appeal Court quoted what the trial judge had concluded:

> In this case, there is no suggestion from any expert that under a therapist-patient relationship, the therapist did not have an existing potential power or authority over the patient. There is also no suggestion from anyone that when a therapist-patient relationship turns into a sexual relationship, that the therapist's power or authority is downgraded or ceased, even though the real therapy has ceased.

> . . .

---

[48]   *Ibid.*, at 566.

The evidence in my view is overwhelming in establishing that there was a substantial imbalance of power between the powers of the accused and each of his alleged victims during the term of real therapy. During the term stated in the indictment, in each one of the charges, he held the power, and he held it by a significant degree. He had the professional status to gain and hold that power, and his alleged victims were vulnerable to that power, and he knew it. As a result of the power imbalance, he had the power to apply pressure to and manipulate those two patients, and he did so. All of that, in my view, means that the exercise of authority, and where it happens for a sexual purpose, there is no consent to an assault for a sexual purpose.[49]

Dr. M lost his appeal and his prison terms were unanimously upheld by the appeal court.

(c) Case Study: Mr. Y, a Nurse in Toronto

(i) RAPE?

In February 1997, Sherrie's mother took her to a hospital because she had stopped having menstrual periods. She was told that her 32-year-old daughter was pregnant and carrying a healthy 15-week-old foetus. "Sherrie" has a congenital malformation of her brain stem with associated hydrocephalus, seizure disorder and severe cerebral palsy.

She uses a wheelchair and is unable to communicate because her throat is paralyzed, although she is alert and oriented. Sherrie is chronically ill and completely dependent on staff for bathing, feeding and diapering at the chronic care facility in Toronto where she lives.

In her report to the Special Task Force on Sexual Abuse of Patients in 2000, Sherrie's mother recalled the decision that she and Sherrie's father had to face in order to save their daughter's life, saying, "[b]ecause her foetus was so far advanced, we had a terrible struggle accepting that Sherrie had to have an abortion."[50]

Very shortly before the therapeutic abortion was scheduled to take place, Sherrie miscarried. A Toronto Police Services detective took the foetus to the Centre for Forensic Science, where DNA evidence was extracted and preserved. In November 1997, Sherrie's mother received a letter from the College of Nurses, stating: "This letter is sent to confirm the details of our telephone conversation last week. I advised the panel of the Discipline Committee that your daughter [Sherrie], while a patient, was sexually abused by [Mr. Y]."[51]

---

[49] *Ibid.*, at 568.
[50] 2001, Task Force at 7.
[51] *Ibid.*

(*ii*) CRIMINAL CHARGES

The nurse who was charged had been part of a team responsible for the care and well-being of Sherrie. This is part of the report that Sherrie's parents gave to the Task Force:

> We trusted [the hospital and the nurse] to give appropriate care for our fragile, vulnerable daughter and he betrayed all of us, especially Sherrie. Sherrie was a tiny, fragile, helpless young woman who could not run away, could not call for help, and could not tell anyone what he was doing to her. He knew it and took advantage of it behind closed doors when he was supposed to be giving her care.[52]

Criminal charges were laid against him for sexual assault. In a plea bargain, he admitted that he had sexual intercourse with Sherrie without her genuine consent. Sherrie's parents were troubled by the reference to consent; Sherrie cannot speak or write, her hips and legs are paralyzed and she has little use of her arms or hands. After a hearing, the College revoked the nurse's licence. He also served four years in prison following his plea of guilt.

(*iii*) INSTITUTIONAL RESPONSIBILITY AND LIABILITY

Sherrie's mother also reported that concerned health professionals, who were working at the institution following the assault, spoke to the family about disparaging, sexualized comments that a small number of other staff members had been heard to make about Sherrie in Sherrie's presence, while she was in great distress and her family members were not present. The family tried to investigate the matter further, but they reported making little progress after exploring a number of avenues. They chose to transfer Sherrie to another institution. Sherrie's mother told the Task Force:

> We might have coped with the rape and pregnancy and eventually put it behind us, but what was unbearable throughout was the way in which [some of the staff of the institution] treated Sherrie. Our only concern was that she receive therapy and good, compassionate care because she was so sick and traumatized. Neither of these happened. She was severely depressed, agitated, stopped eating, and tried to kill herself on numerous occasions by banging her head against the wall — knowing that it could destabilize the shunt implanted in her skull.[53]

---

[52]   *Ibid.*
[53]   *Ibid.*

(*iv*) SCREENING FOR SEX OFFENDERS

Sherrie's parents reported that the family's distress was compounded when they learned that the health professional convicted of preying on their daughter had previous criminal convictions for sexual offences. To her parents, this raised serious concerns that the college, as the licensing body of this professional, and the hospital, as his employer and the caretaker of their disabled daughter, had all been unable to protect Sherrie. They told the Task Force that they did not see this failure to protect as an aberrant isolated incident that could happen only to one disabled patient; they questioned the systemic safeguards for which the college and the institution were respectively responsible, and wanted to know whether changes in licensing and hiring procedures for nurses were being made to protect patients from any nurses with a history of sex offences.

4. Privacy Concerns

In cases where the professional is charged under the *Criminal Code* with sexual offences, including sexual interference, sexual exploitation of a person with a disability, invitation to sexual touching, indecent act or sexual exposure or a form of sexual assault,[54] the court can impose a ban on any information that could identify the complainant or other witnesses, but usually not the accused, when the court is satisfied that justice would be served by such an order. If the charges involve domestic abuse and such a ban is requested then it must be granted by the court and, where identifying the accused would also tend to identify the complainant, then the privacy of the accused is also protected in the ban.[55]

5. Learning Issues and Discussion Points

1. In the Dr. B case study, what do you think of the comparison that Rod and Brenda made between the criminal legal process and the college complaint process? Were they being "fair"? What is the relevance of the fact that Dr. B was generally highly regarded as a professional and as a member of the community at large?

---

[54] R.S.C. 1985, c. C-46, sub. 486(3).
[55] *Ibid.*, sub. 486 (4).

2. In the Dr. M case study, can you see his point of view that both his patients "consented" to sex with him? How would you describe the ways in which transference influenced the professional-patient sexual contact in each of the situations that resulted in the criminal charges? Like Dr. B, Dr. M was highly regarded by many of his peers and patients. Would you have sent Dr. M to jail for what he did?

3. In your opinion, what should be the employer's liability in the Mr. Y case study? If you happened to be the one who overheard sexualized comments being made about a severely disabled patient in her presence, what steps would you take — or not? Is there legislative protection for those who "truth tell" when they make a mandatory report of what they have reason to believe is sexually abusive behaviour on the part of a colleague?

4. Do you think that professionals should have access to a collective legal defence fund that is available to all professionals regulated under the *RHPA*?

5. If professionals have access to legal defence support, should patients have access to similar legal supports? If yes, who should pay for such supports?

Chapter 5

WORKPLACE STRATEGIES FOR THE PREVENTION OF SEXUAL ABUSE[1]

Sexual abuse is an unfortunate but very real and present factor in any workplace. As such, it is imperative that all workplaces, regardless of size, take anticipatory steps to prevent it from happening and deal with it when it occurs. Workplace sexual harassment is very much a boundaries issue. As Marilyn Peterson notes, "[b]oundaries are defined as limits that protect the space between the professional's power and the client's vulnerability" and must be considered in a matter of context rather than content.[2] Peterson explains that:

> Professionals tend to identify and describe boundary violations in term of content. This approach is potentially hazardous, as it provides no early warning system short of the actual event to alert... professionals to impending trouble. Moreover, when violations are defined on the basis of content, those that seem less egregious and visible tend to be ignored, normalized, or dismissed as not serious. Finally, and perhaps most important, placing the primary emphasis on the content of the violation eclipses the more fundamental injury, the injury to the core of the professional-client relationship itself.[3]

Peterson's comments constitute an excellent argument for the development of workplace policies that, among other things, develop an agency-wide understanding of what constitutes sexual harassment, not only between professional and patient, but between employer and employee or between employees.

Before looking at the issue of workplace policies in more detail, this chapter opens with two case studies involving sexual harassment in the

---

[1] The authors are deeply indebted to Alison Engel for her contributions to this chapter.
[2] Marilyn R. Peterson, *At Personal Risk: Boundary Violations in Professional-Client Relationships* (New York: Norton & Co., 1992) at 3.
[3] *Ibid.*, at 3-4.

workplace. The first is set purely in the employment context, in which a female employee is sexually harassed by her supervisor. The second case explores the workplace issues that arise when a psychiatric nurse forms a social relationship with one of her former patients.

A. CASE STUDY: MR. M, EMPLOYER AS ENABLER[4]

Ms. C was transferred from the Toronto office of her company to its Vancouver office at her request. Within one month of beginning work at the Vancouver office, Ms. C was subjected to frequent comments and physical actions of a sexual nature by one of her co-workers, Mr. McL. The harassment included comments such as "blow me," "did you get it last night?" and "did you have oral sex?" as well as grabbing her buttocks, and asking her what she wore underneath her skirt.

Ms. C informed Mr. M, the director of the company's Vancouver branch, about several of the incidents involving Mr. McL. Mr. M responded by telling Ms. C that she was an attractive girl and that he was not surprised the incidents had taken place. Mr. M then stressed the importance of nurturing a team environment. He asked her to perform some "inter-office marketing" by taking Mr. McL out to lunch in order to resolve the problem.

Ms. C refused Mr. M's suggestion because this behaviour would be an invitation for Mr. McL to enter her life. The unwelcome sexual conduct continued and Ms. C tendered a letter of resignation in July 1992, citing the lack of professionalism in the Vancouver office and her discomfort after asking an individual to do things for her and that individual responding by requesting that she "blow him."

Because of Ms. C's value to the company, Mr. M refused to accept the resignation. He promised to promote her and to make progressive changes for the branch. She withdrew her letter of resignation on these and other assurances.

Ms. C received an excellent performance appraisal one month later. Rather than signing it, however, she wrote of her sexual harassment experiences on the employee comments section of the form. Mr. M was furious with her for this action because the comments would reach the head office of the company. Mr. M believed that he had gone the extra mile for Ms. C and that her complaint constituted a betrayal. He threatened to rewrite her performance review, a threat he later recanted.

---

[4] *Clarke v. Command Record Services Ltd.* (1997), 27 C.H.R.R. D/73 (B.C.H.R.C.).

Two weeks later, Mr. M informed Ms. C that she was being terminated due to a stringent cost improvement program as a result of the poor economy.

Ms. C brought her complaint to the British Columbia Human Rights Commission. The Commission found that Ms. C was sexually harassed in her workplace and was terminated because she complained of sexual harassment. The employer was found to have failed to meet its human rights obligations under the British Columbia *Human Rights Code*[5] and was ordered to pay Ms. C for her lost time and suffering.

B. CASE STUDY: MS. H, A PSYCHIATRIC NURSE IN MARKHAM[6]

Ms. H had been practising as a psychiatric nurse for over 15 years when she learned of a job opportunity in a new hospital that was about to open. In 1990, she was hired to work as a staff nurse in the psychiatric department where she worked in a team admitting patients, monitoring them and following the orders of the part-time psychiatrists. Each patient had a primary and secondary nurse and the unit had a full-time social worker and a part-time therapist.

Ms. H met patient Ms. W when she was admitted for depression in 1991 and provided her with care. Following Ms. W's discharge two months later, Ms. H met Ms. W while out shopping and after chatting for a while, the two exchanged telephone numbers. This led to a growing social relationship between the two, and in response to the desire of Ms. W to change residences, she and Ms. H agreed to share an apartment. Ms. H did not disclose the relationship to her superiors at the hospital and asked Ms. S, a friend and former patient at the facility, not to disclose the fact that she and Ms. W were living together.

Eventually, the relationship between Ms. H and Ms. W became known at the hospital and Ms. H was advised that her employment had been terminated and the matter had been reported to the College of Nurses of Ontario. The College found Ms. H guilty of professional misconduct and ordered a reprimand and a two-month suspension of her licence.[7]

---

[5] R.S.B.C. 1996, c. 210.

[6] *Harrop v. Markham Stouffville Hospital*, (1995), 16 C.C.E.L. (2d) 214 (Ont. Gen. Div.).

[7] Note that the term "licence" is referred to in this case. This is because the matter was adjudicated under the *Health Disciplines Act*, R.S.O. 1980, c. 196, which refers to licences as compared to the *Regulated Health Professions Act*, which refers to certificates of registration.

Ms. H brought an action against the hospital for wrongful dismissal, which was heard in 1995. Among the several experts testifying at the trial was a nurse, Ms. R, who testified on behalf of Ms. H. Ms. R noted that although the then-guidelines of the College of Nurses did not prohibit the kind of conduct in which Ms. H engaged, she agreed that it would have been prudent for Ms. H to have consulted her colleagues prior to entering into her relationship with Ms. W. Both Ms. R and Dr. S, expert witnesses for the hospital, agreed on the importance of the concept of transference and counter-transference, and further agreed that they applied in Ms. H's case as she was a psychiatric nurse providing therapeutic treatment to her patients.

In deciding whether the hospital had met its obligation at trial of proving that it had just cause for dismissing Ms. H, the Court noted that the hospital did not set formal standards for its staff regarding patient-staff relationships. At the same time, the Court found that on the basis of her training and her many years of experience, Ms. H understood the concepts — and their associated dangers — of transference and counter-transference. Ms. H also knew her relationship was wrong as proven by the fact that she had attempted to keep it a secret, particularly cautioning Ms. S not to reveal her knowledge of the relationship. Moreover, she knew that patient Ms. S had been upset by her relationship with Ms. W and this constituted a potential source of harm to Ms. S. Ms. H's conduct jeopardized the integrity of her treatment unit. As a result, Ms. H's claim of wrongful dismissal was denied.

C. WHY WORKPLACE POLICIES ARE NECESSARY — THE EMPLOYER AS ENABLER

In his comprehensive, recent work on sexual misconduct in Ontario schools, Mr. Justice Sydney Robins alludes to the importance of effective sexual harassment policy development and implementation by noting that in addition to the direction given by law,

> [c]onduct may also be guided by policies, procedures, guidelines and protocols. Though policies and protocols may not be binding in law, they represent important tools for the prevention and early identification of sexual misconduct, and for protecting those already victimized by such misconduct.[8]

---

[8]   S. Robins, *Protecting Our Students: A Review to Identify and Prevent Sexual Misconduct in Ontario Schools* (Toronto: Ontario Ministry of the Attorney General, 2000) at 287.

Employers in the health professions such as hospitals, health clinics, diagnostic facilities and community health centres play a particularly important role in the prevention of sexual assault and sexual harassment in the health care context. The tone and message that an employer sets for its employees around sexual harassment and sexual assault can help prevent harassment on the one hand, or can enable a perpetrator of harassment on the other. The Law Society of Upper Canada (LSUC), which regulates lawyers practising in Ontario, underscores the obligation employers possess as potential enablers of sexual harassment. In the commentary attached to its policy entitled "A Recommended Personnel Policy Regarding Employment-Related Sexual Harassment for Small Firms," the LSUC states:

> The current law with respect to sexual harassment places an obligation on employers, including law firms, to show "due diligence" with respect to employment-related sexual harassment. This due diligence obligation requires law firms or members of the directing mind of the firm to take proactive steps to prevent sexual harassment and maintain a work environment free from sexual harassment.
>
> The law defines "due diligence" as an obligation to demonstrate that the employer:
>
> 1. made clear to employees that sexual harassment in the workplace would not be condoned;
>
> 2. took active steps to prevent sexual harassment;
>
> 3. attempted to mitigate the effects of any sexual harassment which might exist.
>
> Law firms and lawyers as employers who fail to exercise due diligence will be liable for acts of harassment by agents, employees and partners. Furthermore, partners who are considered to be "the directing mind," may be held liable for such acts by any person who harasses an employee of the firm in the course of the employee's work-related duties.[9]

This is certainly a powerful statement of responsibility that should be heeded by every employer. In doing so, the employer must not only be sure to communicate this message to all involved, but must also be alert to the variety of perspectives that may exist in the workplace. For example, in their study of woman abuse and the workplace, Denham, Gillespie and Cottrell note that woman abuse is largely viewed as a women's issue and those men that take a leadership role in its prevention, often "find themselves marginalized and the issue trivialized

---

[9]   Law Society of Upper Canada, "Preventing and Responding to Workplace Harassment and Discrimination: A Guide to Developing a Policy for Law Firms" (undated) in possession of authors: see further (March 2002) online, Law Society of Upper Canada <http://www.lsuc.on.ca/equity/pdf/equity_modelharassmentpolicy.pdf>.

by their colleagues."[10] The authors further note a number of factors that preclude male involvement in the issue in the workplace, including such things as

- they don't think... [it]... is an extensive or serious problem in the workplace;
- they are in positions of power, feel threatened by change and want to maintain the status quo;
- they don't "know" of anyone who is abused or is an abuser;
- they think it is an issue to be dealt with by human resources, not one in which they should be involved;
- they recognize the importance of the issue but other workplace priorities always take precedence;
- they are not comfortable working with women on what is often labelled "a women's issue;"
- they don't know what to do.[11]

Even employers themselves must test their own attitudes to the problem and often confront their own misperceptions or denials. Arjun Aggarwal notes a number of common themes among the arguments made by employers who believe that they should not be held responsible for sexual abuse in their workplaces:

1. It is a personal affair between the two persons and the company cannot control sexual relations between two adults.

2. The employer never encourages or advocates sexual harassment or, in fact, any kind of harassment of employees.

3. The company has no way of knowing what has been going on between two employees.

4. There is no way an employer can control or interfere with the private or personal lives of its employees.[12]

In addition to the clear destructive impact on individuals as a result of an occurrence of sexual harassment, the consequences of not addressing the issue can also be enormous to the employer. Results can include investigations, litigation, damaged employee morale, unwanted publicity, loss of integrity and the practical fallout of economic loss.[13]

---

[10] B. Denham, J. Gillespie & B. Cottrell, *Workplace Learnings About Woman Abuse: A Guide for Change II* (Ottawa: Health Canada, 1994) at 19.

[11] *Ibid.*

[12] Arjun P. Aggarwal, *Sexual Harassment in the Workplace*, 2nd ed. (Markham, Ont.: Butterworths, 1992) at 181.

[13] *Ibid.*, at 307 *ff.*

Hospitals and other institutional employers owe a legal duty, called a duty of care, to their employees and others that may reasonably enter the premises (such as patients). This duty requires that an employer take steps to prevent and manage risks that are foreseeable in their workplace. In a large institution, such as a hospital, where hundreds of employees, visitors and patients come and go, incidents of sexual assault and harassment are an inevitable reality. An employer must thus have a responsible plan in place both to help prevent sexual assault and to address complaints.

Although the employer itself may not be the perpetrator of the assault or harassment, an employer who is silent on issues of sexual harassment may be an enabler of abuse — a silent bystander who has the power to see and to create an environment that openly condemns sexual harassment, but instead turns a blind eye or fails to take action as a result of ignorance. In order to become an employer who is instead an effective advocate for the safety and well-being of its employees, it is essential to have both a workplace policy on sexual harassment and procedures in place for handling complaints when they do occur. The procedures available for resolving complaints may be either internal workplace procedures or external administrative processes, such as a complaint under human rights legislation.

Although this advice may appear obvious, the case studies described above have been chosen as real-world examples of what happens when managers and those in positions of power do not have either a reasonable understanding of power dynamics and sexual assault, or a clear system in place to address complaints. In the case of Mr. M above, Mr. M clearly valued Ms. C as a top employee — he successfully attempted to dissuade her from resigning and was involved in her promotion. The missing essential component in the situation, however, was a clear and effective workplace policy and procedure for preventing and handling issues of sexual harassment and abuse. In the case of Ms. H, the psychiatric nurse, the absence of clear and defined policies was not only used as a defence by Ms. H, but the lack of them conceivably resulted in harm to both patients and the hospital that could have otherwise been avoided. These cases can only lead to the conclusion that those in positions of power can help create a safe environment for their employees by developing and implementing systems that take issues of sexual harassment and abuse seriously. Furthermore, the *RHPA*,[14] while it does not deal specifically

---

[14]   *Supra* note 7.

with sexual harassment in the workplace as between employees, does have a clear statement of employer responsibility and liability for situations involving sexual harassment of patients by employees.[15] In the case study in Chapter 4, Dr. M also sexually harassed and sexually assaulted women co-workers (a resident and nurses) over whom he had authority reinforced by the employment situation. It should also be noted that the occurrence of harassment between an individual who is both caregiver and employer is not an uncommon dynamic feature of the workplace, as shown in the case studies of Dr. NMRC in Chapter 2, Dr. AM in Chapter 3 and Dr. M in Chapter 4.

D. WORKPLACE POLICY AND PROCEDURE DEVELOPMENT

1. Employers' Legal Obligations

In addition to the common law duty of care owed by employers to their employees, there are a number of statutory requirements that must be met. These requirements are discussed briefly in the following sections.

2. Human Rights Obligations in Ontario

Under the Ontario *Human Rights Code* (Ontario *HRC*), an employer has a legal responsibility to provide a workplace that is free from harassment by the employer, the employer's agents and by other employees.[16] The Ontario *HRC* states:

> Every person who is an employee has a right to freedom from harassment in the workplace by the employer or agent of the employer or by another employee be-cause of race, ancestry, place of origin, colour, ethnic origin, citizenship, creed, age, record of offences, marital status, same-sex partnership status, family status or disability.[17]

The Ontario *HRC* specifically creates the right of every employee to be free from harassment because of the employee's sex. Subsection 7(2) states:

> (2) Every person who is an employee has a right to freedom from harassment in the workplace because of sex by his or her employer or agent of the employer or by another employee.

---

[15] *Health Professions Procedural Code*, *supra* note 7, ss. 85, 93 [hereinafter "the Code"]. (See also the chart in Chapter 3).
[16] Ontario *Human Rights Code*, R.S.O. 1990, c. H.19.
[17] *Ibid.*, sub. 5(2).

In addition the Ontario *HRC* provides specific protections for victims of harassment:

> (3) Every person has a right to be free from,
>
> (a)   a sexual solicitation or advance made by a person in a position to confer, grant or deny a benefit or advancement to the person where the person making the solicitation or advance knows or ought reasonably to know that it is unwelcome; or
>
> (b)   a reprisal on a threat of reprisal for the rejection of a sexual solicitation or advance where the reprisal is made or threatened by a person in a position to confer, grant or deny a benefit or advancement to the person.[18]

These specific prohibitions are an acknowledgment that sexual harassment and assault in the workplace is a consistent problem that must be addressed, that intended or reasonably avoidable abuse must be stopped and that anyone reporting abuse in the workplace is protected by law from retaliation. Taking steps to prevent and handle sexual discrimination in the workplace is part of any employer's human rights obligations in Ontario. On this basis, the Ontario Human Rights Commission states that it is the responsibility of employers to

> (i)   provide a working environment that is free from harassment and discrimination, and
>
> (ii) deal effectively, quickly and fairly with any situations involving claims of harassment or discrimination that come to their attention.[19]

The most effective action an employer can take to create this safe workplace, be it a hospital, physiotherapy clinic or a private practice office, is to have a clear, accessible and transparent policy and procedure in place around sexual harassment and potential complaints. The Ontario Human Rights Commission recommends that the following three elements should be part of any workplace strategy to prevent discrimination in the workplace:

> (i)   an anti-harassment or anti-discrimination policy;
>
> (ii) a complaint resolution procedure; and
>
> (iii) on-going education programmes.[20]

These three elements must not only exist, but employees must know and understand the policy and procedures in place. Open policies,

---

[18]   *Ibid.*, subs. 7(2), (3).

[19]   Ontario Human Rights Commission, *Developing Procedures to Resolve Human Rights Complaints within Your Organization* (June 1996) at 1, online, Ontario Human Rights Commission <http://www.ohrc.on.ca>, click on "Publications," and see under "Plain Language Publications and Guides."

[20]   *Ibid.*, at 2.

accompanied by education, present an opportunity for employers and employees alike to learn about the operation of power dynamics in the workplace.

3. Other Statutory Requirements

In addition to the provisions of the Ontario *Human Rights Code*, a complainant who is considered an employee under the *Employment Standards Act, 2000*,[21] and has resigned from his or her employment as a result of continual harassment or abuse at work, may file a complaint with the Ministry of Labour for constructive dismissal.[22] This type of proceeding may lead to monetary compensation acknowledging that the complainant's resignation was tantamount to a wrongful dismissal. An advisor should be able to explain to a complainant which of these options are available and the details of the administrative procedures under each Act.

It should be noted that there are also federal laws affecting federal employees. Among them are the *Canadian Human Rights Act*[23] and the *Canada Labour Code*,[24] each of which identify the issue of sexual harassment and provide for complaint, investigation and penalty actions. As it pertains to health care, federal employees could be health professionals working in military institutions, serving Aboriginal reserves or working in any federal government agency or enterprise that falls within the jurisdiction of the federal Parliament.

E. COMMON LAW GROUNDS FOR EMPLOYERS' LEGAL LIABILITY FOR SEXUAL ABUSE

The failure of an employer to take steps to prevent and manage sexual abuse in the workplace can result in a finding of liability against the

---

[21] S.O. 2000, c. 41, ss. 1, 2. With a few exceptions, an employee is defined in the legislation as any person who performs work in Ontario or elsewhere for an Ontario employer at the employer's workplace or at home on behalf of the employer or as a trainee of the employer.

[22] *Ibid.*, ss. 96(1), 56(1)(b). "Constructive dismissal" can occur when an employer unilaterally changes the fundamental nature of an employee's job such that the employee is no longer doing the work that he or she originally agreed to do. In this instance, the employee has resigned because of the untenable workplace complication of sexual abuse brought on or allowed to occur by the employer.

[23] R.S.C. 1985, c. H-6.

[24] R.S.C. 1985, c. L-2.

employer in the courtroom or before a human rights or other tribunal. When we talk about the liability of the employer, we must think of the employer not only as an individual but also in the form of an institution. In earlier chapters we discussed how individuals can be held liable for sexual abuse — disciplinary hearings, criminal charges, civil suits — but how are institutions to be held liable? The next two sections examine situations in which institutions were held to be liable for failing to protect their clients.

1. Vicarious Liability

An employer can be held liable for the wrongful actions of the employee even though the employer was not a direct contributor to the wrong. In our case study of Mr. M, he did not harass Ms. C personally, but he ignored her request for his ameliorative intervention as a manager. Only when he saw her complaint in writing did he react (by dismissing her), likely anticipating that those in authority above him in the company — who had no knowledge of what was happening in the workplace he managed — would look to him for a solution. This is known as the vicarious liability of the employer and is described by Grace and Vella in the following way:

> … [T]he common law doctrine of vicarious liability has become one of the most important institutional liability theories in the area of sexual abuse. The doctrine offers plaintiffs accountability and an avenue for recovery of damages against governments, institutions and corporations where recoverability on a judgment would be difficult or impractical against the sexual offenders themselves....[25]

Vicarious liability is the public policy-driven doctrine that extends liability to the employers or principles "… for the tortious [wrongful] conduct of their employees, agents and independent contractors, … provided the misconduct took place within the scope of the [wrongdoer's] duties and responsibilities."[26] Grace and Vella add that liability will be found if "… the employer's enterprise introduced or enhanced the risk of abuse, which then materialized causing harm to another person, and the abuse committed by the employee had a sufficiently close connection with the employment to satisfy the underlying policy rationales."[27] They further note that the doctrine has

---

[25]   Elizabeth K.P. Grace & Susan M. Vella, *Civil Liability for Sexual Abuse and Violence in Canada* (Markham, Ont: Butterworths, 2000) at 43.

[26]   *Ibid.*

[27]   *Ibid.*, at 44.

developed within the last dozen years, and that between 1995 and 2000, some 17 cases of sexual abuse relied on an argument of the vicarious liability against the employer. In the 1997 case of *C. (T.) v. S. (G.D.)*, for example, the complainant sued both the psychiatrist who had abused her and the psychiatric institution at which Dr. Scott worked. The court found, however, that the sexual impropriety was not carried on as a result of the position he held at the institute, and sexual encounters occurred outside the institute. The institute was not vicariously liable for Scott's acts. Scott's misconduct exacerbated TC's condition and led to her present illness, which emerged after 1991. Scott was fully responsible for the global assessment of damages, which totalled $322,000.[28]

2. Fiduciary Duty

In the case study involving Dr. W discussed in Chapter 1, two justices of the Supreme Court of Canada applied the principle of fiduciary duty in finding Dr. W liable for the sexual abuse of Laura. This Court has a long history of consideration of the concept and in one instance has defined fiduciary duty as encompassing the following:

(1) [T]he fiduciary has scope for the exercise of some discretion or power;

(2) The fiduciary can unilaterally exercise that power or discretion so as to affect the beneficiary's legal or practical interests;

(3) The beneficiary is peculiarly vulnerable to or at the mercy of the fiduciary holding the discretion or power.[29]

So how does this apply to an employer? As Grace and Vella point out, although its application to employers and institutions is just emerging,

... [t]he cases decided to date confirm that a breach of fiduciary duty can arise from an act or omission on the part of an institutional fiduciary which is a proximate cause of the abuse, or from breach of a non-delegable duty in which the institution is directly liable for the sexual abuse committed by its delegatee. Under the first theory of liability, the institution does, or omits to do, something which would likely have prevented the abuse or stopped it from continuing, thereby breaching its duty to act in the best interests of the beneficiary.... Under the second theory, the institution is liable for the conduct of its agent, employee or independent contractor, on the basis that the institution, in delegating the execution of the duty entrusted to it, remains directly liable if the duty is improperly discharged because the actions of the wrongdoer are attributed to the institution.[30]

---

[28] *C. (T.) v. S. (G.D.)*, [1997] O.J. No. 2389 (Gen. Div.) (QL).
[29] *Frame v. Smith*, [1987] 2 S.C.R. 99 at 136 per Wilson J.
[30] Grace & Vella, *supra* note 26, at 64.

This means that a hospital, laboratory, clinic or any other health care institution runs the risk of being found liable for failing to protect its clients (its beneficiaries), either knowingly or in a situation where it should have known, from sexual abuse by persons working for it either because it has a direct fiduciary duty to prevent such occurrences or because it is not permitted to avoid liability on the basis that it did not delegate the duty to those workers. It also reinforces for any employer, the wisdom of taking pre-emptive and preventive steps to set guidelines, educate employees about, and implement, proper practices and boundaries within the workplace. Just how this can be done is discussed in the sections that follow.

F. FUNDAMENTAL PRINCIPLES FOR POLICY STATEMENTS

The purpose of the workplace policy is to simplify or clarify the parameters of acceptable behaviour at work.[31] This requirement presents an opportunity for an employer to send a definitive message to its employees that it takes issues of sexual misconduct seriously, setting a tone of respect in the workplace. There are three fundamental principles of effective workplace policies against sexual harassment and abuse. These policies must be:

1. Clear — A policy must define its terms clearly.
2. Accessible — A policy must be accessible to all members of the workplace.
3. Grounded in Action — A policy must detail procedures to deal with harassment and abuse, and consequences for those who are guilty.[32]

1. Clear Policy Statements

Boundaries are defined as "limits that protect the space between the professional's power and the client's vulnerability."[33] One of the central concerns of employers and employees alike is in the understanding of exactly what is meant by sexual harassment in the workplace. Will a compliment on a subordinate's dress constitute harassment? What about

---

[31]   Susan I. Paish & Aiyaz A. Alibhai, *Act, Don't Repeat: Dealing with Sexual Harassment in Your Organization* (Vancouver: Western Legal Publications, 1998) at 9-27.

[32]   The authors are grateful to Alison Engel for her concise description of these principles.

[33]   Peterson, *supra* note 2, at 3.

a pat on the back? Policy statements must be clear that discrimination and harassment are violations of the Ontario *HRC* and will not be tolerated. Specifically, the policy should describe the types of behaviour that are discriminatory, including defining harassment.[34] According to the Ontario *HRC*, "harassment" means "engaging in a course of vexatious comment or conduct that is known or ought reasonably to be known to be unwelcome."[35] The central concept is that the sexual conduct, be it flirtatious comments or too much physical contact, is unwelcome by the recipient. If unwanted conduct continues, it is sexual harassment under the Ontario *HRC*. Clear definitions help all participants in a workplace to understand the type of behaviour that is expected of them.

The Ontario Human Rights Commission has written an excellent publication for organizations to help them develop internal policies and processes for creating a workplace free of discrimination consistent with the Ontario *Human Rights Code*. The guide is useful for all workplaces, from hospitals to private practices and because of this, it is reproduced in full in Appendix III.

2. Accessible Policy Statements

A policy can only be an effective preventative measure and tone-setter against sexual harassment and abuse if all members of a workplace — from the hospital administration, to the residents, to the night-time janitor — know and understand the policy. An organization or employer must make the distribution and explanation of the harassment policy a routine part of any orientation to the workplace. The Ontario Human Rights Commission recommends the following initiatives to disseminate the policy and the message it contains:

    i.   distributing the policy to everyone when it is introduced;

    ii.   sharing it with new employees when they are hired; and

    iii.   training any employee who becomes a member of management, on the contents of the policy.[36]

Further, discussion of rights and responsibilities under the policy can be made the subject of all levels of employee training and orientation.

---

[34] *Developing Procedures to Resolve Human Rights Complaints within Your Organization*, *supra* note 19, at 2-3.

[35] Ontario *Human Rights Code*, *supra* note 17, sub. 10(1).

[36] *Developing Procedures to Resolve Human Rights Complaints within Your Organization*, *supra* note 19.

Employees should be made to feel that the policy and procedures exist for their protection and use at any time.

3. Grounded in Action

When developing a workplace policy on sexual harassment, Mari Florence, author of *Sex at Work*, suggests noting whether the "4 C's" — Clear, Concise Communication, and Consequences have been considered.[37] The final "C," consequences, which attach to failing to follow the policy, are essential for creating a policy that is more than mere lip service. It is the detailed process for complaints and consequences for harassment that give teeth or a tone of seriousness to words on a page. Employees must be told that engaging in prohibited conduct has disciplinary consequences, including potential dismissal, complaints under separate administrative procedures such as the Ontario *Human Rights Code*, and in more serious cases, criminal prosecution. As one author emphasizes, procedure must follow policy in order to prevent double messages:

> By double message, I mean an unwillingness to back up a sexual harassment policy with action. An organization cannot effectively say, "We posted this policy because the law tells us we have to — but please don't even think about bringing us a complaint."[38]

The following discussion thus focuses on the development of the procedures that are necessary to support the policy against harassment.

G. WORKPLACE PROCEDURES

In addition to developing a general policy, it is essential that workplaces, large and small, have more detailed procedures in place for handling allegations. Without a clear system in place to set out the process for investigation and discipline for sexual harassment and abuse, a complainant may be silenced out of uncertainty and fear of mistreatment or retaliation by individual managers and supervisors. Indeed, most employees who choose not to report sexual harassment do not voice their concerns because they do not believe their company has procedures in

---

[37]   Mari Florence, *Sex at Work: Attraction, Orientation, Harassment, Flirtation and Discrimination* (Los Angeles: Silver Lake Publishing, 2001) at 275.

[38]   Peter Rutter, *Sex, Power and Boundaries: Understanding and Preventing Sexual Harassment* (New York: Bantam, 1996) at 139.

place to address the complaint.[39] As a result, the employer may unintentionally become the enabler of the harassment and be liable for the results.

Picture a hospital environment with a myriad of employees and managers bustling around at any given moment. There are doctors on teams with nurses, social workers, physiotherapists and midwives. One social work placement student, for example, may work on a team with doctors and nurses. She may also have a direct Social Work supervisor at the hospital, and a professor who acts as the school liaison to the hospital. In environments as complex as this, employees need to know whose responsibility it is to handle a complaint and how it will subsequently be handled.

As we describe in the case of Dr. M below, the intern who had been assaulted did not complain about the incident until months later when she discovered that other staff had reported him and that a criminal charge had already been laid against him. A clear system encouraging reporting of sexual assault and harassment was not accessible to the intern at the time and she felt silenced by her superior. Further, the case of Mr. M, above, is a strong example of the problems that can arise when the management of sexual harassment allegations is left up to the discretion of an individual who happens to be in charge at a given moment. Mr. M did not understand how power operates in the workplace. His response alienated Ms. C, leaving her to handle the constant harassment on her own. It is apparent, then, that effective prevention of harassment in workplace environments is underscored by clear and known internal and external avenues for managing an incident when it does occur. For internal procedures, both the choice of the investigator and the process of investigation itself can help ensure that the employer is contributing to the creation of a safe work environment for its employees.

1. The Team Involved

Leadership in the workplace has a significant influence on the overall environment and the extent to which employees are prepared to try to resolve issues informally. It is weak leadership that is the root cause of tainted work environments. Clear policies and procedures are particularly needed in times of weak or absent leadership and can, in effect, raise the standards in a work environment and provide some basis for employees

---

[39] Kathleen Neville, *Internal Affairs: The Abuse of Power, Sexual Harassment, and Hypocrisy in the Workplace* (New York: McGraw Hill, 2000) at 225.

to contribute to the management of a workplace because there is an overarching commitment articulated in the policy by those most senior in the organization, even if they are not present on a daily basis.

(a) The Advisor

The Ontario Human Rights Commission recommends that employers appoint a neutral advisor who can provide advice and guidance on the different options available for handling a sexual harassment or assault complaint or response.[40] The information should include a description of the internal complaint procedure if one is available, as well as external administrative options including complaints under the Ontario *HRC* or the *Employment Standards Act*[41] if applicable. A complainant may lodge a complaint under subsection 7(2) of the *Code*, if she has been sexually harassed in the workplace.[42] The Ontario Human Rights Commission has broad remedial powers and may order a variety of measures, including monetary compensation and workplace education. Both the complainant and the employee accused of harassment or assault should have the right to meet with the advisor who should be knowledgeable about internal and external complaint procedures. The advisor can be seen as a confidential ombudsperson, who provides a link to the appropriate channels.

(b) The Investigator

The investigator is responsible for examining the circumstances of the complaint. The employer should choose an impartial third-party investigator who is both familiar with the organization and knowledgeable about the law on sexual misconduct in the workplace and about how power and control operate in a work environment. It is essential that the investigator not be involved in the particular incident and should refrain from making any conclusions until the investigation is entirely complete. The investigator should also *never* be in a position of direct authority over any of the people involved in the complaint.[43]

---

[40] *Developing Procedures to Resolve Human Rights Complaints within Your Organization, supra* note 19.

[41] *Supra* note 22.

[42] For further details on this complaint process, see the Ontario Human Rights Commission's guide to "The Complaints Process" online, Ontario Human Rights Commission <http://www.ohrc.on.ca/english/complaints/index.shtml>.

[43] *Developing Procedures to Resolve Human Rights Complaints within Your Organization, supra* note 19, at 5.

The role of the investigator needs to be clearly defined in the policy of the organization. This role may include:

- fact finding;
- reporting;
- making recommendations; and
- making decisions.[44]

Employees who have been reluctant to report harassment have complained that those appointed to investigate and hear complaints are not adequately trained to investigate them.[45] By having a specific person who is educated about issues of sexual assault and harassment in the workplace, the types of cases described above may be avoided. A vulnerable complainant can be sent the message that there is someone in place who wants to prevent these types of incidents from occurring and the investigator herself or himself will have specific and transparent processes for investigation.

(c) The Investigation

The investigation process itself should also be clearly outlined and explained in a workplace policy. A successful and fair investigation should meet the following four objectives. The process should be:

1. Prompt
2. Thorough
3. Well Documented
4. Confidential[46]

First, a prompt response to an allegation of sexual assault or harassment sends a message to those involved that the employer is taking the allegation seriously.[47] The Ontario Human Rights Commission recommends that the investigation should start immediately after an investigator is chosen and finish within 90 days.[48] Further, a thorough investigation ensures a fair and due process to all involved.

Each person involved in the process should create and keep written documentation of the events that occurred. Important details to include are what happened, when it happened, where it happened and who saw it

---

[44] Paish & Alibhai, *supra* note 31, at 9-23.
[45] Neville, *supra* note 39, at 225.
[46] Paish & Alibhai, *supra* note 31, at 9-25.
[47] *Ibid.*, at 9-25.
[48] *Developing Procedures to Resolve Human Rights Complaints within Your Organization*, *supra* note 19.

happen. In addition, all documentation surrounding the incident, including e-mails and notes, should be kept to support the investigation.

Finally, in addition to being confidential, the organization's policy should contain clear protection from reprisal for all those involved in the complaint. Complainants, in particular, must be sent a clear message that they cannot and will not be penalized for their courage in reporting an incident of harassment in the workplace.

2. Small and Large Workplace Policies

The texts and resources available on preventing sexual harassment in the workplace may appear to be geared towards those working in larger workplaces, such as hospitals. Indeed, the health professionals in small clinics or private practice offices reading this chapter might dismiss ideas of having an advisor or investigator as inapplicable to their small workplace. However, while small and large workplaces differ in their overall organizational needs and goals, employee needs and employer responsibilities around preventing sexual harassment in the workplace are the same in any workplace.[49] Employees need to feel that there is a clear and effective policy and system in place for addressing concerns about sexual harassment and abuse. The power dynamics of a workplace operate in any situation, and thus transparent policies and procedures are needed, particularly in a situation in which there is a lack of obvious support within the workplace itself.

3. Different Workplace Structure but Similar Worker Needs

(a) The Large Institution

(i) CASE STUDY: DR. SM, A PHYSICIAN IN OTTAWA

Dr. SM was a physician who received his licence to practice in 1979. In 1986, he joined the staff of a large urban hospital. In this capacity, Dr. SM saw patients in both the wards of the hospital and in the outpatient clinic, and did on-call work in the emergency room. He was also responsible for supervising interns and residents in the hospital's teaching unit and he worked closely with the nursing and clerical staff in the facility. Dr. SM, at age 43, had separated from his spouse in 1996, and had two young children.

---

[49]   Neville, *supra* note 39, at 217.

In early 1998, Dr. SM went to trial on charges of sexual assault, sexual assault with a weapon, and forcible confinement under the *Criminal Code* for assaulting a female intern, aged 39, who worked in the hospital.[50] The complainant was on internal medicine rotation and Dr. SM was her supervisor. The complainant's story was that on a Friday night, sometime between 9:00 p.m. and 1:00 a.m., she was paged by Dr. SM in the emergency room where she was working. He asked her to meet him in the residents' room the next day to review recently admitted patients. When the complainant arrived, Dr. SM was in the room alone, the lights were on and the door was partially open. The complainant sat down and they began to discuss their patients. At one point, Dr. SM referred to a young male patient with children, whose condition was deteriorating. Dr. SM said he found it hard to give patients bad news and it helped him to discuss the situation in advance with someone who was a "compassionate and empathetic listener." He then put his right hand over the complainant's. When the complainant stood to leave the room, Dr. SM said "You know you want this as much as I do." Dr. SM pulled the complainant away from the door and closed and locked it. He told the complainant that she was "feisty" and he liked it when she struggled. He also said she was "scrawny." At the time of the incident, the complainant was five feet, seven inches tall, and weighed 125 pounds. Dr. SM was six feet, five inches tall, and weighed 240 pounds. Dr. SM attempted to kiss the complainant and remove some of her clothes. While he held the complainant by the back of the neck with one hand, Dr. SM undid the button and zipper of his pants with the other. The complainant protested, saying, "[n]o. Let me go. Leave me alone. I want to get out of here." Dr. SM pinned the complainant on the floor, straddled her and placed his hand over her mouth. With the other he exposed his erect penis. He then held a pair of scissors to her throat and said that if she did not cooperate he would cut off her nipples.

At this point, someone tried to open the door of the residents' room. Dr. SM swore, pulled the complainant to her knees in front of him and said, "[s]uck it and make it fast." The complainant averted her head and Dr. SM began to simultaneously masturbate and hit the complainant on the head with the scissors. Dr. SM ejaculated with most of the semen landing on his clothing although some landed on the complainant's cheek.

---

[50] R.S.C. 1985, c. C-46, ss. 271, 272(1) and 279(2).

The complainant then got up and adjusted her clothing and contact lenses as an intern entered the room and greeted Dr. SM. The complainant spoke briefly with the intern and then all left to resume their duties. The complainant did not report the incident. The next time she saw Dr. SM, he said, "Of course, our little secret will remain quiet." In a subsequent encounter, he said, "If you say anything about this, who would they believe anyway, you an intern, or me, a staff physician?" The complainant said that over the next few weeks she was troubled by nightmares and took all possible steps to avoid Dr. SM or ensure that when she saw him she was not alone. In her second year of residency, she arranged to be supervised by another staff physician.

In June of 1996, the complainant heard that Dr. SM had been criminally charged with assaulting three nurses at the hospital and she contacted the police. Dr. SM was charged with sexual assault, sexual assault with a weapon, and forcible confinement under the *Criminal Code*. The trial took place over 11 days.[51] Dr. SM was found guilty of sexual assault and forcible confinement but acquitted of sexual assault with a weapon. Each of the offences for which he was convicted carried with them sentences of up to ten years in prison. In the complainant's case, the court ordered that Dr. SM serve an 18-month conditional sentence on each charge, to be served concurrently.[52] The conditions on his sentence, which was to be served in the community, included being regularly supervised and keeping his supervisor informed of changes of address or employment; staying in the province unless given permission; keeping the peace and maintaining good behaviour; abstaining from drugs, alcohol or owning, possessing or carrying a weapon; attending a treatment program; carrying a copy of the court order with him whenever he left his home; and refraining from any direct or indirect contact with the complainant.

In August of 1998, a Discipline Panel of the College of Physicians and Surgeons of Ontario met to hear the complaints of six persons against Dr. SM based on incidents that had taken place in the hospital between 1986 and 1996, including that of the complainant.[53] The charges against Dr. SM were brought under Regulations to the *Health Disciplines Act*, in that he had engaged in conduct or an act relevant to his practice that, having regard to all circumstances, would reasonably be regarded by members

---

[51]   *R. v. Markham*, [1998] O.J. No. 5632 (Gen. Div.) (QL).
[52]   *R. v. Markham*, [1998] O.J. No. 5957 (Gen. Div.) (QL).
[53]   *Markham, Re*, [1999] O.C.P.S.D. No. 6 (QL).

(of the College) as disgraceful, dishonourable or unprofessional,[54] and under Regulations to the *Medicine Act, 1991* in that he had engaged in conduct unbecoming of a physician.[55]

The first three complainants were the three nurses involved in the criminal convictions of 1998 discussed above. These nurses alleged that Dr. SM had fondled their breasts and buttocks and made inappropriate comments. Complainants 1, 2, and 3 were the nurses involved in the criminal convictions brought against Dr. SM in 1998. The fifth and sixth complainants, both of whom worked in the hospital, had brought new complaints to the disciplinary process not heard in the earlier criminal actions. They also alleged that Dr. SM had made inappropriate remarks and fondled their breasts. The resident complainant from the criminal trial was the fourth complainant.

Dr. SM admitted that he had engaged in the conduct alleged by Complainants 1, 3, and 6 and admitted only to fondling Complainant 2. He wholly denied the allegations brought by Complainants 4 and 5.

The Discipline Panel stated clearly that its decision must be based purely on the evidence before it and must not take into account Dr. SM's previous criminal convictions. The Panel noted that in order to find Dr. SM guilty, the evidence must be clear and convincing and based on cogent evidence. In concluding that Dr. SM had committed acts of sexual assault and confinement on Complainant 4, the Panel stated that it accepted her credibility over that of Dr. SM. The Panel also found Dr. SM guilty of the complaints alleged by Complainants 2 and 5.

Dr. SM was sentenced in August 1999. The Panel unanimously ordered the revocation of Dr. SM's certificate of registration. In 2001, Dr. SM unsuccessfully attempted to appeal the decision.[56]

A large institutional workplace such as a hospital has hundreds of employees, many of whom will never come in contact with each other. A hospital also generally has sufficient resources to hire an ombudsperson or advisor to provide access to appropriate channels for handling a sexual harassment or assault complaint internally. Overall, then, it is easier for a large institution to provide a properly trained advisor and investigator and a confidential process to those involved in a complaint.

The challenge for a large institution, however, is to ensure that employees themselves know about available procedures and feel that the

---

[54] R.R.O. 448/80, s. 27.32.

[55] O. Reg. 856/93, s. 1(1) 34; *Medicine Act, 1991*, S.O. 1991, c. 30.

[56] *Markham v. College of Physicians & Surgeons (Ontario)*, [2001] O.J. No. 5336 (Div. Ct.) (QL).

issues of sexual assault are taken seriously in a workplace that consistently has other issues at the forefront. Employee attendance at seminars may be less predictable in a larger organization. A hospital may thus need to disseminate its message via more than one avenue — educational seminars, posters, employee training manuals and e-mail can be used to ensure that the message that sexual harassment and assault are not tolerated in the workplace gets across to as many employees as possible. For a list of possible methods of education in the workplace, see Appendix III.

(b) The Small Organization

(i) CASE STUDY: MR. A, A PHYSIOTHERAPIST IN BARRIE[57]

Mr. A was a physiotherapist who ran a practice and owned his own physiotherapy clinic in a mid-sized Ontario town. In the course of his work, Mr. A had acted as a clinic tutor for university students and had also provided co-operative education placements for high school students. In December of 1999, the College Discipline Committee convened a hearing into the conduct of Mr. A. It was alleged by two female students who had been at his clinic on placement that Mr. A had habitually failed to maintain proper professional boundaries in his dealings with patients, students, volunteers, youthful colleagues and employees. This resulted in unprofessional conduct, including sexual impropriety, with these individuals.

Ms. A (not related) observed sexual and flirtatious comments by Mr. A with staff. He commented on his preference for small-breasted women. Ms. A believed these comments referred to herself and another student in the clinic. She believed the comments were made with a humorous intent. Mr. A hugged Ms. A. She felt that the hugs were not professional, but did not find them insulting or threatening. On one occasion, Mr. A slapped or tapped Ms. A's gluteal region despite her explicitly asking him not to. Ms. A understood the touching to be a joke, but felt that it should not have occurred. Ms. A complained to her educational institution about Mr. A. No formal proceedings took place. Mr. A agreed not to take any more students.

Mr. A and Ms. B became friendly during the time of her placement and discussed personal issues, including the fact that Ms. B had been sexually abused. Ms. B became very attached to Mr. A. Mr. A stated that

---

[57] *Asselbergs, Re* (6 December 1999), Case Study 13 (C.P.T.O. Disc. Panel) online <http://www.collegept.org/members/MII_DCASE13.HTML>.

he was not aware of the extent of her attachment to him at this time. During the placement, Mr. A performed physiotherapy procedures on Ms. B for an injury. Although Mr. A denied the physiotherapist-patient relationship, Ms. B viewed herself as his patient. Mr. A created a chart for Ms. B. On some occasions during the placement, Ms. B broke down in tears. Mr. A provided emotional support to Ms. B including stroking her arm, shoulder, hip and knee and holding Ms. B. Mr. A made self-disclosure about his personal problems during at least one of these discussions. Mr. A and Ms. B commenced a personal relationship. There was a progression from casual hugging, to intense hugging, caressing, kissing, disrobing, sexual touching and oral sex. They did not have sexual intercourse.

Mr. A pleaded guilty to the allegation of unprofessional conduct. Mr. A understood that his relationship with Ms. B had caused her great pain. He admitted that he should have never let the relationship take place. The panel gave careful consideration to the facts and Mr. A's plea of guilty. They accepted the plea and found Mr. A guilty of professional misconduct.

During sentencing, the panel considered mitigating factors including the guilty plea, the fact that this was the first complaint lodged against the member, and his commitment to make amends. Aggravating factors justifying a serious penalty were that the member had a duty not to sexualize the relationship, the member sexualized the demonstration of treatments on students and the member did not respect professional boundaries when acting as a clinical instructor.

The panel ordered that Mr. A's certificate of registration be suspended for six months, after which his practice would be monitored for a further 24 months. In addition, Mr. A. was ordered to complete a series of counselling sessions in the area of professional boundaries and was prohibited indefinitely from participating in the training of students. Mr. A was also ordered to write a letter of apology to Ms. B and to pay for her therapy.

In contrast with the large workplace, in a small workplace there may be no available superior in whom a harassed employee can confide. Indeed, the only available superior may be the perpetrator of the unwanted sexual remarks or contact.[58] While the "team work" or "group of friends" workplace model with no clear hierarchy may be desirable in some circumstances for achieving business goals, this model of diffuse

---

[58] Rutter, *supra* note 38, at 129.

control is not what employees require for an ethic around sexual harassment and assault. Employees want a clear mechanism for protection regardless of workplace size.[59]

In very small workplaces, such as private practice offices, these mechanisms may be external procedures, such as complaints to the relevant professional college or under the Ontario *Human Rights Code*. Regardless of workplace size, however, employees must be made aware of these channels of action for handling abuse in the workplace.

Small workplaces can develop the same serious ethic around sexual misconduct in the workplace as large companies. First, a small office or organization can easily send a clear message to all its employees by incorporating education about power in the workplace and sexual harassment into any office training or training manual for new employees.[60] Further, a small office can have a clear written policy listing an outside person, such as a consultant or an agreed-upon third party, who can be contacted regarding issues of sexual harassment or assault. This contact may be an advisor from a community organization specializing in issues of sexual assault or a confidential phone line that acts as an advisor to members of the public around issues of sexual assault. Certain of the professions, like the physiotherapist in this case, are more likely to have members who own or manage small businesses, and in some cases, the colleges have recognized this explicitly in their codes of ethics. For example, the Ontario College of Pharmacists has "Code of Ethics for Pharmacists" which includes a list of ten ethical principles of professional conduct "intended to guide pharmacists in their relationships with patients, other health care practitioners, and the public. Principle ten states: "Pharmacists in control of a pharmacy practice as owner, manager or in-charge pharmacist, ensure that there are no conditions which compromise another pharmacist's ability to practice in accordance with high professional standards and exercise sound professional judgment."[61]

In summary, small and large workplaces have the same responsibility to ensure that their employees work in an environment free of sexual harassment, while each face different challenges in achieving this goal. The specific channels for preventing and handling sexual misconduct

---

[59] Neville, *supra* note 39, at 217.
[60] *Ibid.*
[61] Ontario College of Pharmacists, effective November 1996. Online <http://www.ocpinfo. com>.

will be different, but the general principles of having a clear policy, procedure and concurrent education are applicable to all workplaces.

4. In-Service Training

It is not enough for an employer to create and implement a sexual abuse policy without making a concerted effort to ensure that ongoing and comprehensive education about the issue takes place in the workplace. By ongoing we mean that all those involved, from the CEO to the part-time or volunteer staff to the members of the board be provided with information about what is meant with respect to sexual abuse in the workplace from the moment they apply for the positions and throughout their tenures with the employer. Initially, this process will involve providing all employers with a copy of the approved workplace policy. Later, in-service training should include education about the issue, which can be provided in a wide variety of formats, such as through the distribution of additional written materials, video presentations or lectures. For a comprehensive list of educational resources, see Workplace Policies in Appendix III.

H. LEARNING ISSUES AND DISCUSSION POINTS

In this chapter, we have discussed the complexities of sexual harassment in the workplace and the steps that can be taken to address it when it occurs, and more importantly the steps that can be taken before it ever occurs. In addition to the discussion points below, readers will find helpful information in the appendices relating to the development of effective procedures to prevent workplace sexual harassment.

1. Points to Discuss

- In the two introductory cases of Mr. M and Ms. H there is an interesting contrast in that the offender in the first instance represents the employer who assaulted a subordinate, and the second, a nurse who assaulted a patient. In developing a workplace policy, what issues arise specific to these differing incidents?
- After assaulting the intern, Dr. SM stated: "If you say anything about this, who would they believe anyway, you an intern, or me, a staff physician?" This comment appears to have had the chilling effect on the intern that Dr. SM desired, as she took no steps to report Dr. SM until she heard about other of his victims. Although in the case of Dr.

A, there is no evidence that he made similar comments, did the size of his workplace, that is, his direct and personal control over his employees and volunteers, convey the same message?

- The case studies of Dr. NMRC in Chapter 2, Dr. M in Chapter 4 and Dr. SM in this chapter all involved sexual abuse by a health professional of an individual who was both a patient and an employee. Can you come up with any reasons that might explain this pattern? Are there distinctions among those cases that make a difference?

Chapter 6

EDUCATION

A. OPENING QUOTES

The message to health professions must be given in the context of helping them to provide as good care as possible to all patients, rather than being highly critical and hostile to health professionals for manifesting attitudes that have only recently begun to change in the broader society. Educating about the long-term harmful consequences of sexual abuse is clearly an important step in eliminating this problem but this education must be given in many contexts and situations to accommodate differences in learning styles and educational opportunities, and must recognize the difficulty in changing such long-held social attitudes.[1]

. . .

The College of Nurses of Ontario's Standard of Practice, "Standard for the Therapeutic Nurse-Client Relationship" confirms that the essence of nursing is the establishment of a therapeutic relationship with the client. The ability to establish and maintain the therapeutic boundaries is an essential component of safe, competent and ethical nursing care. Sexual contact with a client is against the interests of the client. It is a fundamental breach of the trust between the nurse and client because it puts the nurse's needs before those of the client and exposes the client to a risk of harm. Sexual contact with a client is a violation of the role of the nurse, which is to use professional knowledge, judgment and skills for the benefit of the client.

Nurses comprise the largest number of regulated health professionals in Ontario and CNO has a good deal of experience in analyzing, adjudicating and educating in the area of sexual abuse and boundary violations. CNO's long-standing abuse prevention programs aimed at helping nurses to prevent abuse and helping employers understand their role in stopping abuse are fundamental to our mandate of public protection. While CNO continues to evaluate and revise these programs, it is critical for all regulators under RHPA to maintain a diligent watch over procedures and particularly to advance the latest forms of education using the best of today's technology.[2]

---

[1] Barbara Lent, M.A., M.D., C.C.F.P., F.C.F.P., Associate Professor, Department of Family Medicine, Faculty of Medicine and Dentistry, University of Western Ontario, and Lead Faculty, for CPSO/UWO course on *Understanding Boundaries and Preventing Boundary Violations in the Doctor-Patient Relationship*. See also note 35, *infra*, and accompanying text.

[2] Anne Coghlan, RN, MScN, Executive Director, College of Nurses of Ontario.

. . .

On my faculty, I have seen women's courses ridiculed at faculty meetings by their male colleagues.... I have seen women faculty members insulted viciously in the public press. I have heard sexual harassment, even rape, trivialized in public by my male colleagues. Inevitably, I have also seen the vast majority of my male colleagues stand silent in observation of this hostile behaviour. I have been guilty of this silence myself. [3]

B. INTRODUCTION: A LITTLE KNOWLEDGE CAN BE DANGEROUS

Most patients are not "educated" in the standards and legal requirements demanded of regulated health professionals. They go to a health professional when they need help. When that help involves some form of psychotherapy, patients are likely most vulnerable, but virtually every professional-patient encounter involves the patient seeking and relying on the professional's particular skills to get what they need for their well-being. Most of the time, patients do not know what will constitute "good" treatment, so often the only way they have of recognizing whether the treatment was abusive is from their feelings of violation and betrayal, often mixed with shock and disbelief, *after* the abuse has occurred — *after the professional has caused the harm*. At the beginning of this book, we alerted the reader to the complexity of the dynamics of sexual abuse of patients. In this chapter, we underscore the crucial role of education and reinforce what has been a consistent theme: sexual abuse is rooted in systemic power dynamics as well as individual mistakes by a sexually abusive professional that may be caused through ignorance, arrogance, illness and/or malfeasance. Regardless of cause, harm results. One professional's abusive application of power creates damage that can ripple through families, communities (of both patient and professional), professions and society at large.

1. The Need for More and Different Education

More than 20 students, practitioners, educators and regulators from a range of professions reviewed this Guide before it was submitted for publication. There was a wide range of feedback on most aspects of the

---

[3] Bruce Feldthusen, Dean of Law, University of Ottawa (2003), in his article "The Gender Wars: 'Where the Boys Are' " (1990) 4 C.J.W.L. 66 at 69.

book, but one point on which everyone agreed was there is a distinct need for more education and practical interactive training — in the degree programs and in continuing education programs for practitioners — on the care of patients needed to prevent sexual abuse, including the dynamics of sexual boundary crossing by health professionals.[4]

Some of our reviewers felt that it was important to include specific information for professionals on providing appropriate care for patients who are survivors of sexual abuse, assault or harassment, many of whom may not disclose their previous history. Students still in their degree programs particularly stressed this need. Ironically though, there seems also to be quite a pervasive "not me" assumption, even among those who articulated strong support for a book of this nature. Again and again, the case studies demonstrate the danger of the potent mix of power dynamics and a professional thinking that he or she can be the exception to the statutory guidelines on professional conduct and sexual boundaries.

2. Why This Chapter's Case Study was Chosen

The case study for this chapter was chosen for several reasons. Unlike Dr. W in our first case study in Chapter 1 — an older male who had been in practice for many years, having graduated from his professional degree program long before any of the task forces or legislative amendments on sexual abuse of patients took place — Dr. AEK in this chapter's case study received her medical education and training some years after the *Related Health Professions Act, 1991 (RHPA)*[5] amendments on sexual abuse came into effect. Unlike the Dr. W case study, in this one the patient/complainant, Mr. X, is male and the professional/respondent, Dr. AEK, is female. Although both professionals were in general practice, Dr. AEK had some specialized "General Practice Psychotherapy" training. While the previous case studies in this Guide raise many questions, this case study prompts this specific query: at a time when the knowledge of a senior student or new graduate in the health professions could be expected to be at its height in such areas of patient care as transference, counter-transference, ethical standards and legislated professional boundaries, what does the Dr. AEK case tell us about the education students in the health professions are receiving?

---

[4]   D.A. Davis, M.A. Thomson, A.D. Oxman & R.B. Haynes, "Changing physician performance. A systematic review of the effect of continuing medical education strategies" (1995) J.A.M.A. 274:9 at 700.

[5]   S.O. 1991, c. 18.

Each profession's college is obligated by the *Health Professions Procedural Code* ("the *Code*") to place on its public register the discipline decisions where there has been a finding of guilt under section 1(3)(a) and (b)[6] — due to sexual contact as specified in sections 51(5) (2) (i) to (v) — excluding section 1(3)(c) which deals with behaviour or comments that do not amount to physical sexual contact. And each such case that a College places on its register presents an opportunity for the profession to learn more about how to educate, train, support and regulate its members more effectively to prevent sexual abuse of patients.

C. CASE STUDY: DR. AEK, A RECENT GRADUATE, FEMALE GP — PSYCHOTHERAPY

Mr. X first saw Dr. AEK in December 1999 concerning a mole he wanted removed. Dr. AEK was in her second year of Family Practice Residency, which had begun in July 1997 but had been interrupted by an 8-month hiatus for an illness that included care by a psychiatrist. She was due to finish in May 2000, but in January 2000, Mr. X phoned Dr. AEK and asked to be referred for psychotherapy. Dr. AEK offered to see him for that purpose and began psychotherapy sessions under the supervision of the Family Medicine program. The sessions were interrupted in May 2000 when Dr. AEK finished her residency and wrote her examinations. In the interim, it was arranged that Dr. M was to care for Mr. X and supervise his medications. When Dr. AEK established an office for a psychotherapy practice (in her home), Dr. M advised Mr. X who contacted Dr. AEK and the psychotherapy sessions were resumed on September 12, 2000.

1. He Says, She Says

There was considerable discrepancy between testimony and other evidence from the patient (his co-worker was also a witness; he provided close-up informal photographs of the professional) as compared to the professional (a colleague, her father and her husband testified; she introduced photographs of her breasts as evidence). The evidence was considered as part of the Discipline Committee's task in defining the nature of the relationship between Dr. AEK and Mr. X, as a patient and as a former patient.

---

[6] Subsection 23(2)(e) of the *Health Professions Procedural Code*, being Sch. 2 to the *Regulated Health Professions Act, ibid.* [hereinafter "the Code"].

Mr. X testified that Dr. AEK commenced a sexual relationship with him while he was a psychotherapy patient (kissing and sexual touching). Dr. AEK denied this. Mr. X also testified that after Dr. AEK terminated their formal psychotherapeutic relationship, she continued to see Mr. X socially, and engaged in a sexual relationship with him, in the period from November 2000 through January 2001. Dr. AEK denied that there had been a sexual relationship at any time.

In December 2000, Dr. AEK billed OHIP for her attendance at a party with Mr. X, which at the time she considered to be "observation" that would help her provide appropriate care for her patient, and for "home calls."

Mr. X alleged that Dr. AEK provided him with cocaine and other drugs to be taken in association with the cocaine, which she denied.

2. What the Discipline Committee had to Decide

It was the duty of the Committee on the evidence before it to determine if Dr. AEK had had a sexual relationship with her patient, or former psychotherapy patient, which would be sexual abuse and disgraceful, dishonourable or unprofessional conduct. In addition to the issue of sexual abuse, the Committee had to determine on the evidence before it whether the conduct of Dr. AEK, in admitting to the disclosure of personal information and to going to a party at a bar with a former psychotherapy patient, and otherwise socializing with him, would be considered by members as disgraceful, dishonourable or unprofessional. The Discipline Committee had to make decisions as to which evidence they found more credible as the basis for the decisions as to whether the professional was guilty of sexual abuse, in accordance with the definitions of sexual abuse and professional misconduct in the *RHPA*. Any consideration as to penalty had to follow a finding of guilt.

The Notice of Hearing alleged that Dr. AEK committed an act of professional misconduct under: 1) clause 51(1)(b.1) of the *Code* in that she engaged in the sexual abuse of a patient; and 2) paragraph 1(1)(33) of Ontario Regulation 856/93 under the *Medicine Act, 1991*[7] for an act or omission relevant to the practise of medicine that, having regard to all the circumstances, would reasonably be regarded by members as "disgraceful, dishonourable or unprofessional."[8] In Appendix I we have

---

[7] S.O. 1991, c. 30.
[8] *College of Physicians & Surgeons (Ontario) v. Koffman*. Indexed as Koffman, Re, Decision/Released June 23, 2003, available online: <http://www.epso.on.ca>.

included the text of the comparable Regulation for midwifery as an example from another discipline.

The Discipline Committee of the College of Physicians and Surgeons of Ontario (CPSO) focused on two main issues:

1. Did the conduct of Dr. AEK constitute sexual abuse?; and
2. Would the conduct of Dr. AEK otherwise be reasonably regarded by members as disgraceful, dishonourable or unprofessional, on the basis of boundary violations, for her interactions with a former psychotherapy patient, for the alleged provision of cocaine to the patient, for an alleged failure to maintain records, and for the alleged improper billing of OHIP?

(a) Risk of Harm — Transference and Counter-transference

In reaching its finding as to guilt in some respects, the Discipline Committee decided that Dr. AEK had not sexually abused her patient such that mandatory revocation of her certificate was required. However, the Committee expressed extensive concern about the lack of judgment on the professional's part. In its deliberations on the appropriate penalty, the Committee took into account in its reasons for the decision concerns about Dr. AEK's naïveté, her lack of understanding and knowledge of transference, her boundary violations, and the fact that she exposed the patient to potential harm. The following paragraphs summarize key points noted by the Discipline Committee in deciding on a penalty.

1. *Boundary violations*, as evidenced by the familiarity in the photographs, the complainant's detailed knowledge of Dr. AEK's personal life, the misguided socialization, setting up an office using the bed in her personal living quarters and the doubtful nature of the house calls, when the patient was already under the care of someone else, were serious professional mistakes. The Committee wrote, "*[t]hey are not mere errors in judgment, but rather are unprofessional acts exposing the patient to potential harm.*"
2. *Poor judgment in agreeing to carry on a relationship with a former patient*, who had admitted he was sexually attracted to her and who already had made a pass at her, including going to his apartment and taking him to social events.
3. *Inadequacy of training and knowledge* that allowed Dr. AEK to believe she was capable of providing psychotherapy to patients suffering from a complex illness.

4. *Continued inability to recognize her inadequacy* and the deleterious effects this had upon the complainant.
5. *Failure to recognize the need for a referral* of a patient who was beyond her skill.
6. *Not meeting criteria that physicians must comport themselves ethically and in the interests of their patients*, as demonstrated by her behaviour with Mr. X.

D. BIG EDUCATIONAL JOB FOR COLLEGES

1. Information, Training, Education Through a Patient Relations Committee in Each College

Section 84(3) of the *Code* gives a complex mandate to the regulatory colleges to provide information, training and education through the establishment of a Patient Relations Committee (PRC) in each college. These new Committees were legislated into being as one of the changes to the *RHPA* designed to improve how the regulatory system dealt with sexual abuse of patients. The law gives each Committee responsibility to develop "measures for preventing or dealing with sexual abuse"[9] through

1. educational requirements for members;
2. guidelines for the conduct of members with their patients;
3. training for the College's staff; and
4. provision of information to the public.

This new statutory obligation came with the implicit expectation that each college, no matter how new or how small, would muster the resources to fulfill its legislated mandate through this new Committee. In its five-year review of the impact of the "sexual abuse amendments" made to the law in 1994, the Health Professions Regulatory Advisory Council (HPRAC) concluded that this separate "new" Committee's mandate be rolled back into the larger college mandate, to let colleges decide how best to use their resources to meet the goals. HPRAC stressed the "utmost importance" for all college activities to be "planned, coordinated and evaluated to achieve the intent of the broad patient relations

---

[9] In Chapter 3, we note how some colleges adopted an "either/or" paradigm by interpreting the term "preventing or dealing" in sub. 84(3) literally as justification for programming that "prevents" *or* "deals" rather than programming that is geared to 'preventing" AND "dealing" with sexual abuse of patients. See "The Role of the Patient Relations Committee" in Chapter 3.

objectives" set out for the Patient Relations Committees (PRC's) — preventing and dealing with sexual abuse of patients.[10]

It is our hope that students, practitioners, regulators and educators will use this Guide. But written materials, while essential for supporting most people in their learning, need to be supplemented. At the present time, educational initiatives are taken by colleges in many different ways and the degree of uptake of the knowledge on prevention of sexual abuse is not at all clear.[11]

(a) The PRC Mandate for Continuing Education for Professionals

Once practitioners have embarked on their busy professional lives, concentrated lengths of time for learning can become rare. Ironically, it seems that what is most familiar as "continuing education," such as a conference, is likely not the most effective learning modality to produce improvements in professional practice. For example, University of Toronto researchers conducted a review of literature on the effectiveness of education strategies in order to assess what approaches seemed most suited to changing physician performance and health care outcomes. Based on 160 educational interventions, they concluded that almost two-thirds (101 of 160) displayed an improvement in at least one major outcome measure: 70 percent demonstrated a change in physician performance, and 48 percent of interventions aimed at health care outcomes produced a positive change. Effective change strategies involved systematic practice-based interventions, including: reminders, patient-mediated interventions, outreach visits, opinion leaders and multi-faceted activities. However, formal continuing education conferences or activities such as audit with feedback had relatively little impact, unless they were combined with enabling or practice-reinforcing strategies.[12]

When the CPSO commissioned the first task force on sexual abuse of patients early in 1991, no Canadian studies or surveys on sexual abuse of patients by professionals had been conducted. We still have a lot to learn. But while comprehensive data on the incidence of sexual abuse of patients by members of the 23 regulated health professions in Ontario have yet to be produced, much more Canadian research and information on this issue has been completed in the past decade. We know that childhood sexual abuse (CSA) can create lifelong health consequences

---

[10] Health Professions Regulatory Advisory Council, *Adjusting the Balance: A Review of the Regulated Health Professions Act* (Toronto: HPRAC, 2001) at 50.

[11] Harry Cummings & Associates, *Evaluation of the Effectiveness of the Patient Relations Program of the Ontario Colleges of Health* (Toronto: HPRAC, 2001).

[12] Davis *et al.*, *supra* note 4.

for survivors.[13] Health professionals now have access to information that can help them respond with compassion and skill when they realize or suspect that a patient is a sex abuse survivor. But health professionals also need to be particularly sensitive to the possibility that a patient with a history of CSA may also be especially vulnerable to boundary testing and boundary crossing, thereby compelling a competent professional to remain alert to the potential risk that may arise in the health professional-patient dynamic. There are a number of resources available to provide some guidance on addressing child sexual abuse issues in practice.

(b) The PRC Mandate for Public Education

When the *RHPA* was proclaimed, the then-Minister of Health Ruth Grier indicated that a comprehensive education program to help the public understand the role of the colleges and the public's rights under the new legislation would be developed. Section 84(3) of the *Code* does charge the PRCs with "provision of information to the public" and section 3(1) of the *RHPA* stipulates that one of the objects of the colleges is to develop, establish and maintain programs to assist individuals to exercise their rights. Nevertheless, the assessments done under the five-year review of the *RHPA* indicated that the public is still poorly informed. For example, only two of the 67 groups and individuals that gave their opinions to HPRAC believed the public was adequately informed.[14] And of those who presented to the public and private hearings that the 2001 Task Force held on sexual abuse of patients, no one was positive about public education by the colleges. HPRAC emphasized the crucial role of public education:

> Public education and access to information are the keys to an informed public, which in turn are absolutely vital to the effectiveness of the regulatory system. In effect, the system cannot be truly accountable to a public that is unaware of the basic elements of the system set out in the *RHPA*.[15]

At one of the roundtables convened by the 2001 Task Force, psychiatrist Dr. Harvey Armstrong referred to the survey of the patient population in Ontario conducted for HPRAC, which concluded that a very small percentage of patients who reported having experienced

---

[13] S. Tudiver, L. McClure, T. Heinonen, C. Scurfield, C. Kreklewetz, *Women Survivors of Childhood Sexual Abuse: Knowledge and Preparation of Health Care Providers to meet Client Needs: Final Report* (Canadian Women's Health Network, April 2000), online: <http://www.cewh.cesf.ca/PDF?pwhce/abuse.pdf.>.

[14] HPRAC, *Adjusting the Balance*, *supra* note 10, at 108, 109.

[15] *Ibid.*

sexual abuse at the hands of their health care providers complained to regulatory colleges or to civil or criminal courts. He said,

> A system designed to protect the public that is not capable of discovering and dis-
> ciplining more than a minuscule percentage of the perpetrators — no matter how
> intelligent, moral, and well motivated its people are — is open to question and
> begs for improvement.[16]

(c) Whose Mandate? — Educating Students

There are some good precedents of professions, with their colleges, that have taken the initiative to fulfill a broader version of the mandate of the "PRCs" than a minimalist interpretation of the law would suggest. For example, students at the University of Toronto Faculty of Pharmacy receive education on sexual abuse of patients as a mandatory part of the curriculum, and then all applicants for registration with the College of Pharmacists are tested on their knowledge of the material as part of the jurisprudence examination.

2. Education on Sexual Abuse and the Ministry of Health and Long-Term Care

The Ministry of Health and Long-Term Care is ultimately responsible for ensuring that public education is carried out in a consistent and cost effective way, but the lack of a centralized and comprehensive system of public information and education is one of the critical deficiencies in the way that government and colleges are implementing the sex abuse prevention goals of the *RHPA*.[17] The Ministry issued detailed instructions to the colleges so that each college's PRC had clear information about the Ministry's expectations for sexual abuse prevention plans, as follows:

> (a)   a statement of philosophy to articulate the college's position on sexual abuse;

---

[16]   Harvey Armstrong, Background Paper for June 9, 2000 Roundtable (Special Task Force on Sexual Abuse of Patients) at 1, 2.

[17]   Some of the colleges expressed this concern to HPRAC during the five-year review of the *RHPA*. Health Professions Regulatory Advisory Council, *Adjusting the Balance: A Review of the Regulated Health Professions Act* (Toronto: HRPAC, 2001) at 109. This may be a particular challenge for the newer colleges or those with smaller member-ships, due to resources. For example, in M. McPhedran, R. Armstrong, B. Long, P. Marshall & R. Roach, *What About Accountability to the Patient? The Independent Final Report of the Special Task Force on Sexual Abuse of Patients* (Toronto: Ministry of Health & Long-Term Care, 2001) the final report of the 2001 Task Force, at page 65, it was noted with approval that the College of Dental Technologists told HPRAC that greater co-ordination and centralization of education by the colleges was needed.

(b) an evaluation of present practices as they relate to sexual abuse, including a review of the complaints and discipline processes, to assess:

— how complaints are investigated,

— communication with complainants,

— practices during discipline hearings, and

— collection of data on receipt of complaints, types of complaints received and the ultimate disposition of complaints, with a view to monitoring trends and identifying problems;

(c) guidelines for professional behaviour and appropriate conduct with patients, covering issues such as:

— who constitutes a patient or a client,

— the special risks to members of the profession of engaging in sexual abuse,

— maintaining appropriate boundaries,

— what constitutes appropriate and inappropriate behaviour with patients,

— initiating, maintaining and terminating personal relationships with patients, and

— multicultural aspects of practice;

(d) professional education programs, including both continuing education of members and education of candidates for registration, the aim of which is to:

— induce an aura of risk as to the real and present danger of slipping into sexually abusive behaviour,

— create an awareness of the consequences of sexually abusing patients,

— sensitize members to conduct which constitutes sexual abuse and to its impact on patients,

— increase knowledge of human sexuality, professional boundaries and appropriate practitioner and patient relations,

— educate practitioners to recognize subtle and indirect disclosure by patients of prior sexual abuse,

— educate practitioners as to how to handle disclosure of prior sexual abuse and how to report it, and

— educate practitioners as to the requirements of the RHPA, including statutory definitions, mandatory reporting requirements and penalties;

(e) education of college staff and committee members who have contact with abused patients or investigate or hear allegations of sexual abuse, including:

— identifying staff and committee members who have direct contact with the public or with abused patients,

> — sensitizing such staff and committee members to issues of sexual abuse, and
>
> — helping such staff and committee members to develop appropriate communication skills;

(f) public education to:

> — communicate the college's zero tolerance policy, and
>
> — increase public awareness as to what constitutes sexual abuse and how to deal with it, through an effective communication plan to members of the public who are in contact with the profession; and

(g) a review of the effect of the sexual abuse provisions and recommendations for changes, including amendments to the relevant regulations.[18]

E. DISTINGUISHING LAWS, REGULATIONS, GUIDELINES, ETHICS AND POLICIES

This section has been added in response to feedback from students who reviewed the manuscript of this Guide. There is a blurring of definition and of understanding related to the terms laws, regulations, guidelines, ethics and policies, and in fact they are often used interchangeably, but not necessarily correctly. As used in this book, these terms are sorted by whether they are statutory in origin or not, as follows:

• Statutory in Origin

1. Laws and regulations — primarily the *RHPA* and its *Code* — as already described in Chapters 1 through 4;
2. Guidelines that each college, through the statutory mandate of its Patient Relations Committee (PRC), is required to develop under section 84.1 of the *Code* (for an example, see Appendix II).

• Voluntary in Origin

1. Ethics or ethical principles found in the codes of ethics voluntarily developed by some of the colleges and some of the professional associations, that are not enforceable as laws or regulations, but serve to define the standards set by self-regulating professions for their members (for an example, see Appendix II);
2. Policies that are also not enforceable as laws or regulations, but which serve to clarify foundational principles that each profes-

---

[18] R.A. Steinecke, *A Complete Guide to the Regulated Health Professions Act*, looseleaf (Aurora, Ont.: Canada Law Book, updated 2002) at paras. 10.100 to 10.11, pp. 10-5 and 10-6.

sion is prepared to follow in making its decisions and carrying out its self-regulatory obligations in the public interest; for example the "Zero Tolerance of Sexual Abuse" policy statements adopted by a number of professional associations and colleges in the early 1990s (See Chapter 1).

This chapter on education and training for prevention of sexual abuse has less reference to the *RHPA*, and more discussion on statutory guidelines and voluntary codes that each self-governing health profession has the authority to develop within part of the regulatory framework of the *RHPA* and its *Code* put in place with the stated purpose of reducing and eradicating sexual abuse of patients.[19] In essence, the law gives the colleges of the professions the discretion to set standards of practice and professional conduct as well as to exercise discretion over how to implement certain aspects of the law.

1. Laws and Regulations

Chapters 1 through 4 focus primarily on laws and their regulations — especially the law (or "statute") that we've been referring to in short form as the *RHPA* (discussed in detail in Chapters 1, 2 and 3), which is the umbrella or omnibus statute governing 23 health professions in Ontario, and its included *Health Professions Procedural Code* ("the *Code*"). We also discuss the *Drugless Practitioners Act*[20] that governs naturopathic doctors in Ontario. In Chapter 2, we provide an example of the individual laws for each profession that pre-dated the *RHPA* and which have been incorporated into its *Code* — for example, the *Medicine Act, 1991.*[21]

Laws or statutes are clarified and complemented by another type of legislation — regulations, which are more administrative in nature, and which cover details needed to implement the larger principles in laws, to make them "work." The procedure for passage of regulations is less public, largely because there is seldom media attention at this stage and because it can be a quicker, less onerous process that is controlled by the

---

[19] Section 1.1 of the *Code* states, "The purpose of the provisions of this Code with respect to sexual abuse of patients by members is to encourage the reporting of such abuse, to provide funding for therapy and counselling for patients who have been sexually abused by members and, ultimately, to eradicate the sexual abuse of patients by members."

[20] R.S.O. 1990, c. D.18.

[21] *Supra* note 7.

minister and civil service, subject to the approval of the Cabinet (described in law as "Lieutenant Governor in Council"), rather than approval by a majority of the legislature as a whole, as required for laws.[22] In certain areas, as part of their self-regulating authority, colleges under the *RHPA* have some authority to pass regulations that are subject to review by the minister. For example, section 85.7 regarding funding for therapy for patients in sexual abuse cases gives the councils of colleges the authority to pass regulations that define eligibility beyond what is specified in the *Code*.[23]

(a) Statutory Guidelines

The *RHPA* requires colleges to prepare "guidelines" regarding sexual abuse of patients.[24] A guideline is typically understood to be a description of the standard or threshold of a professional practice generally recommended to members of that profession, essentially by themselves for themselves. But to reach the objective of prevention of sexual abuse, the *RHPA* directs the PRC of each college to prepare "guidelines" for their members for dealing with or preventing sexual abuse of patients.[25]

2. Codes of Ethics and Codes of Conduct

(a) Code of Ethics

A code of ethics can be used by individual professionals to convert (or modify) personal and professional values into professional practice. Codes can also serve as an indication that professionals practise in the

---

[22] *Regulated Health Professions Act, 1991, supra* note 5, s. 43.1. Subject to the approval of the Lieutenant Governor in Council, the minister may make regulations governing funding under programs required under s. 85.7 of the *Code*, including regulations "(a) prescribing the maximum amount or a means of establishing the maximum amount of funding that may be provided for a person in respect of a case of sexual abuse; (b) prescribing the period of time during which funding may be provided for a person in respect of a case of sexual abuse." [added by S.O. 1993, c. 37, s. 3]. The regulation-making powers assigned to each college by the *Code* enables the college to define what it means by professional misconduct as the offence applies to its particular members. As another example, under the *Medicine Act*, O. Reg. 856/93 lists 34 different forms of professional misconduct.

[23] Subsection 85.7(4) of the *Code*: "A person is eligible for funding *only* if, (a) there is a finding by a panel of the Discipline Committee that the person, while a patient, was sexually abused by a member; or (b) the alternative requirements prescribed in the regulations made by the Council are satisfied" [emphasis added].

[24] Section 84 of the *Code*.

[25] Section 84 of the *Code*.

public interest by going beyond the "bottom line" regulations defining professional misconduct and practising to the highest possible standards. Many but not all regulatory colleges have prepared a code of ethics to help their members to know what is expected of an ethical practitioner. Most of the codes of ethics and *RHPA*-required guidelines are posted on the college websites listed in Appendix II, which also includes some samples of policies and guidelines. Some voluntary membership professional associations have developed their own codes of ethics, separate from the colleges, or they have chosen to adopt a code developed by another body within the profession. The 1987 *Code of Ethics* developed by the Canadian Dietetic Association (currently the Dietitians of Canada) and adopted by the College of Dietitians of Ontario in 1996, describes acceptable professional behaviours for dietitians in Canada.[26]

The Canadian Psychological Association (CPA) is an example of a profession with a code of ethics that has been reviewed and revised regularly. The CPA was the first national professional association in Canada to develop a code of ethics that dealt specifically with sexual abuse.[27] For many years, Canadian organizations of psychologists (both voluntary and regulatory) routinely adopted the various editions of the American Psychological Association code of ethics, until the first edition of the CPA code was published in 1986. The 1977 edition of the APA code was the first version of that code to mention specifically that sexual intimacies with therapy clients were prohibited. The 1986 CPA code of ethics incorporated that standard, which has remained through its three editions (1986, 1991, 2000), and which has been adopted by both the Ontario Psychological Association and the Ontario College of Psychologists. It's interesting to note that the CPA has opted for a higher standard than the APA by specifying that Canadian psychologists must not "encourage or engage in sexual intimacies," whereas the APA code limits its wording to "do not engage in sexual intimacies." Both codes generally prohibit exploitation of any kind, including sexual exploitation, of all persons (not just therapy clients).[28]

---

[26] See the *Code of Ethics Interpretive Guide* available on the College of Dietitians of Ontario website for an excellent discussion of the difference between ethics and values <http://www.cdo.on.ca>.

[27] Canadian Code of Ethics for Psychological, Canadian Psychological Association <http://www.cpa.ca/ethics.2000.html>.

[28] Dr. Carole Sinclair, personal communication with Marilou McPhedran, former president, Ontario Psychological Association (October 14, 2003).

(b) Code of Conduct

In addition to codes of ethics for regulated health professionals, some associations have also developed "codes of conduct," which are designed to clarify what conduct will attract disciplinary scrutiny by that profession's regulatory body. Note in this chapter's case study how the Discipline Committee had to determine whether Dr. AEK was guilty of "professional misconduct" as defined by the *Medicine Act* in aspects of her practice, in addition to the alleged misconduct covered by the sexual abuse definition in the *RHPA*. In Ontario, the statutory guidelines that colleges are required to prepare under section 84 of the *Code* serve the purpose of codes of conduct.

3. Policies

In Chapter 5, we dealt with workplace issues, generally dealt with by "policies" — which are not law — to describe voluntary, self-regulating policies on such issues as sexual harassment in a particular workplace. But in addition to any workplace polices voluntarily created by organizations as part of responsible self-governance, province-wide human rights and labour practices are legislated to create consistent standards for the whole province, across the public and private sectors; for example, the Ontario *Human Rights Code* that is discussed in Chapter 5.

F. WHAT HEALTH PROFESSIONALS NEED TO KNOW ABOUT PROFESSIONAL BOUNDARIES

Boundaries are about "personal space" between two people. Professionals and patients are both entitled to preserve their "private space." But in the patient-professional dynamic, professionals are under an obligation to set and keep boundaries that meet appropriate standards of care. Boundaries differ from person to person, and every professional needs education and training to identify the limit that exists to keep the relationship *professional* in order to ensure that the patient's needs are met in safe, respectful ways. When professional boundaries are crossed, patients may be able to voice that they feel they have been violated, but it is not their "job" to identify or to maintain the boundaries. The first regulatory college in Canada to write guidelines on sexual boundaries was the College of Physicians and Surgeons of Manitoba, the source of the following "plain language" statement:

The nature of any health worker/patient relationship is always unequal because patient is the one seeking help. The trusting relationship and emotional dependence which can exist in the health worker/patient relationship increases the power imbalance. It is never "O.K." for a physician to respond in a sexual way. It makes no difference if the patient agrees to any act or participates actively. *A physician must always maintain professional boundaries and stop the development of any romantic or sexual relationship.*[29]

1. Warning Signs

The crossing of professional boundaries frequently precedes sexual contact; sometimes because the professional may be "setting up" the patient to be used sexually, but often out of an unexamined conviction that "extra effort" needs to be made in that case. As with Dr. AEK, professionals need to learn to apply their skill to examine motivation and, regardless of intense feelings that may be there, use professional judgment to recognize warning signs and act accordingly.

For example, an Ontario professional, and those around the professional, needs to be alert to the context and possible problems if the professional gives a patient "special" status by:

- scheduling appointments after hours or making appointments outside the office (under unusual circumstances for the practice)
- using the patient as a confidant or for personal support
- giving or accepting gifts
- inviting the patient to or attending social engagements with the patient
- borrowing money or getting involved in business dealings with a patient
- confiding a secret to the patient or making secrecy a part of the professional/patient relationship
- inappropriate prescribing of drugs or giving samples of drugs that may not be appropriate for the patient's condition

A colleague might observe or a patient might experience some behaviours that may contribute to a sexually charged environment and some behaviours that create such an inappropriately charged care setting. When any of these behaviours on the part of a professional occur, it is important to pay attention and to call attention to them. Such conscious

---

[29] College of Physicians and Surgeons of Manitoba <http://www.umanitoba.ca/colleges/cps/>.

preventive measures may stop damage that can be done, whether the behaviours are intentional or inadvertent, and which may include:

- no gown or drape sheet provided or watching the patient disrobe or dress;
- breast, genital or anal examinations where the professional has given little or no explanation in advance or where the procedures differ from previous sensitive examinations, but the patient is not informed;
- discussion of a patient's sex life when not related to a clinical problem and/or discussion of the professional's sex life;
- sexually suggestive, demeaning comments or language, or "dirty" jokes;
- ogling (eyeing up and down) or excessive flattery of a patient's physical appearance;
- sexual touching or kissing;
- suggesting that sex with him or her will help the patient heal (as happened with Dr. AB and Dr. M in our case studies in Chapter 4).

Paragraphs 1(3)(a) through (c) of the *Code* clearly define the last four behaviours listed above as "sexual abuse."

(a) Sensitive Care is Not Sexualized Care

All patients deserve sensitive, appropriate care, and health professionals generally strive to provide it. Some patients are more vulnerable than others, for a variety of reasons, and health professionals need skill to identify and respond to such vulnerabilities. Despite the prevalence of abuse in society, sexual abuse is not adequately dealt with in professional schools. Most of the research has focused on child sexual abuse (CSA) and we know that several profound, long-term effects may result from childhood abuse and in turn, may influence current encounters with health care providers without the awareness of one or both parties. Some of the long-term effects of child sexual abuse include post-traumatic stress disorder (PTSD) — PTSD symptoms, psychological problems, interpersonal problems, self-abuse, pain, and other somatic complaints.[30] Awareness of these symptoms as possible sequelae of CSA and the identification of their presence in a patient may evoke the suspicion of CSA, and serve as a "red flag."[31] In an effort to provide appropriate care

---

[30] *Supra*, note 13, at 5.
[31] *Ibid.*

for survivors, whether the sexual abuse occurred in childhood or later, it is essential for health care providers to understand the origin of somatic symptoms, and to consider an abuse history in patients with multiple complaints with no apparent organic cause.

(b) Universal Precautions for Primary Care Providers

The Manitoba study notes that primary care providers, physicians and nurses, are most likely to have the opportunity to build an ongoing professional relationship with patients. The "universal precautions" approach recommended indicates an awareness of the prevalence of abuse, and sensitivity to any signals that may suggest an abuse history. It also demonstrates respect for the patients and offers them control and input into the test, examination, or procedure without necessarily needing to disclose their histories.[32]

2. Ending the Professional-Patient Relationship to Have Sex

In addition to the legally defined boundaries in the *RHPA* attached to a professional's choice to make sexual contact with his or her patients(s), there is an additional aspect to defining the standard of care and the ethical standard required of a professional in putting the needs of his or her patient first. What is the standard of care required when a professional wishes to have sex with a patient? The College of Physicians and Surgeons of Manitoba makes a clear statement on this point:

> It is not acceptable to terminate a physician/patient relationship with the intent of engaging in a sexual relationship. The physician's ethical obligation not to exploit the physician/patient relationship for the physician's personal advantage applies whenever a physician considers termination of the physician/patient relationship to pursue a personal relationship. The physician must recognize the risk of abuse in any such circumstance, and must realistically assess the emotional dependence of the patient. Where a physician/patient relationship is terminated with the intent of entering a personal relationship, the physician is accountable for any exploitation.[33]

---

[32] S. Tudiver, L. McClure, T. Heinonen, C. Kreklewetz, L. Clemente, D. Shilon, C. Scurfield, "Getting Through Medical Examinations: A Resource for Women Survivors of Sexual Abuse and their Health Care Providers" (Canadian Women's Health Network, 2001) <http://www.cwhn.ca/network-reseau/2-11/recherche.html>.

[33] College of Physicians and Surgeons of Manitoba, 2002 Guidelines and Statements: *Sexual Misconduct In the Physician/Patient Relationship* (First Print CC/05-90/RevisionExec/04/02), online <http:/www.umanitoba.ca/colleges/cps/>. Excerpt:
> Sexualizing the physician/patient relationship has no therapeutic value. Physician/patient sexual contact is abusive regardless of whether the physician believes that

This principle needs to be applied to all health professionals. At minimum, from an ethical perspective, it is the responsibility of a professional in a sexually charged relationship to ensure that the points above are considered. In particular, an equivalent and appropriate source of care must be made readily available to the patient and a reasonable amount of time must pass before any attempt is made to assign a sexually attractive patient to the status of "former patient."

The Institute for Clinical Evaluative Studies (ICES) survey[34] (CPSO 2002; discussed in Chapter 1), the survey of emergency physicians (CMAJ 1996), and the survey conducted by the Society of Obstetricians and Gynaecologists of Canada[35] (discussed in Chapter 1) as well as the Ontario Medical Association (OMA) argument in its intervention in the *Mussani* (discussed in chapter 3) appeal, all made reference to exceptional circumstances, such as "rural" or "isolated" community scenarios where professionals faced the dilemma of not being able to choose a sexual partner from among the patient population in such an isolated setting. Yet none of these surveys placed as much emphasis on the dilemma from the perspective of patients who need access to professionals who can be

---

the patient consents. Patient consent is never an acceptable rationalization. It is the physician's responsibility to set and control appropriate boundaries in the physician/patient relationship.

Former Patient

The dynamics of the physician/patient relationship do not necessarily end with the completion of treatment or the transfer of patient care. There is a risk of abuse of power on the part of the physician since, whether intentionally or not, he/she may use or exploit the trust, the confidential information, the emotions or the power created during the professional relationship. In any sexualized conduct with a former patient, the physician has a duty to ensure there is no exploitation by the physician of the power imbalance between the parties resulting from the earlier physician/patient relationship. It is not acceptable to terminate a physician/patient relationship with the intent of engaging in a sexual relationship. The physician's ethical obligation not to exploit the physician/patient relationship for the physician's personal advantage applies whenever a physician considers termination of the physician/patient relationship to pursue a personal relationship. The physician must recognize the risk of abuse in any such circumstance, and must realistically assess the emotional dependence of the patient. Where a physician/patient relationship is terminated with the intent of entering a personal relationship, the physician is accountable for any exploitation.... Given the very special nature of the psychotherapeutic relationship, it is rare for personal relationships to be established between physicians and their former psychotherapy patients in which the previous physician/patient relationship is not exploited in some way.

[34] Unpublished study as reported in College of Physicians and Surgeons of Ontario, "Sexual Abuse of Patients" *Members' Dialogue* (November/December 2002) online, <http://www.cpso.on.ca/Publications/Dialogue/1102/toc.htm>.

[35] J. Lamont & C. Woodward, "Patient-physician Sexual Involvement: A Canadian Survey of Obstetrician-gynaecologists" (1994) 150 C.M.A.J. 1433.

trusted to maintain their professional standards by honouring sexual boundaries that are defined in several ways: in the law, in their profession's code of ethics and in college guidelines mandated by the *RHPA*. Nor was there discussion in the surveys of the inconvenience and potential risk to patients who cannot get the care they need (and presumably used to get) in their communities because their health professional has chosen to cross a sexual boundary, often leaving the (now former) patient(s) with only the option of travelling outside the community for care. Generally speaking, the courts have not been inclined to a more patient-centric view than that found in the research just mentioned. However, in the May 2003 unanimous ruling of the appeal court in the *Mussani* case (the case study in Chapter 3, which has been further appealed by the doctor and the OMA) the judges disagreed with the OMA hypothetical on the right of doctors in rural or isolated communities to consider choosing sexual partners from among their patients, and said

> ...the right to make choices over one's own body does not necessarily implicate the right to make choices with respect to the body of another. In the context of sexual relations between physician and patient there is the further concern that the nature of the relationship will itself improperly affect the choices available to the patient.[36]
>
> . . .
>
> Patients in rural areas are deserving of the same protections as patients in urban ones. The protection... is in place for the patient, not the physician, and their potential impact on a physician's social life is irrelevant.[37]

A patient-centric approach to the isolation scenario produces a number of questions that have not been addressed in the hypothetical examples of the OMA or in the surveys. These questions are raised in the last section of this chapter.

3. Curricula on Boundaries

One interesting initiative is the course "Understanding Boundary Issues" developed by the medical faculty at the University of Western Ontario under the sponsorship of the CPSO. Participants have an opportunity to work with trained standardized patients in the demonstration of respectful clinical interactions and to develop skills in setting appropriate

---

[36] *Mussani v. College of Physicians & Surgeons (Ontario)* (2003), 64 O.R. (3d) 641 at 664 (Div. Ct.).
[37] *Ibid.*, at 669.

boundaries in difficult clinical situations.[38] This course is one valuable model for the kind of continuing education that is essential for prevention of boundary violations in the doctor-patient relationship and sexual abuse of patients. The workshop format and the small tutor/learner ratio mean that the cumulative number of health care professionals who have participated in this initiative is small.[39] Some of the doctors who participated were sent to the course by order of the CPSO Discipline Committee, upon a finding of sexual abuse. However, the course instructors have no way of distinguishing those who have voluntarily elected to take and pay for the course from those who are in the course as a result of a CPSO ruling. This raises a specific question as to how the CPSO can assess the impact of the course on those doctors ordered to attend and a more general question about how regulatory colleges can monitor and assess "rehabilitation" in the event that offending professionals wish to apply for re-entry to practise once the mandatory five-year revocation period is over.

Another curriculum for medicine was developed at the University of Toronto to teach faculty and students about negative consequences of sexual misconduct by physicians, as well as the adverse effects of violations of boundaries between teachers and learners (students, residents, interns and other trainees).[40] There is a didactic portion consisting of lectures on the definitions, causes and consequences of physician-patient sexual misconduct as well as teacher-learner mistreatment and harassment, complemented by an experiential workshop component with case vignettes so the participants have an opportunity to consider their responses in actual clinical and teaching situations. Relationships after termination of treatment and the complaint and discipline procedures of the CPSO are also discussed. In an evaluation of the course, of the 373 participants, 54 percent (15/28) of those attending the course for faculty and 39 percent (133/345) of those at subsequent courses stated that they would change their clinical and

---

[38] *Understanding Boundaries and Preventing Boundary Violations in the Doctor-Patient Relationship.* UWO Contact: Ms. Kavita Sharma at (416) 967-2600 ext. 375, or 1-800-268-7096 ext. 375, or e-mail at ksharma@cpso.on.ca.

[39] With appreciation to Dr. Barbara Lent for providing information on this course. See *supra* note 1.

[40] G.E. Robinson & D.E. Stewart, Department of Psychiatry, University of Toronto, Ontario, "A curriculum on physician-patient sexual misconduct and teacher-learner mistreatment. Part 1: content" (1996) 154:5 C.M.A.J. 643-9, and "A curriculum on physician-patient sexual misconduct and teacher-learner mistreatment. Part 2: Teaching method" (1996) 154:7 C.M.A.J. 1021-5.

teaching practises in positive ways as a result of attending. A further 38 percent (130/345) stated that they already practised in a manner congruent with the model discussed.[41]

4. Discussion Points

1. Do you think the Discipline Committee made the correct decision as to penalty, given the wording of the law?
2. Do you think that there should be any training requirements before general practitioners are allowed to bill OHIP for psychotherapy or counselling?

(a) *Educational Requirements under the Code*

1. Given the legislative requirements regarding education of students, practitioners and the public under section 84 of the *Code*, prepare a report card on the college and/or educational institution of your profession, including answers to the following questions:

    i. Overall, to what extent has each educational requirement in section 84 been met?

    ii. Is there mandatory sexual abuse education in your professional school and for health professionals who have been certified to practise by your College?

    iii. What grade do you assign to the content and accessibility of such programs? For example, where and how frequently are they offered? Are there interactive learning interventions?

    iv. Are the guidelines and policies developed by your health care profession (your college and your association) for the conduct of members with their patients clear about sexual abuse? For example, have you been clearly informed on what you have to consider about possible post-termination relationships?

    v. Do you understand your reporting obligations as a regulated health professional including time frame to report, to whom, and how?

    vi. Do you have information about how members of the public are being educated on sexual boundaries in competent care,

---

[41] *Ibid.* Abstract, "A curriculum on physician-patient sexual misconduct and teacher-learner mistreatment. Part 2: Teaching method" (1996) 154:7 C.M.A.J. 1021-5.

on what constitutes sexual abuse under the Ontario law, and on how to proceed with an inquiry or complaint about sexual abuse?

vii. Have you been adequately educated to assist patients who disclose abuse by health professionals or others? Do you know where you can get ongoing information and support to help you respond to such cases?

5. Critical Analysis of the Zero Tolerance "No Sex With Patients" Rules

2. (a) Approaching the issue of professional-patient sex in rural or isolated community scenarios from a patient-centric angle produces a number of questions that have not been addressed in surveys of the professions (to January 2004 when this book was published). For example:

    i. What happens to the patient's care options when the sexual relationship begins?

    ii. What impact does professional-patient sex have on the level of trust in other professionals to keep sexual and other boundaries intact?

    iii. What of the former patient who then becomes the former sexual partner of a professional in the community — what is the alternative standard of care available under those circumstances in the rural or isolated community?

    iv. What if another professional providing care to that patient wishes to have sex with that patient?

2. (b). Discuss the following "reasonable hypotheticals" — scenarios presented by the OMA in arguing for exceptions to the "no sex with patients" rule:[42]

    i. A professional assesses, diagnoses or treats his or her spouse or partner;

    ii. A brief consensual affair between two colleagues who have provided assessment, diagnosis or treatment to one or each other;

    iii. A single instance of prohibited physical contact, which occurred due to a professional's treatable emotional or mental impairment.

---

[42] Mussani, *supra* note 36, at paras. 88-94.

After your discussion is completed, you may wish to discuss the appeal court's response to each of these scenarios, summarized in the note.[43]

(a) Who Can Best Provide Public Education?

3.   Here are some additional questions geared to develop a broader sense of what education to the public (patients) needs to be and who needs it.[44] These questions have been asked of colleges previously. The actions taken by colleges on these questions varies.

(*i*) ACCESS QUESTIONS

What material is available by each College to patients and to members of the public, and are these materials available in health professionals' offices? Are they produced in different languages? Is the information written in plain language? Are the educational materials available on videotape or cassette for patients who have special needs?

---

[43]   Consider the following summary of the appeal court's response to each of the OMA's "reasonable hypotheticals" in Question 2 at the end of this chapter:

2.(b)(i): Sexual contact between spouses in these circumstances arises from the pre-existing spousal relationship, and not from the treating relationship. As none of the "mischiefs" of sexual abuse arises where treating a pre-existing spouse, the term "sexual abuse" in the *RHPA* could not be reasonably interpreted to capture this conduct. [*Mussani, supra* note 36, at para. 90 in the decision.]

2.(b)(ii): The rules would not apply where the professional/patient relationship is a historical one. The colleagues in this scenario are not precluded from having either type of relationship with each other — they must simply choose which one they wish to maintain. [*Mussani,* at para. 92.]

2(b)(iii): Behaviour due to a treatable mental or emotional impairment would likely be addressed under the incapacity provisions of the *RHPA*. However, the application of the sexual abuse rules in this hypothetical would not necessarily be inappropriate — the objective is the protection of patients from sexual abuse, and the patient in this scenario is no less deserving of protection than the rural patient already discussed. [*Mussani,* at para. 93.]

[44]   Throughout this book, many helpful suggestions have come from members of the task forces on sexual abuse of patients in Ontario, in their previous work and in responses to the manuscript for this book. Our appreciation to Ronda Bessner, Harvey Armstrong, Pat Marshall and Roz Roach for their assistance in developing these questions.

Chapter 7

CONCLUSION

In the Introduction to this book, we promised to examine the intersection of law and practice as a contribution to preventing sexual abuse of patients and thus preventing the harm caused to so many people, not only patients, when health professionals cross the sexual boundary. Abusive behaviour is a facet of our dark side as, humans, and, thus, it is an unpopular issue of public concern about a private matter, affecting thousands of patients *and* thousands of men and women who are licensed or studying to qualify in the 23 professions regulated under Ontario's *The Regulated Health Professions Act, 1991 (RHPA)* as well as other professionals, such as naturopathic doctors, under *The Drugless Practitioners Act.*

As uncomfortable as it makes us, sexual abuse is a topic that just will not go away; it challenges the public, patients, health care practitioners — their educational bodies, regulatory colleges and health care institutions — governments, the legal professions — and the media. Hopefully, the chapters preceding this one have provided detailed and clear information that will enable readers to use the law as a proactive tool in the prevention of such abuse. But knowledge is only as good as its translation, dissemination and uptake. Only a few regulatory colleges or faculties in any of the health disciplines provide substantial course materials or interactive continuing education opportunities on preventing such boundary crossing. The most comprehensive course developed by a college costs more than $1,000. A tiny fraction of the members regulated by that college have actually taken the course or even seen the materials, which are not readily accessible. And in each health regulatory college, the Patient Relations Committees — made mandatory under the *RHPA* in 1994 — have made limited progress in fulfilling their double mandate of professional and public education in the identification and prevention of sexual abuse by health professionals. Thus, a number of troubling questions remain as we begin the second decade since enactment of the law that defines sexual abuse of patients and governs the legal procedures when sexual abuse complaints are made to the regulatory colleges of health professionals in Ontario. In ending this book, we offer a brief synopsis of the context for increased implementation of the law — as a means of reaching the broadly shared goal of preventing sexual abuse of patients.

A. THE STATE OF THE LAW

Every chapter in this book has dealt with aspects of the legislation enacted a decade ago — the *RHPA* and its *Code*. For years now, key provisions dealing with sexual abuse of patients, including the statement of purpose, definition of sexual abuse, and mandatory revocation penalty requirement — have been constitutionally challenged in a number of cases discussed in preceding chapters. As this book goes to press, an upcoming decision by the Ontario Court of Appeal against a CPSO decision in 2000 on the mandatory revocation penalty may come to be considered secondary in influence only to the 1992 decision of the Supreme Court of Canada in *Norberg v. Wynrib*, the first case study in this book.[1]

Ten years after the enactment of the *RHPA*, this book is the first such text devoted to education on the prevention of sexual abuse. As case after case of alleged sexual abuse of patients, often ending with dire consequences for professional and patient alike, becomes a "media event" it is relevant to note how seldom questions are asked about the education and training that health professionals have received on the actual dynamics of sexual boundary crossing. As reported to us by health professionals, much of their education has been "fear-based" and the modest amount of information on this topic covered in training has often focussed on liability in potential "entrapment" scenarios more than on the professional standards of care that are appropriate.

B. MEMBERS OF THE MEDIA AS EDUCATORS

Ironically, because much of the information about the harm — and prevention of the harm — caused by sexual abuse of patients does *not* yet come from educational programs for health professionals or from

---

[1] *Dr. Anil Mussani and the Ontario Medical Association v. The College of Physicians and Surgeons of Ontario and the Attorney General of Ontario* (2004), which is a further appeal to the Ontario Court of Appeal from an earlier decision of the Divisional Court, which was a decision on an appeal from the finding of guilt by the CPSO under the *RHPA*. For more detail, see Chapters 3 and 6 of this book.

public education programs, members of the media covering sexual abuse cases have become *de facto* educators who reach and influence the greatest number of practitioners and students in the health professions and the public at large. In the 10 years since the law was changed, the stigmatization associated with sexual abuse, that can affect patients and professionals, remains a serious barrier to constructive learning about the breadth and depth of this problem. Media professionals are not charged with responsibility for public education, nor are they required to be experts on the topics they choose. But is it reasonable to ask what can be fairly expected of the media in choice of language when covering sexual abuse cases? As a brief exploration of the impact of the media on raising awareness, we look at the power of language through one recent example.[2] Ontario general practitioner and psychotherapist Dr. AA appeared before a CPSO panel in discipline hearings held in 2003 and 2004.[3] The media reported that Dr. AA confirmed through his own evidence (oral testimony and his notes from sessions while he was the health professional responsible for the patient's care, over some 30 months of treatment) that he allowed a number of events to transpire, including occasions when his patient masturbated in his company on the floor of his office. Dr. AA was reported as testifying that he acceded to his patient's opinion that this sexualized behaviour was necessary to facilitate her healing from previous abuse. An expert was quoted as telling the disciplinary panel of the college that the general practitioner psychotherapist had not had sufficient training to provide psychotherapy to a patient with such complex mental health needs. It is important to acknowledge that Dr. AA met all the training requirements set by his profession and the Government of Ontario for providing such care and for billing the Ontario Health Insurance Plan (OHIP). Definitions of prejudice change considerably as more information about the human dimensions of marginalized status, such as mental illness, becomes known. Much of the media commentary on this case made note of the finding that the patient was diagnosed as having a "borderline personality." Not so long ago, it was often acceptable when disabled persons were reduced to the noun "cripples." Coverage of this case was probably not unique and at publication time, it is premature to draw any

---

[2] Christie Blatchford "In a zero-tolerance world, the doctor's no victim" *The Globe and Mail*, 11 entire columns devoted to this case beginning on December 2, 3, 4, 5, 6, 11, 2003, January 6, 7, 8, 9, and 10, 2004, resuming in February 2004.

[3] *College of Physicians and Surgeons of Ontario v. Alan Abelsohn*, hearing commenced December 1, 2003.

conclusions as to outcome. However, it may be instructive to reflect on the impact of language when a widely read journalist chooses to describe patients with this illness by the noun "borderlines"[4] or when the patient in this case is referred to as the "accuser" who is "treated as a helpless lamb, shepherded about by a College support person, not to mention a cooing friend or two, always handled with painful deference."[5]

C. THE NEED FOR EDUCATION

There is an expectation by many that health professionals are being well equipped through education that addresses a wide range of illnesses and disorders among their patient populations, including unpopular or difficult ones. Indeed, this expectation is implicit in much of the law, but society has entrusted the implementation of educational and training programs to institutions of higher learning and regulation. So who should bear the responsibility when a health professional crosses the sexual boundary defined clearly by the law?

At the disciplinary hearing for Dr. AA, an expert witness was reported as having told the discipline panel: "I feel that he had a patient who was very ill and he devised a treatment plan that was unfounded in current clinical and scientific evidence."[6] Many of the case studies in this book — all actual situations experienced by real-life health professionals and patients — indicate varying degrees of awareness and in some cases, profound regret, on the part of professionals found to have sexually abused or assaulted patients, employees or co-workers, or crossed professional boundaries in some other harmful way. Prior to any finding by the discipline panel, Dr. AA was reported as having testified that, "I feel very bad about my poor management of [the woman]. I feel very bad that her suffering has been prolonged and we've heard so much about that."[7]

In a sense, we are closing this book as it began: with questions. To the reader who notes correctly that there are more recorded discipline cases on sexual abuse allegations involving medical doctors than other health professionals, we encourage as part of education an exploration of the impact of hierarchical organizations in which health professionals train

---

[4] *Supra* note 2 (6 January 2004) A7.
[5] Christie Blatchford "What I learned from my psychiatrist" *The Globe and Mail* (6 December 2003).
[6] H. Levy "Doctor endangered patient: Expert" *Toronto Star* (6 January, 2004) B3.
[7] J. Brean "Pity clouded judgment, doctor says" ? *National Post* (9 January 2004).

and work. And we caution against any health professional thinking, perhaps because no patient has ever raised the issue with them, that they do not need education on the dynamics of sexual abuse. As can be seen from Acknowledgements for this book, it has been obvious to us over the years of writing it that educators and regulators in the health professions are well intentioned about developing and maintaining the highest possible standards for their students and colleagues, and that they understand that self regulation of professions is a privilege delegated through legislation that names serving the public interest as its explicit core purpose.

In seeking to understand how best to create learning environments conducive to preventing sexual abuse — be it in a university or a health care institution — we offer the following observation by Canadian experts that could apply to any health profession:

> When these violations occur, there is immense difficulty if the profession or a department ignores the behaviours …Even if they are hushed up, knowledge of their occurrence spreads. Students become acutely aware of the double standard, and teaching about the [professional]-patient relationship and the covenant of care becomes impossible. Since the essence of psychotherapy is based on the integrity of the therapeutic relationship, the teaching of psychotherapy in a department that has not addressed the instances of sexual boundary problems becomes inauthentic and "hollow" … Thus the capacity of even otherwise admirable supervisors to provide effective role models for trainees may be nullified by their collusion and avoidance in addressing boundary violations. This position may leave students confused and disillusioned or with a conscious or unconscious sense of permission regarding violations with their own patients.[8]

Sexual abuse of patients has a high price tag — in financial and human terms — for health care in Canada. If anyone in this country can be identified as the "mother" of publicly funded healthcare, it would be the distinguished former Cabinet minister who oversaw creation of the *Canada Health Act*[9]— The Hon. Monique Bégin — who was good enough to write the Foreword to this book. We join with her in believing that we are "a learning society" and we hope you have found this book to be a helpful educational aide.

---

[8] P. Garfinkel, B. Dorian, J. Sadavoy & M. Bagby "Boundary Violations and Departments of Psychiatry" (1997) 42 Can. J. Psychiatry 764 at 765.
[9] R.S.C. 1985, c. C-6.

Appendix I

EXCERPTS FROM LEGISLATION

1. *HEALTH PROFESSIONS PROCEDURAL CODE*, SCHEDULE 2 OF THE *REGULATED HEALTH PROFESSIONS ACT, 1991*

1. (1) **Interpretation.** — In this Code,

"Board" means the Health Professions Appeal and Review Board under the *Ministry of Health Appeal and Review Boards Act, 1998*; ("Commission")

"by-laws" means by-laws made by the Council; ("règlements administratifs")

"certificate of authorization" means a certificate of authorization issued under the *Regulated Health Professions Act, 1991* or this Code; ("certificat d'autorisation")

"certificate of registration" means a certificate of registration issued by the Registrar; ("certificat d'inscription")

"Council" means the Council of the College; ("conseil")

"drug" means drug as defined in subsection 117 (1) of the *Drug and Pharmacies Regulation Act*; ("médicament")

"health profession corporation" means a corporation incorporated under the *Business Corporations Act* that holds a valid certificate issued under the *Regulated Health Professions Act, 1991* or this Code; ("société professionnelle de la santé")

"incapacitated" means, in relation to a member, that the member is suffering from a physical or mental condition or disorder that makes it desirable in the interest of the public that the member no longer be permitted to practise or that the member's practice be restricted; ("frappé d'incapacité")

"member" means a member of the College; ("membre")

"Minister" means the Minister of Health; ("ministre")

"patient relations program" means a program to enhance relations between members and patients; ("programme de relations avec les patients")

"prescribed" means prescribed in the regulations; ("prescrit")

"quality assurance program" means a program to assure the quality of the practice of the profession and to promote continuing competence among the members; ("programme d'assurance de la qualité")

"Registrar" means the Registrar of the College; ("registrateur")

"registration" means the issuance of a certificate of registration. ("inscription")

(2) **Hearing not required unless referred to.** — Nothing in the health profession Act or this Code shall be construed to require a hearing to be held within the meaning of the *Statutory Powers Procedure Act* unless the holding of a hearing is specifically referred to.

(3) **Sexual abuse of a patient.** — In this Code, "sexual abuse" of a patient by a member means,

    (a)   sexual intercourse or other forms of physical sexual relations between the member and the patient,

    (b)   touching, of a sexual nature, of the patient by the member, or

    (c)   behaviour or remarks of a sexual nature by the member towards the patient.

(4) **Exception.** — For the purposes of subsection (3), "sexual nature" does not include touching, behaviour or remarks of a clinical nature appropriate to the service provided.

1.1 **Statement of purpose, sexual abuse provisions.** — The purpose of the provisions of this Code with respect to sexual abuse of patients by members is to encourage the reporting of such abuse, to provide funding for therapy and counselling for patients who have been sexually abused by members and, ultimately, to eradicate the sexual abuse of patients by members.

College

2.(1) **College is body corporate.** — The College is a body corporate without share capital with all the powers of a natural person.

(2) *Corporations Act.* — The *Corporations Act* does not apply in respect to the College.

3.(1) **Objects of College.** — The College has the following objects:

    1.   To regulate the practice of the profession and to govern the members in accordance with the health profession Act, this

Code and the *Regulated Health Professions Act*, 1991 and the regulations and by-laws.

2. To develop, establish and maintain standards of qualification for persons to be issued certificates of registration.

3. To develop, establish and maintain programs and standards of practice to assure the quality of the practice of the profession.

4. To develop, establish and maintain standards of knowledge and skill and programs to promote continuing competence among the members.

5. To develop, establish and maintain standards of professional ethics for the members.

6. To develop, establish and maintain programs to assist individuals to exercise their rights under this Code and the *Regulated Health Professions Act, 1991*.

7. To administer the health profession Act, this Code and the *Regulated Health Professions Act, 1991* as it relates to the profession and to perform the other duties and exercise the other powers that are imposed or conferred on the College.

8. Any other objects relating to human health care that the Council considers desirable.

(2) **Duty.** — In carrying out its objects, the College has a duty to serve and protect the public interest.

4. **Council.** — The College shall have a Council that shall be its board of directors and that shall manage and administer its affairs.

5. (1) **Terms.** — No term of a Council member who is elected shall exceed three years.

(2) **Multiple terms.** — A person may be a Council member for more than one term but no person who is elected may be a Council member for more than nine consecutive years.

6. **Quorum.** — A majority of the members of the Council constitute a quorum.

7. (1) **Meetings.** — The meetings of the Council shall be open to the public and reasonable notice shall be given to the members of the College and to the public.

(2) **Exclusion of public.** — Despite subsection (1), the Council may exclude the public from any meeting or part of a meeting if it is satisfied that,

(a) matters involving public security may be disclosed;

(b) financial or personal or other matters may be disclosed of such a nature that the desirability of avoiding public disclosure of them in the interest of any person affected or in the public interest outweighs the desirability of adhering to the principle that meetings be open to the public;

(c) a person involved in a criminal proceeding or civil suit or proceeding may be prejudiced;

(d) personnel matters or property acquisitions will be discussed;

(e) instructions will be given to or opinions received from the solicitors for the College; or

(f) the Council will deliberate whether to exclude the public from a meeting or whether to make an order under subsection (3).

(3) **Orders preventing public disclosure.** — In situations in which the Council may exclude the public from meetings, it may make orders it considers necessary to prevent the public disclosure of matters disclosed in the meeting, including banning publication or broadcasting of those matters.

(4) **Reasons noted in minutes.** — If the Council excludes the public from a meeting or makes an order under subsection (3), it shall have its reasons for doing so noted in the minutes of the meeting.

8. **Remuneration and expenses.** — Council members appointed by the Lieutenant Governor in Council shall be paid, by the Minister of Health, the expenses and remuneration the Lieutenant Governor in Council determines.

9. (1) **Employees.** — The Council may employ persons it considers advisable.

(2) **Registrar.** — The Council shall appoint one of its employees as the Registrar.

10. (1) **Committees.** — The College shall have the following committees:

1. Executive Committee.
2. Registration Committee.
3. Complaints Committee.
4. Discipline Committee.
5. Fitness to Practise Committee.
6. Quality Assurance Committee.
7. Patient Relations Committee.

(2) **Appointment.** — The Council shall appoint the members of the committees.

(3) **Composition.** — The composition of the committees shall be in accordance with the by-laws.

11. (1) **Annual reports.** — Each committee named in subsection 10 (1) shall annually submit a report of its activities to the Council.

(2) **Exclusions from reports.** — The Executive Committee shall not submit a report that contains information, other than information of a general statistical nature, relating to,

    (a)   a referral by the Executive Committee to the Discipline or Fitness to Practise Committee until a panel of the Discipline or Fitness to Practise Committee disposes of the matter;

    (b)   an approval for the Registrar to appoint an investigator until the investigation is completed and reported by the Registrar and the Executive Committee decides not to make a referral with respect to the matter to the Discipline Committee or, if the Executive Committee makes a referral with respect to the matter to the Discipline Committee, until a panel of the Discipline Committee disposes of the matter; or

    (c)   an interim order made by the Executive Committee in respect of a member until a panel of the Discipline Committee disposes of the matter.

12. (1) **Executive Committee's exercise of Council's powers.** — Between the meetings of the Council, the Executive Committee has all the powers of the Council with respect to any matter that, in the Committee's opinion, requires immediate attention, other than the power to make, amend or revoke a regulation or by-law.

(2) **Report to Council.** — If the Executive Committee exercises a power of the Council under subsection (1), it shall report on its actions to the Council at the Council's next meeting.

13. (1) **Members.** — A person registered by the College is a member.

(2) **Suspended members.** — A person whose certificate of registration is suspended is not a member.

14. (1) **Continuing jurisdiction.** — A person whose certificate of registration is revoked or who resigns as a member continues to be subject to the jurisdiction of the College for professional misconduct referable to the time when the person was a member.

(2) **Idem.** — A person whose certificate of registration is suspended continues to be subject to the jurisdiction of the College for incapacity and for professional misconduct or incompetence referable to the time when the person was a member or to the period of the suspension.

Registration

15. (1) **Registration.** — If a person applies to the Registrar for registration, the Registrar shall,

    (a)   register the applicant; or

(b)   refer the application to the Registration Committee.

(2) **Referrals to Registration Committee.** — The Registrar shall refer an application for registration to the Registration Committee if the Registrar,

(a)   has doubts, on reasonable grounds, about whether the applicant fulfils the registration requirements;

(b)   is of the opinion that terms, conditions or limitations should be imposed on a certificate of registration of the applicant and the applicant does not consent to the imposition; or

(c)   proposes to refuse the application.

(3) **Notice to applicant.** — If the Registrar refers an application to the Registration Committee, he or she shall give the applicant notice of the statutory grounds for the referral and of the applicant's right to make written submissions under subsection 18 (1).

(4) **Terms, etc., attached on consent.** — If the Registrar is of the opinion that a certificate of registration should be issued to an applicant with terms, conditions or limitations imposed and the applicant consents to the imposition, the Registrar may do so with the approval of a panel of the Registration Committee selected by the chair for the purpose.

(5) **Panels for consent.** — Subsections 17 (2) and (3) apply with respect to the panel mentioned in subsection (4).

16. (1) **Disclosure of application file.** — The Registrar shall give an applicant for registration, at his or her request, all the information and a copy of each document the College has that is relevant to the application.

(2) **Exception.** — The Registrar may refuse to give an applicant anything that may, in the Registrar's opinion, jeopardize the safety of any person.

17. (1) **Panels.** — An application for registration referred to the Registration Committee or an application referred back to the Registration Committee by the Board shall be reviewed by a panel selected by the chair from among the members of the Committee.

(2) **Idem.** — A panel shall be composed of at least three persons, one of whom shall be a person appointed to the Council by the Lieutenant Governor in Council.

(3) **Quorum.** — Three members of a panel constitute a quorum.

18. (1) **Consideration by panel.** — An applicant may make written submissions to the panel within thirty days after receiving notice under subsection 15 (3) or within any longer period the Registrar may specify in the notice.

(2) **Orders by panel.** — After considering the application and the submissions, the panel may make an order doing any one or more of the following:

1. Directing the Registrar to issue a certificate of registration.
2. Directing the Registrar to issue a certificate of registration if the applicant successfully completes examinations set or approved by the panel.
3. Directing the Registrar to issue a certificate of registration if the applicant successfully completes additional training specified by the panel.
4. Directing the Registrar to impose specified terms, conditions and limitations on a certificate of registration of the applicant and specifying a limitation on the applicant's right to apply under subsection 19 (1).
5. Directing the Registrar to refuse to issue a certificate of registration.

(3) **Idem.** — A panel, in making an order under subsection (2), may direct the Registrar to issue a certificate of registration to an applicant who does not meet a registration requirement unless the requirement is prescribed as a non-exemptible requirement.

(4) **Order on consent.** — The panel may, with the consent of the applicant, direct the Registrar to issue a certificate of registration with the terms, conditions and limitations specified by the panel imposed.

19. (1) **Application for variation.** — A member may apply to the Registration Committee for an order directing the Registrar to remove or modify any term, condition or limitation imposed on the member's certificate of registration as a result of a registration proceeding.

(2) **Limitations.** — The right to apply under subsection (1) is subject to any limitation in the order imposing the term, condition or limitation or to which the member consented and to any limitation made under subsection (7) in the disposition of a previous application under this section.

(3) **Panels.** — An application to the Registration Committee under subsection (1) or an application referred back to the Registration Committee by the Board shall be reviewed by a panel selected by the chair from among the members of the Committee.

(4) **Idem.** — Subsections 17 (2) and (3) apply with respect to the panel mentioned in subsection (3).

(5) **Submissions.** — An applicant may make written submissions to the panel.

(6) **Orders.** — After considering the application and the submissions, the panel may make an order doing any one or more of the following:

1. Refusing the application.
2. Directing the Registrar to remove any term, condition or limitation imposed on the certificate of registration.
3. Directing the Registrar to impose terms, conditions or limitations on the certificate of registration.

(7) **Limitations on applications.** — The panel, in disposing of an application under this section, may fix a period of time not longer than six months during which the applicant may not apply under subsection (1).

20. (1) **Notice of orders.** — A panel shall give the applicant notice of an order it makes under subsection 18 (2) or 19 (6) and written reasons for it if the order,

(a) directs the Registrar to refuse to issue a certificate of registration;
(b) directs the Registrar to issue a certificate of registration if the applicant successfully completes examinations or additional training;
(c) directs the Registrar to impose terms, conditions and limitations on a certificate of registration of the applicant; or
(d) refuses an application for an order removing or modifying any term, condition or limitation imposed on a certificate of registration.

(2) **Contents of notice.** — A notice under subsection (1) shall inform the applicant of the order and of the provisions of subsections 21 (1) and (2).

21. (1) **Appeal to Board.** — An applicant who has been given a notice under subsection 20 (1) of an order may require the Board to hold a review of the application and the documentary evidence in support of it, or a hearing of the application, by giving the Board and the Registration Committee notice in accordance with subsection (2).

(2) **Requirements of notice.** — A notice under subsection (1) shall be a written notice, given within thirty days after the notice under subsection 20 (1) was given, specifying whether a review or a hearing is required.

(3) **Order, etc., to Board.** — If the Registration Committee receives a notice that an applicant requires a hearing or review, it shall, within fifteen days after receiving the notice, give the Board a copy of the order made with respect to the application, the reasons for it and the documents and things upon which the decision to make the order was based.

(4) **When order may be carried out.** — An order of a panel, notice of which is required under subsection 20 (1), may be carried out only when,

(a)   the applicant has given the Registrar notice that the applicant will not be requiring a review or hearing;

(b)   thirty-five days have passed since the notice of the order was given under subsection 20 (1) without the applicant requiring a review or hearing; or

(c)   the Board has confirmed the order.

22. (1) **Registration hearings or reviews.** — This section applies to a hearing or review by the Board required by an applicant under subsection 21 (1).

(2) **Procedural provisions.** — The following provisions apply with necessary modifications to a hearing or review:

1.   Subsection 38 (4) (exclusion from panel).
2.   Section 42 (disclosure of evidence).
3.   Section 43 (no communication by panel members).
4.   Section 50 (members of panel who participate).
5.   Section 55 (release of evidence).

(3) **Idem.** — The following provisions also apply with necessary modifications to a hearing:

1.   Section 45 (hearings open).
2.   Section 47 (sexual misconduct witnesses).
3.   Section 48 (transcript of hearings).

(3.1) **Same.** — The following provisions of the *Statutory Powers Procedure Act* also apply with necessary modifications to a review by the Board:

1.   Section 21.1 (correction of errors).
2.   Section 25.1 (rules).

(4) **Findings of fact.** — The findings of fact in a hearing shall be based exclusively on evidence admissible or matters that may be noticed under sections 15 and 16 of the *Statutory Powers Procedure Act.*

(5) **Idem.** — The findings of fact in a review shall be based exclusively on the application and documentary evidence admissible or matters that may be noticed under sections 15 and 16 of the *Statutory Powers Procedure Act.*

(6) **Disposal by Board.** — The Board shall, after the hearing or review, make an order doing any one or more of the following:

1.   Confirming the order made by the panel.
2.   Requiring the Registration Committee to make an order directing the Registrar to issue a certificate of registration to the applicant if the applicant successfully completes any examinations or training the Registration Committee may specify.

3.   Requiring the Registration Committee to make an order directing the Registrar to issue a certificate of registration to the applicant and to impose any terms, conditions and limitations the Board considers appropriate.

4.   Referring the matter back to the Registration Committee for further consideration by a panel, together with any recommendations the Board considers appropriate.

(7) **Idem.** — The Board may make an order under paragraph 3 of subsection (6) only if the Board finds that the applicant substantially qualifies for registration and that the panel has exercised its powers improperly.

(8) **Limitation on order.** — The Board, in making an order under subsection (6), shall not require the Registration Committee to direct the Registrar to issue a certificate of registration to an applicant who does not meet a registration requirement that is prescribed as a non-exemptible requirement.

(9) **Parties.** — The College and the applicant are parties to a hearing or review.

23. (1) **Register.** — The Registrar shall maintain a register.

(2) **Contents of register.** — The register shall contain,

(a)   each member's name, business address and business telephone number and, if applicable, the name of each health profession corporation in which he or she is a shareholder;

(b)   each member's class of registration and specialist status;

(c)   the terms, conditions and limitations imposed on each certificate of registration;

(d)   a notation of every revocation and suspension of a certificate of registration;

(d.1)   the name, business address and business telephone number of every health profession corporation;

(d.2)   the names of the shareholders of each health profession corporation;

(d.3)   a notation of every revocation and suspension of a certificate of authorization;

(e)   the result of every disciplinary and incapacity proceeding;

(e.1)   where findings of the Discipline Committee are appealed, a notation that they are under appeal;

(f)   information that a panel of the Registration, Discipline or Fitness to Practise Committee specifies shall be included; and

(g)   information that is required to be kept in the register in accordance with the by-laws.

(2.1) **Same.** — When an appeal of findings of the Discipline Committee is finally disposed of, the notation added to the register under clause (2) (e.1) shall be removed.

(3) **Access to information.** — A person may obtain, during normal business hours, the following information contained in the register:

1.   Information described in clauses (2) (a), (b), (c), (d.1) and (d.2).

2.   Information described in clause (2) (d) relating to a suspension that is in effect.

2.1   Information described in clause (2) (d.3) relating to a revocation or suspension that is in effect.

3.   The results of every disciplinary and incapacity proceeding completed within six years before the time the register was prepared or last updated,

   i.   in which a member's certificate of registration was revoked or suspended or had terms, conditions or limitations imposed on it, or

   ii. in which a member was required to pay a fine or attend to be reprimanded or in which an order was suspended if the results of the proceeding were directed to be included in the register by a panel of the Discipline or Fitness to Practise Committee.

3.1   For every disciplinary proceeding, completed at any time before the time the register was prepared or last updated, in which a member was found to have committed sexual abuse, as defined in clause 1 (3) (a) or (b), the results of the proceeding.

3.2   Information described in clause (2) (e.1) related to appeals of findings of the Discipline Committee.

4.   Information designated as public in the by-laws.

(3.1) **When information can be withheld.** — The Registrar may refuse to allow a person to obtain a member's business address and business telephone number if the Registrar has reasonable grounds to believe that disclosure of the information may jeopardize the member's safety.

(4) **Panels specifying information in register.** — In disposing of a matter, a panel of the Registration, Discipline or Fitness to Practise Committee may, for the purposes of clause (2) (f), specify information to be included in the register.

(5) **Panels directing results to be public.** — In disposing of a matter, a panel of the Discipline or Fitness to Practise Committee may, for the

purposes of subparagraph ii of paragraph 3 of subsection (3), direct that the results of the proceeding be included in the register.

(6) **Information from register.** — The Registrar shall provide to a person, upon the payment of a reasonable charge, a copy of any information in the register the person may obtain.

(7) **Meaning of "results of proceeding".** — For the purpose of this section and section 56, "result", when used in reference to a disciplinary or incapacity proceeding, means the panel's finding, particulars of the grounds for the finding, and the penalty imposed, including any reprimand.

24. **Suspension for non-payment of fees.** — If a member fails to pay a fee that he or she is required to pay in accordance with the by-laws, the Registrar shall give the member notice of default and of intention to suspend the member and may suspend the member's certificate of registration for failure to pay the fee two months after notice is given.

Complaints

25. (1) **Panel for investigation of complaints.** — A complaint filed with the Registrar regarding the conduct or actions of a member shall be investigated by a panel selected by the chair of the Complaints Committee from among the members of the Committee.

(2) **Composition.** — A panel shall be composed of at least three persons, at least one of whom shall be a person appointed to the Council by the Lieutenant Governor in Council.

(3) **Quorum.** — Three members of a panel constitute a quorum.

(4) **Complaint must be recorded.** — A panel shall not be selected unless the complaint is in writing or is recorded on a tape, film, disk or other medium.

(5) **Notice to member.** — The Registrar shall give the member who is the subject of a complaint notice of the complaint and of the provisions of subsection 26 (1).

26. (1) **Consideration by panel.** — A member who is the subject of a complaint may make written submissions to the panel within thirty days after receiving notice under subsection 25 (5).

(2) **Powers of panel.** — A panel, after investigating a complaint regarding the conduct or actions of a member, considering the submissions of the member and considering or making reasonable efforts to consider all records and documents it considers relevant to the complaint, may do any one or more of the following:

1. Refer a specified allegation of the member's professional misconduct or incompetence to the Discipline Committee if the allegation is related to the complaint.
2. Refer the member to the Executive Committee for incapacity proceedings.
3. Require the member to appear before the panel or another panel of the Complaints Committee to be cautioned.
4. Take action it considers appropriate that is not inconsistent with the health profession Act, this Code, the regulations or by-laws.

(3) **Complaint about sexual abuse.** — In exercising its powers under paragraph 4 of subsection (2), the panel may not refer the matter to the Quality Assurance Committee if the complaint is about sexual abuse as defined in clause 1 (3) (a) or (b).

(4) **Complaint in bad faith, etc.** — If the panel considers a complaint to be frivolous, vexatious, made in bad faith or otherwise an abuse of process, it shall give the complainant and the member notice that it intends to take no action with respect to the complaint and that the complainant and the member have a right to make written submissions within 30 days after receiving the notice.

(5) **Same.** — If the panel is satisfied, after considering the written submissions of the complainant and the member, that a complaint was frivolous, vexatious, made in bad faith or otherwise an abuse of process, the panel shall not take action with respect to the complaint.

27. **Notice of decision.** — A panel shall give the complainant and the member who is the subject of the complaint,

(a) a copy of its decision;
(b) a copy of its reasons, if the panel decided to take no action with respect to a complaint or to do anything under paragraph 3 or 4 of subsection 26 (2); and
(c) a notice advising the member and the complainant of any right to request a review they may have under subsection 29 (2).

28. (1) **Timely disposal.** — A panel shall dispose of a complaint within 120 days after the filing of the complaint.

(2) **If complaint not disposed of.** — If a complaint regarding the conduct or actions of a member has not been disposed of by a panel within 120 days after the filing of the complaint, the Board, on application of the member or the complainant, may require the Complaints Committee to ensure the complaint is disposed of.

(3) **If further delay.** — If the complaint is not disposed of within sixty days after the Board's requirement, the Board shall investigate the

complaint and make an order under subsection (5) within 120 days after the Board's requirement.

(4) **Board's investigatory powers.** — In investigating a complaint, the Board has all the powers of a panel of the Complaints Committee and of the Registrar with respect to the investigation of the matter and, in particular, the Board may appoint an investigator under clause 75 (c).

(5) **Powers of Board.** — After an investigation, the Board may do any one or more of the following:

1. Refer the matter to the Complaints Committee.
2. Make recommendations the Board considers appropriate to the Complaints Committee.
3. Require the Complaints Committee or a panel to do anything the Committee or a panel may do under the health profession Act and this Code except to request the Registrar to conduct an investigation.

29. (1) **Review by Board.** — Subject to section 30, the Board shall review a decision of a panel of the Complaints Committee if the Board receives a request under subsection (2).

(2) **Request for review.** — The complainant or the member who is the subject of the complaint may request the Board to review a decision of a panel of the Complaints Committee unless the decision was,

(a) to refer an allegation of professional misconduct or incompetence to the Discipline Committee; or

(b) to refer the member to the Executive Committee for incapacity proceedings.

(3) **Time limit.** — A request for a review may be made only within thirty days after the receipt of the notice of the right to request a review given under clause 27 (c).

(4) **Parties.** — The complainant and the member who is the subject of the complaint are parties to a review.

30. (1) **When no review.** — The Board shall not review a decision if the party who requested the review withdraws the request and the other party consents.

(2) **Request in bad faith, etc.** — If the Board considers a request to review a decision to have been frivolous, vexatious, made in bad faith or otherwise an abuse of process, it shall give the parties notice that it intends not to proceed with the review and that the parties have a right to make written submissions within thirty days after receiving the notice.

(3) **Idem.** — If the Board is satisfied, after considering the written submissions of the parties, that a request was frivolous, vexatious, made

in bad faith or otherwise an abuse of process, the Board shall not review the decision.

31. **Personal representative as complainant.** — A complainant's personal representative may act as the complainant for the purposes of a review of the decision by the Board if the complainant dies or becomes incapacitated.

32. (1) **Record of decision to be reviewed.** — If the Board is requested to review a decision, the Registrar shall give the Board, within fifteen days after the Board's request, a record of the investigation and the documents and things upon which the decision was based.

(2) **Disclosure.** — Before reviewing a decision, the Board shall disclose to the parties everything given to it by the Registrar under subsection (1).

(3) **Exceptions.** — The Board may refuse to disclose anything that may, in its opinion,

    (a)   disclose matters involving public security;

    (b)   undermine the integrity of the complaint investigation and review process;

    (c)   disclose financial or personal or other matters of such a nature that the desirability of avoiding their disclosure in the interest of any person affected or in the public interest outweighs the desirability of adhering to the principle that disclosure be made;

    (d)   prejudice a person involved in a criminal proceeding or in a civil suit or proceeding; or

    (e)   jeopardize the safety of any person.

33. (1) **Conduct of review.** — In a review, the Board shall consider either or both of,

    (a)   the adequacy of the investigation conducted; or

    (b)   the reasonableness of the decision.

(2) **Procedure.** — In conducting a review, the Board,

    (a)   shall give the party requesting the review an opportunity to comment on the matters set out in clauses (1) (a) and (b) and the other party an opportunity to respond to those comments;

    (b)   may require the College to send a representative;

    (c)   may question the parties and the representative of the College;

    (d)   may permit the parties to make representations with respect to issues raised by any questions asked under clause (c); and

    (e)   shall not allow the parties or the representative of the College to question each other.

34. (1) **Procedural provisions.** — The following provisions apply with necessary modifications to a review by the Board:

1. Section 43 (no communication by panel members).
2. Section 45 (hearings open).
3. Section 47 (sexual misconduct witnesses).
4. Section 50 (members of panel who participate).
5. Section 55 (release of evidence).

(2) **Same.** — The following provisions of the *Statutory Powers Procedure Act* also apply with necessary modifications to a review by the Board:

1. Section 4 (waiver of procedural requirement).
2. Section 4.1 (disposition of proceeding without hearing).
3. Section 5.1 (written hearings).
4. Section 5.2 (electronic hearings).
5. Section 5.3 (pre-hearing conferences).
6. Section 21 (adjournments).
7. Section 21.1 (correction of errors).
8. Section 25.1 (rules).

35. (1) **Powers of Board.** — After conducting a review of a decision, the Board may do any one or more of the following:

1. Confirm all or part of the decision.
2. Make recommendations the Board considers appropriate to the Complaints Committee.
3. Require the Complaints Committee to do anything the Committee or a panel may do under the health profession Act and this Code except to request the Registrar to conduct an investigation.

(2) **Decision in writing.** — The Board shall give its decision and reasons in writing to the parties and the Complaints Committee.

Discipline

36. (1) **Executive Committee referral.** — The Executive Committee may refer a specified allegation of a member's professional misconduct or incompetence to the Discipline Committee.

(2) **Allegations of sexual abuse.** — In deciding whether or not to refer an allegation of the sexual abuse of a patient to the Discipline Committee, the Executive Committee shall take into account any opinion, required under subsection 85.3 (5), as to whether or not the member who is the subject of the report is likely to sexually abuse patients in the future.

37. (1) **Interim suspension.** — The Executive Committee may, subject to subsection (5), make an interim order directing the Registrar to suspend or impose terms, conditions or limitations on a member's certificate of registration if,

(a) an allegation is referred to the Discipline Committee; and

(b) it is of the opinion that the conduct of the member exposes or is likely to expose his or her patients to harm or injury.

(2) **Procedure following interim suspension.** — If an order is made under subsection (1) by the Executive Committee in relation to a matter referred to the Discipline Committee,

(a) the College shall prosecute the matter expeditiously; and

(b) the Discipline Committee shall give precedence to the matter.

(3) **Duration of order.** — An order under subsection (1) continues in force until the matter is disposed of by a panel of the Discipline Committee.

(4) **Panel's order.** — In a matter in which an order under subsection (1) was made, an order of a panel of the Discipline Committee directing the Registrar to revoke, suspend or impose conditions on a member's certificate takes effect immediately despite any appeal.

(5) **Restrictions on orders.** — No order shall be made under subsection (1) with respect to a member by the Executive Committee unless the member has been given,

(a) notice of the Committee's intention to make the order; and

(b) at least fourteen days to make written submissions to the Committee.

38. (1) **Panel for discipline hearing.** — The chair of the Discipline Committee shall select a panel from among the members of the Committee to hold a hearing of allegations of a member's professional misconduct or incompetence referred to the Committee by the Executive or Complaints Committee.

(2) **Composition.** — A panel shall be composed of at least three and no more than five persons, at least two of whom shall be persons appointed to the Council by the Lieutenant Governor in Council.

(3) **Idem.** — At least one of the members of a panel shall be both a member of the College and a member of the Council.

(4) **Exclusion from panel.** — No person shall be selected for a panel who has taken part in the investigation of what is to be the subject-matter of the panel's hearing.

(5) **Quorum.** — Three members of a panel, at least one of whom must be a member who was appointed to the Council by the Lieutenant Governor in Council, constitute a quorum.

39. **Panel members deemed to continue.** — A member of a panel who ceases to be a member of the Discipline Committee after a hearing of a matter has commenced before the panel shall be deemed, for the purposes of dealing with that matter, to remain a member of the panel until the final disposition of the matter.

40. **Amendment of notice of hearing.** — A panel may at any time permit a notice of hearing of allegations against a member to be amended to correct errors or omissions of a minor or clerical nature if it is of the opinion that it is just and equitable to do so and the panel may make any order it considers necessary to prevent prejudice to the member.

41. **Parties.** — The College and the member against whom allegations have been made are parties to a hearing.

41.1 (1) **Non-party participation in hearings.** — A panel may allow a person who is not a party to participate in a hearing if,

    (a)   the good character, propriety of conduct or competence of the person is an issue at the hearing; or

    (b)   the participation of the person, would, in the opinion of the panel, be of assistance to the panel.

(2) **Extent of participation.** — The panel shall determine the extent to which a person who is allowed to participate may do so and, without limiting the generality of this, the panel may allow the person to make oral or written submissions, to lead evidence and to cross examine witnesses.

42. (1) **Disclosure of evidence.** — Evidence against a member is not admissible at a hearing of allegations against the member unless the member is given, at least ten days before the hearing,

    (a)   in the case of written or documentary evidence, an opportunity to examine the evidence;

    (b)   in the case of evidence of an expert, the identity of the expert and a copy of the expert's written report or, if there is no written report, a written summary of the evidence; or

    (c)   in the case of evidence of a witness, the identity of the witness.

(2) **Exception.** — A panel may, in its discretion, allow the introduction of evidence that is inadmissible under subsection (1) and may make directions it considers necessary to ensure that the member is not prejudiced.

42.1 (1) **Disclosure of evidence.** — Evidence of an expert led by a person other than the College is not admissible unless the person gives the College, at least ten days before the hearing, the identity of the expert and a copy of the expert's written report or, if there is no written report, a written summary of the evidence.

(2) **Exception.** — A panel may, in its discretion, allow the introduction of evidence that is inadmissible under this section and may make directions it considers necessary to ensure that the College is not prejudiced.

43. **No communication by panel members.** — No member of a panel holding a hearing shall communicate outside the hearing, in relation to the subject-matter of the hearing, with a party or the party's representative unless the other party has been given notice of the subject-matter of the communication and an opportunity to be present during the communication.

44. **Legal advice.** — If a panel obtains legal advice with respect to a hearing, it shall make the nature of the advice known to the parties and they may make submissions with respect to the advice.

45. (1) **Hearings public.** — A hearing shall, subject to subsection (2), be open to the public.

(2) **Exclusion of public.** — The panel may make an order that the public be excluded from a hearing or any part of it if the panel is satisfied that,

    (a)   matters involving public security may be disclosed;

    (b)   financial or personal or other matters may be disclosed at the hearing of such a nature that the desirability of avoiding public disclosure of those matters in the interest of any person affected or in the public interest outweighs the desirability of adhering to the principle that hearings be open to the public;

    (c)   a person involved in a criminal proceeding or in a civil suit or proceeding may be prejudiced; or

    (d)   the safety of a person may be jeopardized.

(3) **Orders preventing public disclosure.** — In situations in which the panel may make an order that the public be excluded from a hearing, it may make orders it considers necessary to prevent the public disclosure of matters disclosed at the hearing, including orders banning the publication or broadcasting of those matters.

(4) **Public information may be disclosed.** — No order shall be made under subsection (3) that prevents the publication of anything that is contained in the register and available to the public.

(5) **Exclusion of public.** — The panel may make an order that the public be excluded from the part of a hearing dealing with a motion for an order under subsection (2).

(6) **Orders with respect to matters in submissions.** — The panel may make any order necessary to prevent the public disclosure of matters disclosed in the submissions relating to any motion described in

subsection (5), including prohibiting the publication or broadcasting of those matters.

(7) **Reasons for order, etc.** — The panel shall ensure that any order it makes under this section and its reasons are available to the public in writing.

(8) **Reconsidering of order.** — The panel may reconsider an order made under subsection (2) or (3) at the request of any person or on its own motion.

46. **Exception to closed hearings.** — If a panel makes an order under subsection 45 (2) wholly or partly because of the desirability of avoiding disclosure of matters in the interest of a person affected, the panel may allow the person and his or her personal representative to attend the hearing.

47. (1) **Sexual misconduct witnesses.** — A panel shall, on the request of a witness whose testimony is in relation to allegations of a member's misconduct of a sexual nature involving the witness, make an order that no person shall publish the identity of the witness or any information that could disclose the identity of the witness.

(2) **Interpretation.** — In subsection (1), "allegations of a member's misconduct of a sexual nature" include, but are not limited to, allegations that the member sexually abused the witness when the witness was a patient of the member.

48. (1) **Transcript of hearings.** — The panel holding a hearing shall ensure that,

   (a)   the oral evidence is recorded;
   (b)   copies of the transcript of the hearing are available to a party on the party's request at the party's expense; and
   (c)   copies of the transcript of any part of the hearing that is not the subject of an order prohibiting publication are available to any person at that person's expense.

(2) **Transcripts filed with court.** — If a transcript of a part of a hearing that is the subject of an order prohibiting publication is filed with a court in respect of proceedings, only the court and the parties to the proceedings may examine it unless the court orders otherwise.

49. **Admissibility of evidence.** — Despite the *Statutory Powers Procedure Act*, nothing is admissible at a hearing that would be inadmissible in a court in a civil action and the findings of a panel shall be based exclusively on evidence admitted before it.

50. **Members of panel who participate.** — Only the members of a panel who were present throughout a hearing shall participate in the panel's decision.

51. (1) **Professional misconduct.** — A panel shall find that a member has committed an act of professional misconduct if,

  (a) the member has been found guilty of an offence that is relevant to the member's suitability to practise;

  (b) the governing body of a health profession in a jurisdiction other than Ontario has found that the member committed an act of professional misconduct that would, in the opinion of the panel, be an act of professional misconduct as defined in the regulations;

  (b.1) the member has sexually abused a patient; or

  (c) the member has committed an act of professional misconduct as defined in the regulations.

(2) **Orders.** — If a panel finds a member has committed an act of professional misconduct, it may make an order doing any one or more of the following:

  1. Directing the Registrar to revoke the member's certificate of registration.

  2. Directing the Registrar to suspend the member's certificate of registration for a specified period of time.

  3. Directing the Registrar to impose specified terms, conditions and limitations on the member's certificate of registration for a specified or indefinite period of time.

  4. Requiring the member to appear before the panel to be reprimanded.

  5. Requiring the member to pay a fine of not more than $35,000 to the Minister of Finance.

  5.1 If the act of professional misconduct was the sexual abuse of a patient, requiring the member to reimburse the College for funding provided for that patient under the program required under section 85.7.

  5.2 If the panel makes an order under paragraph 5.1, requiring the member to post security acceptable to the College to guarantee the payment of any amounts the member may be required to reimburse under the order under paragraph 5.1.

(3) **Idem.** — In making an order under paragraph 2 or 3 of subsection (2), a panel may specify criteria to be satisfied for the removal of a suspension or the removal of terms, conditions and limitations imposed on a member's certificate of registration.

(4) **Suspension of order.** — A panel may suspend the effect of an order made under subsection (2) for a specified period and on specified conditions.

(5) **Orders relating to sexual abuse.** — If a panel finds a member has committed an act of professional misconduct by sexually abusing a patient, the panel shall do the following in addition to anything else the panel may do under subsection (2):

    1.   Reprimand the member.

    2.   Revoke the member's certificate of registration if the sexual abuse consisted of, or included, any of the following,

        i.   sexual intercourse,

        ii.   genital to genital, genital to anal, oral to genital, or oral to anal contact,

        iii.   masturbation of the member by, or in the presence of, the patient,

        iv.   masturbation of the patient by the member,

        v.   encouragement of the patient by the member to masturbate in the presence of the member.

(6) **Statement re impact of sexual abuse.** — Before making an order under subsection (5), the panel shall consider any written statement that has been filed, and any oral statement that has been made to the panel, describing the impact of the sexual abuse on the patient.

(7) **Same.** — The statement may be made by the patient or by his or her representative.

(8) **Same.** — The panel shall not consider the statement unless a finding of professional misconduct has been made.

(9) **Notice to member.** — When a written statement is filed, the panel shall, as soon as possible, have copies of it provided to the member, to his or her counsel and to the College.

52. (1) **Incompetence.** — A panel shall find a member to be incompetent if the member's professional care of a patient displayed a lack of knowledge, skill or judgment or disregard for the welfare of the patient of a nature or to an extent that demonstrates that the member is unfit to continue to practise or that the member's practice should be restricted.

(2) **Order.** — If a panel finds a member is incompetent, it may make an order doing any one or more of the following:

    1.   Directing the Registrar to revoke the member's certificate of registration.

    2.   Directing the Registrar to suspend the member's certificate of registration.

    3.   Directing the Registrar to impose specified terms, conditions and limitations on the member's certificate of registration for a specified or indefinite period of time.

(3) **Idem.** — In making an order under subsection (2), a panel may specify criteria to be satisfied for the removal of a suspension or the removal of terms, conditions and limitations imposed on a member's certificate of registration.

53. **Costs if proceedings unwarranted.** — If a panel is of the opinion that the commencement of proceedings was unwarranted, it may make an order requiring the College to pay all or part of the member's legal costs.

53.1 **College's costs.** — In an appropriate case, a panel may make an order requiring a member who the panel finds has committed an act of professional misconduct or finds to be incompetent to pay all or part of the following costs and expenses:

1. The College's legal costs and expenses.
2. The College's costs and expenses incurred in investigating the matter.
3. The College's costs and expenses incurred in conducting the hearing.

54. **Decision to complainant.** — A panel shall give its decision and reasons in writing to the parties and, if the matter had been referred to the Discipline Committee by the Complaints Committee, to the complainant in the matter.

55. **Release of evidence.** — The Discipline Committee shall release documents and things put into evidence at a hearing to the person who produced them, on request, within a reasonable time after the matter in issue has been finally determined.

56. (1) **Publication of decisions.** — The College shall publish a panel's decision and its reasons, or a summary of its reasons, in its annual report and may publish the decision and reasons or summary in any other publication of the College.

(2) **Publication of member's name.** — In publishing a decision and reasons or summary under subsection (1), the College shall publish the name of the member who was the subject of the proceeding if,

(a)   the results of the proceeding may be obtained by a person from the register; or

(b)   the member requests the publication of his or her name.

(3) **Withholding of member's name.** — The College shall not publish the member's name unless it is required to do so under subsection (2).

Incapacity

57. **Registrar's inquiry.** — If the Registrar believes that a member may be incapacitated, the Registrar shall make inquiries he or she considers

appropriate and shall report the results of the inquiries to the Executive Committee.

58. (1) **Appointment of board of inquiry.** — The Executive Committee may appoint a board of inquiry to inquire into whether a member is incapacitated if it receives,

(a)   a report from the Registrar under section 57; or

(b)   a referral from a panel of the Complaints Committee under paragraph 2 of subsection 26 (2).

(2) **Notice to member.** — The Executive Committee shall give a member notice that it intends to appoint a board of inquiry to inquire into whether the member is incapacitated before it appoints a board.

(3) **Composition of board.** — A board of inquiry shall be composed of one member of the Council who was appointed by the Lieutenant Governor in Council and two or more members of the College.

59. (1) **Inquiries by board.** — A board of inquiry shall make inquiries it considers appropriate.

(2) **Physical or mental examinations.** — If, after making inquiries, a board of inquiry has reasonable and probable grounds to believe that the member who is the subject of the inquiry is incapacitated, the board may require the member to submit to physical or mental examinations conducted or ordered by a health professional specified by the board and may, subject to section 63, make an order directing the Registrar to suspend the member's certificate of registration until he or she submits to the examinations.

60. **Board's report.** — A board of inquiry shall report to the Executive Committee and shall give a copy of its report and a copy of any report on an examination required under subsection 59 (2) to the member who was the subject of the inquiry.

61. **Referral to Fitness to Practise Committee.** — After receiving the report of a board of inquiry, the Executive Committee may refer the matter to the Fitness to Practise Committee.

62. (1) **Interim suspension.** — The Executive Committee may, subject to section 63, make an interim order directing the Registrar to suspend or impose terms, conditions or limitations on a member's certificate of registration if,

(a)   it has referred a matter involving the member to the Fitness to Practise Committee; and

(b)   it is of the opinion that the physical or mental state of the member exposes or is likely to expose his or her patients to harm or injury.

(2) **Procedure following interim suspension.** — If an order is made under subsection (1) by the Executive Committee in relation to a matter referred to the Fitness to Practise Committee,

    (a)   the College shall prosecute the matter expeditiously; and

    (b)   the Fitness to Practise Committee shall give precedence to the matter.

(3) **Duration of order.** — An order under subsection (1) continues in force until the matter is disposed of by a panel of the Fitness to Practise Committee.

63. **Restrictions on orders.** — No order shall be made with respect to a member by a board of inquiry under subsection 59 (2) or by the Executive Committee under subsection 62 (1) unless the member has been given,

    (a)   notice of the intention of the board or Committee to make the order;

    (b)   at least fourteen days to make written submissions to the board or Committee; and

    (c)   in the case of an order by the Executive Committee under subsection 62 (1), a copy of the provisions of section 62.

64. (1) **Panels for Fitness to Practise hearings.** — The chair of the Fitness to Practise Committee shall select a panel from among the members of the Committee to hold a hearing of any matter referred to the Committee by the Executive Committee.

(2) **Composition.** — A panel shall be composed of at least three persons, one of whom shall be a person appointed to the Council by the Lieutenant Governor in Council.

(3) **Quorum.** — Three members of a panel constitute a quorum.

65. **Parties.** — The College, the member who is alleged to be incapacitated and any other person specified by the panel are parties to a hearing.

66. (1) **Reports of health professionals.** — A report prepared and signed by a health professional containing his or her findings and the facts upon which they are based is admissible as evidence at a hearing without proof of its making or of the health professional's signature if the party introducing the report gives the other parties a copy of the report at least ten days before the hearing.

(2) **Testimony of health professionals.** — A health professional may not give evidence in his or her professional capacity at a hearing unless a report, prepared and signed by the health professional containing his or her findings and the facts upon which they are based, is introduced as evidence.

(3) **Cross-examination.** — If a report described in subsection (1) is introduced by a party, the other parties may summon and cross-examine the person who prepared the report.

(4) **Exception.** — A panel may, in its discretion, allow a party to introduce evidence that is inadmissible under this section and may make directions it considers necessary to ensure that the other parties are not prejudiced.

67. **Procedural provisions.** — The following provisions apply with necessary modifications to a hearing by a panel:

1. Subsection 22 (4) (findings of fact).
2. Subsection 38 (4) (exclusion from panel).
3. Section 39 (panel members deemed to continue).
4. Section 42 (disclosure of evidence).
4.1 Section 42.1 (disclosure of evidence by member).
5. Section 43 (no communication by panel members).
6. Section 44 (legal advice).
7. Section 47 (sexual misconduct witnesses).
8. Section 50 (members of panel who participate).
9. Section 55 (release of evidence).

68. (1) **Hearings closed.** — A hearing shall, subject to subsection (2), be closed to the public.

(2) **Open on request of member in some cases.** — A hearing shall be open to the public if the person who is alleged to be incapacitated requests it in a written notice received by the Registrar before the day the hearing commences, unless the panel is satisfied that,

(a) matters involving public security may be disclosed;
(b) financial or personal matters or other matters may be disclosed at the hearing of such a nature, having regard to the circumstances, that the desirability of avoiding disclosure thereof in the interest of any person affected other than the person whose capacity is being investigated or in the public interest outweighs the desirability of adhering to the principle that hearings be open to the public;
(c) a person involved in a criminal proceeding or civil suit may be prejudiced; or
(d) the safety of any person may be jeopardized.

69. (1) **Orders.** — If a panel finds that a member is incapacitated, it shall make an order doing any one or more of the following:

1. Directing the Registrar to revoke the member's certificate of registration.

2. Directing the Registrar to suspend the member's certificate of registration.

3. Directing the Registrar to impose specified terms, conditions and limitations on the member's certificate of registration for a specified or indefinite period of time.

(2) **Idem.** — In making an order under subsection (1), a panel may specify criteria to be satisfied for the removal of a suspension or the removal of terms, conditions and limitations imposed on a member's certificate of registration.

Appeals to Court

70. (1) **Appeals from decisions.** — A party to proceedings before the Board concerning a registration hearing or review or to proceedings before a panel of the Discipline or Fitness to Practise Committee, other than a hearing of an application under subsection 72 (1), may appeal from the decision of the Board or panel to the Divisional Court.

(2) **Basis of appeal.** — An appeal under subsection (1) may be made on questions of law or fact or both.

(3) **Court's powers.** — In an appeal under subsection (1), the Court has all the powers of the panel that dealt with the matter and, in an appeal from the Board, the Court also has all the powers of the Board.

71. **No stay of certain orders pending appeal.** — An order made by a panel of the Discipline Committee on the grounds of incompetence or by a panel of the Fitness to Practise Committee on the grounds of incapacity, directing the Registrar to revoke, suspend or impose terms, limitations or conditions on a member's certificate, takes effect immediately despite any appeal.

71.1 **No stay of certain orders pending appeal.** — Section 71 also applies to an order made by a panel of the Discipline Committee because of a finding that a member has committed sexual abuse of the kind described in subparagraph i, ii, iii or iv of paragraph 2 of subsection 51 (5).

Reinstatement

72. (1) **Applications for reinstatement.** — A person whose certificate of registration has been revoked or suspended as a result of disciplinary or incapacity proceedings may apply in writing to the Registrar to have a new certificate issued or the suspension removed.

(2) **Time of application.** — An application under subsection (1) shall not be made earlier than,

    (a)   one year after the revocation or suspension; or

    (b)   six months after a previous application under subsection (1).

(3) **Time of application, sexual abuse cases.** — An application under subsection (1), in relation to a revocation for sexual abuse of a patient, shall not be made earlier than,

    (a)   five years after the revocation; or

    (b)   six months after a previous application under subsection (1).

73. (1) **Referral to Committee.** — The Registrar shall refer the application, if the revocation or suspension was on the grounds of,

    (a)   professional misconduct or incompetence, to the Discipline Committee; or

    (b)   incapacity, to the Fitness to Practise Committee.

(2) **Hearings.** — The chair of a committee to which an application is referred shall select a panel from among the members of the committee to hold a hearing of the application.

(3) **Procedural provisions.** — The following provisions apply with necessary modifications to a hearing of an application by a panel of the Discipline Committee:

    1.   Subsection 22 (4) (findings of fact).
    2.   Subsection 38 (2) (composition).
    3.   Subsection 38 (3) (composition).
    4.   Subsection 38 (5) (quorum).
    5.   Section 43 (no communication by panel members).
    6.   Section 44 (legal advice).
    7.   Section 45 (hearings open).
    8.   Section 47 (sexual misconduct witnesses).
    9.   Section 48 (transcript of hearings).
    10. Section 50 (members of panel who participate).
    11. Section 55 (release of evidence).

(4) **Idem.** — The following provisions apply with necessary modifications to a hearing of an application by a panel of the Fitness to Practise Committee:

    1.   Subsection 22 (4) (findings of fact).
    2.   Section 43 (no communication by panel members).
    3.   Section 44 (legal advice).
    4.   Section 47 (sexual misconduct witnesses).
    5.   Section 48 (transcript of hearings).
    6.   Section 50 (members of panel who participate).
    7.   Section 55 (release of evidence).
    8.   Subsection 64 (2) (composition).
    9.   Subsection 64 (3) (quorum).

10. Section 68 (hearings closed).

(5) **Order.** — A panel may, after a hearing, make an order doing any one or more of the following:

1. Directing the Registrar to issue a certificate of registration to the applicant.
2. Directing the Registrar to remove the suspension of the applicant's certificate of registration.
3. Directing the Registrar to impose specified terms, conditions and limitations on the applicant's certificate of registration.

(5.1) **Limitation for sexual abuse cases.** — A panel may not make an order directing that the Registrar issue a new certificate of registration to an applicant whose certificate had been revoked for sexual abuse of a patient unless the prescribed conditions are met.

(6) **Decision.** — A panel that held a hearing of an application shall give its decision and reasons in writing to the applicant and the Registrar.

74. (1) **Orders without hearing.** — The Council or Executive Committee may, without a hearing, with respect to a person whose certificate of registration has been revoked or suspended as a result of disciplinary or incapacity proceedings, make an order doing any one or more of the following:

1. Directing the Registrar to issue a new certificate of registration to the applicant.
2. Directing the Registrar to remove the suspension of the applicant's certificate of registration.
3. Directing the Registrar to impose specified terms, conditions and limitations on the applicant's certificate of registration if an order is made under paragraph 1 or 2.

(2) **Limitation.** — This section does not apply with respect to a revocation for sexual abuse of a patient.

Registrar's Powers of Investigation

75. **Investigators.** — The Registrar may appoint one or more investigators to determine whether a member has committed an act of professional misconduct or is incompetent if,

(a) the Registrar believes on reasonable and probable grounds that the member has committed an act of professional misconduct or is incompetent and the Executive Committee approves of the appointment;

(b) the Executive Committee has received a report from the Quality Assurance Committee with respect to the member and has requested the Registrar to conduct an investigation; or

     (c)   the Complaints Committee has received a written complaint about the member and has requested the Registrar to conduct an investigation.

76. (1) **Powers of investigators.** — An investigator may inquire into and examine the practice of the member to be investigated and has, for the purposes of the investigation, all the powers of a commission under Part II of the *Public Inquiries Act.*

(2) **Idem.** — An investigator may, on the production of his or her appointment, enter at any reasonable time the business premises of the member and may examine anything found there that is relevant to the investigation.

(3) **Obstruction prohibited.** — No person shall obstruct an investigator or withhold or conceal from him or her or destroy anything that is relevant to the investigation.

(4) **Conflicts.** — This section applies despite any provision in any Act relating to the confidentiality of health records.

77. (1) **Entries and searches.** — A justice of the peace may, on the application of the investigator, issue a warrant authorizing an investigator to enter and search a place and examine anything that is relevant to the investigation if the justice of the peace is satisfied that the investigator has been properly appointed and that there are reasonable and probable grounds for believing that,

     (a)   the member being investigated has committed an act of professional misconduct or is incompetent; and

     (b)   there is something relevant to the investigation at the place.

(2) **Searches by day unless stated.** — A warrant issued under subsection (1) does not authorize an entry or search after sunset and before sunrise unless it is expressly stated in the warrant.

(3) **Assistance and entry by force.** — An investigator entering and searching a place under the authority of a warrant issued under subsection (1) may be assisted by other persons and may enter a place by force.

(4) **Investigator to show identification.** — An investigator entering and searching a place under the authority of a warrant issued under subsection (1) shall produce his or her identification, on request, to any person at the place.

78. (1) **Copying of documents and objects.** — An investigator may copy, at the College's expense, a document or object that an investigator may examine under subsection 76 (2) or under the authority of a warrant issued under subsection 77 (1).

(2) **Removal for documents and objects**. — An investigator may remove a document or object described in subsection (1) if,

(a)   it is not practicable to copy it in the place where it is examined; or

(b)   a copy of it is not sufficient for the purposes of the investigation.

(3) **Return of documents and objects or copies.** — If it is practicable to copy a document or object removed under subsection (2), the investigator shall,

(a)   if it was removed under clause (2) (a), return the document or object within a reasonable time; or

(b)   if it was removed under clause (2) (b), provide the person who was in possession of the document or object with a copy of it within a reasonable time.

(4) **Copy as evidence.** — A copy of a document or object certified by an investigator to be a true copy shall be received in evidence in any proceeding to the same extent and shall have the same evidentiary value as the document or object itself.

(5) **Definition.** — In this section,

"document" means a record of information in any form and includes any part of it.

79. **Report of investigation.** — The Registrar shall report the results of an investigation to,

(a)   the Executive Committee if the investigator was appointed under clause 75 (a) or (b);

(b)   the Complaints Committee if the investigator was appointed under clause 75 (c), at the request of the Complaints Committee; or

(c)   the Board if the investigator was appointed under clause 75 (c) by the Board exercising the Registrar's powers under subsection 28 (4).

Quality Assurance Committee

79.1 **Reference to Quality Assurance Committee.** — When the Executive Committee, Complaints Committee or Board receives a report under section 79 of the results of an investigation conducted into a possible act of sexual abuse as defined in clause 1 (3) (c), it may refer the matter to the Quality Assurance Committee.

80. **Quality assurance program required.** — The Council shall make regulations under clause 95 (1) (r) prescribing a quality assurance program.

81. **Assessors.** — The Quality Assurance Committee may appoint assessors for the purposes of a quality assurance program.

82. (1) **Co-operation with Committee and assessors.** — Every member shall co-operate with the Quality Assurance Committee and with any assessor it appoints and in particular every member shall,

(a) permit the assessor to enter and inspect the premises where the member practises;

(b) permit the assessor to inspect the member's records of the care of patients;

(c) give the Committee or the assessor the information in respect of the care of patients or in respect of the member's records of the care of patients the Committee or assessor requests in the form the Committee or assessor specifies;

(d) confer with the Committee or the assessor if requested to do so by either of them; and

(e) participate in a program designed to evaluate the knowledge, skill and judgment of the member, if requested to do so by the Committee.

(2) **Inspection of premises.** — Every person who controls premises where a member practises, other than a private dwelling, shall allow an assessor to enter and inspect the premises.

(3) **Inspection of records.** — Every person who controls records relating to a member's care of patients shall allow an assessor to inspect the records.

(4) **Exception.** — Subsection (3) does not require a patient or his or her representative to allow an assessor to inspect records relating to the patient's care.

(5) **Conflict.** — This section applies despite any provision in any Act relating to the confidentiality of health records.

83. (1) **Confidentiality of information.** — Except as provided in this section, the Quality Assurance Committee and any assessor appointed by it shall not disclose, to any other committee, information that,

(a) was given by the member; or

(b) relates to the member and was obtained under section 82.

(2) **Exception if member gave false information.** — Information described in subsection (1) may be disclosed for the purpose of showing that the member knowingly gave false information to the Quality Assurance Committee or an assessor.

(3) **Referrals to Executive Committee.** — If the Quality Assurance Committee is of the opinion, based on an assessment, that a member may have committed an act of professional misconduct or may be

incompetent or incapacitated, the Committee may disclose the name of the member and allegations against the member to the Executive Committee.

(4) **Use in other Committees.** — Information that was disclosed contrary to subsection (1) shall not be used against the member to whom it relates in a proceeding before the Discipline or Fitness to Practise Committees.

(5) **Evidence in proceedings.** — Without limiting the generality of section 36 of the *Regulated Health Professions Act*, 1991, information described in subsection (1) or information held by a member for the purpose of complying with the requirements of a prescribed quality assurance program mentioned in section 80 is not admissible in evidence in a civil proceeding except in a proceeding under a health profession Act and to the extent permitted by that Act or a regulation made under that Act.

Patient Relations Program

84. (1) **Patient relations program.** — The College shall have a patient relations program.

(2) **Measures for sexual abuse of patients.** — The patient relations program must include measures for preventing or dealing with sexual abuse of patients.

(3) **Same.** — The measures for preventing or dealing with sexual abuse of patients must include,

    (a) educational requirements for members;
    (b) guidelines for the conduct of members with their patients;
    (c) training for the College's staff; and
    (d) the provision of information to the public.

(4) **Report on program.** — The Council shall give the Health Professions Regulatory Advisory Council a written report describing the patient relation program and, when changes are made to the program, a written report describing the changes.

85. **Advice to Council.** — The Patient Relations Committee shall advise the Council with respect to the patient relations program.

Reporting of Health Professionals

85.1 (1) **Reporting by members.** — A member shall file a report in accordance with section 85.3 if the member has reasonable grounds, obtained in the course of practising the profession, to believe that another member of the same or a different College has sexually abused a patient.

(2) **If name not known.** — A member is not required to file a report if the member does not know the name of the member who would be the subject of the report.

(3) **If information from a patient.** — If a member is required to file a report because of reasonable grounds obtained from one of the member's patients, the member shall use his or her best efforts to advise the patient of the requirement to file the report before doing so.

85.2 (1) **Reporting by facilities.** — A person who operates a facility where one or more members practise shall file a report in accordance with section 85.3 if the person has reasonable grounds to believe that a member who practises at the facility has sexually abused a patient.

(2) **When non-individuals have reasonable grounds.** — For the purposes of subsection (1), a person who operates a facility but who is not an individual shall be deemed to have reasonable grounds if the individual who is responsible for the operation of the facility has reasonable grounds.

(3) **If name not known.** — A person who operates a facility is not required to file a report if the person does not know the name of the member who would be the subject of the report.

85.3 (1) **Requirements of required reports.** — A report required under section 85.1 or 85.2 must be filed in writing with the Registrar of the College of the member who is the subject of the report.

(2) **Timing of report, sexual abuse.** — The report must be filed within thirty days after the obligation to report arises unless the person who is required to file the report has reasonable grounds to believe that the member will continue to sexually abuse the patient or will sexually abuse other patients, in which case the report must be filed forthwith.

(3) **Contents of report.** — The report must contain,

    (a)   the name of the person filing the report;
    (b)   the name of the member who is the subject of the report;
    (c)   an explanation of the alleged sexual abuse;
    (d)   if the grounds of the person filing the report are related to a particular patient of the member who is the subject of the report, the name of that patient, subject to subsection (4).

(4) **Patients not named without consent.** — The name of a patient who may have been sexually abused must not be included in a report unless the patient, or if the patient is incapable, the patient's representative, consents in writing to the inclusion of the patient's name.

(5) **If reporter providing psychotherapy.** — If a member who is required to file a report under section 85.1 is providing psychotherapy to the member who would be the subject of the report, the report must also

contain the opinion of the member filing the report, if he or she is able to form one, as to whether or not the member who is the subject of the report is likely to sexually abuse patients in the future.

85.4 (1) **Additional reports, psychotherapy.** — A member who files a report in respect of which subsection 85.3 (5) applies, shall file an additional report to the same College if the member ceases to provide psychotherapy to the member who was the subject of the first report.

(2) **Timing of additional report.** — The additional report must be filed forthwith.

85.5 (1) **Reporting by employers, etc.** — A person who terminates the employment or revokes, suspends or imposes restrictions on the privileges of a member or who dissolves a partnership, a health profession corporation or association with a member for reasons of professional misconduct, incompetence or incapacity shall file with the Registrar within thirty days after the termination, revocation, suspension, imposition or dissolution a written report setting out the reasons.

(2) **Same.** — If a person intended to terminate the employment of a member or to revoke the member's privileges for reasons of professional misconduct, incompetence or incapacity but the person did not do so because the member resigned or voluntarily relinquished his or her privileges, the person shall file with the Registrar within thirty days after the resignation or relinquishment a written report setting out the reasons upon which the person had intended to act.

(3) **Application.** — This section applies to every person, other than a patient, who employs or offers privileges to a member or associates in partnership or otherwise with a member for the purpose of offering health services.

85.6 **Immunity for reports.** — No action or other proceeding shall be instituted against a person for filing a report in good faith under section 85.1, 85.2, 85.4 or 85.5.

Funding for Therapy and Counselling

85.7 (1) **Funding provided by College.** — There shall be a program, established by the College, to provide funding for therapy and counselling for persons who, while patients, were sexually abused by members.

(2) **Funding governed by regulations.** — The funding shall be provided in accordance with the regulations made under the *Regulated Health Professions Act, 1991*.

(3) **Administration.** — The Patient Relations Committee shall administer the program.

(4) **Eligibility.** — A person is eligible for funding only if,

   (a)   there is a finding by a panel of the Discipline Committee that the person, while a patient, was sexually abused by a member; or

   (b)   the alternative requirements prescribed in the regulations made by the Council are satisfied.

(5) **Effect of appeal.** — A person's eligibility for funding under clause (4) (a) is not affected by an appeal from the panel's finding.

(6) **No assessment.** — A person is not required to undergo a psychological or other assessment before receiving funding.

(7) **Choice of therapist or counsellor.** — A person who is eligible for funding is entitled to choose any therapist or counsellor, subject to the following restrictions:

   1.   The therapist or counsellor must not be a person to whom the eligible person has any family relationship.

   2.   The therapist or counsellor must not be a person who, to the College's knowledge, has at any time or in any jurisdiction been found guilty of professional misconduct of a sexual nature or been found civilly or criminally liable for an act of a similar nature.

   3.   If the therapist or counsellor is not a member of a regulated health profession, the College may require the person to sign a document indicating that he or she understands that the therapist or counsellor is not subject to professional discipline.

(8) **Payment.** — Funding shall be paid only to the therapist or counsellor chosen by the person.

(9) **Use of funding.** — Funding shall be used only to pay for therapy or counselling and shall not be applied directly or indirectly for any other purpose.

(10) **Same.** — Funding may be used to pay for therapy or counselling that was provided before the person became eligible under subsection (4) but after the panel began its hearing into the matter.

(11) **Other coverage.** — The funding that is provided to a person shall be reduced by the amount that the Ontario Health Insurance Plan or a private insurer is required to pay for therapy or counselling for the person during the period of time during which funding may be provided for him or her under the program.

(12) **Right of recovery.** — The College is entitled to recover from the member, in a proceeding brought in a court of competent jurisdiction,

money paid in accordance with this section for therapy or counselling for an eligible person referred to in clause (4) (a).

(13) **Person not required to testify.** — The eligible person shall not be required to appear or testify in the proceeding.

Health Profession Corporations

85.8 **Professional corporations.** — Subject to the regulations made under subsection 43 (1) of the *Regulated Health Professions Act*, 1991 and the by-laws, one or more members of the same health profession may establish a health profession corporation for the purpose of practising their health profession, and the provisions of the *Business Corporations Act* that apply to professional corporations within the meaning of that Act apply to such a corporation.

85.9 **Notice of change of shareholder.** — A health profession corporation shall notify the Registrar within the time and in the form and manner determined under the by-laws of a change in the shareholders of the corporation.

85.10 **Application of Act, etc.** — The following things apply to a member who practises a health profession through a health profession corporation:

1. This Act and the regulations.
2. The statute governing the member's health profession, and the regulations and by-laws made under that statute.

85.11 (1) **Professional, fiduciary and ethical obligations to patients.** — The professional, fiduciary and ethical obligations of a member to a person on whose behalf the member is practising a health profession,

(a) are not diminished by the fact that the member is practising through a health profession corporation; and

(b) apply equally to the corporation and to its directors, officers, shareholders, agents and employees.

(2) **Investigation.** — Subsections (3) and (4) apply if an action or the conduct of a member practising on behalf of a health profession corporation is the subject of one of the following:

1. A complaint.
2. A mandatory report.
3. A specified allegation of professional misconduct or incompetence.
4. An investigation, review or hearing by the Board.
5. An investigation, inspection or assessment by an investigator or assessor appointed under the Code.
6. An inquiry by a board of inquiry or by the Registrar.

7.   A referral to the Discipline Committee or the Fitness to Practise Committee.

8.   A hearing by a committee of the college.

(3) **Same.** — In the circumstances described in subsection (2), any power that the College may exercise in respect of the member may be exercised in respect of the health profession corporation.

(4) **Liability.** — In the circumstances described in subsection (2), the health profession corporation is jointly and severally liable with the member for all fines, costs and expenses that the member is ordered to pay.

85.12 **Conflict in duties.** — If there is a conflict between a member's duty to a patient, the college or the public and the member's duty to a health profession corporation as a director or officer of the corporation, the duty to the patient, the college or the public prevails.

85.13 **Restrictions apply to corporation's certificate.** — A term, condition or limitation imposed on the certificate of registration of a member practising a health profession through a health profession corporation applies to the certificate of authorization of the corporation in relation to the practice of the health profession through the member.

85.14 (1) **Prohibition, professional misconduct.** — In the course of practising a health profession, a health profession corporation shall not do, or fail to do, something that would constitute professional misconduct if a member of the health profession did, or failed to do, it.

(2) **Prohibition, contraventions.** — A health profession corporation shall not contravene any provision of,

(a)   this Act or the regulations; or

(b)   the statute governing the health profession or the regulations or by-laws made under that statute.

(3) **Prohibition, corporate matters.** — A health profession corporation shall not practise a health profession when it does not satisfy the requirements for a professional corporation under subsection 3.2 (2) of the *Business Corporations Act*.

Miscellaneous

86. (1) **Right to use French.** — A person has the right to use French in all dealings with the College.

(2) **Council to ensure right.** — The Council shall take all reasonable measures and make all reasonable plans to ensure that persons may use French in all dealings with the College.

(3) **Definition.** — In this section,

"dealings" means any service or procedure available to the public or to members and includes giving or receiving communications, information or notices, making applications, taking examinations or tests and participating in programs or in hearings or reviews.

(4) **Limitation.** — A person's right under subsection (1) is subject to the limits that are reasonable in the circumstances.

87. **Injunctions.** — The College may apply to the Ontario Court (General Division) for an order directing a person to comply with a provision of the health profession Act, this Code, the *Regulated Health Professions Act, 1991*, the regulations under those Acts or the by-laws made under clause 94 (1) (1.2), (1.3) (s), (t), (t.1), (t.2), (v), (w) or (y).

88. **Evidence of Registrar.** — A statement purporting to be certified by the Registrar under the seal of the College as a statement of information from the records kept by the Registrar in the course of his or her duties is admissible in court as proof, in the absence of evidence to the contrary, of the information in it without proof of the Registrar's appointment or signature or of the seal of the College.

89. (1) **Limitation period.** — No person who is or was a member is liable to any action arising out of negligence or malpractice in respect of professional services requested of or rendered by the person unless the action is commenced within one year after the date when the person commencing the action knew or ought to have known the fact or facts upon which the negligence or malpractice is alleged.

(2) **Transition.** — During the first year this section is in force, it does not operate to shorten the time period, provided by statutory law as it was immediately before this section comes into force, during which an action could be brought.

(3) **Limitation of liability.** — A health profession corporation that holds or held a certificate of authorization is not liable to any action arising out of negligence or malpractice in respect of professional services requested of, or rendered by, the corporation unless the action is commenced within one year after the date when the person commencing the action knew or ought to have known the fact or facts upon which the alleged negligence or malpractice is based.

Note: On a day to be named by proclamation of the Lieutenant Governor, section 89 is repealed by the Statutes of Ontario, 2002, chapter 24, Schedule B, section 25.

90. **Repealed:** [1993, c. 37, s. 24].

91. (1) **Service by mail.** — A notice or a decision to be given under the health profession Act, this Code or the regulations to a person may be given by mail.

(2) **Idem.** — If a notice or decision under the health profession Act, this Code or the regulations is sent by prepaid first class mail addressed to the person at the person's last known address, there is a rebuttable presumption that the notice was received by the person on the fifth day after the notice was mailed.

92. (1) **Making false representations to obtain certificates.** — Every person who makes a representation, knowing it to be false, for the purpose of having a certificate of registration or a certificate of authorization issued is guilty of an offence and on conviction is liable to a fine of not more than $10,000.

(2) **Assisting the making of false representation.** — Every person who knowingly assists a person in committing an offence under subsection (1) is guilty of an offence and on conviction is liable to a fine of not more than $10,000.

92.1 **Protection for reporters from reprisals.** — No person shall do anything, or refrain from doing anything, relating to another person's employment or to a contract providing for the provision of services by that other person, in retaliation for that other person filing a report or making a complaint as long as the report was filed, or the complaint was made, in good faith.

93. (1) **Offence.** — Every person who contravenes an order made under section 45 or 47 is guilty of an offence and on conviction is liable to a fine of not more than $10,000 for a first offence and not more than $20,000 for a subsequent offence.

(2) **Idem.** — Every person who contravenes subsection 76 (3) is guilty of an offence and on conviction is liable to a fine of not more than $10,000.

(3) **Idem.** — Every person who contravenes subsection 82 (2) or (3) is guilty of an offence and on conviction is liable to a fine of not more than $5,000 for a first offence and not more than $10,000 for a subsequent offence.

(4) **Same.** — Every person who contravenes subsection 85.1 (1), 85.2 (1), 85.4 (1) or 85.5 (1) or section 92.1 is guilty of an offence and on conviction is liable to a fine of not more than $25,000.

93.1 **Forms.** — The College may require that forms approved by the College be used for any purpose under the Act.

94. (1) **By-laws.** — The Council may make by-laws relating to the administrative and internal affairs of the College and, without limiting the generality of the foregoing, the Council may make by-laws,

    (a)   adopting a seal for the College;

    (b)   providing for the execution of documents by the College;

    (c)   respecting banking and finance;

(d)   fixing the financial year of the College and providing for the audit of the accounts and transactions of the College;

(d.1)   respecting the election of Council members, including the requirements for members to be able to vote, electoral districts and election recounts;

(d.2)   respecting the qualification and terms of office of Council members who are elected;

(d.3)   prescribing conditions disqualifying elected members from sitting on the Council and governing the removal of disqualified Council members;

(e)   providing procedures for the election of the President and Vice-President of the College, the selection of the chairs of the committees, the filling of a vacancy in those offices, and setting out the duties and powers of the President, Vice-President and the chairs;

(f)   respecting the calling, holding and conducting of the Council meetings and respecting the duties of the Council's members;

(g)   respecting the calling, holding and conducting of meetings of the members;

(g.1)   providing that a meeting of the Council or of members or a meeting of a committee or of a panel that is held for any purpose other than for the conducting of a hearing may be held in any manner that allows all the persons participating to communicate with each other simultaneously and instantaneously;

(g.2)   prescribing what constitutes a conflict of interest for members of the Council or a committee and regulating or prohibiting the carrying out of the duties of those members in cases in which there is a conflict of interest;

(h)   providing for the remuneration of the members of the Council and committees other than persons appointed by the Lieutenant Governor in Council and for the payment of the expenses of the Council and committees in the conduct of their business;

(h.1)   respecting the filling of vacancies on the Council or on committees;

(h.2)   providing for the composition of committees;

(h.3)   respecting the qualification, selection, appointment and terms of office of members of committees required by subsection 10 (1) who are not members of the Council;

(h.4)   prescribing conditions disqualifying committee members from sitting on committees required under subsection 10 (1) and governing the removal of disqualified committee members;

(i)   providing for the appointment, powers and duties of committees other than the committees required by subsection 10 (1);

(j)   delegating to the Executive Committee powers and duties of the Council, other than the power to make, amend or revoke regulations and by-laws;

(k)   providing for a code of ethics for the members;

(l)   providing for the appointment of inspectors for the purposes of regulations made under clause 95 (1) (h);

(l.1)   respecting the maintenance of the register kept by the Registrar and providing for the issuing of certificates when information contained in the register is made available to the public under subsection 23 (3);

(l.2)   prescribing information as information to be kept in the register for the purposes of clause 23 (2) (g) and designating information kept in the register as public for the purposes of paragraph 4 of subsection 23 (3);

(l.3)   requiring members to give the College their home addresses and such other information as may be specified in the by-law about themselves and the places they practise the profession, the services they provide there, their participation in continuing education programs and the names, business addresses, telephone numbers and facsimile numbers of their associates, partners, employers and employees and prescribing the form and manner in which the information shall be given;

(l.4)   respecting the duties and office of the Registrar;

(m)   providing procedures for the making, amending and revoking of by-laws;

(n)   prescribing forms and providing for their use;

(o)   respecting the management of the property of the College;

(p)   authorizing the College to make arrangements for the indemnity of members against professional liability and providing levies to be paid by members;

(q)   respecting membership of the College in a national organization of bodies with similar functions, the payment of annual assessments and representation at meetings;

(r)   authorizing the making of grants to advance scientific knowledge or the education of persons wishing to practise the profession, to maintain or improve the standards of practice of the profession or to provide public information about, and encourage interest in, the past and present role of the profession in society;

(s) requiring members to pay annual fees, fees upon application for a certificate and upon registration and fees for examinations, appeals from examinations, election recounts and continuing education programs and for anything the Registrar or a committee of the College is required or authorized to do and requiring members to pay penalties for the late payment of any fee;

(t) specifying the amount of any fee or penalty required under clause (s);

(t.1) prescribing the form and manner in which a health profession corporation shall notify the Registrar of a change in the shareholders of the corporation and the time period for doing so;

(t.2) requiring the payment of fees upon application for a certificate of authorization and for the issue or renewal of a certificate of authorization and specifying the amount of such fees;

(u) requiring persons to pay fees, set by the Registrar or by by-law, for anything the Registrar is required or authorized to do;

(v) requiring members to pay specified amounts to pay for the program required under section 85.7, including amounts that are different for different members or classes of members and including amounts,

    (i) that are specified in the by-law,

    (ii) that are calculated according to a method set out in the by-law, or

    (iii) that are determined by a person specified in the by-law;

(w) requiring members to participate in an arrangement set up by the College in which members pay a person such amounts as may be determined by the person for the members or for classes of members and the person pays amounts to the College to pay for the program required under section 85.7;

(x) authorizing the Patient Relations Committee to require therapists and counsellors who are providing therapy or counselling that is funded through the program required under section 85.7 and persons who are receiving such therapy or counselling, to provide a written statement, signed in each case by the therapist or counsellor and by the person, containing details of the therapist's or counsellor's training and experience, and confirming that therapy or counselling is being provided and that the funds received are being devoted only to that purpose;

(y) requiring members to have professional liability insurance that satisfies the requirements specified in the by-laws or to belong to a specified association that provides protection against professional liability and requiring members to give proof of the insurance or membership to the Registrar in the manner set out in the by-laws;

(z) respecting the designation of life or honourary members of the College and prescribing their rights and privileges;

(z.1) exempting any member or class of member from a by-law made under this section;

(z.2) specifying or setting out anything that is required to be specified or set out under this subsection.

(2) **Circulation of certain by-laws.** — A by-law shall not be made under clause (1) (l.2), (l.3), (s), (t), (v), (w) or (y) unless the proposed by-law is circulated to every member at least 60 days before it is approved by the Council.

(2.1) **Exception.** — Despite subsection (2), the Council may, with the approval of the Minister, exempt a by-law from the requirement that it be circulated or abridge the 60-day period referred to in subsection (2) to such lesser period as the Minister may determine.

(3) **Copies of by-laws.** — A copy of the by-laws made by the Council shall be given to the Minister and to each member and shall be available for public inspection in the office of the College.

(4) **Unanimous by-laws, etc.** — A by-law or resolution signed by all the members of the Council is as valid and effective as if passed at a meeting of the Council called, constituted and held for the purpose.

(5) **Application.** — Subsections (3) and (4) apply to by-laws made under this section or under a health profession Act.

95. (1) **Regulations.** — Subject to the approval of the Lieutenant Governor in Council and with prior review of the Minister, the Council may make regulations,

(a) prescribing classes of certificates of registration and imposing terms, conditions and limitations on the certificates of registration of a class;

(b) respecting applications for certificates of registration or classes of them and the issuing, suspension, revocation and expiration of the certificates or classes of them;

(c) prescribing standards and qualifications for the issue of certificates of registration;

(d) prescribing certain registration requirements as non-exemptible requirements for the purposes of subsection 18 (3) and 22 (8);

(e) defining specialties in the profession, providing for certificates relating to those specialties, the qualifications for and suspension and revocation of those certificates and governing the use of prescribed terms, titles or designations by members indicating a specialization in the profession;

(f) requiring, for purposes associated with the registration of members, the successful completion of examinations as set, from time to time, by the College, other persons or associations of persons and providing for an appeal of the results of the examinations;

(g) governing or prohibiting the delegation by or to members of controlled acts set out in subsection 27 (2) of the *Regulated Health Professions Act, 1991*;

(h) requiring and providing for the inspection and examination of premises used in connection with the practice of the profession and of equipment, books, accounts, reports and records of members relating to their practices;

(i) prescribing what constitutes a conflict of interest in the practice of the profession and regulating or prohibiting the practice of the profession in cases in which there is a conflict of interest;

(j) defining professional misconduct for the purposes of clause 51 (1) (c);

(k) designating acts of professional misconduct that must be reported;

(l) respecting the promotion or advertising of the practice of the profession;

(m) respecting the reporting and publication of decisions of panels;

(n) prescribing the standards of practice of the profession and prohibiting members from acting beyond the scope of practice of the profession in the course of practising the profession;

(o) requiring members to keep prescribed records in respect of their practice;

(p) regulating or prohibiting the use of terms, titles and designations by members in respect of their practices;

(q) prescribing alternative requirements for eligibility for funding under clause 85.7 (4) (b);

(r) prescribing a quality assurance program;

(s) respecting the giving of notice of meetings and hearings that are to be open to the public;

(t) providing for the exemption of any member from the regulations made by the Council;

(u) prescribing anything that is referred to in the health profession Act or this Code as being prescribed.

(1.1) Standards of practice. — A regulation under clause (1) (n) may adopt by reference, in whole or in part and with such changes as are considered necessary, any code, standard or guideline relating to standards of practice of the profession and require compliance with the code, standard or guideline as adopted.

(1.2) Rolling incorporation. — If a regulation under subsection (1.1) so provides, a code, standard or guideline adopted by reference shall be a reference to it, as amended from time to time, and whether the amendment was made before or after the regulation was made.

(1.3) Copies available for inspection. — A copy of a code, standard or guideline adopted by reference under subsection (1.1) shall be available for public inspection during normal business hours in the office of the College.

(1.4) Circulation. — A regulation shall not be made under subsection (1) unless the proposed regulation is circulated to every member at least 60 days before it is approved by the Council.

(1.5) Same. — Subsection (1.4) does not apply to a regulation if the Minister required that the Council make the regulation under clause 5 (1) (c) of the *Regulated Health Professions Act, 1991*.

(1.6) Exception. — Despite subsection (1.4), the Council may, with the approval of the Minister, exempt a regulation from the requirement that it be circulated or abridge the 60-day period referred to in subsection (1.4) to such lesser period as the Minister may determine.

(2) Idem. — Regulations made under clause (1) (r) may require members to participate in continuing education programs.

(2.1) Same. — Regulations made under clause (1) (r) of subsection (1) may,

    (a)   authorize the Quality Assurance Committee to require individual members whose knowledge, skills and judgment have been assessed under section 82 and found to be unsatisfactory to participate in specified continuing education programs;

    (b)   authorize the Quality Assurance Committee to direct the Registrar to impose terms, conditions or limitations, for a specified period not exceeding six months, on the certificate of registration of a member whose knowledge, skills and judgment have been assessed or reassessed under section 82 and found to be unsatisfactory, or who has failed to participate in specified continuing education programs as required by the Committee or has not completed those programs successfully;

    (c)   authorize the Quality Assurance Committee to direct the Registrar to remove terms, conditions or limitations imposed under a regulation made under clause (b) before the end of the specified period, if the Committee is satisfied that the member's knowledge, skills and judgment are now satisfactory;

(d) authorize the Quality Assurance Committee to require a member to undergo a psychological or other assessment if a matter respecting the member is referred to the Committee under subsection 26 (3) or section 79.1;

(e) authorize the Quality Assurance Committee, after receiving a report of an assessment required under a regulation made under clause (d), to require the member to undertake specified measures, such as receiving education, therapy or counselling;

(f) authorize the Quality Assurance Committee to direct the Registrar to impose terms, conditions or limitations on the member's certificate of registration, for a specified period not exceeding six months, if,

    (i) the member refuses to undergo an assessment,

    (ii) the Committee has required the member to undertake specified measures which have not yet been completed, or

    (iii) the member refuses to undertake the specified measures;

(g) authorize the Quality Assurance Committee to direct the Registrar to remove terms, conditions or limitations imposed under a regulation made under clause (f) before the end of the specified period, if the Committee is satisfied that the terms, conditions or limitations are no longer needed.

(2.2) **Same.** — If the Council makes a regulation as described in clause (2.1) (b) or (f), it shall also make a regulation providing that no direction shall be given to the Registrar unless the member has been given notice of the Quality Assurance Committee's intention to give the direction and at least fourteen days to make written submissions to the Committee.

(3) **Scope of regulations.** — A regulation may be general or particular in its application.

2. SAMPLE REGULATION 858/93 UNDER THE *MIDWIFERY ACT, 1991*: PROFESSIONAL MISCONDUCT

1. The following are acts of professional misconduct for the purposes of clause 51 (1) (c) of the Health Professions Procedural Code:

The Practice of the Profession and the Care of, and Relationship with, Clients

1. Contravening a term, condition or limitation imposed on the member's certificate of registration.

2. Contravening a standard of practice of the profession.

3. Doing anything to a client for a therapeutic, preventative, palliative, diagnostic, cosmetic or other health-related purpose in a situation in which a consent is required by law, without such a consent.

4. Delegating a controlled act in contravention of the Act, the *Regulated Health Professions Act, 1991*, or the regulations under either of those Acts.

5. Abusing a client, physically or verbally, or taking unfair advantage of the position of confidence and authority in relation to a client which the midwife has as a professional.

6. Practising the profession while under the influence of any substance, or while suffering from illness or other dysfunction which the member knows or ought to know impairs the member's ability to practise.

7. Prescribing, dispensing or selling drugs for an improper purpose.

8. Discontinuing professional services that are needed unless,
   i.   the client requests the discontinuation,
   ii.   alternative services acceptable to the client are arranged,
   iii. there is no longer a relationship of trust and confidence between the midwife and the client and the client is given a reasonable opportunity to arrange alternative services, or
   iv.   the client requests services inconsistent with the standards of practice of the profession and the midwife has adhered to the standard of practice for discontinuing care in such circumstances.

9. Discontinuing professional services provided to a community or clientele without reasonable cause, unless adequate notice has been given or adequate alternative arrangements for services have been made.

10. Failing without reasonable cause to provide to a client continuity of care as defined in College practice guidelines.

11. Failing without reasonable cause to provide services to a client during labour and birth in the client's chosen birthplace.

12. Practising the profession while the member is in a conflict of interest.

13. Giving information about a client to a person other than the client or his or her authorized representative except with the consent of the client or his or her authorized representative or as required or allowed by law.

14. Breaching an agreement with a client relating to professional services for the client or fees for such services.

15. Inappropriately using a term, title or designation in respect of the member's practice.

16. Using a name other than the member's name as set out in the register, in the course of providing or offering to provide services within the scope of practice of the profession.

Record Keeping and Reports

17. Failing to keep records as required by the regulations.

18. Falsifying a record relating to the member's practice.

19. Failing, without reasonable cause, to provide a report or certificate relating to an examination or treatment performed by the member, within a reasonable time to the client or his or her authorized representative after a client or his or her authorized representative has requested such a report or certificate.

20. Signing or issuing, in the member's professional capacity, a document that the member knows contains a false or misleading statement.

Business Practices

21. Submitting an account or charge for services that the member knows is false or misleading.

22. Charging a fee that is excessive in relation to the services charged for.

23. Failing to inform the client of the fee to be charged for services before the commencement of the services.

24. Charging a fee or accepting payment from a client in respect of a service for which the member has been paid by the Ministry of Health.

25. Charging for midwifery services on a fee for service arrangement.

26. Charging a block fee without specifying,
    i.   the services covered by the fee,
    ii.   the amount of the fee,
    iii.   the arrangements for paying the fee,
    iv.   the rights and obligations of the midwife and the client if the relationship between them is terminated before all the services are provided.

27. Charging a fee, in addition to a block fee described in paragraph 26, for an undertaking to be available to provide services to the client.

28. Failing to itemize an account for professional services, if requested to do so by the client or the person or agency who is to pay, in whole or in part, for the services.

Miscellaneous Matters

29. Contravening the Act, the *Regulated Health Professions Act, 1991* or the regulations under either of those Acts.

30. Contravening a federal, provincial, or territorial law, or a municipal by-law so as to prejudice the interests of a client.

31. Influencing a client to change his or her will or other testamentary instrument.

32. Engaging in conduct or performing an act, in the course of practising the profession, that, having regard to all the circumstances, would reasonably be regarded by members as disgraceful, dishonourable or unprofessional.

3. HOW TO FIND LEGISLATION ONLINE

Three Websites That are Thorough and Easy to Use

Access to Justice Network provides comprehensive legislative materials from all provinces and the federal government, including regulations, and other legal information.

Go to <http://www.acjnet.org>.

Through this network, or independently, you can also access the following:

Government of Ontario e-laws website allows you to easily search Ontario statutes, regulations, bills and legislative records.

Go to <http://www.e-laws.gov.on.ca>.

Canadian Legal Information Institute (CanLII) not only provides statutes, but is a free site for accessing a growing body of case law from courts and tribunals across the country.

Go to <http://www.canlii.org/index_en.html>.

Appendix II

CONTACTS AND CHECKPOINTS

COLLEGE CONTACT INFORMATION

	College	Address	Telephone	Fax	Website
1	College of Audiologists and Speech-Language Pathologists of Ontario	160 Bloor St. East, Suite 1125 Toronto, Ontario M4W 1B9	(416) 975-5347 or 1-800-993-9459	(416) 975-8394	www.caslpo.com
2	College of Chiropodists of Ontario	180 Dundas St. West, Suite 2102 Toronto, Ontario M5G 1Z8	(416) 542-1333 or toll free (in Ontario) 1-877-232-7653	(416) 542-1666	www.cocoo.on.ca
3	College of Chiropractors of Ontario	130 Bloor St. West, Suite 902 Toronto, Ontario M5S 1N5	(416) 922-6355	(416) 925-9610	www.cco.on.ca
4	College of Dental Hygienists of Ontario	69 Bloor St. East, Suite 300 Toronto, Ontario M4W 1A9	(416) 961-6324 or toll-free (in Ontario) 1-800-268-2346	(416) 961-6028	www.cdho.org

	College	Address	Telephone	Fax	Website
5	Royal College of Dental Surgeons of Ontario	6 Crescent Road Toronto, Ontario M4W 1T1	(416) 961-6555 or 1-800-565-4591	(416) 961-5814	www.rcdso.org
6	College of Dental Technologists of Ontario	2100 Ellesmere Road Suite 260 Scarborough, Ontario M1H 3B7	(416) 438-5003 or (within Canada) 1-877-391-CDTO (2386)	(416) 438-5004	www.cdto.ca
7	College of Denturists of Ontario	180 Bloor St. West, Suite 903 Toronto, Ontario M5S 2V6	(416) 925-6331 or toll-free 1- 888-236-4326	(416) 925-6332	www.denturists-cdo.com
8	College of Dietitians of Ontario	438 University Avenue Suite 1810 (Box 40) Toronto, Ontario M5G 2K8	(416) 598-1725 or 1-800-668-4990	(416) 598-0274	www.cdo.on.ca
9	College of Massage Therapists of Ontario	1867 Yonge St., Suite 810 Toronto, Ontario M5S 1Y5	(416) 489-2626 or toll-free (in Ontario) 1-800-465-1933	(416) 489-2625	www.cmto.com
10	College of Medical Laboratory Technologists of Ontario	10 Bay St., Suite 330 Toronto, Ontario M5J 2R8	(416) 861-9605 or toll-free 1-800-323-9672	(416) 861-0934	www.cmlto.com
11	College of Medical Radiation Technologists of Ontario	170 Bloor St. West, Suite 1001 Toronto, Ontario M5S 1T9	(416) 975-4353 or toll-free 1-800-563-5847	(416) 975-4355	www.cmrto.org

	College	Address	Telephone	Fax	Website
12	College of Midwives of Ontario	55 St. Clair Avenue West Suite 812, Box 27 Toronto, Ontario M4V 2Y7	(416) 327-0874	(416) 327-8219	www.cmo.on.ca
13	College of Nurses of Ontario	101 Davenport Road Toronto, Ontario M5R 3P1	(416) 928-0900 or toll-free (in Ontario) 1-800-387-5526	(416) 928-6507	www.cno.org
14	College of Occupational Therapists of Ontario	20 Bay St., Suite 900 Toronto, Ontario M5J 2N8	(416) 214-1177 or toll-free 1-800-890-6570	(416) 214-1173	www.coto.org
15	College of Opticians of Ontario	85 Richmond St. West Suite 902 Toronto, Ontario M5H 2C9	(416) 368-3616 or toll-free (in Ontario) 1-800-990-9793	(416) 368-2713	www.coptont.org
16	College of Optometrists of Ontario	6 Crescent Road Second Floor Toronto, Ontario M4W 1T1	(416) 962-4071 or toll-free 1-888-825-2554	(416) 962-4073	www.collegeoptom.on.ca
17	Ontario College of Pharmacists	483 Huron St. Toronto, Ontario M5R 2R4	(416) 962-4861 or 1-800-220-1921	(416) 847-8200	www.ocpinfo.com
18	College of Physicians and Surgeons of Ontario	80 College St. West 10th Floor Toronto, Ontario M5G 2E2	(416) 967-2603 or 1-800-268-7096	(416) 961-3330	www.cpso.on.ca

19	College of Physiotherapists of Ontario	230 Richmond St. West 10th Floor Toronto, Ontario M5V 1V6	(416) 591-3828 or 1-800-583-5885	(416) 591-3834	www.collegept.org
20	College of Psychologists of Ontario	110 Eglinton Avenue West Suite 500 Toronto, Ontario M4R 1A3	(416) 961-8817 or 1-800-489-8388	(416) 961-2635	www.cpo.on.ca
21	College of Respiratory Therapists of Ontario	180 Dundas St. West Suite 2103 Toronto, Ontario M5G 1Z8	(416) 591-7800 or toll-free (in Ontario) 1-800-261-0528	(416) 591-7890	www.crto.on.ca
22	Board of Directors of Drugless Therapy – Naturopathy	112 Adelaide St. East Toronto, Ontario M5C 1E2	(416) 866-8383	(416) 866-2175	Website address not available

SAMPLE POLICIES: ZERO TOLERANCE OF SEXUAL ABUSE/ HARASSMENT

The College of Dental Technologists — a college regulated under the *RHPA*

The College of Dental Technologists of Ontario has a policy of "zero tolerance" for sexual abuse and harassment of patients, clients, and co-workers in the practice of dental technology.

The College's Policy on sexual abuse and harassment is set out below:

1. Prevent sexual abuse and harassment by educating and informing members of policy development, complaints processes and guidelines for proper professional relationships;
2. Train College staff, Council and Committee members to be responsive, sensitive and supportive to the needs of complainants and members;
3. Inform the public and the target groups mentioned above of their rights, the College's policies and the complaints processes.

Definition

"Patient" as an individual receiving professional treatment referred by a dentist or a health practitioner;

"Client" as a dentist or a health practitioner primarily responsible for the treatment of a patient;

"Co-worker" as a person working in the same place as the dental technologist, including employee of the dental technologist, or a person working in a place where the dental technologist would have professional contact in his/her practice;

"Sexual Abuse" as defined in the *Regulated Health Professions Act, 1991*:

- Sexual intercourse or other forms of physical sexual relations between the member and the patient;
- touching, of a sexual nature, of the patient by the member; or
- behaviour or remarks, of a sexual nature by the member towards the patient;

"Sexual Harassment in the workplace" includes:

- unwelcome sexual advances (verbal, written or physical);
- requests or demands for sexual favours;
- any other type of sexually oriented conduct;
- verbal abuse or "kidding" that is sex oriented;

when

- the conduct has the purpose or the effect of interfering with an individual's work performance or creating an intimidating, hostile, or offensive work environment/relation; and/or
- submission to such conduct is either an explicit or implicit term or condition of employment; and/or
- submission to or rejection of the conduct is used as a basis for making employment decisions.

NO. 6

PREVENTION OF SEXUAL ABUSE

The goal of these guidelines is to:

- Protect the public
- Respond promptly and sensitively to a complainant while protecting the rights of the accused Naturopathic Doctor to a fair hearing
- Safeguard the privacy of the complainant and the Naturopathic Doctor
- Avoid delays; complete the investigation within a reasonable time frame
- Have as non-confrontational an investigation as possible

Sexual Abuse includes, but is not limited to:

- Sexual intercourse or other forms of physical relations between a Naturopathic Doctor and a client
- Sexual touching of the client by the Naturopathic Doctor
- Behaviour or remarks of a sexual nature by the Naturopathic Doctor towards the client

Examples of inappropriate behaviour include:

- Sex between a Naturopathic Doctor and a client, whether it is initiated by the client or not
- Engaging in any conduct with a client which is sexual, or may be reasonably interpreted as sexual, including but not limited to sexual intercourse, genital to genital contact, genital to anal contact, oral to genital contact, oral to anal contact, oral to oral contact except for CPR, touching breasts or genitals except for the purpose of appropriate physical examination or treatment or where the client has refused or withdrawn consent
- Encouraging the client to masturbate in the presence of the Naturopathic Doctor or masturbation by the Naturopathic Doctor when the client is present
- Any behaviour, gestures or expressions that are seductive or sexually demeaning to a client
- Inappropriate procedures including, but not limited to, inappropriate disrobing or draping practices that reflect a lack of respect for the client's privacy or deliberately watching a client dress or undress instead of providing privacy
- Subjecting a client to a genital, breast, anal or rectal examination in the presence of medical students or other parties without the explicit written consent of the client, or when consent has been withdrawn
- Examination or touching of the genitals without gloves
- Inappropriate comments about or to a client including, but not limited to, making sexual comments, or comments that could be interpreted as sexual, about a client's body or clothing
- Making sexual or sexually demeaning comments to a client, sexual innuendo or jokes, or criticism of the client's sexual orientation
- Making comments about sexual performance during an examination or consultation, except when the examination or consultation is pertinent to the issue of sexual function or dysfunction
- Requesting details of sexual history or sexual likes or dislikes, when not clinically indicated for the type of consultation, other than the normal questions associated with gathering information during a history or homeopathic consultation
- Making a request to date

- Initiation by the Naturopathic Doctor of conversation regarding the sexual problems, preferences or fantasies of the Naturopathic Doctor
- Kissing

Any conduct will be considered 'sexual in nature' if it is inherently sexual conduct, e.g. touching the client's sexual organs other than when warranted or called for in the course of an examination; or it is potentially neutral contact done with a sexual motivation, e.g. patting the client's knee.

'Sexual in nature' does not include touching, behaviour or remarks of a clinical nature appropriate to the service provided.

The penalty for infractions could include revocation of the Naturopathic Doctor's license.

Naturopathic Doctors are required to report any instances of abuse by a colleague or other health care provider. Complaints will be acted upon but the name of the complainant will be kept confidential until formal charges are laid.

To avoid unintentional transgressions, Naturopathic Doctors are required to:

- Have someone else in the examination room when doing examinations of the genitals, breasts or anus, unless the client specifically requests otherwise (this might include a support person of the client or a member of the Naturopathic Doctor's office staff and should be handled in such a way that the privacy of the client is protected as much as possible)
- Explain all procedures in detail prior to the examination, no matter how routine

Naturopathic Doctors should:

- Ask permission before asking questions of an intimate nature, or before touching
- Create a climate of open communication to reduce the power imbalance inherent in the practitioner/client relationship

- Encourage clients to ask questions, express any discomfort, and to take personal responsibility in making health care choices

When a professional association and a friendship exist at the same time, the Naturopathic Doctor should ensure that they are kept quite separate.

If a more intimate relationship is to develop, the Naturopathic Doctor is responsible for terminating the professional relationship and providing appropriate referral. After such closure, a cooling off period of at least two years must be respected before proceeding with any further relationship. However, if counseling has been a major component of the professional relationship, sexual contact is prohibited for all time.

June 25, 1999

SAMPLE STATUTORY PRACTICE GUIDELINES OF A COLLEGE UNDER *THE REGULATED HEALTH PROFESSIONS ACT, 1991, HEALTH PROFESSIONS PROCEDURAL CODE*, SECTIONS 85.1, 85.2

College of Medical Laboratory Technologists of Ontario

Practice Guidelines for the Prevention of Sexual Abuse: Guidelines for Professional Behaviour for Medical Laboratory Technologists

College of Medical Laboratory Technologists of Ontario

OVERVIEW

These Practice Guidelines were developed to set the standard for professional conduct among all MLTs. The Regulated Health Professions Act, 1991 (the RHPA) requires that each College have guidelines for the conduct of members with their patients aimed specifically at preventing or dealing with sexual abuse of patients. These guidelines, which have been developed by the Patient Relations Committee, have 5 specific purposes.

- To ensure members understand the CMLTO's philosophy of zero tolerance as it relates to sexual abuse.

- To provide members with a clear understanding of what is meant by "sexual abuse".
- To ensure members are aware of their reporting obligations regarding sexual abuse and child abuse.
- To provide members with guidelines for appropriate behaviour.
- To outline the penalties for failing to comply with these guidelines.

Practice Guidelines for the Prevention of Sexual Abuse

INTRODUCTION
ZERO TOLERANCE

The CMLTO has adopted a philosophy of zero tolerance as it relates to sexual abuse. This means that:

- No act of sexual abuse is ever acceptable and sexual abuse must never be tolerated;
- The College recognizes the seriousness and extent of injury sexual abuse causes the victim and others related to the victim;
- Medical laboratory technologists must accept that broad definitions of sexual abuse capture a diversity of individual and cultural viewpoints;
- If a patient is uncomfortable with words or behaviour used by a technologist, then the technologist must be sensitive to the discomfort and change the words or behaviour.

DEFINITION OF SEXUAL ABUSE

Sexual abuse is defined in the RHPA to include sexual intercourse or other forms of sexual relations; touching of a sexual nature and behaviour and remarks of a sexual nature.

The RHPA states that "sexual nature" does not include touching, behaviour or remarks of a clinical nature appropriate to the service provided. It is important for a member to understand that it is always inappropriate for a health professional to have a sexual relationship with a patient and that a patient can never consent to sexual abuse. This is a reflection of the real and perceived power imbalances that exist between health professionals and their patients.

REPORTING OBLIGATIONS REPORTING OF SEXUAL ABUSE

The RHPA requires members to file a written report if they have reasonable grounds, obtained in the course of their practice, that a patient has been sexually abused by another regulated health professional. Failure to comply with these reporting obligations carries a potential $25,000.00 fine and may also result in charges of professional misconduct. If you have reasonable grounds, obtained in the course of your practice that a patient has been sexually abused by another health professional, you must:

- Submit a written report within 30 days to the Registrar of that health professional's College.
- Submit the report forthwith if you have reason to believe that the abuse will continue, or abuse of other patients will occur.
- Only include the name of the patient if you have her/his written consent to do so.
- Use your best efforts to advise the patient of the requirement to file a report before doing so if the information the report is based on was obtained from the patient.
- Remember that you are not required to file a report if you do not know the name of the health professional in question.
- Keep in mind that the RHPA provides protection to a person who files a report in good faith.

REPORTING OF CHILD ABUSE

Under the Child and Family Services Act (CFSA) health professionals, including Medical Laboratory Technologists, are required to report when a child is in need of protection. Failure to report is an offence that carries a potential penalty of $1,000.00. If you suspect a child is or may be in need of protection you must report immediately and directly to the Children's Aid Society. Remember you have an ongoing duty to report, despite previous reports that may have been made, and you cannot rely on others to make the report. The CFSA also provides protection to individuals who file reports in good faith.

If a member is in doubt about their reporting obligations, they may contact the College or the Children's Aid Society for guidance.

GUIDELINES FOR APPROPRIATE BEHAVIOUR

Members are expected to conduct their practice at all times in keeping with the Professional Code of Ethics, RHPA, and standards of practice of the profession. Members should familiarize themselves with the MLT Boundaries of Practice Guidebook, which provides solid advice and information that can assist them to manage their relationships with patients.

Members should keep the following principles in mind at all times;

- Talk before you touch
- Touch only when necessary
- Get the patient's consent
- Assume nothing
- Show respect for the patient
- Maintain the patient's dignity
- Respect cultural diversity
- Create a safe environment
- Maintain confidentiality
- Remember patients can change their mind

PENALTIES

Sexual abuse is a serious offence. If a panel of the Discipline Committee finds a member guilty of sexually abusing a patient, it must:

- Reprimand the member
- Revoke the member's certificate of registration if the sexual abuse consisted of, or included, any of the following:
    - Sexual intercourse
    - Genital to genital, genital to anal, genital to oral, oral to genital, or oral to anal contact
    - Masturbation of the member by, or in the presence of, the patient
    - Masturbation of the patient by the member
    - Encouragement of the patient by the member to masturbate in the presence of the member

In addition, the panel may:

- Revoke the member's certificate of registration (even if the abuse does not meet the above criteria)
- Suspend the member's certificate of registration
- Impose specified terms, conditions and limitations on the member's certificate of registration
- Require the member to pay a fine of not more than $35,000.00
- Require the member to pay all or part of the costs incurred by the College in investigating the matter and conducting the hearing
- Require the member to reimburse the College for funding provided to the patient under the program for therapy and counseling for patients to a maximum of $10,000.00 per patient. A member who has had his/her certificate of registration revoked for sexual abuse of a patient may not re-apply to the College for reinstatement for a period of five years.

SUMMARY

Sexual abuse has no place in the delivery of health care services. Medical Laboratory Technologists are among the professionals who have declared a zero tolerance for sexual abuse. We are each responsible to ensure that our own behaviour conforms to the statutory, ethical and practice standards expected of our profession. Together we must strive to eradicate the sexual abuse of patients by health care professionals.

MLT Boundaries of Practice Guidebook

OVERVIEW

The MLT Boundaries of Practice Guidebook is intended to provide regulated Medical Laboratory Technologists (MLTs) working in Ontario laboratories, with solid advice and information that can assist them to manage their relationships with patients. The Guidebook provides Ontario MLTs with:

- a boundary framework that identifies the major areas where boundary risks take place
- principles of safe practice in each boundary area
- indicators of unsafe practice in each boundary area
- case studies for learning more about boundaries, and

- a decision-making tool to assist MLTs to avoid risks in patient-professional relationships

The Guidebook builds upon the CMLTO Standards of Practice for Medical Laboratory Technologists (MLTs) and the CMLTO MLT Code of Ethics which both suggest that MLTs are expected to interact with the patient in ways that ensure the patient's needs are met in a respectful, caring and professional manner.

The Guidebook also builds upon the Guidelines for Professional Behaviour for Medical Laboratory Technologists-Prevention of Sexual Abuse, issued in 1995, which begins to address boundaries in MLT / patient relationships, particularly in the areas of sexual abuse prevention, cross cultural sensitivity and respect for patient confidentiality. The Guidebook also builds on the CMLTO's Quality Assurance Program which requires all MLTs to complete a checklist annually where they identify, among other things, the learning required to maintain competence in areas of sexual abuse prevention, respect for the dignity, values, privacy and beliefs of the individual, and the demonstration of effective interpersonal skills with patients and peers.

Appendix III

WORKPLACE POLICIES FOR THE PREVENTION OF SEXUAL ABUSE

1. ONTARIO HUMAN RIGHTS COMMISSION: DEVELOPING PROCEDURES TO RESOLVE HUMAN RIGHTS COMPLAINTS WITHIN YOUR ORGANIZATION[1]

PLEASE NOTE

This policy reflects the Commission's interpretation of the Ontario Human Rights Code provisions and should be read in conjunction with the specific provisions of the Code. Any questions regarding this policy should be directed to the staff of the Ontario Human Rights Commission.

Introduction

The Ontario Human Rights Code (the "Code") states that it is public policy in Ontario to recognize the dignity and worth of every person and to provide equal rights and opportunities without discrimination. The aim is to create a climate of understanding and mutual respect for the dignity and worth of each person so that each person feels a part of the community and feels able to contribute to the community.

The purpose of this booklet is to help organizations develop effective and fair ways to deal with claims of harassment or discrimination that may arise in the workplace. Since most of the questions that the Commission receives deal with human rights issues arising in employment, these guidelines focus on the workplace. However, the principles in these guidelines may also apply in some circumstances to other areas covered by the Code, such as a rental accommodation situation.

Ignoring acts of harassment and discrimination has a bad effect on the workplace. Low employee morale, high stress, damaged professional

---

[1]   <http://www.ohrc.on.ca>.

reputations and employee absences are a few of the results of not paying attention to discrimination and harassment.

Dealing promptly with these issues will save you time and money. By letting everyone know what the rules are and what forms of behaviour are not acceptable, you may avoid costly and upsetting procedures in the courts or before special tribunals. In other words, strong policies and programmes prevent human rights complaints and make good business sense.

The Commission suggests that employers develop internal anti-discrimination policies and procedures to solve complaints that may arise as part of a broad program to build an environment that is free from discrimination and harassment. Such a program should be:

(i)   based on a strong message against discrimination and harassment;
(ii) effective in investigating and settling specific complaints;
(iii) told clearly to all staff or members of the organization;
(iv) respectful of the privacy of all the individuals taking part in the process; and
(v)   wherever possible, part of an ongoing educational programme in the workplace.

WHO IS RESPONSIBLE?

1. Employer Responsibility

Employers have a responsibility to:

(i) provide a working environment that is free from harassment and discrimination; and
(ii) deal effectively, quickly and fairly with any situations involving claims of harassment or discrimination that come to their attention.

Employers could be held liable by a court or tribunal if they or their managers do not act to put an end to discrimination or harassment in their workplaces.

2. The Role of the Ontario Human Rights Commission

Internal policies and procedures sometimes fail to resolve a problem of harassment and discrimination. If such a problem is brought to the attention of the Commission, it may be necessary for the Commission to intervene to try to settle the complaint.

GUIDELINES FOR DEVELOPING INTERNAL PROCESSES IN YOUR ORGANIZATION

Several factors, including how complex or how large your organization might be, could determine the kind of procedures you use. These guidelines should provide a useful framework for any organization to use. The following elements should be part of any complete strategy to resolve human right issues that may arise in the workplace:

    (i)   an anti-harassment or anti-discrimination policy;

    (ii)   a complaint resolution procedure; and

    (iii) on-going education programmes.

These elements should be developed together with the union or other employees' organizations where they may exist in any given workplace.

1. Policy

A policy statement should make it clear that discrimination and harassment are violations of the Code and will not be tolerated. The policy should describe the types of behaviour that are discriminatory, and should send the message that management takes this issue seriously. The policy should spell out what disciplinary measure would be applied, including the possibility of the loss of employment, if a claim of harassment or discrimination is proven.

It is important to make it clear to employees that having an internal complaint resolution procedure in place does not in any way stop an individual from going to the Commission, if she or he wants to. [See endnote 1 (in original; other notes added to this reproduction for this Guide).] Some employees may also have rights under employee collective agreements that will give them other choices for dealing with a problem.

Policies should include:

    (i)   a list of the prohibited grounds of discrimination listed in the Code (see Appendix "A");

    (ii)   a definition of "harassment" as defined by the Code (subsection 10(1); see Appendix "B");

(iii) an explanation of the notion of a "poisoned environment" [See endnote 2 (in original; other notes added to this reproduction for this Guide).] as a violation of the Code (see Appendix "C"); and

(iv) an explanation of the liability of corporations for the behaviour of their officers, managers, employees, etc. (see Appendix "B").

All employees should be aware of this internal policy and of any procedures in place for resolving complaints. You can do this by:

(i) distributing the policy to everyone when it is introduced;

(ii) sharing it with new employees when they are hired; and

(iii) training any employee who becomes a member of management, on the contents of the policy.

2. Complaint Resolution Procedures

(a) Appoint an Advisor

Anyone who feels that she or he has been discriminated against or harassed in the workplace may want to discuss the situation with someone in the company who is familiar with the policy. This person is called an "advisor", and should be able to provide advice on how to deal with the problem, including information on how to file an internal complaint with management. A person who has been accused of harassment or discrimination should also have the right to meet with an advisor.

The advisor is supposed to be neutral, objective and knowledgeable about human rights issues. The person should be able to provide information and explain choices for dealing with a problem, including the option to approach the Commission for help.

The advisor should also know about grievance procedures under collective agreements or other internal complaint procedures that may apply to the situation.

The advisor should be professional and experienced. He or she also has to make sure that all issues are kept strictly confidential.

(b) Documentation

For everyone involved in the process, it is important to make and keep written notes about the events leading to the complaint. These details should include:

(i) what happened — a description of the events or situation;

(ii) when it happened — dates and times of the events or incidents;

(iii) where did it happen; and

(iv) who saw it happen — the names of any witnesses, if any.

As well, any other documents or materials, such as letters, notes, offensive pictures, etc., that may have something to do with the complaint should be kept.

(c) Protection from Reprisal

Persons who make a complaint, as well as anyone else who is involved, should not be penalized for doing so. This is called "reprisal". Protection from reprisal covers:

(i) complainants,

(ii) witnesses,

(iii) advisors,

(iv) representatives of complainants and witnesses,

(v) investigators, and

(vi) decision makers/management.

(d) Representation

The people involved in an internal complaint resolution process should be allowed to have someone represent them if they wish. Representatives may include union stewards or a colleague.

(e) Investigators

Investigators are responsible for examining the circumstances of a complaint. They should therefore be, and be seen to be as independent and objective as possible. Wherever possible, an investigator should not be in a position of direct authority over any of the people involved in a complaint, but should report to someone with the authority to make decisions and have them enforced. If not, the process will be seen to be weak and without "teeth".

An investigation should not be carried out by anyone who is seen as taking sides with either party. For example, it is not very likely that a lawyer who often represents management in labour disputes will be seen as being objective by non-management employees. Also, the investigator should not be someone in a position to have any power or influence over the career progress of either of the parties.

Investigators must:

(i) know about human rights in general, and what the Code says, in particular; and

(ii) make sure that the investigation process is confidential.

In most cases, investigations should start immediately after an investigator is chosen, and finish within ninety days.

(f) Resolution

If a complaint can not be settled through the internal procedure, the employee should be told that a complaint may be filed with the Commission or a grievance filed with the union if one exists in the particular workplace.

3. Education Programmes

Education is an important part of preventing harassment in the workplace. Training programmes for all staff ensure that everyone knows what the rules are and how they will be applied.

Everyone responsible for enforcing the policy or advising on procedures should be thoroughly aware of the policies and procedures that are part of the workplace rules. The organization can:

(i) provide up-to-date information about human rights issues and important court decisions or board of inquiry decisions in this area of the law;

(ii) make sure that all staff are trained on how to deal with discrimination and harassment in the workplace;

(iii) measure the effectiveness of the policies and procedures, and change them if necessary; and

(iv) respond immediately to any claim of discrimination or harassment.

Both the person making a complaint and the person against whom it is made should know how the internal procedure works. This includes information like:

(i) who will investigate;

(ii) how long the process is likely to take;

(iii) what you will receive at the end of the investigation;

(iv)   who will decide what action the employer will take; and

(v)   what solutions or results are possible.

The person making the complaint should also be told about the time limits that apply with the other choices available for the enforcement of human rights, such as filing a grievance with the union or a complaint with the Commission.

For example, complaints under the Code must be filed within six months from the date the last act of alleged discrimination occurred. The Commission has the choice, under section 34(1)(d) of the Code, as to whether or not to deal with complaints which are filed past this time limit. For a grievance under a collective agreement, employees should be aware that a much shorter time limit (days or weeks) may apply.

THE ONTARIO HUMAN RIGHTS COMMISSION

A person who wishes to complain directly to the Commission may do so, even if she or he has used, or has chosen not to use the company's internal procedures.

If a person believes that he or she has been harassed or discriminated against, the Commission will try to settle the dispute, if possible. If that fails, the complaint will then be investigated by the Commission.

WILL THE COMMISSION DEAL WITH ALL COMPLAINTS?

According to the Code, the Commission does not have to deal with all complaints. The Code allows the Commission to decide not to deal with a complaint in certain situations:

(i)   if another provincial law, such as the Employment Standards Act or the grievance procedure under the Labour Relations Act, would be a better law for dealing with the complaint;

(ii)   if the complaint is trivial, petty, bothersome or made in bad faith;

(iii) if the employer is outside provincial law and therefore the Code does not apply (for example, if someone has a complaint against a bank or an airline, that complaint would be dealt with under federal jurisdiction); or

(iv)   if an individual files a complaint more than six months after the events upon which the complaint is based. The Commission will decide not to deal with complaints of this kind if the complainant's delay was in bad faith (for example, if a person delays the filing of a complaint on purpose), or if the delay causes significant prejudice to the employer (for example, if after six months, important documents are destroyed or witnesses are no longer available).

Only the Commissioners have the right to make a decision not to deal with a complaint. In such situations, the Commission will decide each case on its own merit or value. The Commission by law has to provide reasons to the parties when a decision is made not to deal with a case under section 34. If a decision is made not to deal with a complaint, this does not mean the complaint has been dismissed or evaluated on its merits. It simply means that the complaint is outside of the Commission's control, or that it would be unfair to the parties to go ahead with the complaint for the reasons outlined above.

THE COMMISSION AND THE BOARD OF INQUIRY

The Commission is required by the Code to try to settle complaints and to conduct investigations. If the Commission cannot settle a complaint and if there is enough evidence, the Commission may refer the complaint to a board of inquiry.

Boards of inquiry are separate decision-making bodies or tribunals, that are completely independent from the Commission. The board of inquiry has a wide range of powers to make orders against the employer, organization or individual who is named as a respondent to the complaint. Orders may include offers of employment or job reinstatement, financial compensation for lost wages, mental anguish, etc. A board of inquiry can also order an employer to adapt the workplace to accommodate the needs of a person with a disability.

FOR FURTHER INFORMATION

The Ontario Human Rights Commission has offices in several locations across the province. For more information about the Commission or this policy statement, please call the office most convenient for you during regular office hours from Monday to Friday. The addresses and telephone numbers of our offices are listed in this document.

Commission Offices

APPENDIX "A"

Under Ontario's Human Rights Code, a person has the right to equal treatment in a number of social areas:

(i)   services
(ii)   accommodation (where you live)
(iii)   employment
(iv)   contracts
(v)   membership in trade unions and vocational associations

based on the following grounds:

(i)   race
(ii)   ancestry
(iii)   place of origin
(iv)   colour
(v)   ethnic origin
(vi)   citizenship
(vii)   creed (religion)
(viii)   sex
(ix)   sexual orientation
(x)   age
(xi)   record of offenses (in employment)
(xii)   marital status
(xiii)   family status (being in a parent-child relationship)
(xiv)   receipt of public assistance (in housing)
(xv)   mental or physical handicap

APPENDIX "B"

RELEVANT ONTARIO HUMAN RIGHTS CODE PROVISIONS

Section 10
(1)   "Harassment" means engaging in a course of vexatious comment or conduct that is known or ought reasonably to be known to be unwelcome.

Section 34

(1)   Where it appears to the Commission that,

   (a)   the complaint is one that could or should be more appropriately
         dealt with under an Act other than this Act;

   (b)   the subject-matter of the complaint is trivial, frivolous, vexatious
         or made in bad faith;

   (c)   the complaint is not within the jurisdiction of the Commission;
         or

   (d)   the facts upon which the complaint is based occurred more than
         six months before the complaint was filed, unless the Commission
         is satisfied that the delay was incurred in good faith and no
         substantial prejudice will result to any person affected by the
         delay,

the Commission may, in its discretion, decide not to deal with the
complaint.

Section 41

(2) If the board of inquiry finds that a right of a complainant under Part I
has been infringed by an employer that has an employment equity plan
under the Employment Equity Act, 1993, the board may make an order
that has the effect of imposing requirements on the employer that are in
addition to those contained in the employment equity plan.

Section 45

(1) For the purposes of this Act, except subsection 2(2), subsection 5(2),
section 7 and subsection 44(1), any act or thing done or omitted to be
done in the course of his or her employment by an officer, official,
employee or agent of a corporation, trade union, trade or occupational
association, unincorporated association or employers' organization shall
be deemed to be an act or thing done or omitted to be done by the
corporation, trade union, trade or occupational association, unincorporated
association or employers' organization.

ENDNOTES

1. *Ontario Human Rights Commission v. Etobicoke (Borough)*, [1982]
1 S.C.R. 202. This case states that one cannot contract out of the rights
under the Code.
2. A "poisoned environment" is a form of discrimination. It may be
created by comments or actions of any person regardless of her/his

position or status. These offensive comments or actions spoil the work, housing or other environment. The poisoned environment forms an unequal term or condition of employment, accommodation, etc. and is therefore a violation of the right to be free from discrimination. See further *Wei Fu v. Ontario Government Protective Services* (1985), 6 C.H.R.R. D/2797 (Ont. Bd. of Inquiry); *Dhillon v. F.W. Woolworth Co.* (1982), 3 C.H.R.R. D/743 (Ont. Bd. of Inquiry); *Lee v. T.J. Applebee's Food Conglomeration* (1987), 9 C.H.R.R. D/4781 (Ont. Bd. of Inquiry).

IF YOU HAVE A HUMAN RIGHTS COMPLAINT

1. If you have a human rights complaint, you may contact the regional office closest to you. A Commission staff person will tell you if your concerns are covered by the Ontario Human Rights Code (the "Code").

2. Commission staff will explain how the Code applies to your situation and how the complaint procedure works. Commission staff will work with you and the other party to resolve the concerns. The Commission also offers mediation services.

3. If you want the Commission to address your concerns, you should file a complaint within 6 months from the last incident of discrimination. This time limit is set out in section 34 of the Code.

4. "Filing a complaint" means that you have completed the Commission's complaint form and provided all requested details. You must have signed, dated and returned the form to the Commission.

5. When you file a complaint, Commission staff will work with you and the person/company you have filed against, to try and resolve the complaint through mediation.

6. The Commission may consider not to deal with a complaint under section 34 if:

   (a) another Ontario law would be better suited to deal with the situation, such as the Labour Relations Act;

   (b) you have no reasonable basis to support a claim of discrimination, or that you have made the complaint in bad faith, or that you have already obtained a remedy somewhere else;

   (c) the matter is outside the Commission's legal authority;

   (d) you have waited longer than 6 months from the last incident of discrimination to file a complaint.

7. The Commission is neutral and does not take sides in the complaint. Commission staff will assist you with questions about the complaint procedure. However, if you require legal advice, please contact a lawyer.

IF A HUMAN RIGHTS COMPLAINT IS MADE AGAINST YOU

1. If the Commission receives a complaint against you, Commission staff will contact you to discuss the matter.
2. Commission staff will explain how the Code applies to the situation and how the complaint procedure works. Commission staff will work with you and the person making the complaint to try and resolve the concerns. The Commission also offers mediation services.
3. If the concerns cannot be resolved and mediation is not successful, the complaint may proceed to the investigation stage.
4. You can ask the Commission not to deal with the complaint under section 34 of the Code if:

   (a) another Ontario law would be better suited to deal with the situation, such as the Labour Relations Act;
   (b) you believe that the person making the complaint has no reasonable basis to support a claim of discrimination, or that the complaint is in bad faith, or that a remedy has already been obtained by the complainant somewhere else;
   (c) the matter is outside the Commission's legal authority;
   (d) the person making the complaint waited longer than 6 months from the last incident of discrimination to file a complaint.

5. The Commission is neutral and does not take sides in the complaint. Commission staff will assist you with questions about the complaint procedure. However, if you require legal representation or advice, please contact a lawyer.

2. SAMPLE POLICY FOR THE LARGE WORKPLACE

Preamble

It is the goal of (Employer) to promote a workplace that is free of sexual harassment and abuse. Sexual harassment and abuse of employees is unlawful and will not be tolerated by (Employer).

This Policy responds to the (Employer's) responsibility under the *Ontario Human Rights Code* to prevent sexual harassment and to provide procedures to handle complaints. The (Employer) will offer education and training programs to support the administration of this Policy and to ensure that all members of the (Employer's) workplace are aware of their rights and responsibilities and have access to the appropriate procedures.

Definitions

1. Sexual Harassment

Harassment is defined by the Ontario Human Rights Commission as engaging in a course of vexatious comment or conduct that is known or ought reasonably to be known to be unwelcome.[2] Sexual harassment is thus engaging in a course of conduct of a sexual or gender related nature that is known or should reasonably be known to be unwelcome. For example, someone who makes unwelcome sexual or gender-related remarks and gestures by:

- making offensive jokes
- being verbally abusive based on gender
- making unwanted comments about one's body
- staring or making unwanted gesters
- displaying offensive pictures or depictions
- making inappropriate sexual suggestions or requests
- touch inappropriately or in an unwanted fashion

2. Sexual Solicitation or Advance

A person suggests that if you become sexually involved with him or her, he or she will give you a raise or provide you with some other type of incentive.

3. Reprisal

A person who has authority or power denies you something important, punishes or threatens you for refusing a sexual request, or for complaining about inappropriate sexual behaviour or comments.[3]

4. Sexual Harassment and a "Poisoned Environment"

Even if the harassment is not directed at you, it can still create an uncomfortable, intimidating, humiliating or intolerable work environment

---

[2]   Section 10(1) of the Ontario *Human Rights Code*, R.S.C. 1990, c. H.19, available online <www.ohrc.on.ca>.

[3]   OHRC, s. 3(b).

for you or for others. This type of environment is considered a poisoned work environment.[4]

Principles

Pursuant to the Ontario *Human Rights Code*, (Employer) is responsible in law for ensuring that its employees are free from sexual harassment and abuse in the workplace. It is unlawful for (Employer) to retaliate against any employee because she or he has opposed discriminatory employment practices, filed a complaint about sexual harassment internally, or filed a complaint of sexual harassment under an external administrative procedure.

(Employer) is committed to providing a workplace that is free from sexual harassment and abuse. (Employer) is committed to providing education about power and sexual harassment, and to providing a fair and transparent complaints procedure for handling sexual harassment allegations.

Internal Complaints Procedure

If you believe that you have been sexually harassed or abused in the workplace, you have the right to file a complaint with (Employer). This complaint may be filed orally or in writing by contacting:

> (names of internal Human Resources person in charge of managing complaints and phone number)

A. The Advice Stage

Both the complainant and the respondent have the right to meet with an advisor.

Advisors are neutral liaisons in the complaint process. The advisors are knowledgeable about the internal and external avenues available for a complainant or respondent and will discuss these options with you.

B. The Investigation Stage

Once (Employer) has received the complaint, an appropriate investigator will be appointed and the complaint will be fairly and promptly investigated.

---

[4] Ontario Human Rights Commission, *Guide to the Human Rights Code*, May 26, 1991 at 11.

Investigators are internal employees who have been chosen by the organization to examine the circumstances of the complaint. Investigators are knowledgeable about the law on sexual misconduct in the workplace. The investigators' role includes fact finding, reporting, and making recommendations about discipline if applicable.

An investigator is never involved in the incident he or she is investigating. An investigator will also never be in a position of direct authority over any of the people involved in the complaint.

The investigator will conduct a private interview with both the complainant and the respondent, as well as with any witnesses.

The results of the investigation will be communicated to the complainant and the respondent.

C. The Discipline Stage

If it is determined that inappropriate conduct has been perpetrated by an employee, disciplinary action will be taken. The discipline may include:

- mandatory counseling for the perpetrator
- an apology letter from the perpetrator to the complainant
- an official reprimand documented in the perpetrator's file
- a transfer of the perpetrator to another department, if appropriate
- suspension
- dismissal

External Administrative Proceedings

In addition to the above internal complaints procedure, if you believe you have been subjected to sexual harassment, you may file a formal complaint with the Ontario Human Rights Commission or with (relevant Professional College). Using the internal complaint procedure does not prohibit you from filing a complaint with the Commission or College.

(contact information for Ontario Human Rights Commission)
(contact information for the relevant Professional College)

3. SAMPLE POLICY FOR THE SMALL WORKPLACE

Preamble

It is the goal of (Employer) to promote a workplace that is free of sexual harassment and abuse. Sexual harassment and abuse of employees is unlawful and will not be tolerated by (Employer).

This Policy responds to the (Employer's) responsibility under the Ontario Human Rights Code to prevent sexual harassment and to provide procedures to handle complaints. The (Employer) will ensure that all members of the (Employer's) workplace are aware of their rights and responsibilities and have access to the appropriate procedures.

Definitions

1. Sexual Harassment

Harassment is defined by the Ontario Human Rights Commission as engaging in a course of vexatious comment or conduct that is known or ought reasonably to be known to be unwelcome.[5] Sexual harassment is thus engaging in a course of conduct of a sexual or gender related nature that is known or should reasonably be known to be unwelcome. For example, someone who makes unwelcome sexual or gender-related remarks and gestures by:

- touching you inappropriately
- making offensive jokes or remarks about women or men
- making sexual requests or suggestions
- staring at or making unwelcome comments about your body
- displaying sexually offensive pictures
- being verbally abusive to you because of your gender[6]

2. Sexual Solicitation or Advance

A person suggests that if you become sexually involved with him or her, he or she will give you a raise or provide you with some other type of incentive.

3. Reprisal

A person who has authority or power denies you something important, punishes or threatens you for refusing a sexual request, or for complaining about inappropriate sexual behaviour or comments.[7]

4. Sexual Harassment and a "Poisoned Environment"

Even if the harassment is not directed at you, it can still create an uncomfortable, intimidating, humiliating or intolerable work environment

---

[5] *Ibid.*, section 10(1).
[6] *Ibid.*
[7] *Ibid.*

for you or for others. This type of environment is considered a poisoned work environment.[8]

Principles

Pursuant to the Ontario *Human Rights Code*, (Employer) is responsible in law for ensuring that its employees are free from sexual harassment and abuse in the workplace. It is unlawful for (Employer) to retaliate against any employee because she or he has opposed discriminatory employment practices, filed a complaint about sexual harassment internally, or filed a complaint of sexual harassment under an external administrative procedure.

(Employer) is committed to providing a workplace that is free from sexual harassment and abuse. (Employer) is committed to providing access to fair complaints procedures for its employees. Although this is a small workplace, (Employer) believes that its employees must have access to the same rights to be free from harassment in the workplace, as those in larger institutions.

Internal Complaints Procedures

If you believe that you have been sexually harassed or abused in the workplace, you have the right to file a complaint with (Employer). This complaint may be filed orally or in writing by contacting any member of management. This manager will then contact our outside consultant (name) from (Community Organization) who will be responsible for the complaint from this stage forward.

In the alternative, you may contact our outside consultant (name) from (Community Organization) to file a harassment complaint yourself. The member of management or outside person will provide you with the information regarding the different options available for filing a complaint.

Both the complainant and the respondent have the right to meet with the outside Consultant for information about available complaint processes.

The Consultant will interview the complainant, the respondent, and any available witnesses. The Consultant's role includes fact finding, reporting, making recommendations and making decisions about discipline if applicable.

---

[8]   *Ibid.*

Discipline

If the Consultant determines that inappropriate conduct has been perpetrated by an employee, disciplinary action will be taken. This action may include:

- mandatory counseling for the perpetrator
- an apology letter from the perpetrator to the complainant
- official reprimand documented in the perpetrator's file
- suspension
- dismissal

External Administrative Procedures

(Employer) encourages its employees to use the external avenues available for handling complaints, particularly in light of the small size of our organization and potential discomfort with using an internal procedure.

These external procedures are open to employees whether or not they choose to file a complaint internally with our Consultant. These options include filing a complaint with the Ontario Human Rights Commission and/or reporting the misconduct to the (relevant professional college).

(phone number for the Ontario Human Rights Commission)
(phone number for the Professional College)

4. EDUCATIONAL TOOLS

The following list contains suggested tools for educating about workplace sexual abuse and its prevention:[9]

- Invite a guest speaker
- Hold workshops
- Show films or videos
- Develop a library of relevant materials
- Make continuing education and conference opportunities available
- Work with other groups
- Consult with survivor groups
- Have professional publications and relevant documents readily available
- Ensure professionals can consult about sexual abuse concerns, including confidential access
- Provide self-assessment tools
- Hold regular training sessions

---

[9] Consolidated and adapted from B. Laskin & P. Klein, "Sexual Abuse Prevention Plans of the Regulated Health Professions: Recommended Approaches and Evaluation Methods" (Report to the Health Professions Regulatory Advisory Council, 1996).

Appendix IV

CASE STUDIES AND DISCUSSION POINTS[*]

A. DR. W, A PHYSICIAN

This case is Canada's leading judicial decision on sexual abuse of patients. Dr. W was sued by his former patient, Laura, who lost her case in the British Columbia trial and appeal courts. Her final appeal to the Supreme Court of Canada reversed the lower courts' rulings, and held Dr. W liable for paying damages to his patient for harm done to her as a result of his abrogation of his duty as a health professional. The Supreme Court decision in *Norberg*[1] stands as the definitive analysis by our highest court (as of January 2004 when this Guide was published) on the fiduciary duty owed by health professionals to their patients and on how the Court found the doctor's defence argument that the patient gave her "consent" to sexual contact to be "inherently suspect."

Dr. W had been in practice for many years and maintained his office in conjunction with his home. The patient, Laura, came to see Dr. W, complaining of severe headaches, for which previous physicians had prescribed strong medications, such as Fiorinal. It became clear that she wanted greater access to such drugs and when Dr. W confronted his patient, she admitted to him that she was addicted. Dr. W made suggestions of a

---

Explanatory Note: This Appendix is a compilation of the case studies found in the body of the Guide. For educational purposes, they have been collected here to augment course materials. We remind instructors that each regulatory college is obligated under the *Regulated Health Professions Act, 1991* to make available summaries of all findings in sexual abuse cases, except where the alleged abuse was limited to comments, gestures or behaviour, meaning no physical sexual contact between professional and patient. Most colleges fulfil this obligation by including discipline case summaries in a regular publication to their members; for example, the magazine published by the College of Physicians and Surgeons of Ontario, *Members' Dialogue*. In Appendix II you will find contact information for each of the regulated colleges to facilitate your access to additional, more recent cases in a particular discipline.

[1] *Norberg v. Wynrib*, [1992] 2 S.C.R. 226.

sexual nature by pointing upstairs where his apartment was located, but he did not at any time use physical force. Initially Laura resisted, but after trying and then failing to obtain enough medication from other doctors, Laura returned to Dr. W. An exchange of sex for drugs evolved, continuing for more than a year, and included sexual behaviour that consisted of fondling and simulated intercourse, prior to the patient receiving a prescription renewal or a supply of medication from the doctor.

Dr. W refused to prescribe to Laura when he learned that she was under criminal investigation for "double doctoring," but when she visited upstairs with him, he continued to give her pills. Laura told Dr. W that she needed help with her addiction. Dr. W advised her to "just quit." Laura stopped coming to him and took the initiative to enter a rehabilitation centre after being charged with obtaining narcotic prescription drugs without disclosing particulars of prescriptions from other doctors.

Some time after entering treatment, Laura sued Dr. W in a civil suit on the grounds of negligence, breach of fiduciary duty, breach of contract and sexual assault as the tort of battery, which is the intentional infliction of force on another person. Laura lost her case at trial and again on appeal to the British Columbia Court of Appeal. However, the judges of the Supreme Court of Canada unanimously agreed that the lower courts were wrong and ordered the doctor to pay damages as well as legal costs to the patient.

1. Discussion Points

1. Under what circumstances does the law in Ontario allow a professional to have sexual contact with a patient? With a former patient?
2. What right does a professional have to earn his or her livelihood as a registered and regulated health professional under the *RHPA?*
3. What should a professional reasonably expect from his or her professional association when charged with sexual abuse by their regulatory college?
4. How is the public interest served through self-regulation by the health professions?

B. DR. G, AN ONTARIO PHYSICIAN DISCIPLINED IN ARIZONA (INTERJURISDICTIONAL CASE)

Annually, the College of Physicians and Surgeons of Ontario (CPSO) asks each of its members to complete a questionnaire as a requirement of having his or her membership renewed. When Dr. G, a physician registered in Ontario but working in Arizona, completed his 2000 questionnaire, he provided a number of negative answers to questions about any disciplinary actions in which he was involved when in fact, he was immersed in a disciplinary process conducted by the Arizona State College. When the CPSO became aware of the Arizona process and its outcome, which found Dr. G guilty, and noted that Dr. G had misinformed the College when he responded to its questionnaire, the CPSO commenced an investigation and subsequently set a date for a disciplinary hearing. Dr. G pled not guilty to the charges.

The disciplinary panel ruled on two allegations against Dr. G. The first involved the determination on whether, by falsifying his questionnaire responses, he was guilty of professional misconduct under the *Regulated Health Professions Act, 1991 (RHPA)*.[2] Second, the panel considered whether the finding of professional misconduct in Arizona and the fact that Dr. G had disobeyed the Arizona Board's orders constituted a similar finding under the Ontario legislation.

Dr. G did not attend the hearing and the panel relied on evidence that it had gathered in its investigation. The panel concluded that Dr. G was guilty, and ordered that a reprimand be placed on the register against him and that he pay costs in the amount of $5,000.

1. Discussion Points

The cases of Dr. G and Dr. NMRC (following) deal with professional misconduct that was also confirmed by a regulatory body in another jurisdiction.

1. What would be the implications if the issue was the discovery by an Ontario college that one of its members was guilty of sexual abuse outside the province but that the abuse was not recognized by the regulator in the other jurisdiction?

---

[2] S.O. 1991, c. 18.

2. Would the Ontario college have any jurisdiction over Dr. G or Dr. NMRC if they had not renewed their certificates of registration in Ontario?

C. DR. NMRC, A PSYCHIATRIST PRACTISING IN QUEBEC

Dr. NMRC was a member of the College of Physicians and Surgeons of Ontario (CPSO) at the time that she was practising in the province of Quebec. She had been treating Mr. A for anxiety and alcohol-related problems for several years, when he called her for help. Dr. NMRC advised Mr. A to come to her home so that she could assess his condition. After seeing Mr. A, Dr. NMRC urged him to go to hospital, but he refused. Instead, Dr. NMRC administered Ativan, which is used to treat anxiety, and allowed Mr. A to stay in her home, which he did. Dr. NMRC continued to lodge Mr. A and treated him as an employee by providing him with a variety of jobs. Mr. A had stayed with Dr. NMRC for a month when the relationship between them became sexual and it continued for the next six months.

Dr. NMRC was eventually convicted under Quebec law of a violation of ethics as a result of her relationship with Mr. A. The matter came to the attention of the CPSO, which convened a disciplinary hearing and rendered a decision in July of 2001. The grounds for the hearing were based on the requirements under the *RHPA Code,*[3] section 51(1), which states:

> A panel shall find that a member has committed an act of professional misconduct if
>
> . . .
>
> (b) the governing body of a health profession in a jurisdiction other than Ontario has found that the member committed an act of professional misconduct that would, in the opinion of the panel, be an act of professional misconduct as defined in the regulations;
>
> (b.1) the member has sexually abused a patient....

Dr. NMRC admitted her guilt and the disciplinary panel found that she had committed an act of professional misconduct as alleged. It ordered that her certificate of registration be revoked immediately and that she be reprimanded and that the reprimand be recorded in the College register.

---

[3] *Health Professions Procedural Code*, being Sch. 2 to the *Regulated Health Professions Act, ibid.*, hereinafter "the *Code.*"

1. Discussion Points

Compare the cases of Dr. G and Dr. NMRC. While they are similar in the jurisdictional sense, how do they differ? Do you think the penalties are appropriate in comparison?

D. DR. AB, A PSYCHOLOGIST IN OTTAWA

1. Civil lawsuit and College Discipline Processes

Dr. AB (his actual initials) was a prominent, respected member of Ottawa's professional community for many years. In addition to his private practice as a registered psychologist, he lectured at a university and was often invited to speak at conferences and meetings. The identity of the patient who brought the civil lawsuit against him for harm caused due to his sexual abuse in the course of her treatment was protected by court order. She will be named "Nora" and her husband will be named "James" in this case study. The following description of the circumstances in this case is taken from the judicial decision, which found Dr. AB to be in breach of his duty as a health professional in a position of authority and to have been grossly negligent in the standard of care he provided to Nora.

> Following more than two years of care — and after slowly eroding "Nora's" personal, physical and psychological boundaries and grooming her for sexual exploitation—her therapist initiated a sexual relationship. Nora was in a state of deep transference. She was convinced that she was in love and was important and special to him. At that time, Nora told herself that she "willingly" consented to the "relationship" and was reassured when he said that he "loved" her too.[4]

The following quote from Nora is from her statement to the Ontario Special Task Force on Sexual Abuse of Patients. She describes in her own words her experience of transference exploitation and one aspect of the harm caused by her psychologist's exploitation of her trust:

> When I heard the expert witness describe how he turned me into a little girl, I flashed on how he kept trying to get me to perform oral sex on him in his office and I could only nod my head "no" back and forth, back and forth, like a little girl. Listening to the expert, I realised then that he planned all along to be able to abuse the little girl in me. Even now, years later, I wake up in a sweat remembering. I feel raped. When he had sex with me, he was raping me. He knew what he was doing, but he didn't care. It never leaves me. Never a day goes by that I think about

---

[4] *C. (N.) v. Blank*, [1998] O.J. No. 2544 (Div. Ct).

it, but now I see it for what it was. I have never felt such deep, deep pain to the core of my being.[5]

Dr. Iris Jackson, a psychologist herself and former president of the Ontario Psychological Association, assessed Nora's situation and gave expert testimony in the lawsuit explaining how "consent" could not have been given:

> (Nora) could not have made a free choice to consent in the sexual relationship with (her therapist). She was in a sexual relationship with a man who had power over her psychological state of mind and her treatment process. He had initiated erotic contact after a process of grooming her for exploitation and slowly eroding her personal, physical and psychological boundaries and implying that she was special to him and that he "loved her although he was not in love with her."[6]

2. Secondary Victims: Trauma to People who Have Not Been Sexually Abused

Dr. Gary Schoener, a psychologist based in Minnesota who is widely consulted on sexual abuse of patients, uses the term "associate victims." Dr. Harvey Armstrong, one of Canada's foremost authorities on treating sexual abuse survivors, notes that: "Secondary or vicarious victimisation occurs when a second person, on learning of the extent and severity of the trauma of a person they care about and are involved with, becomes traumatized and develops post traumatic symptoms."[7]

(a) Nora's Husband, James

Nora also made a complaint to the College of Psychologists of Ontario, a process that went on longer than the civil lawsuit. In his testimony to the Special Task Force, Nora's husband "James" spoke of his experience:

> It is only recently that I understand that I am a victim of this abuse....The college process affects the whole family, not just the victim. There are many victims within a family unit. I felt impotent because I could not protect my wife through the process. I had no power to act — to fulfil my role as her husband. It was all done through another party, like a puppeteer.[8]

---

[5]   2001 Task Force, at 11-12.
[6]   *Supra* note 4 at 18.
[7]   2001 Task Force, at 12.
[8]   *Ibid.*

3. A Judge's Perspective on Dr. AB

Few patients reach the point of being able to marshal their resources to sue for damages, separate from or in addition to the college process and possibly also the criminal law process. Few judicial decisions have examined the dynamics of sexual abuse by a health professional thoroughly. The following excerpt is from the judgment in Nora's civil lawsuit against Dr. AB, rendered by Justice J. Aitken of the Ontario Court of Justice (General Division) in 1998.

> She went to him for help at a time when she was particularly vulnerable and insecure. He had the professional knowledge to help her, but instead used that knowledge to manipulate the situation to his own advantage, playing on [her] lack of confidence, her search for a positive father-figure and her sexual inhibitions. In these circumstances, as has been attested by Dr. Jackson and Dr. Freebury, [the patient] could not exercise free will. Her participation in sexual activities with Dr. B. [a psychologist] was not based on any understanding on her part as to what was really happening. He kept her in a constant state of confusion as to whether his advances were part of her treatment, evidence of his love for her, or something else. This was coupled with her overwhelming dependency on him, which he let develop unchecked, so that she was rendered incapable of coming to her own assessments or conclusions. There could be no genuine consent in these circumstances. Therefore everything from the initial touching to the hugging, kissing, fondling, masturbating and finally intercourse were all forms of battery. I agree with McLachlin J. that "...where such a power imbalance exists it matters not what the patient may have done, how seductively she may have dressed, how compliant she may have appeared, or how self interested her conduct may have been — the doctor will be at fault if sexual exploitation occurs." Exploitation did occur in this case, and the sole responsibility for that rests with Dr. B. There can be no doubt that [the therapist] owed fiduciary obligations to [the patient] when he took her on as a client within his clinical psychology practice. It is also equally clear that he breached those obligations by totally ignoring what were appropriate therapist-client boundaries and particularly by initiating and maintaining a sexual relationship with her. The obligation was on him and him alone to ensure the appropriate boundaries were maintained. By breaching them, he put his own needs ahead of those of [his patient]. He did not do this on just one occasion. He did it repeatedly from August 1990 to August 1995, and arguably beyond.[9]

(b) An Example of Damages Awarded to a Patient /Plaintiff

Madame Justice Aitken concluded her written decision by quantifying the damages Dr. AB was ordered to pay as a result of the harm done to his patient. The judge's disapproval of what Dr. AB was found to have done is reflected in the fact that Dr. AB was ordered to pay several types

---

[9]   *C. (N.) v. Blank, supra* note 4, at paras. 169, 174, 175.

of damages, to demonstrate how repugnant his abuse was to the Court. The Court awarded the plaintiff damages of $326,275.98, including aggravated damages of $100,000, punitive damages of $25,000, and special damages of approximately $200,000. The Court awarded the plaintiff's husband $30,000 in damages as compensation for the losses he had suffered and would suffer in the future as a result of the defendant's treatment of his wife. The judge noted that the plaintiff's injuries were the foreseeable result of the defendant's negligence. In assessing damages, the Court started from the premise that absent the defendant's involvement, the plaintiff would have been living a normal, healthy life by December 1993. She would have been working full time. She may have needed supportive counselling from time to time, but nothing in the nature of the intensive psychotherapy she had required since December 1993, and continued to require. The judge was of the opinion that Dr. AB had breached virtually all standards of professional conduct; that his negligence was so reckless and audacious as to shock the Court, meriting aggravated damages, in addition to the other kinds of damages also awarded.

E. DR. B, A CHIROPRACTOR IN ST. CATHARINES

1. College Discipline Hearing and Criminal Trial — Jail Terms

Dr. B negotiated guilty pleas on nine charges of sexual assault committed while he was purporting to treat nine women in his capacity as a licensed chiropractor. His abusive conduct took several forms, including breast fondling, genital manipulation, digital penetration of the vagina and digital penetration of the rectum. Dr. B persisted in the sexual misconduct despite being questioned about it by some of his patients, and despite being warned to stop; once by a senior medical practitioner from the community and once from the College of Chiropractors. Victim impact statements were filed at the criminal trial, detailing the harm suffered as a result of Dr. B's mistreatment of those patients, including: sexual dysfunction, termination of marriages and long-term relationships, disharmony within the family, loss of trust in the health professions, loss of self-worth and dignity and overwhelming feelings of shame, humiliation and embarrassment.

The trial judge gave Dr. B an 18-month conditional sentence plus three years' probation. The Crown appealed the conditional sentence and asked the Court of Appeal to use its authority to replace the conditional sentence with a prison sentence of nine months because the conditional sentence failed to "adequately reflect the principles of general deterrence and denunciation and that it is manifestly unfit having regard to the gravity and seriousness of the offences and the respondent's degree of moral blameworthiness."[10]

The trial judge had decided on the conditional sentence after taking into consideration evidence about Dr. B's particular circumstances as a popular practitioner in a small Ontario city. The trial judge heard testimony from a noted psychologist who reported that Dr. B had marital problems and that he suffered from a sexual disorder known as "toucherism." The psychologist told the judge that, in his expert opinion, Dr. B needed therapy to prevent relapsing but that he did not present a danger to the community at large. The trial judge also took into account the remorse that Dr. B expressed at trial and the fact that he acknowledged assaulting 13 patients over a ten-year period and that he entered nine guilty pleas at trial, which in turn spared the victims from having to relive their experiences in a public forum.

The three Court of Appeal judges unanimously decided to set aside the conditional sentence and substitute a sentence of nine months' imprisonment, while keeping the terms of three years' probation and a weapons prohibition put in place by the trial judge. In giving reasons for the Appeal Court making this decision, Moldaver J. said:

> The crimes committed by the respondent were extremely serious. As indicated, over the course of ten years, he sexually assaulted thirteen female patients and in doing so, he repeatedly broke the sacred bond that forms the essence of a doctor/patient relationship. By any measure, this was a gross breach of trust and, as is all too often the case, it has resulted in tragic consequences for the victims.[11]

2. Dr. B, the Criminal Court and the College

A "360 degree" view of these cases, such as with Dr. B's, is difficult to achieve. Each of his patients had a unique experience that traumatized them and affected their personal circles extending out into the community at large. Dr. B expressed remorse over his violations of professional standards and the trust of his patients. He was married with children; his family had to make the best of their lives in the same community as his victims, without his financial support. And like many professionals found guilty of sexually abusing one or some of their

---

[10] *R. v. Bedard* (23 May 2001), Doc. No. C35494 (Ont. C.A.), online <http://www.canlii.org/on/cas/onca255.html> at para. 2.

[11] *Ibid.*, at para. 18.

patients, Dr. B was popular with many of his patients and generally well regarded, which set up another kind of dissonance within the community at large. This was recognized by the trial judge, and on appeal Modaver J. noted:

> Because these offences occurred in a small Ontario community, many of the victims harbour concerns about meeting the respondent in public. For some, this has led to a form of self-imposed house arrest. For example, Ms. H states:
>
>> ...[I] have felt petrified to go out in public, even with my family because I'm afraid I'll run into him and I don't know how I would react. So ever since the charges were laid against [Dr. B] last year I haven't really been out other than doctors appointments and medical tests and on occasion since we have a new 24 hours grocery store my husband will take me at 1:00 or 2:00 a.m.,. All this worry and stress has made my physical condition much worse....
>
> Another example is found in Ms. S's victim impact statement:
>
>> ...Or when you go out into a mall and the whole time you're looking around to see if you are going to run into someone who works at the chiro [sic] office or [Dr. B] himself which has happened to me at Christmas and you completely lose it in a public place. I find that I tend to avoid a lot of situations...[12]

Moldaver J. also acknowledged the impact of community dissonance on the victims:

> In addition to feeling like prisoners in their own community, several of the victims report that because of the respondent's [Dr. B] otherwise unblemished professional reputation and his strong support in the community, they have had to contend with comments from others, including relatives and friends, to the effect that the respondent is innocent and that the charges against him have been concocted for purposes of personal gain.[13]

After the criminal process was well underway, the College of Chiropractors followed up in accordance with the mandate given under the *RHPA*. Some colleges take the position that it is better to wait until a criminal process is complete before undertaking the college complaint process under civil law. Other colleges decide — on a case-by-case basis — whether or not to use executive authority to temporarily suspend a professional's practice, out of concern for immediate harm to patients. There is no set rule as to what colleges must do when one or more complaint is received about a member of that college. The decision to intervene is left to the judgment of the Registrar and the Executive Committee of the particular college.

---

[12] *Ibid.*, at para. 8.
[13] *Ibid.*, at para. 9.

The following excerpts, from testimony given to the 2001 Task Force by one of the women victimized by Dr. B and her husband, a police officer, are taken from the transcript of a public hearing held by the Task Force in Toronto on May 9, 2000, to illustrate some of what was experienced by them as a result of the College's decision to have the criminal investigation proceed in advance of the college process. Brenda and Rod asked that their real names be used.

Brenda commented on her experience of the college process, after she had participated in the criminal trial.

> His other victims and I were put through the criminal process; he finally came before the college where he admitted guilt in all cases. Along with other victims, I was at the college hearing when they revoked his licence for five years. This whole process continues to be like a nightmare — weird and hard to predict. It's been a real eye opener for me to see how these people being paid good money to process our cases treat victims — they act like they're doing us a big favour, they take months to respond, months to proceed on very serious charges and months to reimburse our expenses.[14]

At the public hearing, Rod expressed concerns from his perspective as a husband, a member of the community and a police officer:

> I have been a policeman for 25 years and continue to be one. For eight of the years, I specialized in investigating sexual assaults. Because of the difficulty in dealing with such cases, each of us that investigate sexual assaults is forced to undergo extensive training. Police receive training in cognitive interviewing skills. Yet, the person who interviewed Brenda in the hotel room had no training, no video, no recording....The only sanction placed on this man was by the courts — controlling his behaviour with other patients. The college has yet to do a single thing. He's allowed to resign. If that isn't a PR move.... When a complaint comes from a member of the same college, it must have been the hardest thing that member has to do, to complain about a fellow college member in a small community. He knows this man personally. Mandatory revocation of an abuser's license is a must in order to instill any confidence in the public. These are the procedures already in place, but it seems there is no standardization that happens between the colleges. From our experience, we've gone into great detail and we've been pushed on this right to the hills.
>
> At the date that the information is officially sworn in court, he is officially charged with the criminal offences, yet there are no sanctions from the college to protect the public from this man. Since the college has interviewed the victims, not a single thing has been done. It seems illogical that the college wouldn't act upon the charges being officially laid and have an interim sanction in place pending the outcome. This is not one isolated incident. At the time, there were at least nine other victims. It's now a matter of law whether this person is going to be found

---

14   2001 Task Force at 18.

guilty or not. But there's [sic] reasonable grounds to believe, as far as the college goes, that something has to be done, first to protect the public and the second, to protect the remaining members of the profession who are truly doing a decent job.[15]

F. DR. M, A PSYCHOLOGIST IN TORONTO

1. College Discipline and Criminal Trial — Jail Terms

Dr. M was the chief psychologist at a large general hospital in Metropolitan Toronto and he maintained a private practice. He was 47 years old when he was charged with two counts of sexual assault of two patients — Ms. U and Ms. V — whose names were protected by publication bans made by the trial judge. Both patients were married with families and both had histories of sexual abuse, which they disclosed to Dr. M early in their psychotherapeutic relationship with him. Dr. M chose not to testify at his criminal trial.

(a) What Happened with Patient U

In 1987, Ms. U was dismissed from her job of 22 years. She was devastated. She could not sleep or eat and felt suicidal when she was referred to Dr. M. She commenced seeing him twice a week at his office at the hospital and disclosed her personal background, including the fact that as a young person she had been physically and sexually abused while under the care of the Children's Aid Society.

The trial judge accepted her testimony when she described the gradual process that led to sex with Dr. M. During therapy sessions, Ms. U and Dr. M sat in chairs facing each other. As time passed, he would move closer while she would push her chair away from him. During particularly difficult sessions, when Ms. U discussed painful incidents, the appellant would touch Ms. U on the foot or leg with his own foot or leg. He told her that it would be easier for her to talk if he touched her. One day Dr. M asked for a kiss because it was his birthday. Ms. U presented her cheek but he turned her face and kissed her on the lips. In therapy, when Ms. U described her husband as a person with problems of his own who was not supportive of her, Dr. M told her that she would never get better unless she left her husband. In the same month as the first kiss, Dr. M came to his patient's house, at night, uninvited; he returned several times, sometimes with food and wine. On one such

---

occasion, he told his patient that his marriage was a mistake and that he was in love with her. Ms. U told Dr. M that it would not be difficult for her to get a lover, but that what she wanted and needed was a therapist. Nonetheless, Dr. M started coming to U's house almost every night and eventually they started having sexual intercourse there. She continued to see him at the hospital for therapy. After about a month, Dr. M went to Europe to attend an International Society of Hypnosis meeting. Before he left, Ms. U told him again that she only wanted him to be her therapist. He agreed. However, while he was gone, she received notes, telephone calls and gifts from him, with some sexual messages on some of the postcards he sent. When Dr. M returned from Europe, both the sexual and therapeutic relationships resumed. Ms. U told the judge that she had had no intention of continuing with the sexual relationship and that she repeatedly asked to be sent to another therapist. Furthermore, when she was suicidal, she asked him to admit her to the hospital's psychiatric unit.

The trial judge described Dr. M's response. "He would explain about the length of time it took to develop trust with him and to talk about what had happened in her background." The trial judge wrote, "whatever the accused said to her made sense to her."[16] More than a year after sexual contact with Dr. M had begun, Ms. U and her husband separated. The psychologist-patient sexual contact in therapy continued for almost four years after that. Finally, in September 1992, the sexual relationship ended when Ms. U found Dr. M in bed with another one of his patients.

(b) What Happened with Patient V

Ms. V was a 29-year-old registered nurse, who was married to a medical doctor and was the mother of two children, when she became a private patient of Dr. M in March 1992. She remained his patient for only seven months. Ms. V had been sexually victimized as a young girl, which caused depression and suicidal tendencies. As a teenager, Ms. V had difficulty saying "no" to sexual overtures. As an adult, these earlier traumatic events contributed to a depression that affected her sexual relationship with her husband. Her husband suggested hypnotherapy and they sought a female hypnotist who had experience dealing with survivors of child sexual abuse. The Ontario Society for Clinical Hypnosis recommended they contact Dr. M because he had a female associate who might be available. Ms. V approached her first appointment with Dr. M

---

[16] *R. v. Matheson* (1999), 44 O.R. (3d) 557 at 562 (C.A.).

carefully. Before seeing him, she sent him a fax in which she outlined in detail her background and present difficulties. At their initial meeting Ms. V told Dr. M that she wanted a female therapist. She agreed to let Dr. M hypnotize her, under which she was returned to a child-like state in which she felt the experience of desperately needing someone to rescue her. Ms. V agreed to continue seeing Dr. M because she believed hypnosis would be helpful. During those initial therapy sessions, there was non-sexual touching by Dr. M, which comforted Ms. V when she talked of something troubling or painful. However, over time, the touching grew more intimate. Dr. M started to rest his hand on her knee or shoulder and he pulled his chair closer, placed his arm around her and pulled her onto his lap, in a manner that the patient found comforting, allowing her to speak more freely. Dr. M suggested that they embrace at the outset of each session and Ms. V complied. During one session, while the patient recounted childhood abuses, Dr. M stroked her arm. When she told him that she was sexually aroused by this, he responded that it was normal for patients to develop strong feelings for their therapists. Ms. V told the appellant that she felt guilty and distressed because she did not want to have sexual feelings for him. She had told Dr. M of her sexual difficulties as a teenager and he knew that she valued her 12 years of fidelity to her husband. In spite of knowing this, he continued to touch her in this manner, explaining to her that she needed therapy and he was helping her. After one of these sessions, Ms. V decided to send Dr. M a fax saying that she wanted to end therapy with him because it was having a harmful effect on her. She also told her husband how she felt about the touching, but he did not agree that she should end the therapy, telling her the touching was a therapeutic tool used to trigger positive feelings of comfort. Her husband encouraged her to discuss her feelings with Dr. M. After that, her sessions were increased to two a week. The patient realized that the touching was really about her therapist's desire for sex, but she was unable to talk to anyone about her realization and felt powerless to alter the course of action. Thus began the three-month period of psychologist-patient sexual contact in the course of psychotherapy.

During one session, Dr. M embraced Ms. V and stroked her while she spoke of the childhood abuse. She asked him to touch her, because she was upset. He told her he did not want to do anything to hurt her. She asked if his touching would hurt her. He said he did not know. He touched her breasts and she rubbed his chest for 10 or 15 minutes. In the subsequent session, they eventually started touching each other, then stood up, took off their clothes and had sex on the floor of his office.

After that previous session, the patient had anticipated that Dr. M would want to have intercourse so she brought a condom. After the sex, Ms. V told Dr. M that she felt very distressed and he assured her he was going to provide her with therapy.

By the next session, the patient decided that sex was not a price she wanted to pay for therapy. She wanted to phone the appellant to tell him but feared that her husband would again intervene. Instead, she went to the appellant's office. She placed her chair as far away from him as she could and would not look at him. She was crying while she told him how terrible she felt about what they had done and said that they could not do it again. She said she needed therapy and that she did not want him to touch her. She also told him she did not want to have sex with him. Dr. M told Ms. V that she did need therapy, that she was very close to being better and that he could help her. He told her she did not have to disclose anything to her husband. He sat on the floor next to her and touched her knee. She kept telling him she did not want him to touch her. He spoke to her throughout in a very reassuring tone, repeatedly telling her that he cared a great deal for her and was going to help her. By the end of the session, Ms. V had "agreed to" continue seeing Dr. M twice a week, one day for sex and the other for therapy. She later told him that if sex was going to continue she did not want to have sex on the floor of his office because she found it humiliating. She "agreed to" and did have the "sex sessions" in his apartment about five times. Her next attempt to stop the sex came when she sent Dr. M a fax telling him that she desperately needed therapy, but that he had betrayed her, that she felt he had manipulated her and was not helping her. Ms. V wrote to Dr. M saying that she felt trapped because there was nobody else in the world she could talk to except him. Once again he assured her that she was getting better.

That summer, Dr. M went away for three weeks. While he was gone, Ms. V resolved once again that she was not going to resume therapy with him. Upon his return, Dr. M called Ms. V at her home and she agreed to meet him because she did not want to be rude. They met and had sex, after which she had a panic attack, rolled off the bed and pulled a blanket around herself. She told Dr. M that she was very frightened and to leave her alone. Again, he was very reassuring, saying it was all right, he was going to help her and she did not have anything to fear. The following month, seven months after she first saw Dr. M, Ms. V read the book *Sex in the Forbidden Zone*, which explained transference, making it clear why a therapist cannot have sex with a patient and provide competent therapy to that patient at the same time. Ms. V gave this book to Dr. M and told him that what he had done was harmful. He became apologetic and acknowledged that he had done something wrong, and he offered to find her another therapist. After this meeting, Ms. V did not see Dr. M again.

(c) The Criminal Trial

As is standard in sexual assault trials, Ms.V was closely questioned by the defence lawyer about her willingness to have sex with Dr. M. She acknowledged that Dr. M had not expressly asked for sex; she testified that she "always went more by his actions and behaviour than his words." Ms. V also testified that during the time that the sexual activity was happening she never in any way evidenced that she did not wish to have it, explaining that she did not believe that she could stop Dr. M from touching her or having sex with her.

(d) Why the Courts Decided Against Dr. M

A primary defence argument on behalf of Dr. M was that both women patients "consented" to sex with him, over a considerable period of time, when they could have declined or walked away. The reasons for judgment, both at trial and on the appeal by Dr. M against his conviction, focused on whether there was consent on the part of the two patients. The judges had to look at whether there was consent and whether it could be recognized as genuine and mutual consent or whether it was the kind of "consent" that was vitiated by the authority held by professionals. According to paragraph 265(3)(d) of the *Criminal Code*,[17] "no consent is obtained where the complainant submits or does not resist by reason of... the exercise of authority." Dr. M's defence counsel argued that the relationship of therapist and patient does not involve authority and that the patients in question consented freely to their sexual relationship with their therapist.

The central issue raised by this appeal was about the meaning of the word "authority" as used by Parliament in enacting paragraph 265(3)(d). Dr. M's argument was that as a psychologist he had neither the power nor the right to enforce obedience, and thus he did not have "authority," therefore conduct could not fall within the ambit of paragraph 265(3)(d). His defence counsel pointed out to the trial judge that "authority relationships" are numerous, for example, parent and child, teacher and pupil, employer and employee, superior and junior ranks in military and

---

[17] R.S.C. 1985, c. C-46.

other organizations, and in each of these organizations there is a power or right to enforce obedience in some respect — but that is not true of the doctor-patient relationship nor of the therapist-patient relationship. The defence argued that a doctor may prescribe, but he or she has no power or right to enforce obedience.

Dr. Gail Robinson was one of the expert witnesses at trial and her explanation of the transference and the power dynamics in psychotherapeutic relationships was accepted by the trial judge, and respected by the appeal judges in their conclusions that the boundaries crossed by Dr. M brought his exercise of his professional authority within the meaning of the *Criminal Code*. The courts noted the following explanation of transference with approval, citing Phyllis Coleman's article on sexual abuse:

> Transference refers to the phenomenon whereby the patient begins to relate to the psychotherapist as if he were a parent or some other significant person in her life. The degree of transference involved places this relationship close to that of the parent-child on the continuum of exploitation. To benefit from psychotherapy, the patient must reveal intimate information about herself. Because these revelations are so personal, and often involve information which could be damaging to the patient, she must develop a strong sense of trust in her psychotherapist before she makes such disclosures. Consequently, she is likely to "fall in love" with her psychotherapist, fantasizing that he will be able to make her well. The patient's fantasy is similar to the belief of a child that the parent can solve any problem. As a result of the transference, adult patients may attempt to change the relationship from therapeutic to sexual. Such behaviour is analogous to the "flirtatious" behaviour of a daughter with her father. Nevertheless, just as the father must encourage his daughter to develop her sexuality without responding to her in an overtly sexual manner, the psychotherapist must deny the patient sexual gratification while providing a safe place for exploration of her sexual nature. ...

> The therapist must reject any overt response to sexual feelings because, as a result of transference, the patient's consent to a sexual relationship is inherently suspect. As with the child incest victim, coercion ordinarily is not required. The dependent person's "consent", or even her initiation of sexual contact, is not voluntary because she cannot make a mature decision based on existing information. Rather, she "agrees" as a result of unconscious factors, and therefore lacks the state of mind necessary to consent. Sex under these circumstances is tantamount to sex without consent and should result in liability for damages. [P. Colman, "Sex in Power Dependency Relationships: Taking Unfair Advantage of the 'Fair' Sex" (1988) 53 Alta. L. Rev. 95 at 103-4.][18]

In its judgment on whether the trial judge had erred, the Appeal Court quoted what the trial judge had concluded:

---

[18] *R. v. Matheson*, *supra* note 16, at 566.

In this case, there is no suggestion from any expert that under a therapist-patient relationship, the therapist did not have an existing potential power or authority over the patient. There is also no suggestion from anyone that when a therapist-patient relationship turns into a sexual relationship, that the therapist's power or authority is downgraded or ceased, even though the real therapy has ceased.

. . .

The evidence in my view is overwhelming in establishing that there was a substantial imbalance of power between the powers of the accused and each of his alleged victims during the term of real therapy. During the term stated in the indictment, in each one of the charges, he held the power, and he held it by a significant degree. He had the professional status to gain and hold that power, and his alleged victims were vulnerable to that power, and he knew it. As a result of the power imbalance, he had the power to apply pressure to and manipulate those two patients, and he did so. All of that, in my view, means the exercise of authority, and where it happens for a sexual purpose, there is no consent to an assault for a sexual purpose.[19]

Dr. M lost his appeal. The appeal court unanimously upheld his prison terms.

G. MR. Y, A NURSE IN TORONTO

1. Rape?

In February 1997, Sherrie's mother took her to a hospital because she had stopped having menstrual periods. She was told that her 32-year-old daughter was pregnant and carrying a healthy 15-week-old foetus. "Sherrie" has a congenital malformation of her brain stem with associated hydrocephalus, seizure disorder and severe cerebral palsy. She uses a wheelchair and is unable to communicate because her throat is paralyzed, although she is alert and oriented. Sherrie is chronically ill and completely dependent on staff for bathing, feeding and diapering at the chronic care facility in Toronto where she lives.

In her report to the Special Task Force on Sexual Abuse of Patients in 2000, Sherrie's mother recalled the decision that she and Sherrie's father had to face in order to save their daughter's life, saying, "[b]ecause her foetus was so far advanced, we had a terrible struggle accepting that Sherrie had to have an abortion."[20]

Very shortly before the therapeutic abortion was scheduled to take place, Sherrie miscarried. A Toronto Police Services detective took the foetus to the Centre for Forensic Science, where DNA evidence was

---

[19] *Ibid.*, at 568.
[20] 2001 Task Force, at 7.

extracted and preserved. In November 1997, Sherrie's mother received a letter from the College of Nurses, stating: "This letter is sent to confirm the details of our telephone conversation last week. I advised the panel of the Discipline Committee that your daughter [Sherrie], while a patient, was sexually abused by [Mr.Y]."[21]

2. Criminal Charges

The nurse who was charged had been part of a team responsible for the care and well-being of Sherrie. This is part of the report that Sherrie's parents gave to the Task Force:

> We trusted [the hospital and the nurse] to give appropriate care for our fragile, vulnerable daughter and he betrayed all of us, especially Sherrie. Sherrie was a tiny, fragile, helpless young woman who could not run away, could not call for help, and could not tell anyone what he was doing to her. He knew it and took advantage of it behind closed doors when he was supposed to be giving her care.[22]

Criminal charges were laid against him for sexual assault. In a plea bargain, he admitted that he had sexual intercourse with Sherrie without her genuine consent. Sherrie's parents were troubled by the reference to consent; Sherrie cannot speak or write, her hips and legs are paralyzed and she has little use of her arms or hands. After a hearing, the College revoked the nurse's licence. He also served four years in prison following his plea of guilt.

3. Institutional Responsibility and Liability

Sherrie's mother also reported that concerned health professionals, who were working at the institution following the assault, spoke to the family about disparaging, sexualized comments that a small number of other staff members had been heard to make about Sherrie in Sherrie's presence, while she was in great distress and her family members were not present. The family tried to investigate the matter further, but they reported making little progress after exploring a number of avenues. They chose to transfer Sherrie to another institution. Sherrie's mother told the Task Force:

> We might have coped with the rape and pregnancy and eventually put it behind us, but what was unbearable throughout was the way in which [some of the staff of

---

[21] *Ibid.*
[22] *Ibid.*

the institution] treated Sherrie. Our only concern was that she receive therapy and good, compassionate care because she was so sick and traumatized. Neither of these happened. She was severely depressed, agitated, stopped eating, and tried to kill herself on numerous occasions by banging her head against the wall — knowing that it could destabilize the shunt implanted in her skull.[23]

4. Screening for Sex Offenders

Sherrie's parents reported that the family's distress was compounded when they learned that the health professional convicted of preying on their daughter had previous criminal convictions for sexual offences. To her parents, this raised serious concerns that the college, as the licensing body of this professional, and the hospital, as his employer and the caretaker of their disabled daughter, had all been unable to protect Sherrie. They told the Task Force that they did not see this failure to protect as an aberrant isolated incident that could happen only to one disabled patient; they questioned the systemic safeguards for which the college and the institution were respectively responsible, and wanted to know whether changes in licensing and hiring procedures for nurses were being made to protect patients from any nurses with a history of sex offences.

5. Privacy Concerns

In cases where the professional is charged under the *Criminal Code* with sexual offences, including sexual interference, sexual exploitation of a person with a disability, invitation to sexual touching, indecent act or sexual exposure or a form of sexual assault the court can impose a ban on any information that could identify the complainant or other witnesses, but usually not the accused, when the court is satisfied that justice would be served by such an order. If the charges involve domestic abuse and such a ban is requested then it must be granted by the court and, where identifying the accused would also tend to identify the complainant, then the privacy of the accused is also protected in the ban.

6. Points for Discussion and Learning on Criminal Cases

1. In the Dr. B case study, what do you think of the comparison that Rod and Brenda made between the criminal legal process and the

---

[23] *Ibid.*

college complaint process? Were they being "fair"? What is the relevance of the fact that Dr. B was generally highly regarded as a professional and as a member of the community at large?

2. In the Dr. M case study, can you see his point of view that both his patients "consented" to sex with him? How would you describe the ways in which transference influenced the professional-patient sexual contact in each of the situations that resulted in the criminal charges? Like Dr. B, Dr. M was highly regarded by many of his peers and patients. Would you have sent Dr. M to jail for what he did?

3. In your opinion, what should be the employer's liability in the Mr. Y case study? If you happened to be the one who overheard sexualized comments being made about a severely disabled patient in her presence, what steps would you take — or not? Is there legislative protection for those who "truth tell" when they make a mandatory report of what they have reason to believe is sexually abusive behaviour on the part of a colleague?

4. Do you think that professionals should have access to a collective legal defence fund that is available to all professionals regulated under the *RHPA*?

5. If professionals have access to legal defence support, should patients have access to similar legal supports? If yes, who should pay for such supports?

H. MR. M, AN EMPLOYER AND ENABLER

Ms. C was transferred from the Toronto office of her company to its Vancouver office at her request. Within one month of beginning work at the Vancouver office, Ms. C was subjected to frequent comments and physical actions of a sexual nature by one of her co-workers, Mr. McL. The harassment included comments such as "blow me," "did you get it last night?" and "did you have oral sex?" as well as grabbing her buttocks, and asking her what she wore underneath her skirt.

Ms. C informed Mr. M, the director of the company's Vancouver branch, about several of the incidents involving Mr. McL. Mr. M responded by telling Ms. C that she was an attractive girl and that he was not surprised the incidents had taken place. Mr. M then stressed the importance of nurturing a team environment. He asked her to perform some "inter-office marketing" by taking Mr. McL out to lunch in order to resolve the problem.

Ms. C refused Mr. M's suggestion because this behaviour would be an invitation for Mr. McL to enter her life. The unwelcome sexual conduct continued and Ms. C tendered a letter of resignation in July 1992, citing the lack of professionalism in the Vancouver office and her discomfort after asking an individual to do things for her and that individual responding by requesting that she "blow him."

Because of Ms. C's value to the company, Mr. M refused to accept the resignation. He promised to promote her and to make progressive changes for the branch. She withdrew her letter of resignation on these and other assurances.

Ms. C received an excellent performance appraisal one month later. Rather than signing it, however, she wrote of her sexual harassment experiences on the employee comments section of the form. Mr. M was furious with her for this action because the comments would reach the head office of the company. Mr. M believed that he had gone the extra mile for Ms. C and that her complaint constituted a betrayal. He threatened to rewrite her performance review, a threat he later recanted. Two weeks later, Mr. M informed Ms. C that she was being terminated due to a stringent cost improvement program as a result of the poor economy.

Ms. C brought her complaint to the British Columbia Human Rights Commission. The Commission found that Ms. C was sexually harassed in her workplace and was terminated because she complained of sexual harassment. The employer was found to have failed to meet its human rights obligations under the British Columbia *Human Rights Code*[24] and was ordered to pay Ms. C for her lost time and suffering.

1. Discussion Points

1. Mr. M clearly valued Ms. C as a top employee — he successfully attempted to dissuade her from resigning and was involved in her promotion. What were the missing essential components in the situation that might have protected Ms. C?
2. How would you describe Mr. M's attitude to Ms. C's plight?

---

[24] R.S.B.C. 1996, c. 210.

I. MS. H, A PSYCHIATRIC NURSE IN MARKHAM

Ms. H had been practising as a psychiatric nurse for over 15 years when she learned of a job opportunity in a new hospital that was about to open. In 1990, she was hired to work as a staff nurse in the psychiatric department where she worked in a team admitting patients, monitoring them and following the orders of the part-time psychiatrists. Each patient had a primary and secondary nurse and the unit had a full-time social worker and a part-time therapist.

Ms. H met patient Ms. W when she was admitted for depression in 1991 and provided her with care. Following Ms. W's discharge two months later, Ms. H met Ms. W while out shopping and after chatting for a while, the two exchanged telephone numbers. This led to a growing social relationship between the two, and in response to the desire of Ms. W to change residences, she and Ms. H agreed to share an apartment. Ms. H did not disclose the relationship to her superiors at the hospital and asked Ms. S, a friend and former patient at the facility, not to disclose the fact that she and Ms. W were living together.

Eventually, the relationship between Ms. H and Ms. W became known at the hospital and Ms. H was advised that her employment had been terminated and the matter had been reported to the College of Nurses as required by the *Regulated Health Professions Act*. The College found Ms. H guilty of professional misconduct and ordered a reprimand and a two-month suspension of her licence.

Ms. H brought an action against the hospital for wrongful dismissal, which was heard in 1995. Among the several experts testifying at the trial was a nurse, Ms. R, who testified on behalf of Ms. H. Ms. R noted that although the then-guidelines of the College of Nurses did not prohibit the kind of conduct in which Ms. H engaged, she agreed that it would have been prudent for Ms. H to have consulted her colleagues prior to entering into her relationship with Ms. W. Both Ms. R and Dr. S, expert witnesses for the hospital, agreed on the importance of the concept of transference and counter-transference, and further agreed that they applied in Ms. H's case as she was a psychiatric nurse providing therapeutic treatment to her patients.

In deciding whether the hospital had met its obligation at trial of proving that it had just cause for dismissing Ms. H, the Court noted that the hospital did not set formal standards for its staff regarding patient-staff relationships. At the same time, the Court found that on the basis of her training and her many years of experience, Ms. H understood the concepts — and their associated dangers — of transference and counter-transference. Ms. H also knew her relationship was wrong as proven by the fact that she had attempted to keep it a secret, particularly cautioning Ms. S not to reveal her knowledge of the relationship. Moreover, she knew that patient Ms. S had been upset by her relationship with Ms. W and this constituted a potential source of harm to Ms. S. Ms. H's conduct jeopardized the integrity of her treatment unit. As a result, Ms. H's claim of wrongful dismissal was denied.

1. Discussion Points

1.   The absence of clear and defined policy was used as a defence by Ms. H but the court did not accept it because it believed that Ms. H understood the concept of sexual abuse. If the facts of the situation were different, do you think the defence would be successful?
2.   The lack of a workplace policy resulted in harm to both patients and the hospital. What could have been put in place to ensure that both were protected?
3.   In the two cases of Mr. M and Ms. H above, there is an interesting contrast in that the offender in the first instance represents an employer who assaulted a subordinate and in the second, a nurse who assaulted a patient. In developing a workplace policy, what issues arise specific to these differing incidents?

J. DR. SM, A PHYSICIAN IN OTTAWA

Dr. SM was a physician who received his licence to practice in 1979. In 1986, he joined the staff of a large urban hospital. In this capacity, Dr. SM saw patients in both the wards of the hospital and in the outpatient clinic, and did on-call work in the emergency room. He was also responsible for supervising interns and residents in the hospital's teaching unit and he worked closely with the nursing and clerical staff in the facility. Dr. SM, at age 43, had separated from his spouse in 1996, and had two young children.

In early 1998, Dr. SM went to trial on charges of sexual assault, sexual assault with a weapon, and forcible confinement under the *Criminal Code* for assaulting a female intern, aged 39, who worked in the hospital. The complainant was on internal medicine rotation and Dr. SM was her supervisor. The complainant's story was that on a Friday night, sometime between 9:00 p.m. and 1:00 a.m., she was paged by Dr.

SM in the emergency room where she was working. He asked her to meet him in the residents' room the next day to review recently admitted patients. When the complainant arrived, Dr. SM was in the room alone, the lights were on and the door was partially open. The complainant sat down and they began to discuss their patients. At one point, Dr. SM referred to a young male patient with children, whose condition was deteriorating. Dr. SM said he found it hard to give patients bad news and it helped him to discuss the situation in advance with someone who was a "compassionate and empathetic listener." He then put his right hand over the complainant's. When the complainant stood to leave the room, Dr. SM said "You know you want this as much as I do." Dr. SM pulled the complainant away from the door and closed and locked it. He told the complainant that she was "feisty" and he liked it when she struggled. He also said she was "scrawny." At the time of the incident, the complainant was five feet, seven inches tall, and weighed 125 pounds. Dr. SM was six feet, five inches tall, and weighed 240 pounds. Dr. SM attempted to kiss the complainant and remove some of her clothes. While he held the complainant by the back of the neck with one hand, Dr. SM undid the button and zipper of his pants with the other. The complainant protested, saying, "[n]o. Let me go. Leave me alone. I want to get out of here." Dr. SM pinned the complainant on the floor, straddled her and placed his hand over her mouth. With the other he exposed his erect penis. He then held a pair of scissors to her throat and said that if she did not cooperate he would cut off her nipples.

At this point, someone tried to open the door of the residents' room. Dr. SM swore, pulled the complainant to her knees in front of him and said "[s]uck it and make it fast." The complainant averted her head and Dr. SM began to simultaneously masturbate and hit the complainant on the head with the scissors. Dr. SM ejaculated with most of the semen landing on his clothing although some landed on the complainant's cheek.

The complainant then got up and adjusted her clothing and contact lenses as an intern entered the room and greeted Dr. SM. The complainant spoke briefly with the intern and then all left to resume their duties. The complainant did not report the incident. The next time she saw Dr. SM, he said, "Of course, our little secret will remain quiet." In a subsequent encounter, he said, "If you say anything about this, who would they believe anyway, you an intern, or me, a staff physician?" The complainant said that over the next few weeks she was troubled by nightmares and took all possible steps to avoid Dr. SM or ensure that when she saw him she was not alone. In her second year of residency, she arranged to be supervised by another staff physician.

In June of 1996, the complainant heard that Dr. SM had been criminally charged with assaulting three nurses at the hospital and she contacted the police. Dr. SM was charged with sexual assault, sexual assault with a weapon, and forcible confinement under the *Criminal Code*. The trial took place over 11 days. Dr. SM was found guilty of sexual assault and forcible confinement, but acquitted of sexual assault with a weapon. Each of the offences for which he was convicted carried with them sentences of up to ten years in prison. In the complainant's case, the court ordered that Dr. SM serve an 18-month conditional sentence on each charge, to be served concurrently. The conditions on his sentence, which was to be served in the community, included being regularly supervised and keeping his supervisor informed of changes of address or employment; staying in the province unless given permission; keeping the peace and maintaining good behaviour; abstaining from drugs, alcohol or owning, possessing or carrying a weapon; attending a treatment program; carrying a copy of the court order with him whenever he left his home; and refraining from any direct or indirect contact with the complainant.

In August of 1998, a Discipline Panel of the College of Physicians and Surgeons of Ontario met to hear the complaints of six persons against Dr. SM based on incidents that had taken place in the hospital between 1986 and 1996, including that of the complainant. The charges against Dr. SM were brought under Regulations to the *Health Disciplines Act*,[25] in that he had engaged in conduct or an act relevant to his practice that, having regard to all circumstances, would reasonably be regarded by members (of the College) as disgraceful, dishonourable or unprofessional, and under Regulations to the *Medicine Act, 1991*[26] in that he had engaged in conduct unbecoming of a physician.

The first three complainants were the three nurses involved in the criminal convictions of 1998 discussed above. These nurses alleged that Dr. SM had fondled their breasts and buttocks and made inappropriate comments. Complainants 1, 2, and 3 were the nurses involved in the criminal convictions brought against Dr. SM in 1998. The fifth and sixth complainants, both of whom worked in the hospital, had brought new complaints to the disciplinary process not heard in the earlier criminal actions. They also alleged that Dr. SM had made inappropriate remarks

---

[25] R.R.O. 448/80, s. 27.32.
[26] O. Reg. 856/93, s. 1(1) 34; *Medicine Act, 1991*, S.O. 1991, c. 30.

and fondled their breasts. The resident complainant from the criminal trial was the fourth complainant. Dr. SM admitted that he had engaged in the conduct alleged by Complainants 1, 3, and 6 and admitted only to fondling Complainant 2. He wholly denied the allegations brought by Complainants 4 and 5.

The Discipline Panel stated clearly that its decision must be based purely on the evidence before it and must not take into account Dr. SM's previous criminal convictions. The Panel noted that in order to find Dr. SM guilty, the evidence must be clear and convincing and based on cogent evidence. In concluding that Dr. SM had committed acts of sexual assault and confinement on Complainant 4, the Panel stated that it accepted her credibility over that of Dr. SM. The Panel also found Dr. SM guilty of the complaints alleged by Complainants 2 and 5.

Dr. SM was sentenced in August 1999. The Panel unanimously ordered the revocation of Dr. SM's certificate of registration. In 2001, Dr. SM unsuccessfully attempted to appeal the decision.

1. Discussion Points:

1. After assaulting the intern, Dr. SM stated: "If you say anything about this, who would they believe anyway, you an intern, or me, a staff physician?" This comment appears to have had the chilling effect on the intern that Dr. SM desired, as she took no steps to report Dr. SM until she heard about his other victims. If a colleague confided this kind of occurrence to you, what would you do?

2. As a new employee, what are the difficulties you anticipate might exist in trying to have a small workplace that does not have a sexual abuse prevention policy, to develop and implement one?

K. MR. A, A PHYSIOTHERAPIST IN BARRIE

Mr. A was a physiotherapist who ran a practice and owned his own physiotherapy clinic in a mid-sized Ontario town. In the course of his work, Mr. A had acted as a clinic tutor for university students and had also provided co-operative education placements for high school students. In December of 1999, the College Discipline Committee convened a hearing into the conduct of Mr. A. It was alleged by two female students who had been at his clinic on placement that Mr. A had habitually failed to maintain proper professional boundaries in his dealings with patients, students, volunteers, youthful colleagues and employees. This resulted in unprofessional conduct, including sexual impropriety, with these individuals.

Ms. A (not related) observed sexual and flirtatious comments by Mr. A with staff. He commented on his preference for small-breasted women. Ms. A believed these comments referred to herself and another student in the clinic. She believed the comments were made with a humorous intent. Mr. A hugged Ms. A. She felt that the hugs were not professional, but did not find them insulting or threatening. On one occasion, Mr. A slapped or tapped Ms. A's gluteal region despite her explicitly asking him not to. Ms. A understood the touching to be a joke, but felt that it should not have occurred. Ms. A complained to her educational institution about Mr. A. No formal proceedings took place. Mr. A agreed not to take any more students.

Mr. A and Ms. B became friendly during the time of her placement and discussed personal issues, including the fact that Ms. B had been sexually abused. Ms. B became very attached to Mr. A. Mr. A stated that he was not aware of the extent of her attachment to him at this time. During the placement, Mr. A performed physiotherapy procedures on Ms. B for an injury. Although Mr. A denied the physiotherapist-patient relationship, Ms. B viewed herself as his patient. Mr. A created a chart for Ms. B. On some occasions during the placement, Ms. B broke down in tears. Mr. A provided emotional support to Ms. B including stroking her arm, shoulder, hip and knee and holding Ms. B. Mr. A made self-disclosure about his personal problems during at least one of these discussions. Mr. A and Ms. B commenced a personal relationship. There was a progression from casual hugging, to intense hugging, caressing, kissing, disrobing, sexual touching and oral sex. They did not have sexual intercourse.

Mr. A pleaded guilty to the allegation of unprofessional conduct. Mr. A understood that his relationship with Ms. B had caused her great pain. He admitted that he should have never let the relationship take place. The panel gave careful consideration to the facts and Mr. A's plea of guilty. They accepted the plea and found Mr. A guilty of professional misconduct.

During sentencing, the panel considered mitigating factors including the guilty plea, the fact that this was the first complaint lodged against the member, and his commitment to make amends. Aggravating factors justifying a serious penalty were that the member had a duty not to sexualize the relationship, the member sexualized the demonstration of treatments on students, and the member did not respect professional boundaries when acting as a clinical instructor.

The panel ordered that Mr. A's certificate of registration be suspended for six months, after which his practice would be monitored for a further 24 months. In addition, Mr. A was ordered to complete a series of counselling sessions in the area of professional boundaries and was prohibited indefinitely from participating in the training of students. Mr. A was also ordered to write a letter of apology to Ms. B and to pay for her therapy.

1. Discussion Points

1. Although there is no evidence that Dr. A made similar comments to those of Dr. SM above, did the size of his workplace; that is, his direct and personal control over his employees and volunteers, convey the same message?
2. As a new employee, what are the difficulties you anticipate might exist in trying to have a small workplace that does not have a sexual abuse prevention policy to develop and implement one?

L. DR. AEK, A RECENT GRADUATE, FEMALE GENERAL PRACTITIONER — PSYCHOTHERAPY

Mr. X first saw Dr. AEK in December 1999 concerning a mole he wanted removed. Dr. AEK was in her second year of Family Practice Residency, which had begun in July 1997 but had been interrupted by an 8-month hiatus for an illness that included care by a psychiatrist. She was due to finish in May 2000, but in January 2000, Mr. X phoned Dr. AEK and asked to be referred for psychotherapy. Dr. AEK offered to see him for that purpose and began psychotherapy sessions under the supervision of the Family Medicine program. The sessions were interrupted in May 2000 when Dr. AEK finished her residency and wrote her examinations. In the interim, it was arranged that Dr. M was to care for Mr. X and supervise his medications. When Dr. AEK established an office for a psychotherapy practice (in her home), Dr. M advised Mr. X who contacted Dr. AEK and the psychotherapy sessions were resumed on September 12, 2000.

1. He Says, She Says

There was considerable discrepancy between testimony and other evidence from the patient (his co-worker was also a witness; he provided close-up informal photographs of the professional) as compared to the professional (a colleague, her father and her husband testified; she introduced photographs of her breasts as evidence). The evidence was considered as part of the Discipline Committee's task in defining the nature of the relationship between Dr. AEK and Mr. X, as a patient and as a former patient.

Mr. X testified that Dr. AEK commenced a sexual relationship with him while he was a psychotherapy patient (kissing and sexual touching). Dr. AEK denied this. Mr. X also testified that after Dr. AEK terminated their formal psychotherapeutic relationship, she continued to see Mr. X socially, and engaged in a sexual relationship with him, in the period from November 2000 through January 2001. Dr. AEK denied that there had been a sexual relationship at any time.

In December 2000, Dr. AEK billed OHIP for her attendance at a party with Mr. X, which at the time she considered to be "observation" that would help her provide appropriate care for her patient, and for "home calls." Mr. X alleged that Dr. AEK provided him with cocaine and other drugs to be taken in association with the cocaine, which she denied.

2. What the Discipline Committee Had to Decide

It was the duty of the Committee on the evidence before it to determine if Dr. AEK had had a sexual relationship with her patient, or former psychotherapy patient, which would be sexual abuse and disgraceful, dishonourable or unprofessional conduct. In addition to the issue of sexual abuse, the Committee had to determine on the evidence before it whether the conduct of Dr. AEK, in admitting to the disclosure of personal information and to going to a party at a bar with a former psychotherapy patient, and otherwise socializing with him, would be considered by members as disgraceful, dishonourable or unprofessional. The Discipline Committee had to make decisions as to which evidence they found more credible as the basis for the decisions as to whether the professional was guilty of sexual abuse, in accordance with the definitions of sexual abuse and professional misconduct in the *RHPA*. Any consideration as to penalty had to follow a finding of guilt.

The Notice of Hearing alleged that Dr. AEK committed an act of professional misconduct under: 1) paragraph 51(1)(b.1) of the *Code* in that she engaged in the sexual abuse of a patient; and 2) paragraph 1(1)(33) of Ontario Regulation 856/93 under the *Medicine Act* for an act or omission relevant to the practice of medicine that, having regard to all the circumstances, would reasonably be regarded by members as "disgraceful, dishonourable or unprofessional."

The Discipline Committee of the CPSO focused on two main issues:

1. Did the conduct of Dr. AEK constitute sexual abuse?; and
2. Would the conduct of Dr. AEK otherwise be reasonably regarded by members as disgraceful, dishonourable or unprofessional, on the basis of boundary violations, for her interactions with a former psychotherapy patient, for the alleged provision of cocaine to the patient, for an alleged failure to maintain records, and for the alleged improper billing of OHIP?

3. Risk of Harm — Transference and Counter-transference

In reaching its finding as to guilt in some respects, the Discipline Committee decided that Dr. AEK had not sexually abused her patient such that mandatory revocation of her certificate was required. However, the Committee expressed extensive concern about the lack of judgment on the professional's part. In its deliberations on the appropriate penalty, the Committee took into account in its reasons for decision concerns about Dr. AEK's naïveté, her lack of understanding and knowledge of transference, her boundary violations, and the fact that she exposed the patient to potential harm. The following paragraphs convey key points noted by the Discipline Committee in deciding on penalty.

1. *Boundary violations*, as evidenced by the familiarity in the photographs, the complainant's detailed knowledge of Dr. AEK's personal life, the misguided socialization, setting up an office using the bed in her personal living quarters and the doubtful nature of the house calls, when the patient was already under the care of someone else, were serious professional mistakes. *The Committee wrote, "They are not mere errors in judgment, but rather are unprofessional acts exposing the patient to potential harm."*
2. *Poor judgment in agreeing to carry on a relationship with a former patient,* who had admitted he was sexually attracted to her and who already had made a pass at her, including going to his apartment and taking him to social events.

3.   *Inadequacy of training and knowledge* that allowed Dr. AEK to believe she was capable of providing psychotherapy to patients suffering from a complex illness.

4.   *Continued inability to recognize her inadequacy* and the deleterious effects this had upon the complainant.

5.   *Failure to recognize the need for a referral* of a patient who was beyond her skill.

6.   *Not meeting criteria that physicians must comport themselves ethically and in the interests of their patients*, as demonstrated by her behaviour with Mr. X.

4. Educational Requirements under the *Code*

1.   Given the legislative requirements regarding education of students, practitioners and the public under section 84 of the *Code*, prepare a report card on the college and/or educational institution of your profession, including answers to the following questions:

   i.   Overall, to what extent has each educational requirement in section 84 been met?

   ii.   Is there mandatory sexual abuse education in your professional school and for health professionals who have been certified by your college to practise?

   iii. What grade do you assign to the content and accessibility of such programs. For example, where and how frequently are they offered? Are there interactive learning interventions?

   iv.   Are the guidelines and policies developed by your health care profession (your college and your association) for the conduct of members with their patients clear about sexual abuse? For example, have you been clearly informed on what you have to consider about possible post-termination relationships?

   v.   Do you understand your reporting obligations as a regulated health professional, including time frame to report, to whom, and how?

   vi.   Do you have information about how members of the public are being educated on sexual boundaries in competent care, on what constitutes sexual abuse under the Ontario law, on how to proceed with an inquiry or complaint about sexual abuse?

vii. Have you been adequately educated to assist patients who disclose abuse by health professionals or others? Do you know where you can get ongoing information and support to help you respond to such cases?

5. Critical Analysis of the Zero Tolerance "No Sex With Patients" Rules

2.(a) Approaching the issue of professional-patient sex in rural or isolated community scenarios from a patient-centric angle produces a number of questions that have not been addressed in surveys of the professions (to January 2004 when this book was published). For example:

(i) What happens to the patient's care options when the sexual relationship begins?

(ii) What impact does professional-patient sex have on the level of trust in other professionals to keep sexual and other boundaries intact?

(iii) What of the former patient who then becomes the former sexual partner of a professional in the community — what is the alternative standard of care available under those circumstances in the rural or isolated community?

(iv) What if another professional providing care to that patient wishes to have sex with that patient?

2.(b) Discuss the following "reasonable hypotheticals" — scenarios presented by the Ontario Medical Association in arguing for exceptions to the "no sex with patients" rule:

(i) A professional assesses, diagnoses or treats his or her spouse or partner;

(ii.) A brief consensual affair between two colleagues who have provided assessment, diagnosis or treatment to one or each other;

(iii) A single instance of prohibited physical contact, which occurred due to a professional's treatable emotional or mental impairment.

After your discussion is completed, you may wish to discuss the appeal court's response to each of these scenarios, which are summarized in note 42 in Chapter 6.

6. Who Can Best Provide Public Education?

Here are some additional questions geared to develop a broader sense of what education needs to be and who needs it.

1. What material is available by each College to patients and to members of the public, and are these materials available in health professional's offices?
2. Are they produced in different languages?
3. Is the information written in plain language?
4. Are the educational materials available on videotape or cassette for patients who have special needs?

Appendix V

ESSENTIAL READING

Aggarwal, A.P., *Sexual Harassment: A Guide for Understanding and Prevention* (Toronto: Butterworths, 1992).

Armstrong, H., "Fear and Denial: Grappling with the Reality of Abusive Physicians" (1995) 152:2 Can. Med. Assoc. J. 177.

Bohnen, L., *Regulated Health Professions Act: A Practical Guide* (Aurora, Ont.: Canada Law Book, 1994).

Braverman, L., *Administrative Tribunals: A Legal Handbook* (Aurora, Ont.: Canada Law Book, 2001).

Carr, M. & Robinson, G., "Fatal Attraction: The Ethical and Clinical Dilemma of Patient-Therapist Sex" (1990) 35 Can. J. Psychiatry 122.

Carr, M., Robinson, G., Stewart, D. *et al.*, "A Survey of Canadian Psychiatric Residents Regarding Resident-educator Sexual Contact" (1991) 148 Am. J. Psychiatry 216.

College of Physicians and Surgeons of Ontario, "Sexual Abuse of Patients" in College of Physicians and Surgeons of Ontario, *Member Dialogue* (November/December 2002) online, College of Physicians and Surgeons of Ontario <http//www.cpso.on.ca/Publications/Dialogue/1102/study.htm>.

Cullen, R.M., "Arguments for Zero Tolerance of Sexual Contact between Doctors and Patients" (1999). J. of Med. Ethics 482.

Davis, D.A., Thomson, M.A., Oxman, A.D., & Haynes, R.B., "Changing physician performance. A systematic review of the effect of continuing medical education strategies" (1995) 274:9 J.A.M.A. 700.

Gartrell, N. *et al.*, "Psychiatrist-Patient Sexual Contact: Results of a National Survey-Prevalence" (1986) 143:9 Am. J. Psychiatry 1126.

Gartrell, N., Herman, J., Olarte, S., *et al.*, "Psychiatrist-patient Sexual Contact: Results of a National Survey" (1988) 145 Am. J. Psychiatry 690.

Gartrell, N., Milliken, N., Goodson, III, W., *et al.*, "Physicians-patient Sexual Contact — Prevalence and Problems" (1992) 157 West J. Med. 139.

Health Professions Regulatory Advisory Council, *Adjusting the Balance: A Review of the Regulated Health Professions Act* (Toronto: Health Professions Regulatory Advisory Council, 2001).

Health Professions Regulatory Advisory Council, *Weighing the Balance: A Review of the Regulated Health Professions Act* (Toronto: Health Professions Regulatory Advisory Council, 1999).

Herman, J., *Trauma and Recovery: The Aftermath of Violence — From Domestic Abuse to Political Terror* (New York: Basic Books, 1997).

Herman J., Gartrell, N., Olarte, S., Feldstein, M. & Localio, R., "Psychiatrist-Patient Sexual Contact: Results of a National Survey, II: Psychiatrists' Attitudes" (1987) Am. J. Psychiatry 144.

Lamont, J. & Woodward, C., "Patient-physician sexual involvement: a Canadian survey of obstetrician-gynecologists" (1994) 150 Can. Med. Assoc. J. 1433.

McNamara, L. & Nelson, E., "Regulation of Health Care Professionals" in J. Downie & T. Caulfield, eds. *Canadian Health Law and Policy* (Toronto: Butterworths, 1999).

McPhedran, M., "Investigating Sexual Abuse of Patients: The Ontario Experience" (1992) 1 Health Law Review 3.

McPhedran, M., Armstrong, H., Edney, R., Long, B., Marshall, P., Roach, R., *The Final Report of the Independent Task Force on Sexual Abuse of Patients* (College of Physicians & Surgeons of Ontario, November 25, 1991).

McPhedran, M., Armstrong, R., Long, B., Marshall, P. & Roach, R., *What About Accountability to the Patient?* (Toronto: Independent Final Report of the Special Task Force on Sexual Abuse of Patients, 2001).

O'Reilly, P.L., *Health Care Practitioners: An Ontario Case Study in Policy Making* (Toronto: University of Toronto Press, 2000).

Penfold, P.S., *Sexual Abuse by Health Professionals: A Personal Search for Meaning and Healing* (Toronto: University of Toronto Press, 1998).

Peterson, M.R., *At Personal Risk: Boundary Violations in Professional-Client Relationships* (New York: Norton & Co., 1992).

Schwartz, A., *Striking a New Balance: A Blueprint for the Regulation of Ontario's Health Professions* (Toronto: Ministry of Health, 1989).

Steinecke, R.A., *A Complete Guide to the Regulated Health Professions Act*, looseleaf (Aurora, Ont.: Canada Law Book, updated 2002).

Appendix VI

PREVENTING SEXUAL ABUSE OF PATIENTS AN IMPORTANT NOTE FOR PATIENTS

We haven't met and I can't tell you my name, but you are reading this handout from *Preventing Sexual Abuse of Patients — A Legal Guide for Health Care Professionals*, so I know that you (or someone close to you) are concerned about sexual abuse, assault or harassment in a health care setting and you have probably received this handout from a concerned health professional who has the Prevention Guide. There are a dozen "real-life" case studies in the Prevention Guide, and my case is one of them. Authors Marilou McPhedran and Wendy Sutton asked me to write this message to you — as one patient to another. Although the Prevention Guide is a textbook for health professionals, I was one of the reviewers of the manuscript because I lived through (and yes, "survivor" is certainly a good description!) many of the different legal processes that can be triggered when a patient is sexually abused by a health professional. There is little information readily available to the public about sexual abuse of patients, and the options available for patients who have had this terrible experience can seem quite intimidating. I wish I had a source of information like this book when I became able to tell the truth about what happened to me, but I wish even more that the sexual abuse had never happened at all. That is why this handout is designed to do two things — in an abbreviated form: 1) give you basic contact information about the regulatory colleges that are legally responsible for responding to patients who report experiences of sexual abuse, and 2) give you some basic information that I think may be helpful to a patient recovering from sexual abuse, or someone who may be in a position to stop or prevent such abuse. The "public interest" described in the Ontario law that governs 23 health professions in Ontario (the *Regulated Health Professions Act* and its included *Health Professions Procedural Code*)[1] is really about *our* interest — we are all patients of one or more regulated health professionals and *we are the "public"*. I hope this information is helpful to you, and although we don't know each other — remember: you are not alone in this — it's patients, working in partnership with the very many health professions who are not abusers, who will help to make the regulatory system more responsive to patients and more capable of stopping abusers.

Sincerely, "Nora"

Taking Action on Sexual Abuse by a Health Professional

Remember: It is critical for the professional to appreciate that there may be a sexualized environment with some patients, that this is within the realm of a reasonable possibility for a number of possible reasons, and that it is always the responsibility of the professional to focus on providing appropriate care for the individual patient.

A few Points to Keep in Mind if you are Considering Action

If you have experienced abuse then you may want to visit a number of websites that are listed below to gather information to help you decide on what you need to do to get the assistance you need to heal. Unfortunately, although the Ontario Government supports many health professions and their institutions financially, there is currently (at the time of publication in 2004) no Government funded independent support or advocacy program for sexually abused patients, although some colleges try to provide such support.

Websites

See "Choosing a Family Physician for Survivors" in the Sexual Abuse Reading Centre on the Recovery Canada Wellness Network website.[2] As well, the Canadian Women's Health Network has published a Manitoba

---

[1]   *Regulated Health Professions Act, 1991* — available online <http://www.gov. on.ca/mbs/english/publications> or through the Government of Ontario Bookstore Tel: 1-800-377-7746 toll-free or TTY 1-800-387-5559.

[2]   <http://www.vansondesign.com/RecoveryCanada/SexualAbuse/Library/choosingadoctor. html>.

study with practical, detailed guidelines in "A Resource for Women Survivors of Abuse and Their Care Providers" [3] with specific sections for physicians, primary care nurses, breast screening nurses, mammographers, sonographers and dental care providers. According to the authors, "it is essential for health care providers to understand the origin of somatic symptoms, and to consider an abuse history in patients with multiple complaints without an organic cause." There are also a number of American websites, such as AdvocateWeb, which offers extensive free resources for victims, survivors, and their families, friends, victim advocates, and professionals. [4]

Good News, Bad News: Therapeutic Support Funds at the Colleges

The legislation[5] requires colleges — through "Patient Relations Committees" to establish funds for sexually abused patients, but be prepared: access to funding for therapy and counselling is limited by the law and by some colleges in a number of ways. Even though those who have been sexually abused by a health care professional usually require treatment from the date the incident occurred, in most cases, there is no access to the college funding for a patient whose complaint did not proceed to a formal hearing. If a plea bargain is reached, a member voluntarily resigns, or the college decides not to proceed with the complaint, then the patient can expect to be denied access to counselling funds. Only those elected to represent us in the Ontario Legislature can change the law. To contact your Member of Provincial Parliament (MPP), consult your telephone directory under Government of Ontario.

How to Contact a College

Each regulated health profession is related to a regulatory college for that profession, and the colleges have a legal responsibility to provide public education and to process complaints about sexual abuse of patients. Some colleges are better than others in providing this public service.

---

[3] S. Tudiver *et al.* Available on paper from the Prairie Women's Health Centre of Excellence and online <http//:www.cwhn.ca/resources/csa>.

[4] <http://www.advocateweb.org>.

[5] *Regulated Health Professions Act, 1991* — available online <http:www.gov.on.ca/mbs/english/publications> or through the Government of Ontario Bookstore Tel: 1-800-377-7746 toll-free or TTY 1-800-387-5559.

Health Professions Regulatory Advisory Council (HPRAC)

If you contact a college and you do not feel you have been helped, one option would be to contact the Health Professions Regulatory Advisory Council (HPRAC) — which must report to the minister of health annually on how the colleges are fulfilling their legal obligations in the public interest.[6] If you do contact HPRAC, remember to record and keep the date of your contact, the name(s) of HPRAC staff with whom you communicated and, if you sent HPRAC any written information, make sure you keep a complete copy for your own future reference. If you are comfortable disclosing your identity, you can tell HPRAC staff to mail the HPRAC annual report to you so you can see how your concerns were addressed, or if you wish to maintain your privacy, you can access the annual report on the HPRAC website <http://www.hprac.org>.

---

[6] HPRAC Tel: Toll-Free 1-888-377-7746, or 416-326-1550, Fax: 416-326-1549; E-mail: <http://info@hprac.org>; Website: <http://www.hprac.org>; Mail: 55 St. Clair Avenue West, Suite 806, Box 18, Toronto, Ontario, Canada M4V 2Y7.

INDEX

Law perspective — *cont'd*
• SCC pronouncements, 37-38

Legislation, online, 254

Liability. *See* Workplace policies

Limitation periods, 82, 243

M

Mandatory reporting, 71, 73-75, 89

Mandatory revocation, 41, 42, 109-10

Media, 200-202

Misconduct. *See* Professional misconduct

O

Offences and penalties, *see also* Criminal offences
• chart re, 95-99
• failure to file report, 95
• false reporting, 95
• mandatory revocation, 109-12
• • Charter rights and freedoms and, 109-10
• • college vs. court approach to, 110-11

P

Patient Relations Committee
• education and. *See* Education
• generally. *See* Complaints
• HPP Code provisions re, 33, 237
• RHPA provisions re, 73

Patient Relations Program, 33, 71, 73 237

Policy samples
• dental technologists, college of, 259-63
• • definitions, 259-60
• • prevention guidelines, 260-62
• Human Rights Commission, 280-86
• large workplace, 280-3
• • definitions, 281
• • employer's responsibilities, 282
• • external administrative proceedings, 283

• • internal complaints procedure, 282-3
• • preamble, 280
• small workplace, 283-86
• • definitions, 284
• • employer's responsibilities, 285
• • external administrative proceedings, 286
• • internal complaints procedure, 285-86
• • preamble, 283

Policy statement
• generally. *See* Workplace policies
• *Human Rights Code* requirements, 271-72

Practice guidelines
• medical laboratory technologists, sample, 263-68
• • appropriate behaviour, guidelines for, 266
• • boundaries of practice guidebook, 267-68
• • child abuse, reporting of, 265
• • overview, 263
• • penalties, 266-67
• • reporting obligations, 265
• • sexual abuse defined, 264
• • zero tolerance, 264

Prevention program
• blame issue, 35
• consent issue, 34-35
• coverage, 33
• HPRAC assessment, 34
• key questions, 34
• regulatory college programs, 34
• vulnerability issue, 34

Prevention strategies
• boundary issues, 145
• employer as enabler, case study re, 146-47, 307-308
• psychiatric nurse, case study re, 147-48, 309-10
• workplace policies. *See* Workplace policies

Privacy
• admissibility of evidence, 127
• criminal proceedings and, 126, 142, 306
• generally, 126
• media attention, 128
• personal information, privileged or protected, 127
• publication bans, 126

Sex with patients — *cont'd*
• Charter freedom of association argument, 42-43
• mandatory revocation provision, 41, 42
• zero tolerance policy. *See* **Zero tolerance policies**

Sexual abuse, *see also Regulated Health Professions Act*

• allegations. *See* **Allegations**
• causes of re patients, 13-14
• • counter-transference, 14
• • transference, 14
• cost of, 203
• defined, 13, 32, 206
• education re. *See* **Education**
• gender-based analysis, 19
• impact on patients, 23-24
• • risk of harm, 23, 36-37
• • secondary/vicarious victimization, 24
• policies re. *See* **Policy samples; Policy statement**
• poverty and, 19
• prevalence of, 15-20
• • diversity, 19-20
• • generally, 15
• • incidence, 15-18
• • 1991 CPSO survey, 16
• • "sexual contact" issue, 18
• • 2000 HPRAC survey, 16
• • 2001 Task Force report, 17-18
• • U.S. data, 15
• problem of, 9
• types of, 13

Sexual assault, 38-9, 129

Sexual contact

• prohibition of, 20-22

Statutory guidelines, 186

Statutory obligations, 184

Statutory practice guidelines. *See* **Practice guidelines**

Students, medical, *see also* **Education**

• ignorance of, 22

V

Victim

• protection for, 75
• secondary, 24, 116, 292

W

Websites, 330

Whistle blowing, 71, 73-75, 86-87

Workplace policies

• complaint procedures, 159-63
• • advisor, appointment of neutral, 161
• • generally, 159-60
• • hospital environment, in, 160
• • investigation process, 162-63
• • investigator, role and training of, 161-62
• • team involvement, 160-63
• development of, 145
• due diligence requirement, 149
• duty of care issue, 151
• employer as enabler issue, 148-52
• employer legal liability, 152
• • common law grounds for, 154-57
• • fiduciary duty, 156-57
• • vicarious liability, 155-56
• employer responsibility, 149-50
• *Human Rights Code* obligations, 152-54
• in-service training, 170
• large workplace, in, 163
• • case study, 163-67, 310-13
• • necessity for, 148-52
• • policy statements, principles for, 157-59
• • accessibility and dissemination of policy, 158
• • boundaries, clear establishment of, 157-58
• • consequences of prohibited behaviour, action re, 159
• • generally, 157
• • sexual harassment, meaning of, 157-58
• power dynamics, understanding of, 151
• sexual abuse as "women's issue", 149-50
• silence as enablement, 151
• small workplace, in, 163, 168-69
• • case study, 167-68, 313-15
• statutory obligations, 154

Workplace prevention strategies. *See* **Prevention strategies**